OXFORD LEGAL HISTORY SERIES

General Editors

PAUL BRAND
JOSHUA GETZLER
AND
DANIEL HULSEBOSCH

Contract before the Enlightenment

OXFORD LEGAL HISTORY SERIES

General Editors
Paul Brand, Joshua Getzler, and Daniel Hulsebosch

This series presents original work in legal history from all periods. Contributions to the series analyze diverse legal traditions, including common law; *ius commune*, civilian, and canon law; colonial, imperial, and international law; and customary, religious, and non-Western cultures of law. The series embraces methods ranging from doctrinal and juristic analysis through to every variety of historical, social-scientific, and philosophical enquiry. A leading purpose of the series is to investigate how legal ideas and practices operated in larger historical contexts. Our authors trace changes in legal thought and practice and the interactions of law with political and constitutional institutions and wider movements in social, economic, cultural, and intellectual life.

Contract before the Enlightenment

The Ideas of James Dalrymple, Viscount Stair,
1619–1695

STEPHEN BOGLE

OXFORD
UNIVERSITY PRESS

OXFORD
UNIVERSITY PRESS

Great Clarendon Street, Oxford, OX2 6DP,
United Kingdom

Oxford University Press is a department of the University of Oxford.
It furthers the University's objective of excellence in research, scholarship,
and education by publishing worldwide. Oxford is a registered trade mark of
Oxford University Press in the UK and in certain other countries

Published in the United States of America by Oxford University Press
198 Madison Avenue, New York, NY 10016, United States of America

British Library Cataloguing in Publication Data
Data available

Library of Congress Control Number is on file at the Library of Congress

ISBN 978-0-19-288496-1

DOI: 10.1093/oso/9780192884961.001.0001

Printed and bound by
CPI Group (UK) Ltd, Croydon, CR0 4YY

James Pierre Bogle

beloved son,

lived thirty-three minutes, loved forever

Preface

In 2010, Dr Dot Reid suggested that I read James Gordley's *The Philosophical Origins of Modern Contract Doctrine*[1] along with Alasdair MacIntyre's *Whose Justice? Which Rationality?*[2] I had previously studied philosophy as an undergraduate—and, despite all the analytical philosophy taught on that degree, I was enthralled by historical explanations of ideas throughout my studies. I was therefore gripped by Gordley's approach to law and MacIntyre's analysis of Stair, but was also left with a sense that there was a great deal more to say. It was clear to me that the complexity and role of Protestant natural law theories in the development of modern ideas of law and not just private law were not fully appreciated.

After some sage warnings from Professor Paul du Plessis about transplanting grand theories of European legal development into Scottish legal history, I returned to the sources and cautiously queried the role that philosophy, theology, and political theory played in developing the *ideas* of contract law—or style of legal thought—found in the *Institutions of the Law of Scotland* (*Institutions*) by James Dalrymple, Viscount Stair (1619–95). Under the guidance of Professors Martin Hogg, who had already chartered aspects of this terrain himself, and John Cairns, I was able to complete my doctoral studies and answer some of these queries, but I was unable to fully answer all my questions.

A surprisingly enjoyable viva—I was not aware it could be—conducted by Professors Catharine MacMillan and Hector MacQueen who encouraged me to go further, specifically in understanding the legacy of Stair's contractual thought and situating his *Institutions* within the context of his other extant works, particularly the *Divine Perfections*. Indeed, I am particularly grateful to Professor MacQueen who suggested at the outset that I write this book and for his kind assistance in proposing this project to OUP.

Yet, following the viva, I wanted to sharpen my methodology and approach to intellectual history, something which although not exhaustively explained in the pages that follow was a major preoccupation of my research between 2014 and 2018. It was only after several years of further research and, for the most part, writing between 2019 and 2021, that I completed this manuscript in late 2021. Throughout this period, I benefited greatly from the insightful counsel and invaluable input of Professor Joshua Getzler as the series editor. He read everything twice, and undoubtedly improved this manuscript with his careful and thoughtful guidance, particularly suggesting the inclusion of Chapters 2 and 3.

And so, this book explores the contractual thought of Viscount Stair and its relationship to the intellectual context of northern Europe and specifically

---

[1] (OUP 1991).
[2] (Duckworth 1988).

mid-seventeenth-century Scotland. In writing this book, I have been aware that, to some, Stair is 'obscure'[3] and 'barely known, except to specialists',[4] whereas to others he is an 'oracle'[5] or an 'idol'.[6] While I try to steer clear of replicating enthusiastic praise of Stair, I do try to establish the value of examining his contractual thought and suggest that his ideas about the law of contract should be known beyond Scottish legal history. I try to demonstrate in these chapters how Stair developed the notion that individuals have a right to trade and contract, and how this relates to the intellectual climate of the seventeenth century and to writers such as Hugo Grotius and Thomas Hobbes. After highlighting how distinctive Stair was in comparison to his legal contemporaries, the middle chapters explain how philosophy and theology contributed to what was, in seventeenth-century Scotland, an innovative approach to contract law. It is in the penultimate chapter that I explore how Grotius's notions of free trade and commerce were adapted by Stair for a Calvinist audience. On that basis, I conclude that his contractual thought is an example of a genre of seventeenth- and eighteenth-century theories which covered far more than just contracts, but nonetheless included consideration of contracting and the importance of commerce for the establishment of a civil society.[7] From the perspective of legal history, these natural law theories contributed to various developments within legal thought, offering a means by which political or legal rules, practices and institutions, including the law of contract, could be explained, justified, or indeed criticized.[8] If this is accepted, then I hope this book demonstrates that Stair is a noteworthy but possibly overlooked example of this development.

A note should be made about the conventions I have adopted. Unless dates are used within quotations, any reference to a specific date is given in the post-1600 format. On the whole, the original spelling and grammar found within primary sources has been maintained and silent emendation used very sparingly. Any uncertainty of transcription has been indicated with a question mark enclosed within square brackets. Generally, authors' names have been provided in a format which will be familiar to English readers or the most frequently used form within the literature. For instance, where a Latinized version of a jurist's name is more frequently used than its native iteration, the latter has been chosen. Similarly, noble titles have often been used where persons are more easily identifiable by such titles, such as Stair rather than Dalrymple.

---

[3] Martha C Nussbaum, *Philosophical Interventions: Reviews 1986–2011* (OUP 2012) 58.

[4] Bernard Williams, *Essays and Reviews, 1959–2002* (Princeton University Press 2014) 284.

[5] *Routledge v Carruthers* 19 May 1812 FC at 588 per Lord President Blair.

[6] A C Black, 'Institutional Writers' in *An Introductory Survey of the Sources and Literature of Scots Law*, vol 1 (Stair Society 1936) 63.

[7] Richard Tuck, *Natural Rights Theories* (CUP 1979); Knud Haakonssen, *Natural Law and Moral Philosophy: From Grotius to the Scottish Enlightenment* (CUP 1996) 15–61; Knud Haakonssen, 'Protestant Natural Law Theory: A General Interpretation' in Natalie Brender and Larry Krasnoff (eds), *New Essays on the History of Autonomy* (CUP 2004) 92–109; Knud Haakonssen and Michael J Seidler, 'Natural Law: Law, Rights and Duties' in Richard Whatmore and Brian Young (eds), *A Companion to Intellectual History* (Wiley-Blackwell 2015) 383–94.

[8] Knud Haakonssen, 'What Might be Called Natural Jurisprudence?' in R H Campbell and Andrew Skinner (eds), *The Origins and Nature of the Scottish Enlightenment* (John Donald 1982) 205–25; Tim J Hochstrasser, *Natural Law Theories in the Early Enlightenment* (CUP 2000) 1–39; István Hont, 'Needs and Justice in the *Wealth of Nations*: An Introductory Essay' in István Hont and Michael Ignatieff (eds), *Wealth and Virtue: The Shaping of Political Economy in the Scottish Enlightenment* (CUP 1983) 1–44.

In many places, the book opts for the masculine noun or pronoun, where a modern reader might expect a gender-neutral reference. Primarily this is because the texts discussed in this book did not consider the position of women, implicitly subjugating female existence. Of course, whether this gives a true account of the legal and social position of women in seventeenth-century society is a very different question. In passing, for example, it is worth noting that several cases referenced in Chapters 1 and 4 involve women acting as relicts or executors. Nonetheless, when it comes to systematic texts or juristic overviews of the law, such women, in effect, disappear. To be clear, none of this implies that the ideas expressed in the texts considered in this book could not be equally applied to women—but only that their authors did not, as far as I could determine, consider them as being applicable to women.

Stephen Bogle
January 2023
Glasgow

Acknowledgements

I am grateful to many colleagues and institutions for their support and help over the last ten or so years. I owe my thanks to several funders who have provided me with support at various points, including the Edinburgh Legal Education Trust, the University of Edinburgh College of Humanities and Social Science Studentship Bursary, the Revd Dr Murray McGregor Memorial Scholarship and the School of Law Research Fund, University of Glasgow.

My thanks are also due to the National Library of Scotland, Registers of Scotland, the Advocates Library, the Signet Library, the University of Edinburgh Special Collections, Boston Public Library, the Archives and Special Collections of the University of Glasgow, Hunterian Art Gallery of the University of Glasgow, and the Gladstone Library for access and use of their collections.

Dr Stephen Rawles shared with me a printed (unpublished) copy of the University of Glasgow's 1691 library catalogue. Originally, I believe, it was Professor Olivia Robinson who prompted Dr Rawles to produce such a document. It proved to be vital. Many thanks are due to Dr Rawles for his generosity and Professor Robinson for her foresight.

Small but thoughtful gestures can make a huge difference. Indeed, special thanks are due to Dr Madeleine Pennington (Ward) whose insightful comments at the Society for Reformation Studies in 2015 opened a new vista through which to view Stair's theory of human action. Additionally, my conversations with Dr Anat Rosenberg at the Association of Young Legal Historians Conference in Tel Aviv in 2015 left a strong impression on me—whether it was her intention or not—about the importance of understanding how lawyers *think* about the law.

I was fortunate to receive perceptive and immensely helpful feedback on draft chapters from several colleagues and friends who work across different disciplines touched upon in this book, including Dr Neil MacIntyre, Dr Giovanni Gellera, Professor Adelyn Wilson, Dr Graeme Cunningham, and Dr Paul Scott. As this book stretches across history, philosophy, and political theory, the comments of these scholars were precious. I also benefited greatly from four separate referees' reports. Each report undoubtedly improved the argument and assisted me both at an early and later stage of writing. I am also obliged to Professor John Blackie and Dr Ilya Kotlyar for their help in translating certain Latin passages. Any errors are, of course, my own.

In early 2020, I enlisted the help of Mr Ivor Normand as I prepared the manuscript. He was the most diligent of copyeditors, and I am very grateful for his patience and meticulousness. Moreover, in the final stages of preparation, during the late summer of 2021, two additional chapters were added. I am forever grateful to Dr Chloë Kennedy, who at the shortest of notice, read and reviewed these chapters providing wonderfully helpful guidance and comments, carrying me over the finishing line of this project—at least in terms of writing.

Many thanks are due to Mr Ewan Easton for suggesting that I use George Henry's (1858–1943) 'River Landscape by Moonlight' also known as 'Sundown' (1887), which is held by the Hunterian Art Gallery of the University of Glasgow (and who kindly provided the image). I am also grateful to Mr Brian Stone, Ms Paulina dos Santos Major, Ms Prajkta, Ms Meiling Voon, and the cover art designer from OUP for their superb production support. I was also fortunate to have the assistance of Ms Kate McIntosh with the production of the index.

It remains for me to give heartfelt thanks to my colleagues within the School of Law at the University of Glasgow, many of whom have discussed aspects of this book—whether knowingly or not—with me over the years, including, Mrs Jennifer Crawford, Drs Dot Reid, John Macleod (now of the University of Edinburgh), Jill Robbie, Bobby Lindsay, Mat Campbell, and Marco Goldoni and Professors George Pavlakos, Emilios Christodoulidis, Lindsay Farmer, Fiona Leverick, Frankie McCarthy, James Chalmers, Mark Furse, Adam Tomkins, Akbar Rasulov, Jane Mair, Mark Godfrey, and Andreas Rahmatian. The School has provided a generous and vibrant environment within which to write this book.

My deepest gratitude goes to my wife, Anne-Claire. She has scarificed a great deal in order for me to write this book. I could not have done this without her.

Contents

List of Abbreviations

Adv MS	Manuscript of the Faculty of Advocates held by the National Library of Scotland
Balfour Practicks	James Balfour, *Practicks: Or, a system of the more ancient law of Scotland. Compiled by Sir James Balfour of Pettindreich, carefully published from several manuscripts* (Thomas & Walter Ruddimans 1754).
Calvin Inst	John Calvin, *Institutes of the Christian Religion* (first published 1536, Eerdmans Publishing, 1994)
Craig *Jus feudale*	Thomas Craig, *Jus Feudale Tribus Libris Comprehensum Quibus Non Solùm Consuetudines Feudales & Prædiorum Lura* (first published 1655, Leslie Dodd tr, Stair Society 2017)
De Jure Belli Ac Pacis	Hugo Grotius, *The Rights of War and Peace* (first published 1625, Liberty Fund 2005)
Digest	*The Digest of Justinian*, vol 4 (Alan Watson tr, University of Pennsylvania Press 1998).
Durie's Practicks	A Gibson (ed), *The Decision of the Lords of Council and Session in Most Cases of Importance, Debated, and Brought before Them; from July 1621 to July 1642* (Andrew Anderson 1690)
Erskine *Institute*	John Erskine, *An Institute of the Law of Scotland* (first published 1773, Edinburgh Legal Education Trust 2014)
EUL	Edinburgh University Library
Forbes *Institutes*	William Forbes, *Institutes of the Law of Scotland* (first published 1722, Edinburgh Legal Education Trust 2012)
Gaius Inst	*The Institutes of Gaius* (Francis de Zulueta tr, OUP 1946)
GUL	Glasgow University Library
Hope's Minor Practicks	Alexander Bayne (ed), *Minor Practicks, or, a Treatise of the Scottish Law* (Thomas Ruddiman 1726).
Hope's Major Practicks	James A Clyde (ed), *Hope's Major Practicks, 1608–1633*, vol 2 (Stair Society 1937).
Justinian Inst	Justinian's Institutes (Peter Birks and Grant McLeod trs, Cornell University Press 1987)
Mackenzie *Institutions*	George Mackenzie, *The Institutions of the Law of Scotland* (John Reid 1684)
Mor	William M Morison (ed), *Decisions of the Court of Session, from its First Institutions to the Present Time* (2nd edn, Archibald Constable 1811)
NLS Ms	Manuscript held by the National Library of Scotland

RPS   Keith M Brown et al (eds) *The Records of the Parliaments of*
                                   Scotland to 1707 (St Andrews 2007–21) <http://www.rps.ac.uk>
                                   accessed 13 April 2021

Spotiswoode *Practicks*   John Spotiswoode (ed), *Practicks of the Laws of Scotland Observed*
                                   and Collected by Sir Robert Spotiswoode (James Watson 1706)

Stair *Inst*   James Dalrymple, Viscount Stair, *Institutions of the Law of Scotland*
                                   (2nd edn, Andrew Anderson 1693)

Stair *Divine Perfections*   James Dalrymple, Viscount Stair, *A Vindication of the Divine*
                                   Perfections: Illustrating the Glory of God in Them by Reason
                                   and Revelation: Methodically Digested Into Several Mediations
                                   (Brabazon Aylmer 1695)

Introduction

Transforming the Law of Contract

In the early manuscripts of what was to become the *Institutions of the Law of Scotland* (*Institutions*) drafted by James Dalrymple (1619–95), Viscount Stair, there is a transformation in how the law of contract is described. Stair rejected a legal tradition of a thousand years, arguing that in Scots law bare promises were legally enforceable. In contrast to many of his European counterparts, he spoke of a generalized law of contract, not contracts and, importantly, subverted the familiar taxonomy of Justinian, placing obligations before his account of property. Moreover, Stair adopted the language of the 'will' in his explanation of contractual formation, moving the focus from external factors, such as physical transfer or formal writs to an internal mental trigger. Indeed, it is notable and yet thus far unexplained why the language of liberty to contract can be found in a natural law treatise of a Calvinist jurist like Stair, where you might otherwise expect regulation and restriction of individual decision-making.

This book explains the circumstances and context within which these developments happened, paying particular attention to what these ideas and this language meant to Stair and his contemporaries.[1] In order to do this, this book examines not only Stair's own published work but also the mid- to late seventeenth-century context within which he wrote, particularly the theological, philosophical, and political environment of this period. It describes how Stair developed his understanding of contract while working against the backdrop of Calvinist theology, Aristotelian philosophy, Grotian natural law, and the early modern notions of Roman law that were used by mid-seventeenth-century Scots lawyers. It also suggests how Stair's project relates to the natural law jurisprudence which emerged in Scotland in the late seventeenth century, and to its recharacterization of law, trade, and virtue.

The 'Founding Father of Scots Law'

Scots lawyers often speak of Stair as the founding father of Scots law. Indeed, Sheriff Black once remarked: 'Every body of men has its own special idol, and of Scots lawyers it is safe to say that Stair's position is impregnable . . .'.[2] Lord Cooper has described

---

[1] Quentin Skinner, 'Meaning and Understanding in the History of Ideas' (1969) 8 (1) History and Theory 3–53. Of course, the literature on historical methodology is vast particularly when considering ideas. It is unnecessary to rehearse this literature, yet it is worth noting that, in general, the approach taken in this book follows that which is plotted out by Dunn: John M Dunn, 'The Identity of the History of Ideas' in *Political Obligation in its Historical Context* (OUP 1980) 13–28. Originally published John Dunn, 'The Identity of the History of Ideas' (1968) 43 (164) Philosophy 85–104.

[2] A C Black, 'Institutional Writers' in *Introductory Survey of the Sources and Literature of Scots Law*, vol 1 (Stair Society 1936) 63.

Contract before the Enlightenment. Stephen Bogle, Oxford University Press. © Stephen Bogle 2023.
DOI: 10.1093/oso/9780192884961.003.0001

Stair's *Institutions*, published in 1681, as marking 'the creation of Scots Law'[3] and Professor Walker has said the *Institutions* inaugurated 'the beginning of modern Scots law ... '.[4] In 1981, Lord Cameron said that it is 'difficult to exaggerate the impact of Stair's great work both on the development and indeed the continued survival of Scots law'.[5] Yet in the same year, John Blackie offered a crucial re-evaluation of Stair's status. In an analysis of how judges used the *Institutions* throughout the eighteenth and nineteenth centuries, Blackie stressed that the 'present day views of Stair are grounded in the 19th century understanding of his work, which was itself an elaboration on an earlier understanding'.[6] Blackie's work offers a vital counterbalance to the otherwise romanticized notion of Stair's place within Scottish legal history, yet it is remarkable that unlike other areas of private law in Scotland, judges and jurists continue to note that Stair laid the foundations for and had a lasting impact upon the law of contract in Scotland.

'[I]n his magisterial *Institutions of the Law of Scotland*' says William McBryde, '[Stair] was the first to establish a coherent system for the Scots law of obligations'.[7] Martin Hogg has said, 'Any understanding of the nature of the Scots law of obligations, including the theory of Scots contract, must begin with the *Institutions of the Law of Scotland* of James Dalrymple, Viscount Stair ... '.[8] Describing the contemporary law relating to promising in Scots law, McBryde says 'theoretical discussion [of promising] at any length in Scots law has been limited. Stair's pronouncement was sufficiently authoritative to be followed by others and to represent the modern law'.[9] Hogg agrees, saying 'Stair's magisterial treatment of voluntary obligations gave Scots law a distinctive approach to promise that was to endure ...'.[10] In relation to the question of whether a recipient needs to have knowledge of a promise made in their favour for it to be legally binding, the Lord President (Gill) was confident, remarking 'In my opinion, a promise in the law of Scotland is a unilateral juristic act. It acquires its binding force by reason of the declarant's expression of his will to be bound. Stair tells us that a promise is obligatory per se (*Institutions*, I. 10. 4). He says that "the will of the promiser constitutes a right in the other" (ibid)'.[11] Indeed, Reinhard Zimmermann said 'the

---

[3] Lord Cooper, 'The Scottish Legal Tradition' in Lord Cooper (ed), *Selected Papers, 1922–1954* (Oliver Boyd 1957) 172, 177.

[4] David M Walker, 'Introduction' in David M Walker (ed), *Institutions of the Law of Scotland* (Stair Society 1981) 37.

[5] Lord Cameron, 'Advertisement' in David M Walker (ed), *The Institutions of the Law of Scotland* (Stair Society 1981). Indeed, it is an indication of his standing within Scottish legal thought that some judges and jurists have advocated that as an 'institutional writer' Stair's opinion is of the highest authority akin to a source of law: Thomas B Smith, *A Short Commentary on the Law of Scotland* (W Green & Son 1962) 32; David M Walker, *The Scottish Legal System* (1997); for discussion, see Andreas Rahmatian, 'The Role of Institutional Writers in Scots Law' (2018) 1 Juridical Review 42–63. For an important examination of this concept, see John W Cairns, 'Institutional Writings in Scotland Reconsidered' (1984) 4 Journal of Legal History 76.

[6] John W G Blackie, 'Stair's Later Reputation as a Jurist' in David M Walker (ed), *Stair Tercentenary Studies* (Stair Society 1981) 237. Also see Cairns 'Institutional Writings in Scotland Reconsidered' (n 5).

[7] William W McBryde, 'Promises in Scots Law' (1993) 42 (1) International Comparative Law Quarterly 48–66, 54.

[8] Martin Hogg, 'Perspectives on Contract Theory from a Mixed Jurisdiction' (2009) 29 (3) Oxford Journal of Legal Studies 643, 648.

[9] McBryde 'Promises in Scots Law' (n 7) 56.

[10] Martin Hogg, *Promises and Contract Law: Comparative Perspectives* (CUP 2011) 142.

[11] *Regus (Maxim) Ltd v Bank of Scotland Plc* 2013 SC 331 at 338.

doctrine of promise as expounded by Stair has survived and it remains useful, not only as far as the analysis of promises for a reward is concerned'.[12] When addressing the issue of specific implement for an obligation to do something (ie continue performance of a contract) rather than to give (ie to pay a monetary debt), the Lord President (Rodger) said: 'The controversy was pursued in succeeding generations, but for Scots law the basic approach was settled by Stair *Institutions* 1.17.16'.[13] A few years later in the House of Lords, he observed that at 'the heart of Scots property law ... lies the maxim *traditionibus, non nudis pactis, transferuntur reum ...* ' and the 'adoption of this rule of Roman law as part of Scots law' he explained 'can be traced at least as far back as Stair, *The Institutions of the Law of Scotland* (III, iii, 5)'.[14] Indeed, in terms of the taxonomy of the Scots law of obligations, Hector MacQueen suggests 'The beginning of the modern Scottish approach, and perhaps the only serious attempt at its philosophical justification, is to be found in Stair's *Institutions*.'[15] Niall Whitty and Danie Visser have also observed that ' ... the outline of Stair's system [of obligations] has survived [into the modern law]'.[16] If modern doctrinal accounts of the Scots law of contract identify some of its distinctive features as arising in Stair's *Institutions*, then it could be said that this book offers an explanation as to why Stair wrote what he did about the law of contract.

The Distinctiveness of Contract Law in Scotland

Yet it is not only Scots lawyers who are interested in Stair's contribution. Since the 1930s, comparative lawyers and judges have suggested that the private law of Scotland, including its approach to promises and contracts,[17] is different from both Common law systems and Civilian systems of law.[18] Prior to this, the external

---

[12] Reinhard Zimmermann, *Roman law, Contemporary Law, European Law the Civilian Tradition Today* (OUP 2001) 159.

[13] *Highland and Universal Properties Ltd v Safeway Properties Ltd* 2000 SC 298 at 298 per Lord Rodger.

[14] *Burnett's Trustee v Grainger* 2004 SC (HL) 19 at para 12 per Lord Rodger.

[15] Hector L MacQueen, 'The Law of Obligations in Scotland' in Reiner Schulze and Fryderyk Zoll (eds), *The Law of Obligations in Europe: A New Wave of Codifications* (De Gruyter 2013) 213–43.

[16] Niall Whitty and Danie Visser, 'The Structure of the Law of Delict in Historical Perspective' in Reinhard Zimmermann and Kenneth Reid (eds), *A History of Private Law in Scotland*, vol 2 (OUP 2000) 422, 467.

[17] For ease, from here on, I will refer to the 'law of contract' or 'Scots contract law' but I am including within those phrases, promises or unilateral obligations.

[18] Lord Normand, 'Consideration in the Law of Scotland' (1939) 55 Law Quarterly Review 358, 365; Thomas A Cooper, 'The Common and the Civil Law. A Scot's View' (1950) 63 (3) Harvard Law Review 468; David M Walker, 'Some Characteristics of Scots Law' (1955) 18 (4) The Modern Law Review 321–37; Thomas B Smith, *Scotland: The Development of its Laws and Constitution* (Stevens 1962) 742; Smith *A Short Commentary* (n 5) Ch 32; Reinhard Zimmermann and Phillip Hellwege, 'Belohnungsversprechen: "Pollicitatio", "Promise" or "Offer"' (1998) 39 Zeitschrift für Rechtsvergleichung 133; Hector L MacQueen, 'Scots Law and the Road to the New Ius Commune' in Martijn Hesselink (ed), *The Ius Commune Lectures*, vol 1 (Unigraphic 2000) 19; Jans Smits, The *Making of European Private Law: Toward a Ius Commune. European as a Mixed Legal System* (Intersentia 2002) 112; David V Synder, 'Hunting Promissory Estoppel' in Vernon Palmer and Elspeth Reid (eds), *Mixed Jurisdictions Compared: Private Law in Louisiana and Scotland* (2009) 281; Martin Hogg, 'Promise: The Neglected Obligation in European Private Law' (2010) 52 (1) International & Comparative Law Quarterly 461; Lord Hope, 'The Role of the Judge in Developing Contract Law' (Contract Law Conference, Jersey, 15 October 2010) (unpublished, available at <Microsoft Word - Contract Law Conference - Jersey 15 Oct 10.doc (supremecourt.uk)> accessed 19 October 2022); Pierre de Gioia-Carabellese, 'The Concepts of the Scottish (and Italian)

identity of Scots law or legal thought in Scotland, in comparison to other bodies of law or jurisdictions, meant different things to different generations.[19] Today, one of the prevailing views is that Scots private law is distinctive, in part, due to its apparent mix of Civilian and Common law ideas,[20] including the law of contract.[21] Yet the designation of Scotland as a 'mixed legal system' is as much to do with legal thought, including legal history, as it is to do with legal propositions. Stair is undoubtedly an important part of the story of how Scots understand the law of contract but the intentions of Stair when he wrote about contractual obligations is unexplored.

Hence, this book explains Stair's contribution to the law of contract in Scotland by examining the complex context within which it was written and published, highlighting the philosophical and theological nature of four central ideas found in Stair's account: agreements are binding, the will is the trigger for creation of contractual obligations, man has a God-given freedom by which to create contractual obligations that he should use to bring glory to God, and the rules of contract should be informed by the needs of commerce as much as equity. The first three chapters of this book therefore explain contractual thought before Stair, how Roman law was utilized by Stair's contemporaries, and how Stair described the law of contract in the *Institutions*. Here Stair took a distinctive path compared to his contemporaries, and we will see that it is necessary to search beyond legal sources to explain Stair's radical reformulation of the law of contract in Scotland. It will be argued that Stair's contractual thought was shaped not only by influential legal texts of the mid-seventeenth century but also by a gamut of theological and philosophical impulses. Chapters 4 to 8 examine the key theological and philosophical elements in the formation of Stair's contractual thought. But first it will be valuable to broach the life and times of Stair when he wrote the *Institutions*, embedded as this juristic work was within a context of theology and natural philosophy addressed to a wider audience. We mistake Stair's life and work if we consider him only as a jurist.

looking for philosophical and theological impulses underlying his idea of contract

---

Unilateral Promise and the English Unilateral Contracts' (2011) 22 (3) European Business Law Review 381; Nils Jansen and Reinhard Zimmermann (eds), *Commentaries on European Contract Laws* (OUP 2018) Art 2: 107. MacQueen gives a useful overview of comparative law in Scotland since the 1920s: Hector L MacQueen, 'Public, Private, and National Identity' in Cormac M Amhliagh, Claudio Michelon, and Neil Walker (eds), *After Public Law* (Edinburgh University Press 2013) 168.

[19] John W Cairns, 'Development of Comparative Law in Great Britain' in Reinhard Zimmermann and Mathias Reimann (eds), *The Oxford Handbook of Comparative Law* (OUP 2006) 132–74; John W Cairns, 'Attitudes to Codification in Scotland' (2007) 22 Tulane European & Civil Law Forum 1; John D Ford, 'Four Models of Union' in Hector L MacQueen (ed), *Miscellany VII*, vol 62 (Stair Society 2015) 179. For example, both editions of William Gloag's *The Law of Contract: A Treatise on the Principles of Contract in the Law of Scotland*, published in 1914 and 1929 describe the law of Scotland without much care or reference to its uniqueness; it generally lacks a self-consciousness which you find in later works on private law in Scotland.
[20] Konrad Zweigert and Hein Kötz, *An Introduction to Comparative Law* (Tony Weir tr, 3rd edn, OUP 1998) 204.
[21] MacQueen, 'Scots Law and the Road to the New Ius Commune' (n 18).

The Public Life of Stair

Stair's life was eventful.[22] Born James Dalrymple in 1619 in Ayrshire on the west coast of Scotland, he studied at Glasgow University from 1633 to 1637, graduating top of his year.[23] In his early twenties, he fought in the Bishops' Wars as a Covenanter, and, upon peace being restored, was elected a regent in 1641 at Glasgow University, where he taught for six years.[24] Upon resigning from his post, he was admitted advocate in 1648.[25] He sought entry to the Faculty of Advocates by delivering a lesson to the Lords of Session in February 1648.[26] The intention of this admission process was for the candidate to demonstrate his learning in the law—and evidently Stair impressed some of the Lordships, as a record of his address was preserved by the Lord Ordinary, Sir John Scot of Scotstarvet.[27] However, not long into Stair's career at the bar, Charles I was executed, and Stair found himself in Edinburgh during the midst of a constitutional crisis.[28] Notably, he played a role in its resolution; Stair was appointed Secretary to the Commission to Breda and was sent by the Scots Parliament to negotiate with the Prince of Wales the terms of his reign in Scotland.[29] That year, he was also appointed to the Radical Parliament's law commission, which sought to review the laws of Scotland in light of godly rule.[30] From 1651 until 1657, he practised as an advocate but refused to take the Oath of Allegiance to the Commonwealth in 1654.[31]

Stair otherwise fared reasonably well during Cromwell's Commonwealth, establishing a good relationship with the governor of Scotland, George Monk.[32] Importantly, during the Interregnum, Cromwell closed the Court of Session but in its place established a Commission for the Administration of Justice in Scotland.[33]

---

[22] For fuller accounts of Stair's life and politics, see Aeneas J G Mackay, *Memoir of Sir James Dalrymple, First Viscount Stair* (Edmonston & Douglas 1873); John M Graham (ed), *Annals and Correspondence of the Viscount and the First and Second Earls of Stair* (William Blackwood & Sons 1875) vol 1, 1–94; Gordon M Hutton, 'The Political Thought of Sir James Dalrymple, First Viscount Stair (1619–1695)' (DPhil thesis, University of Birmingham 1971) 1–116; Gordon M Hutton, 'Stair's Public Career' in David M Walker (ed), *Stair Tercentenary Studies* (Stair Society 1981) vol 33, 1–65; John D Ford, 'Dalrymple, James, first Viscount Stair (1619–1695)' in *Oxford Dictionary of National Biography* (OUP 2004) <https://www.oxforddnb.com/> accessed 8 April 2021. Also see Stair's own account, *An Apology for Sir James Dalrymple of Stair, President of the Session, by Himself* (first published 1690, J Ballantyne & Co 1825).

[23] Cosmo Nelson, *Munimenta Alme Universitatis Glasguensi: Records of the University of Glasgow from its Foundation until 1727* (Maitland Club 1854) vol 3, 22.

[24] Mackay, *Memoir of Sir James Dalrymple* (n 22) 7–9.

[25] John D Ford, *Law and Opinion in Scotland during the Seventeenth Century* (Hart 2007) 2–7.

[26] For discussion of Stair's address to the Lords of Session, see Ford, *Law and Opinion* (n 25) 2–21.

[27] 'Scotstarvet's "Trew Relation"' (1916) 13 (52) Scottish Historical Review 380–92.

[28] See Samuel R Gardiner, *History of the Great Civil War, 1642–1649* (Longmans, Green & Co 1901) vol 4, 574–81; David Stevenson, *Revolution and Counter-Revolution in Scotland, 1644–1651* (John Donald 2003) 103–41; Allan I Macinnes, *The British Revolution, 1629–1660* (Macmillian 2005).

[29] For account of his time as secretary, see Hutton 'The Political Thought of Sir James Dalrymple' (n 22) 12–32; and, for a summary, Hutton 'Stair's Public Career' (n 22) 3–4.

[30] Regarding the Radical Parliament, see Stevenson *Revolution and Counter-Revolution* (n 28) 135; Michael Lynch, 'The Wars of Covenant' in Michael Lynch (ed), *The Oxford Companion to Scottish History* (OUP 2007) 112; Neil McIntyre, 'Saints and Subverters: The Later Covenanters in Scotland c. 1648–1682' (DPhil thesis, University of Strathclyde 2016) 29–41.

[31] Hutton 'Stair's Public Career' (n 22) 5.

[32] Mackay *Memoir of Sir James Dalrymple* (n 22) 62–70.

[33] Ford *Law and Opinion* (n 25) 91–151.

Staffing this Commission proved very difficult, and in 1657 Stair was appointed a Commissioner despite having less than seven years' legal experience.[34] Following the failure of the Commonwealth, in 1661 the Court of Session reopened and Charles II appointed Stair as a Lord Ordinary, becoming Lord Stair.[35] Stair's experience during the Restoration was mixed. Refusing to take the Declaration in 1663, Stair was not prepared to undermine or renounce the 1560 Scots Confession and the National Covenant of 1637. However, after a private meeting with Charles II, he was allowed to continue as a Lord Ordinary during the Restoration.[36] He was closely associated with Lord Lauderdale during this period, often pleading for moderation with regard to Covenanters.[37] In 1671, he was appointed Lord President of the Court of Session; this appointment was at the expense of Peter Wedderburn, Lord Gosford, a more experienced advocate and the preferred candidate of the outgoing President, John Gilmour. However, as the Duke of York exerted his influence over Scotland in the early 1680s, Stair found himself in a difficult political situation as a moderate Presbyterian sympathetic to the Covenanters and concerned about the preservation of Protestantism in Scotland.[38] In 1681, Stair's political position deteriorated as his family came into direct conflict with the powerful John Claverhouse, a close ally of the Duke of York, who was tasked with the suppression of Covenanters in Scotland.[39] Stair and his family fled to the Dutch Provinces, taking residence in Leiden in 1681.[40] He remained in the Dutch Provinces until 1688, when he returned to England as part of William of Orange's invading army, landing at Torbay on William's flagship.[41] Upon his return to Scotland in 1689, he was controversially reappointed Lord President of the Court of Session. In 1690, he took the title Viscount Stair.[42] He died in 1695 after a short illness.

Literature

It is not only the context of Stair's life that suggests looking beyond conventional legal sources. In addition to his *Institutions*, Stair published other texts during his lifetime.[43]

---

[34] Graham *Annals* (n 22) 14–15; Mackay *Memoir of Sir James Dalrymple* (n 22) 58–68; Ford *Law and Opinion* (n 25) 113–15.

[35] Graham *Annals* (n 22) 17–28; Mackay *Memoir of Sir James Dalrymple* (n 22) 70–71.

[36] Stair *Apology* (n 22) 9; Graham *Annals* (n 22) 18–28; Hutton 'Stair's Public Career' (n 22) 5–6.

[37] Stair, *Apology* (n 22) 11–13; Graham *Annals* (n 22) 50–60; Mackay *Memoir of Sir James Dalrymple* (n 22) 93–130; Hutton 'Stair's Public Career' (n 22) 6–31.

[38] Graham *Annals* (n 22) 61–72; Mackay *Memoir of Sir James Dalrymple* (n 22) 139–50; Hutton 'Stair's Public Career' (n 22) 33–39.

[39] Graham *Annals* (n 22) 63–67; Mackay *Memoir of Sir James Dalrymple* (n 22) 179–86; Hutton 'Stair's Public Career' (n 22) 6–31.

[40] Graham *Annals* (n 22) 63–71; Mackay *Memoir of Sir James Dalrymple* (n 22) 182–93; Hutton 'Stair's Public Career' (n 22) 39–49.

[41] Mackay *Memoir of Sir James Dalrymple* (n 22) 213.

[42] Graham *Annals* (n 22) 88–93; Ford 'Dalrymple, James, first Viscount Stair (1619–1695)' (n 22).

[43] Some of Stair's correspondence can be found in the Lauderdale, Leven and Melville, and Dundas Papers held by the National Library of Scotland. A small collection is also available in the National Records of Scotland: GD1/520. The New Hailes Collection has papers relating to the Dalrymple family but nothing that relates directly to Stair or is of any significance for present purposes. A fire in 1716 at Castle Kennedy, the residence of John Dalrymple, Stair's eldest son, may have destroyed any of Stair's own individual papers, manuscripts, or correspondence if they were in existence at the time (Graham *Annals* (n 22) 327).

Often overlooked but noteworthy is that as a regent at Glasgow, Stair published his student graduation theses in 1646.[44] They intimate he was an enquiring and innovating teacher who, although working within the paradigms of scholastic natural philosophy, was critical and sought new ways to describe, for example, causation.[45] Stair did not return to publishing anything on natural philosophy until 1686, when he published in Leiden his *Physiologia nova experimentalis*,[46] prefaced with a letter to the Royal Society of London. The impression given is that he continued in his later years to engage with contemporary theories and approaches to natural philosophy, provided, of course, that they could be interpreted in a theistic manner.[47] Shortly after his death, an anonymous treatise on theology was also published in Leiden, entitled *A Vindication of Divine Perfections*.[48] Several anonymous pamphlets have also been associated with Stair from around the time of the 1688 revolution, justifying the Convention of Estates.[49] In 1690, he published a pamphlet entitled *An Apology for James Dalrymple, Viscount Stair* where he sought to respond to various tracts which questioned his honesty and political motivations.[50] Less well known, but important in

Generally, the extant correspondence does not shed too much light upon his intellectual or philosophical positions but relates solely to public affairs.

[44] James Dalrymple, *Theses Logicæ, Metaphysicæ, Physicæ, Mathematicæ* (George Anderson 1646). See David S Sytsma's translation of Dalrymple's ethical theses: David S Sytsma, ' "Ethical Theses" in *Theses Logicae, Metaphysicae, Physicae, Mathematicae, et Ethicae* (George Anderson 1646) (2020) <https://tci. academia.edu/DavidSytsma/Translations> accessed 15 April 2021.

[45] For a crucial examination, see Giovanni Gellera, 'Natural Philosophy in the Graduation Theses of the Scottish Universities in the First Half of the Seventeenth Century (DPhil thesis, University of Glasgow 2012) 63 ff.

[46] James Dalrymple, *Physiologia Nova Experimentalis in qua, Generales Notions Aristotelis, Epicuri, & Cartesii Supplentur: Errores Derterguntur & Emendantur* (Cornelium Boutesteyn 1686). Indeed, he offers an interesting history in the *Physiologia* of natural philosophy suggesting that incremental knowledge of the natural world is gained over centuries through different ideas and methods used by man. He speaks of the mysteries of God's creation being revealed and discovered over time through man's investigation. Interestingly, as part of his history of natural philosophy Stair says it is a far less certain science in contrast to theology, metaphysics, and moral sciences, which are self-evident and therefore have, historically, attracted closer study from scholars.

[47] For some brief discussion, see Mackay *Memoir of Sir James Dalrymple* (n 22) 197–206.

[48] Although anonymous, it has been associated with Stair since the early eighteenth century—and with good reason. First, Stair concluded a contract with an Edinburgh publisher in the spring of 1681 promising several books, including his *Institutions* and 'a Treatise contain four Inquires concerning Humane Knowledge, Natural Theologie, Morality and Phisiologie … ' (George Dallas, *System of Stiles* (Andrew Anderson 1697) 152–53; Alastair Mann, *The Scottish Book Trade, 1500 to 1720* (Tuckwell 2000) 114). Second, in 1695, the same year the *Divine Perfections* was published, the London publisher, Brabazon Aylmer, advertised the *Divine Perfections* as being written 'By the Right Honourable the Lord President' (John Tillotson, *Sermons concerning the Divinity and Incarnation of our Blessed Saviour* (Aylmer, 1695) 305; Tillotson died in 1694 and was, at the time, the archbishop of Canterbury). Third, some years after his death, William Forbes, under the patronage and supervision of Stair's son, wrote a relatively detailed biography of Stair and unquestionably attributed the authorship of the *Divine Perfections* to Stair (William Forbes, *A Journal of the Session* (Edinburgh 1714) xi). Mackay, Hutton, and Ford all agree that Stair produced this treatise: Mackay *Memoir of Sir James Dalrymple* (n 22) 272–73; Hutton 'Stair's Public Career' (n 22) 65; Ford 'Dalrymple, James, first Viscount Stair (1619–1695)' (n 22).

[49] Including *A Vindication of the Proceedings of the Convention of the Estates in Scotland* (Ric Chinwell 1689) (William Forbes, *A Journal of the Session* (Faculty of Advocates 1714) xi). Hutton suggests that another three political pamphlets can be connected to Stair, but his evidence for this is more speculative than probable: Hutton 'The Political Thought of Sir James Dalrymple' (n 22) 553–58.

[50] (First published 1690, J Ballantyne & Co 1825).

terms of his contemporary legal contribution, is his *Decisions of the Court of Session*, the first volume being published in 1681 and the second two years later.[51] This leaves Stair's printed work as the most direct means by which to study his ideas and intentions. However, this is far from straightforward when it comes to Stair's *Institutions* because of both the manuscript tradition, which garnered around forty copies of what was to become the *Institutions*,[52] and the various posthumous republications of the *Institutions* since 1693. A great deal of painstaking scholarly work has been undertaken of late, which has peeled back the layers of uncertainty that have existed around the pre-1681 copies of Stair's original manuscript that he finished in 1662.[53] It is therefore important, before discussing Stair's contractual thought, that the different contexts and texts of the *Institutions* are explained.

Different Texts of the *Institutions*

Stair published two versions of the *Institutions* in his lifetime: one in 1681 and a second edition in 1693.[54] Four posthumous republications were produced, each carrying with them edits, alterations and notes. In 1759, an edition was prepared and edited by two Scots advocates, John Gordon and William Johnstone. In the advertisement, it was explained that a new edition was necessary 'to remove, by the Help of Several Manuscripts, the Obscurity which every where occurred in the former Editions of this valuable System of Law; and to add, in Notes, the Alterations which have been introduced since the 1693 [edition]'.[55] In 1826–27, another advocate, George Brodie, published a further edition, having 'constantly collated the three former editions with nine manuscript copies from the Advocate's Library', and gaining 'greater confidence in the accuracy of the 1693 edition, which was the last published by the author himself'. On that basis, Brodie only made alterations 'where it is obvious, from the sense or the decision referred to, that a slight inaccuracy exists', and he criticized the 'liberties used with text by the last editors' (Gordon and Johnstone) and their attempt to integrate alterations taken from various manuscripts.[56] A fifth edition was published in 1832 and edited by the Edinburgh Professor of Scots Law, John Shank More, which attempted to reproduce the 1693 edition but with additional discussion and notes appended at the

---

[51] James Dalrymple, *The Decisions of the Lords of Council and Session in the Most Important Cases Debate before them, with Acts of Sederunt* (Andrew Anderson 1683); *The Decisions of the Lords of Council & Session, In the most Important Cases Debate before them, From July 1671 to July 1681* (Andrew Anderson 1687). Also worth noting is that, in 1681, Stair published a book on the Court of Session process: *Modus Litigandi or Form of Process observed Before the Lords of Council and Session in Scotland* (Andrew Anderson 1681). For discussion of the *Modus Litigandi*, see Alan Watson, *The Making of the Civil Law* (Harvard University Press 1981) 30–31; Ford *Law and Opinion* (n 25) 70–71, 377.

[52] Ford *Law and Opinion* (n 25) 574–79.

[53] Ford, *Law and Opinion* (n 25) 59–89; Adelyn L M Wilson, 'The Sources and Method of the *Institutions of the Law of Scotland* by Sir James Dalrymple, 1st Viscount Stair, with Specific Reference to the Law of Obligations' (DPhil thesis, Edinburgh University 2011); Adelyn L M Wilson, 'The Textual Tradition of Stair's *Institutions*, with Reference to the Title "Of Liberty and Servitude"' in Hector L MacQueen (ed), *Miscellany Seven* (Stair Society 2015) vol 62, 1–125.

[54] (Andrew Anderson 1681); (Edinburgh: Andrew Anderson 1693).

[55] (G Hamilton and J Balfour 1759) iii.

[56] (Thomas Clark 1826) iv.

back. Although there is yet to be a detailed analysis or comprehensive examination of any of the posthumous editions, More's edition appears to offer the most sensitive of the posthumous reproductions of the 1693 edition. The sixth edition was published in 1981[57] in celebration of the tercentenary of the 1681 original, and was edited by David Walker, Professor of Scots Law at the University of Glasgow. Unfortunately, Walker's edition is not without criticism, because it did nothing to untangle the knots tied by previous editors' intermingling of the 1693 edition with previous manuscript versions, or to pinpoint the unidentified edits of subsequent editors and avoid the modernizing updates which hinder a historical reading of the text.[58] As Wilson has noted, 'each of the new versions of the *Institutions* had changes made to the text, and many passages significantly altered between versions'.[59] It is with this background in mind that this study primarily draws upon the 1693 edition published by Stair but also, importantly, with reference to several manuscripts. Indeed, the approach taken in this book and the history of these manuscripts warrants further explanation.

As Gordon and Johnstone's first posthumous edition suggests, it has long been known that manuscript copies of earlier versions of the *Institutions* circulated within the Faculty of Advocates from 1662 onwards. Several comprehensive studies of the *Institutions*' drafting and the textual development of individual titles have been undertaken by Hutton[60] and Gordon.[61] More recently, there has been an intensification of such studies by Ford[62] and Adelyn Wilson.[63] Importantly, Ford has shown that there were two distinct manuscript editions produced by Stair before the publication of the first edition in 1681: one being an earlier 1662 version, and the other a 1671 edition.[64] In broad terms, these studies confirm that there were three versions of the *Institutions* before the second printed edition of 1693. Ford's research clarifies the question of when Stair began drafting his *Institutions*. According to him, the first version of the *Institutions* is the manuscript which Stair drafted during or sometime between 1659 and 1661.[65] Ford concludes it was finished sometime after the winter session of the Court of Session in 1661–62.[66] The first version of the *Institutions*, several copies of which survive today, then circulated within the Faculty from around 1662. The second manuscript is a revision of this first version. Ford believes that Stair revised this copy between 1666 and 1667.[67] There appear to have been no substantive changes to the structure, theoretical ideas, or substantive propositions of law, but rather minor

---

[57] (University Presses of Glasgow and Edinburgh 1981).

[58] Alan Watson, 'The Institutions of the Law of Scotland (1693) by James Viscount of Stair, David M. Walker' (1983) 27 (2) *The American Journal of Legal History* 214.

[59] Wilson 'The Textual Tradition of Stair's *Institutions*' (n 53) 2.

[60] Gordon M Hutton, 'Stair's Aim in Writing the *Institutions*' in David M Walker (ed), *Stair Tercentenary Studies* (Stair Society 1981) vol 33, 79 ff.

[61] William M Gordon, 'Stair, Grotius and Sources of Stair's *Institutions*' in William M Gordon (ed), *Roman Law, Scots Law and Legal History* (Edinburgh University Press 2007) 225–66.

[62] Ford *Law and Opinion* (n 45) 63–73.

[63] Wilson 'Sources and Method' (n 53) 14–32. Also see Wilson 'The Textual Tradition of Stair's *Institutions*' (n 53).

[64] Ford *Law and Opinion* (n 25) 68–73.

[65] Ford *Law and Opinion* (n 25) 72.

[66] Ford *Law and Opinion* (n 25) 73.

[67] Ford *Law and Opinion* (n 25) 70.

alterations and, importantly, some 500 additional citations.[68] The third version of the *Institutions* is the first published copy of 1681. There were significant alterations made to this version, which included the addition of more decisions made by the Court of Session between 1667 and 1681. Lastly, the fourth version was revised in 1692 and published in 1693. Wilson demonstrates that from 1663 to 1693, with the important exception of citations and references to decisions of the Court of Session, there were very limited substantive changes made to Stair's title on conventional obligations.[69]

Contractual Thought before Stair

In order fully to understand the significance to Stair's contractual thought, Chapter 1 explores the texts used by his legal contemporaries and what they themselves wrote about contracting. It demonstrates that Stair had several other examples of Scottish legal literature to draw upon when he first drafted the *Institutions*, including, importantly, the *Jus feudale* of James Craig (1538–1608).[70] Although he took inspiration from Craig's project, Stair's approach was different. Chapter 1 demonstrates that in the context of mid-seventeenth-century writing about contract, he is remarkable for several reasons. First, he departed from previous legal writing, including that of Craig, by making it clear that in Scotland customary law rather than Roman law applied to contractual and promissory obligations. Second, Stair's *Institutions* are distinctive because they emphasize explicitly that, in Scots customary law, a *nudum pactum* was enforceable within a secular court. Third, Stair is notable for adopting a unique structure and organization for his description of the law practised in Scotland when compared with those of his near contemporaries. Fourth, in comparison with his peers he is unique in adopting a relatively sophisticated theory of human action when describing the creation of a voluntary obligation. Fifth, by connecting the concepts of commerce, freedom, and contract in his explanation of the legal system in Scotland, Stair gives his *Institutions* a social and political significance. These are important differences. The mid-seventeenth-century literature of which the first draft of the *Institutions* is part does not offer much instruction as to how or why Stair came to offer a distinctive account of the law of obligations—but, as will be demonstrated, the intellectual context of Scotland in the mid- to late seventeenth century does.

Roman Law as a Source of Law

As Chapter 1 explains, Roman law was the central source of inspiration when novel legal questions relating to contract arose. Yet what is noteworthy is that Stair does not position Roman law in this manner. Thus, Chapter 2 examines Stair's express

---

[68] Ford *Law and Opinion* (n 25) 70. This being said, the introduction of the 1662 manuscripts and the introduction of the 1666 manuscripts differ.

[69] Wilson 'Sources and method' (n 53).

[70] Thomas Craig, *Jus Feudale Tribus Libris Comprehensum Quibus Non Solùm Consuetudines Feudales & Prædiorum Lura* (first published 1655, Leslie Dodd tr, Stair Society 2017).

objectives in writing the *Institutions* and how these aims relate to his handling of Roman law. It is evident that in realizing these objectives, it resulted in a reconfiguration, in the *Institutions*, of the traditional approach Scots lawyers would otherwise take to their sources of law. By placing Scots customary law at the forefront of his account of law in Scotland, Stair sought to demonstrate that Roman law played a supplementary role and was not the primary source of contract law in Scotland. In turn, this connected with his second express aim which was to demonstrate the equity of Scots law and offer an account of how human law, including the law of contract, related to natural law. A new philosophical basis for the law of contract in Scotland was therefore established by Stair, which framed Roman law sources as a possible source of equity rather than the embodiment of it. Thus, he urged judges to consider turning directly to equity when seeking out a solution to a novel issue of contract law, which involved an assessment of its utility as well as its equity. Stair thus offers a means by which solutions to new questions of contract law could be assessed, including those found in the Roman law sources often used by Scots lawyers. Hence Chapter 2 concludes by noting that Stair could rightly be understood as innovating within the Roman law tradition, offering a new way by which to justify the use of such sources that was more aligned to his conceptualization of natural law and legal reasoning.

A New Philosophical Basis for Contract Law in Scotland

A summary of Stair's account of contracting is given in Chapter 3, paying particular attention to key concepts which he brought from natural law and into the foreground. This chapter makes it clear that, when compared with his legal contemporaries, Stair is distinctive in terms of his language, structure, and approach: his description of contract is sophisticated and uses ideas and language taken from medieval theology, scholastic philosophy, and modern natural law theories. Stair also wished to demonstrate that the law of Scotland was based on foundational principles, which were derived from equity and honed by utility—something that he developed in detail throughout the *Institutions*. Hence to determine the solution to a novel legal situation or to justify the approach taken by the existing law, Stair sought to demonstrate that legal propositions should be evaluated, not only for their equity but also their utility. In this regard, Stair saw equity as a means by which you could realize natural law and utility as a model by which to ensure workable solutions were found within a political community formed out of necessity.

Upon this observation that natural law can only be partially implemented by human law for society to remain stable and peaceful, Stair then deployed three central ideas relating to contract: that the will is the primary trigger for the creation of offers, promises, and contracts; that man has a God-given freedom by which to bind himself; and that this freedom should be directed towards bringing glory to God. In relation to this last idea, Stair was ever conscious of the fact that there were limits to the jurisdiction and capabilities of human law therefore making it clear to his readers that it should be man's conscience that directs his use of his freedom to contract. Later chapters expand upon this interpretation of Stair's account, whereas Chapter 3 explains how he deployed these concepts as well as his equity-utility axis to key doctrines of contract law, such as formation, formality, third-party rights, *laesio enormis*, and the nominate contracts of Roman law. Indeed Chapter 3 stresses that the footprint of Roman law is unmistakable within Stair's description of contract law in Scotland, but that as subsequent chapters argue he reformulated the justification, understanding, and use of Roman law in Scotland according to his new philosophical system.

Standing by the Faith of Pactions and Promises

Chapter 4 examines a central claim within Stair's *Institutions*: there is nothing more natural than standing by one's pactions, and so a *nudum pactum*, including a promise, is enforceable in a secular Scots court.[71] From the point of view of legal history, this was a significant development in Scotland. For centuries prior to this, *nuda pacta* were, by their definition, unenforceable in secular courts. Although such developments had happened in other courts around Europe, it is difficult to find any indication of their enforcement in Scotland before Stair's *Institutions*. On this basis, Chapter 4 suggests that Stair differs from his contemporaries because he was prepared to apply his natural law theory to the law of Scotland directly and, if necessary, in contradiction to both the Roman law and traditional notions of the Court of Session's temporal jurisdiction. It is here that equity came before the requirements of utility.

This chapter demonstrates, however, that no matter whether Stair's contemporaries understood the law of Scotland to enforce *nuda pacta*, when viewed through the lens of Stair's natural law theory that was a small step. Of course, as will be acknowledged, Roman law could be viewed by lawyers and theologians in the early modern period as a near-embodiment of natural law; but Stair did not share that perspective. Rather, he drew from the Calvinist notion that some basic principles of natural law, ie the Moral Law, were known to man without reasoning, observation, the wisdom of antiquity or Roman law, or Scripture. Simply by the innate sense of the basic principles of morality imprinted on man's heart, ie conscience, which included standing by the faith of our pactions, man knew what he should do, at least in very basic terms. If Stair was to demonstrate that the law of Scotland related to the nature of man and the Moral Law of God, it was imperative that *nuda pacta* were, at least in theory, enforceable. In taking this approach, Stair minimized the otherwise received wisdom and equity of Roman law that dominated a great deal of Scottish legal thinking in the mid-seventeenth century.

It will also be suggested that this strong sense of the moral imperative of standing by the faith of one's pactions meant that Stair differed from Grotius and others by suggesting that promises, even without acceptance, were, theoretically, enforceable in Scots law. This chapter concludes that it was crucial to Stair's contractual thought that the law of contract was connected to a basic principle of natural law, which could be known without reasoning. That was a significant step, as it demonstrated that Stair was also prepared to leave behind the conventional wisdom of Roman law in order to give an account of the law of contract in Scotland.

---

[71] Stair *Inst* 1.10.4–6.

Stair's 'Plain Method' and Structure

Chapter 5 argues that Stair developed an innovative structure for the *Institutions* and contract due to his blend of legal humanism and Aristotelianism.[72] The opening passage of the 1681 edition of the *Institutions* extols the virtues of a 'Plain, Rational, and Natural Method'.[73] At several points, Stair indicates that he is consciously moving from self-evident general principles to their natural consequences which manifest in particulars.[74] Stair explained: 'I have chosen the method I thought fittest for this purpose, and the terms most intelligible in common use, and have as much as I could, forborne the terms of art'.[75]

Prior to Stair's *Institutions*, the law of Scotland had an overlapping and disparate collection of rules and legal orders applying to the creation of an obligation. For example, one could create a bond or an oath; register a contract; or physically transfer a moveable. Each of these different modes of creating an obligation carried with it a different set of rules, including both cause and the appropriate jurisdiction wherein one might pursue the performance of that obligation. It is argued that there was no generalized mode of thinking about these different legal orders in Scottish legal literature. Stair himself noted that the traditional approach of Roman law was confused. However, in Chapter 4 it is argued that his understanding of Aristotelian reasoning, coupled with a Calvinist reading of what the Moral Law was, helped him to link these otherwise different legal orders and rules. Against this backdrop, one can see the generalized notion of contract found in the *Institutions* as a likely consequence of, and being shaped by, Stair's Aristotelianism and Calvinist understanding of the basic principles of Moral Law.

Human Action, the Will, and Freedom

Stair did not only introduce the terminology of 'conventional' and 'obediential obligation' into the lexicon of Scottish legal discourse, but also, he used the terminology of the 'will' when describing legally relevant voluntary acts, which is a notable development within legal language. Of course, the idea that contracts were created by the consent or agreement of individuals was a familiar notion to lawyers who studied either Roman or canon law in the early modern period. There is no examination or description of consent or human action within existing literature used by Scots lawyers in the mid-seventeenth century. However, in the first version of the *Institutions*, Stair offers a relatively sophisticated description of human action for a legal treatise.

The use of the term 'will' is itself distinctive. Lawyers in the seventeenth century would have drawn from canon law to describe the will within the act of marriage but

---

[72] In the 1980s, John Ford suggested that 'in keeping with his academic training and with Duarenus' recommendation' Stair followed 'the method attributed to Aristotle': John D Ford, 'The Rational Discipline of Law' (DPhil thesis, University of Cambridge 1988) 44.

[73] Stair *Inst* Dedication.

[74] Stair *Inst* Dedication; 1.1; 1.1.17; 1.1.23.

[75] Stair *Inst* 1.1.1.

would not normally use canonist ideas to describe contracting. Rather more widely, the concept of will would have been associated with theological descriptions of human decision-making. In addition, the way in which Stair uses a three-stage description of human action—desire, resolution, and will—to explain the steps towards the conclusion of a conventional obligation is useful, not only analytically and linguistically but also practically, in helping to distinguish between different types of actions that do or do not create a contract.

This chapter explains how philosophical theology from the medieval period relates to Stair's discussion of the human will, freedom, and liberty. It describes how different senses of freedom and liberty are used in early modern literature, and which should inform our understanding of Stair's uses of these terms. By exploring the heritage of these concepts and their use in contemporary seventeenth-century literature, the chapter argues that Stair shared the same metaphysical and ethical toolbox as many of the Jesuit theologian-cum-jurists of the early modern period.

Freedom, Liberty, and Conscience

It is central to this book's analysis of Stair's contractual thought to explain how he understood liberty and freedom. Chapter 7 seeks to shed new light on this by examining how Stair described these concepts in his *Divine Perfections*. Additionally, other mid-seventeenth-century theological texts are considered, including the Westminster Confession of Faith (1647), each demonstrating what liberty and freedom would have meant to his mid-seventeenth-century audience. Taking this approach, demonstrates the complex and sophisticated conception of liberty that Stair describes in his *Divine Perfections* and that his theological account is consistent with his legal account in the *Institutions*. Although a modern reading of Stair would understand his use of liberty in a rather one-dimensional (Hobbesian) negative sense, ie liberty from external interference, Stair in fact used the concept of liberty in the full knowledge that, to his readers, it would have a two-dimensional sense, ie a rich theological meaning. His readers would have unmistakably known that he was invoking the idea that man should use his liberty not only to tend to his own needs and necessities but also, importantly, to bring glory to God. In other words, when Stair used the concept of liberty with relation to the law of contract, he did so with a thick notion of liberty or a positive conception that differed from the Hobbesian sense.

But, importantly, given his political perspective, Stair did not suggest that the human law or a civil authority should guide the use of liberty; rather, that it should be man's conscience. On this reading, it is suggested that he understood our freedom to contract as being shaped by a personal ethics. However, our personal ethics should not be left untutored, according to Stair. Rather, when reading Stair in the context of the mid-seventeenth century, it is clear that, for a Calvinist like him, an individual's decision to use their liberty should be informed by their conscience and guided by the preaching, detailed catechisms and the burgeoning casuistry literature of Protestant ministers and theologians that addressed, inter alia, contracting. But, importantly, Stair did not suggest that this should be done by civil authorities or the positive law. This leaves a space within his account of the freedom of contract for individuals to make their own decisions about how they contract with others.

Freedom to Contract in the Seventeenth Century

One of the most important influences on Stair is Hugo Grotius. Hence, Chapter 8 explains what of freedom of contract meant to Grotius in comparison with Stair. Noting that the idea of freedom of contract can have numerous different meanings, either contemporaneously or historically, this chapter nonetheless argues that it is profitable to compare Stair with these writers but also to consider, if possible, what relationship these early modern writers might have with contemporary notions of freedom of contract.

The chapter argues that although statements of free trade are commonplace within Classical literature, from Aristotle to the *Institutes* of Justinian, there is a notable reformulation of this notion in Grotius and, to an extent, Stair. They attach this notion of free trade to an individual rather than a state or community; they formulate it in terms of a right of an individual; they say that it is right for man to trade; and they do so using juristic concepts such as a contract and the interpersonal language of private law.

However, as the chapter demonstrates, although there are similarities, there are very important differences between the work of Stair and that of Grotius. In comparing and contrasting the writers, it becomes evident that each was informed by different theological and ecclesiastical perspectives, which set different limits and jurisdictions around man's liberty to contract. Stair gave an account of liberty and contracting in the *Institutions* that left space for ecclesiastical authorities to shape the conscience of parishioners but, importantly, without the use of civil authority or human law. Grotius did not make such space. Chapter 8 demonstrates that the respective theological and political viewpoints of Grotius and Stair undoubtedly shape the extent to which they see another person or institution shaping or guiding the use of man's liberty, but that they nonetheless shared a theoretical standpoint in the connection between liberty, trade and contract that at least resembles modern notions of freedom of contract. Importantly, in their natural law theories, they made a division between aspects of natural law that can be enforced by a civil authority and those that cannot, therefore setting up a familiar distinction between personal ethics or imperfect duties and (civil) legal duties or perfect duties.

The Reception of Stair's Contractual Thought

The immediate reception of Stair's contractual thought is usefully considered by comparing Stair's approach to that of George Mackenzie and Gershom Carmichael. Although a comparison between Stair and Carmichael may not be immediately obvious, as the latter is known as a moral philosopher, whereas Stair was a jurist, Chapter 9 explains why it is an illuminating comparison. On this basis, Chapter 9 argues that it was moral professors who sustained the form of natural law enquiry into law that we find in Stair's work. In the teachings and writings of late seventeenth and early eighteenth-century moral philosophers, we find exploration of the origins of civil society and discussion of the concepts of justice, property, liberty, rights, trade, and, importantly, contract as building blocks of society. In other words, it may not necessarily have been jurists, such as Mackenzie, who continued Stair's contractual project but rather moral professors, who themselves were engaged in a natural law exploration of the origins of civil society, including consideration of the aforementioned concepts. Therefore Chapter 9 argues for a wider definition of what counts as legal writing or legal thought in the eighteenth century.

Once the field of enquiry is broadened to include natural law writing, the chapter demonstrates that Stair's approach to the law of contract was received as part of a burgeoning literature known today as Protestant natural law theories; such writing included consideration of basic juristic concepts of, inter alia, rights, property, and contracts. If viewed from this broader angle, Stair's contractual thought is one instance of an otherwise growing interest in natural law in Scotland and indeed northern Europe that continued into the eighteenth century. Chapter 9 shows that Carmichael's work can be viewed as an example of Stair's style of contractual thought being sustained and developed in Scotland. In particular, central aspects of Stair's contractual thought continued to be discussed, adapted, and considered in Scotland during the eighteenth century, including: his engagement with axiomatic principles, ie standing by the faith of a paction or performing promises; his organization of these principles around a primary duty to God and then secondary duties and rights owed to our neighbours; his organization of the basic principles of civil society around property, contract, and rights; his division between natural and juristic obligations; and his concern with the internal triggers for the creation of obligations and responsibility. Stair may not have influenced Carmichael, but they did share a similar project: a reworking of Grotius's natural law theory for theological and philosophical reasons. Indeed, Stair's engagement with Grotius, which included consideration of contracting and commerce, was something that Scots and others beyond Scotland continued within the Protestant natural law tradition well into the eighteenth century.

Stair within a Wider European Context

The chapters of this book therefore build towards arguing that we should not only return to Stair to properly understand an often-lauded source of law in Scotland but is valuable to our understanding of how notions of freedom to contract developed in northern Europe.[76] Of note is that Stair's *Institutions* represents a Calvinist reworking of the natural law theory of Hugo Grotius (1583–1645), which inspired, influenced, and shaped Stair's account of contracting. In 1937, Henderson remarked, in his study

---

[76] Of note is the impact of Grotian legal thought upon the development of contract law within various different European legal cultures. See the special edition of Grotiana which investigates Grotian notions of consent, promising and contract: Wim Decock, 'Hugo Grotius's Views on Consent, Contract and the Christian Commonwealth' (2020) 41 (1) Grotiana 1–12.

of Scottish religious and intellectual culture, that 'one Dutch name which affected all classes and schools [in Scotland] was that of Hugo Grotius'.[77] Despite this acknowledged influence, the relationship between Grotius's natural law theory and Scottish Calvinist understandings of human nature have never been fully explored.[78] For that reason, this book is a detailed examination of a particular variant of Protestant natural law,[79] which shaped ideas about the law of contract in Scotland.[80] It demonstrates how Stair's adherence to the main tenets of Calvinism, and particularly the doctrines of the Church of Scotland, coupled with his continual engagement with scholastic philosophy, shaped his approach to natural law and the law of contract. From a political and legal perspective, it can be said that Stair offered an account of the temporal rights and freedoms of individuals, in Scotland, which dovetailed with the Church of Scotland's spiritual instruction of how to use those rights and freedoms in accordance with one's conscience.

Stair also demonstrates the existence of non-confessional connections between a Calvinist and Jesuit account of contracting.[81] Our historical knowledge of how contracting has been understood by different European legal cultures has been significantly enriched through the work of Wim Decock. He has documented in great detail the reform of Catholic legal thought by early modern Jesuits who reclaimed Roman law for theological purposes. Re-reading sources of positive law which were used during the early modern period, including Roman law and canon law, with the renewed energy of the Counter-Reformation, Decock has shown how these juristically

---

[77] George D Henderson, *Religious Life in Seventeenth-Century Scotland* (CUP 1937) 75. It appears that German Lutherans in the mid-to-late seventeenth century also turned to Grotius, particularly because he was understood to be a more palatable alterative to Pufendorf: Paolo Astorri, 'Grotius's Contract Theory in the Works of His German Commentators: First Explorations' (2020) 41 (1) Grotiana 88–107.

[78] In offering an analysis of how Stair reworked Grotius's natural law theory, this book makes a contribution to the somewhat neglected intellectual history of seventeenth-century Scotland. For discussion, see: John Coffey, *Politics, Religion and the British Revolutions: The Mind of Samuel Rutherford* (CUP 1997) 1–29; Clare Jackson, *Restoration Scotland, 1660–1690: Royalist Politics, Religion and Ideas* (Boydell Press 2003) 1–13; Neil McIntyre, 'Saints and Subverters: The Later Covenanters in Scotland c. 1648–1682' (DPhil thesis, University of Strathclyde 2016) 1–19.

[79] Indeed, it compares Grotius's and Stair's different responses to what Haakonssen has described as 'a continuing ambiguity in Protestantism towards natural law as a rational account of morals' (Knud Haakonssen, *Natural Law and Moral Philosophy: From Grotius to the Scottish Enlightenment* (CUP 1996) 25).

[80] As a specific investigation into Stair's natural law theory of contracting, it arguably examines in detail a particular strand of what Gordley, and Hogg identify, as the 'Northern natural law school'. See James Gordley, *The Philosophical Origins of Modern Contract Doctrine* (OUP 1991) 5–7; Hogg *Promises and Contract* (n 10) 127; Randall Lesaffer, *European Legal History: A Cultural and Political Perspective* (CUP 2009) 448–50. It is worth remarking that although Stair comfortably fits within this definition, other jurists working within Northern Europe do not. Or at least Stair's open acknowledgment of Grotius is noteworthy. Interesting, several studies has identified a great deal of hesitancy when dealing with Grotius in the seventeenth century: Sören Koch, 'Grotius's Impact on the Scandinavian Theory of Contract Law' (2020) 41 (1) Grotiana 59–87.

[81] These chapters contribute to our understanding of the relationship between Catholic and Protestant reformers' writings about private law during the sixteenth and seventeenth centuries (at least from a Scottish perspective): Harold Berman, *Law and Revolution II: The Impact of the Protestant Reformation in the Western Legal Tradition* (Harvard University Press 2006) 70; Wim Decock, *Theologians and Contract Law: The Moral Transformation of the Ius Commune* (ca. 1500–1650) (Brill 2013) 14–20; Wim Decock, Jordan J Ballor, M Germann, and Laurent Waelkens (eds), *Law and Religion: The Legal Teachings of the Protestant and Catholic Reformations* (Vandenhoeck & Ruprecht 2014) 7–8; Stephen Bogle, 'Law and Religion' (2015) 19 (2) Edinburgh Law Review 285–87.

inclined Jesuits produced key juristic ideas and principles of contract law, including a notion that individuals had a freedom to contract which is realized by the exercise of the will.[82]

Additionally, Paolo Astorri's examination of Lutheran theology and contract law, has offered important insights into how jurists, lawyers, and theologians, predominately within what is now modern-day Germany, understood contracting in the early modern period maintaining a strict divide between the legal and the spiritual aspects of a contract.[83] In his rich and wide-ranging study, he demonstrates a distinctively Lutheran viewpoint of contract law, including their approach to interest and usury, but equally a cross-confessional affinity between Lutherans and early modern Jesuits: each offered a sophisticated moral interpretation of the existing doctrines and practice of contract law, providing an extensive repository of ethical direction about the purpose, use, and nature of contracts.

Significantly, this book investigates similar developments to those identified by Decock and Astorri, but within the Calvinist context of Scotland in the mid-seventeenth century. It is not, however, a comparative study matching and contrasting these diverse and individual approaches to the law of contract; but it does, particularly within the footnotes, begin to gesture towards the similarities and dissimilarities between these approaches. Indeed, if such a study were to be undertaken it would enrichen our appreciation of both the diversity but also the commonalities of various legal cultures within Europe. It would underscore that the development of legal systems, and particularly our understanding of law, in Europe, has been profoundly shaped by what might be called external intellectual developments that have their roots in philosophical theology.

Lastly, Stair's ideas of commerce and freedom of contract, which are found in copies of Stair's manuscripts which circulated from the 1660s onwards, are significant. They are suggestive of the more developed ideas of a commercial society and natural jurisprudence that emerged in the eighteenth century.[84] By demonstrating the existence of these ideas in Stair's *Institutions*, this book begins the process of exploring the relationship between Stair and eighteenth-century conceptions of commerce and sociability. It does so by clarifying what contracting meant to Stair and offering an interpretation

---

[82] Wim Decock, *Theologians and Contract Law: The Moral Transformation of the Ius Commune (ca. 1500–1650)* (Brill 2013).

[83] Paolo Astorri, *Lutheran Theology and Contract Law in Early Modern Germany (ca. 1520—1720)* (Brill 2020).

[84] This is to take seriously MacCormick's remark that Stair's natural law account of the positive law in Scotland was in some ways an anticipation of the ideas of a commercial society associated with the eighteenth century: Neil MacCormick, 'The Rational Discipline of Law' (1982) 26 Juridical Review 146, 159. However, in identifying this connection, such an argument also needs to be mindful of Hont's insights that such ideas are presented in the seventeenth century: István Hont and Michael Ignatieff, 'Needs and Justice in the *Wealth of Nations*: An Introductory Essay' in István Hont and Michael Ignatieff (eds), *Wealth and Virtue: The Shaping of Political Economy in the Scottish Enlightenment* (CUP 1983) 1–44; István Hont, 'The Language of Sociability and Commerce' in Anthony Pagden (ed), *The Languages of Political Theory in Early-Modern Europe* (CUP 1987) 253–76.

of his concept of freedom to contract. This interpretation stresses the philosophical theological meaning of freedom and Stair's Calvinist world view that said that freedom should be used to bring glory to God.[85] But it also helps to explain how elements of Stair's reformulation of contracting relate to later developments in both the characterization and legal regulation of commerce in the eighteenth century.

---

[85] In making this argument, there are similarities between what Dunn has identified as Locke's conception of freedom to achieve 'your calling' and what Stair calls freedom to 'bring glory to God': John Dunn, *The Political Thought of John Locke* (OUP 1969) 245–61.

1

Contractual Thought before Stair

This chapter aims to provide a picture of contractual thought in Scotland in the mid-seventeenth century, around the time Stair drafted the first version of his *Institutions of the Law of Scotland* (*Institutions*). It begins by summarizing the existing secondary literature and suggests how the interpretation offered here differs from previous studies of the law of contract in seventeenth-century Scotland.[1] The primary material selected for examination here has been identified in separate studies by John Ford and Adelyn Wilson as being used in or around the 1650s in Scotland.[2] Such texts were reprintings of medieval statutes, more recent legislation, or different types of legal manuscripts produced by previous generations of lawyers and used as current legal literature.[3] There were also compilations which incorporated various types of legal sources into one document, or more substantive digests written by advocates or judges working in the Court of Session.[4] Many other texts are not considered here, but it is hoped that the interpretation offered here can give sufficient context against which to understand Stair's contractual thought.

This chapter examines what David Ibbetson has described as the 'frameworks' through which lawyers approach the rules of law which they used.[5] Hence, this chapter investigates the sources, structure, and style of legal writing found in these texts. That is: what sources of law did Scots lawyers use, and what authority did they attribute to them; how did lawyers or jurists organize the law applying to contracting behaviour; and is there any indication of theoretical considerations within these sources, such as an account of what consent is, any express or implied normative justification for the enforcement of contracts or promises, and any general account of what a contract is

---

[1] cf Kenneth Reid and Reinhard Zimmermann, 'The Development of Legal Doctrine in a Mixed System' in Kenneth Reid and Reinhard Zimmermann (eds), *A History of Private Law in Scotland* (OUP 2000) vol 1, 1; John D Ford, *Law and Opinion in Scotland during the Seventeenth Century* (Hart 2007) x.

[2] NLS Ms 8490 (John Nisbett?); Adv Ms 24.4.14 (George Lockhart?); Ad Ms 24.3.9 (George Lockhart?); Adv Ms 25.4.2 (John Nisbet?); Adv Ms 24.2.3 (John Thomson); Adv Ms 24.3.2 (Thomas Wallace?); Ad Ms 24.1.3 (Thomas Wallace?); NLS Ms 3171 (Thomas Wallace?); NLS Ms 943 (Thomas Wallace?) Adv Ms 24.1.3 (Peter Wedderburn?); NLS MS 5435 (Robert Ker?).

[3] See Andrew R C Simpson and Adelyn L M Wilson, *Scottish Legal History Volume 1: 1000–1707* (Edinburgh University Press 2017) 276–88, who generally divide legal literature during the seventeenth century into five categories: editions of laws; collections of decisions; digests or digest practicks; manuals for practice; treatise or institutional writing.

[4] Ford, *Law and Opinion* (n 1) 1–89; Adelyn L M Wilson, 'The Sources and Method of the *Institutions of the Law of Scotland*, by Sir James Dalrymple, 1st Viscount Stair, with Specific Reference to the Law of Obligations (DPhil thesis, University of Edinburgh 2011); Simpson and Wilson *Scottish Legal History* (n 3) 257–328. Of course, there were other sources used and written during this period, but the selection adopted in this chapter is taken to be generally indicative of a style of legal writing which emerged in the 1650s around the time that Stair wrote the first draft of the *Institutions*; see Ford *Law and Opinion* (n 1) 73–84.

[5] David Ibbetson, 'What is Legal History a History of?' in Andrew Lewis and Michael Lobban (eds), *Law and History: Current Legal Issues 2003* (Oxford 2004), vol 6, 38.

Contract before the Enlightenment. Stephen Bogle, Oxford University Press. © Stephen Bogle 2023.
DOI: 10.1093/oso/9780192884961.003.0002

and how it relates to other doctrines or concepts of private law. This helps to demonstrate, by means of comparison, the distinctiveness of Stair's account of contracting and the need to explain Stair's approach by appealing to the wider political, theological, and philosophical context within which he operated. Indeed, Stair's approach to the law of contract, which emerges when compared to his contemporaries, strongly suggests that he was drawing upon ideas beyond legal sources and was more receptive in comparison to others in offering a philosophical and theologically informed account of private law.

Contract Law before Stair

Sources and methods

It is important to start with the insights that can be taken from Wilson's examination of the sources and methods used by Stair when drafting his title on conventional obligations.[6] First, she identifies that Stair drew the majority of his citations for the decisions of the Court of Session from judicial notes and reports, that were collected together in manuscript papers and known as practicks; these included Lord Durie's practicks, but also practicks produced by or associated with Thomas Hope, Robert Spotiswoode, Thomas Hamilton (Earl of Haddington), and Thomas Nicholson.[7] This suggests, as will be discussed below, that an examination of the approach to the law of contract found in Durie, but also others such as Hope are particularly significant. Second, Wilson finds that Stair often referred to Hugo Grotius on points of natural law (although not always agreeing with him), and that Petrus Gudelinus was his principal source of Roman law, but that he also used Arnold Vinnius and Arnold Corvinus in a similar manner (with the latter also used for propositions of canon law).[8] What Wilson stresses is that Stair's use of 'continental sources was typical of Scottish jurists of the period', emphasizing connections between legal writing in Scotland and particularly in the Low Countries.[9] As is also clear from the *Institutions* and Wilson's examination, it was not restricted to jurists from the Low Countries, as Stair also cited Jesuits, French jurists, and from what is modern-day Germany. But Wilson is keen to demonstrate that it is highly likely that, in numerous places, Stair lifted his citation of one writer from another, and so caution should be exercised when examining Stair's references. Third, from an examination of libraries available to Scots lawyers during the mid- to late seventeenth century, she has also suggested that 'some Scots jurists did have extensive knowledge of [continental legal] literature and incorporated this into their writing'.[10] A final few points should be stressed. Wilson demonstrates that Stair

---

[6] Wilson 'Sources and Method' (n 4).

[7] Wilson 'Sources and Method' (n 4) 29. Interestingly, Wilson has also highlighted that Stair was unconcerned about citing decisions made by the interregnum court that was established during the 1650s under Cromwell's protectorate, although he did conceal the source of these decisions: A Wilson, 'Practicks in Scotland's Interregnum' (2012) Juridical Review 319.

[8] Wilson 'Sources and Method' (n 4) 253–55.

[9] Wilson 'Sources and Method' (n 4) 262.

[10] Wilson 'Sources and Method' (n 4) 47.

vastly increased his references to continental literature in his title on conventional obligations between the 1660s and the 1680s. However, it is also clear that his underlying structure and general propositions of law did not change: in other words, Stair sought to strengthen the original draft of the *Institutions* with supplementary references rather than fundamentally alter his approach to conventional obligations. Importantly, for this book, this suggests that Stair's contractual thought did not significantly change from the late 1650s to the publication of the first printed edition of the *Institutions* in 1681. Overall, Wilson demonstrates that some lawyers in Scotland, mostly advocates and judges, had access to various forms of legal literature from around Europe and importantly, relatively up-to-date literature too, which would convey to Scots, if they had not already gathered these from travel and study abroad, contemporary notions about the traditional sources of the *ius commune* and ideas about customary law found in other jurisdictions, including ideas and practices relating to contracting.

Doctrines and rules

what is Ford's methodology?

We here follow Ford's and Wilson's historical methodologies for the examination of doctrinal sources.[11] In general, when the circumstances within which Stair wrote his title on conventional obligations are analyzed, it has been from the viewpoint of specific rules or doctrines. Such an approach neglects analysis of Stair's contractual thought or wider legal writing; it views things from the perspective not of what Stair and his contemporaries thought they were doing but rather of how the rules and doctrines Stair describes relate to modern-day doctrines of contract law.[12] Such work does, nonetheless, stress that Stair introduced an innovative and distinctive mode of contractual thought, without examining the historical qualities of Stair's *Institutions* comprehensively.[13] In other words, there have been several doctrinal histories of Scots contract law but very few legal histories and limited exploration of the legal thought of the key contributors.[14] Moreover, one of the persistent conclusions which emerges from this literature is that both canon and Roman law shaped and, in some places, determined the rules and doctrines of contract law which were used in Scotland

[11] Such an intimate attention to detail in terms of manuscripts, libraries, and the working methods of a writer offers a new way to approach many writers within Scots legal history, which John Ford has masterfully demonstrated in his monograph *Law and Opinion* and which Wilson expertly demonstrated in her doctoral thesis. Some earlier examples of this approach, which often sheds much-needed light on otherwise intractable doctrinal debates, include, importantly: William M Gordon, 'Stair, Grotius and the Sources of Stair's *Institutions*' in William M Gordon (ed), *Roman Law, Scots Law and Legal History: Selected Essays* (EUP 2007) 255; and Alan Rodger, 'Molina, Stair and the jus quaesitum tertio' (1969) Juridical Review 34 and 128.

[12] See Alexander J Mackenzie Stuart, 'Contract and Quasi Contract' in *An Introduction to Scottish Legal History*, vol 20 (Stair Society 1958) 241; James J Gow, 'The Constitution and Proof of Voluntary Obligations' (1961) 1 Juridical Rreview; Gerhard Lubbe, 'Formation of Contract' in Kenneth Reid and Reinhard Zimmermann (eds), *A History of Private Law in Scotland*, vol 1 (OUP 2000) 1.

[13] MacKenzie Stuart 'Contract and Quasi Contract' (n 12) 253; Lubbe 'Formation of Contract' (n 12) 44–46; William D H Sellar, 'Promise' in Kenneth Reid and Reinhard Zimmermann (eds), *A History of Private Law in Scotland*, vol 1 (OUP 2000) 252, 226.

[14] For discussion of doctrinal history in Scotland, see Reid and Zimmermann 'The Development of Legal Doctrine in a Mixed System' (n 1) 8. For a general discussion about doctrinal history, see Ibbetson 'What is Legal History a History of?' (n 5) 33–40.

in the early modern period. Of course, this is no surprise: the legal tradition which mid-seventeenth-century Scots lawyers inherited was one which had been in various ways drawing from *ius commune* sources of opinion and law for well over a century.[15] However, the purpose here is not to designate one or other doctrine according to modern conceptions of heritage—Roman law, canon law, English law, and so on—but to examine the writing, texts, and contractual thought of mid-seventeenth-century lawyers. We need to understand how Stair and his contemporaries used and understood the *ius commune* and its sources, and not view mid-seventeenth-century contractual thought as another phase of simple 'reception'.

Ius commune tradition in Scotland

Later chapters will explore the place of Roman law within seventeenth-century Scottish legal practice of contract law. But for now, it is important to note that there are numerous reasons why the *ius commune* more generally influenced the law of Scotland; but, by the middle of the sixteenth century, Scotland faced several deficiencies within its native legal sources, particularly its statutory law which acted as a catalyst for Scots to draw more liberally and creatively from the *ius commune*.[16] It also provided an educational and intellectual fabric to legal practice in Scotland. Indeed, in the mid-seventeenth century, entry into the Scots bar was gained almost exclusively by providing the Lords of Session with a lesson upon a particular title of the *Digest*.[17] Scots lawyers did not just study the *ius commune* sources, they cited it copiously in their pleadings at the bar,[18] and when they wrote about the law applying to contracting in Scotland they often used its language, structure, and propositions of law. In terms of what lawyers meant by *ius commune*, it appears that by the start of the seventeenth century the phrase 'common law' or *ius commune* meant Roman law rather than canon law.[19] Stair was to innovate in this

[15] John W Cairns, 'The Civil Law Tradition in Scottish Legal Thought' in David L Carey Miller and Reinhard Zimmermann (eds), *The Civilian Tradition and Scots Law: Aberdeen Quincentenary Essays* (Duncker & Humblot 1995) 191; Gero Dolezalek, 'Introduction: The Purpose of this Book' in Gero Dolezalek (ed), *Scotland under the Ius Commune*, vol 55 (Stair Society 2010) 1–12.

[16] John Cairns, 'Historical Introduction' in Kenneth Reid and Reinhard Zimmermann (eds), *A History of Private Law in Scotland*, vol 1 (OUP 2000) 14–184 at 73. Also see Peter Stein, 'The Influence of Roman Law' (1963) 8 Juridical Review 205; Gero Dolezalek, 'The Court of Session as a Ius Commune Court—Witnessed by "Sinclair's Practicks", 1540–1549' in Hector L MacQueen (ed), *Miscellany Four*, vol 49 (Stair Society 2002) 72–75; John W Cairns, 'Jus Civile in Scotland, ca. 1600' (2004) 2 Roman Legal Tradition 136.

[17] John W Cairns, 'The Law, the Advocates and the Universities in Late Sixteenth-Century Scotland' (1994) 73 (196) Scottish Historical Review 171; Ford *Law and Opinion* (n 1) 1–29.

[18] Durie *Practicks*; Spotiswoode *Practicks*; Anonymous, *The Decisions of the English Judges, during the Usurpation, from the Year 1655, to His Majesty's Restoration, and the Sitting Down of the Session in June 1661* (Hamilton & Balfour 1762); James Dalrymple, Viscount Stair, *The Decisions of the Lords of Council & Session, in the Most Important Cases Debate before Them with the Acts of Sederunt* (Anderson 1681); John Lauder, Lord Fountainhall, *The Decisions of the Lords of Council and Session, from June 6th, 1678, to July 30th, 1712*, vols 1 and 2 (Hamilton & Balfour 1759–61).

[19] Cairns 'Jus Civile in Scotland' (n 16) 135–70. However, as Cairns makes clear, this designation should not suggest a clear disambiguation between Roman law and canon law; it is important to remember that Roman law and canon law had been mixing and moulding together for centuries prior to this definitive move towards a Roman law *simpliciter* definition. Hence, when Scots used the term *ius commune* or Roman

regard:[20] he sought to establish that the 'common law' of Scotland could be found in the decisions of the Session. Ford has argued that in Hope's *Major Practicks* we find a foreshadowing of this understanding of the common law of Scotland.[21] However, in terms of framing contractual thought in the mid-seventeenth century, it is far safer to assume that, by and large, common law was taken to mean, by the majority of Scots, the Roman law. Therefore, although Roman law and canon law should not be treated as separate legal regimes in the early modern period and should not always be reduced to specific source documents, it is possible to say that the basic notions of contracting found in the primary texts of, and commentaries on, the *Corpus iuris civilis* and the *Corpus iuris canonici* served as the intellectual backdrop—language, concepts, and taxonomy—to the native legal thinking about contracting in Scotland during the early modern period; and, by the mid-seventeenth century, Roman law was a more dominant source of law.

In terms of rules and doctrines, there has been a great deal of research into the influence of 'Roman law' upon the private law of Scotland.[22] As already noted, the focus in this chapter is not to trace or identify the place of Roman or canon law in the making of native customary law in Scotland or to define what they are in relation to the practice of mid-seventeenth-century law in Scotland. It remains a tricky topic in terms of measuring the extent of that influence, pinpointing points of contact and assessing its modern-day legacy.[23] Additionally, unlike much of the existing literature on the history of the law of contract in Scotland, the approach taken in this chapter is horizontal; that is, comparing Stair to near-contemporaries rather than to predecessors or subsequent jurists. Specific rules or doctrines are not the focus here. Our attention will be upon contractual thought more generally. By examining the patterns of citation, styles of writing, methods compilation, and existing legal texts used by Scots lawyers, it is possible to identify if there were any substantive theoretical ideas about the law of contract held during this period. Indeed, given Scotland's long connections with the *ius commune* legal tradition and the extent to which, as Wilson demonstrated, Stair had access to modern commentaries upon Roman law, it is significant that Stair focused upon the law in Scotland and institutions of law creation within Scotland, such as the Court of Session. Hence, writing about customary law in the way Stair did is an important development.[24]

---

law in the mid-seventeenth century, they were referring to what was in effect the product of centuries of cross-fertilization of Roman law and canon law.

[20] Ford *Law and Opinion* (n 1) Ch 6.

[21] Ford *Law and Opinion* (n 1) 281.

[22] Miller and Zimmermann *The Civilian Tradition and Scots Law* (n 15); Kenneth Reid and Reinhard Zimmermann (eds), *A History of Private Law in Scotland*, vol 1 (OUP 2000).

[23] For example, John D Ford 'The Civilian Tradition and Scots Law: Aberdeen Quincentenary Essays. Edited by David L Carey Miller and Reinhard Zimmermann' (1998) 57 (2) Cambridge Law Journal 415–18; John D Ford, 'A History of Private Law in Scotland, 2 vols' (2001) 60 (3) Cambridge Law Journal 630; Robert Feenstra, 'The Development of European Private Law: A Watershed?' in Carey Miller and Reinhard Zimmermann, *The Civilian Tradition and Scots Law* (n 15) 103; Paul J du Plessis, 'Legal History and Method(s)' (2010) 16 (1) Fundamina 47; John W Cairns, 'National, Transnational and European Legal Histories: Problems and Paradigms. A Scottish Perspective' (2012) 5 Clio@Themis: Revue Électronique D'histoire du Droit 1.

[24] Simpson and Wilson *Scottish Legal History* (n 3) 273–90.

Writing about Customary Law in Scotland

Stair is noteworthy, in comparison to his contemporaries, because he provided a comprehensive account of private law in Scotland and explained its historical origins, albeit briefly, and its theoretical roots far more extensively. In comparison both to previous generations of Scots lawyers and to his contemporaries, it is remarkable the depths Stair plumbed in providing an original theoretical framework and analytical scheme for the law used and developed in Scotland. However, in comparison to European colleagues, he may not be unique: he could be recognized as part of an important group of jurists who moved the focus away from the *ius commune* tradition towards local customary law.[25] Across western areas of Europe in the mid-seventeenth century, various ideas were emerging about the importance and place of local customary law and how it related to the otherwise dominant sources and ideas of the *ius commune* tradition.[26] There was an emerging literature, known as the Institutions or Institutes, which by the end of the seventeenth century focused solely on the independent law of European principalities, much like Stair's own *Institutions*.[27] As national legal literature emerged, there was a growing sense of nation states but also of the need to rationalize and explain native customary law in comparison to other bodies of customary law and learned sources of law, such as the Roman law and canon law.[28] This can be compared to previous generations of lawyers in Scotland and around Europe who would engage with transnational legal systems in a direct manner and in preference for customary law. Therefore, this is an important context to have in mind when understanding the legal background against which Stair wrote his *Institutions*. Stair, as will be argued, is the most developed and pronounced example of this within mid-seventeenth-century Scottish legal writing—by finding a structure, theory, and collection of sources which was capable of serving as an extensive body of law for Scotland—but there were others who, to varying degrees, attempted similar things to Stair.

Contemporary Legal Writing in the 1650s

Stair was not the first Scots lawyer to write about Scots customary law. As already noted, when he came to write about the law in Scotland, previous attempts were available to him in the form practicks. Although far from exhaustive, Hector McKechnie has suggested that the extant practicks could be divided into decision practicks and digest practicks—the first being judicial notes of decisions, whereas the second is a

---

[25] Klaus Luig, 'The Institutes of National Law in the Seventeenth and Eighteenth Centuries' (1972) Juridical Review 193; Alan Watson, *The Making of the Civil Law* (Harvard University Press 1981) 62–82. Jean-Louis Halpérin reads this as state intervention because it was often legal professionals, judges, or jurists who, associated in some way or funded by the state, initiated such literature: *Five Legal Revolutions Since the 17th Century: An Analysis of Global Legal History* (Springer 2014) 30.

[26] Peter Stein, *Roman Law in European History* (CUP 1999) 104–05; Ford, *Law and Opinion* (n 1) 181–247.

[27] Luig 'Institutes of National Law' (n 25).

[28] Luig 'Institutes of National Law' (n 25).

compilation of various reports written up retrospectively.[29] Dolezalek explains that during the sixteenth and seventeenth centuries in Scotland 'the term was on the one hand applied to general digests of domestic law which collected legal rules from all available sources: statutes, "auld lawis" and judicial precedent'[30] while also being used to describe 'digests which only collected judicial precedents'.[31] Some of the practicks used during the mid-seventeenth century included what are now known as Sir James Balfour's practicks,[32] Hope's practicks,[33] and Spotiswoode's practicks.[34] In comparison to practicks, Craig's *Jus Feudale*[35] was one of the only Scots texts prior to the 1650s which sought to cover a specific area of law comprehensively by bringing together *ius commune* sources of law with domestic law applied in Scotland.[36] Often practicks were written against the backdrop of the *ius commune* or a conception of legal learning, and often they did not make explicit or express how the practick operated in relation to other sources of law. In comparison, Craig's treatise offered a comprehensive local account of feudal law in Scotland and was clear about each individual source of law's authority in Scotland. These rough distinctions, however, are not exhaustive, as there are other examples of practicks which do not fit neatly into McKechnie's rough distinction because they contain not always exclusively decisions of the Court of Session or judicial reports but also legislation, citation of learned authority, and commentaries. As Wilson and Andrew Simpson warn, some caution should be exercised in terms of using McKechnie's rough distinction, but nonetheless for the purposes of this chapter it gives a starting point from which to approach these texts and examine contractual thought.[37]

Of note is that some of these practicks were produced by their authors decades before Stair or his peers came to write their own manuscripts. Indeed, the fact that

---

[29] Hector McKechnie, 'Practicks, 1469–1700 Part 1. Native Sources' in *An Introductory Survey of the Sources and Literature of Scots Law*, vol 1 (Stair Society 1936) 28. Simpson and Wilson are more cautious, suggesting that this rough distinction does not satisfactorily describe the complexity and differences between the various styles of legal literature which may fall into the general category of practice: Simpson and Wilson, *Scottish Legal History* (n 3) 284. However, for present purposes the rough distinction is a useful starting point from which to investigate more closely the different styles of contractual writing which can be found within these manuscripts.

[30] Dolezalek 'Introduction: The Purpose of this Book' (n 15) 7.

[31] Dolezalek 'Introduction: The Purpose of this Book' (n 15) 7.

[32] First published: James Balfour, *Practicks: Or, a System of the More Ancient Law of Scotland. Compiled by Sir James Balfour of Pettindreich, Carefully Published from Several Manuscripts* (Edinburgh: Thomas & Walter Ruddimans, 1754).

[33] First published: James A Clyde (ed), *Hope's Major Practicks, 1608–1633*, vol 3 (Stair Society 1937).

[34] First published: John Spotiswoode (ed), *Practicks of the Laws of Scotland Observed and Collected by Sir Robert Spotiswoode* (James Watson 1706).

[35] First published: Thomas Craig, *Jus Feudale Tribus Libris Comprehensum quibus non Solùm Consuetudines Feudales & Prædiorum Lura* (Impensis Societatis Stationariorum 1655); James A Clyde, *Sir Thomas Craig of Riccarton The Jus Feudal with an Appendix Containing the Books of the Feus*, 2 vols (Stair Society 1934). Also see the English translation: Thomas Craig, *Jus Feudale*, book 1, vol 64 (Leslie Dodd tr, Stair Society 2017).

[36] For discussion, see John D Ford (ed), *Alexander King's Treatise on Maritime Law*, vol 65 (Stair Society 2018).

[37] Simpson and Wilson *Scottish Legal History* (n 3) 284. Also see Adelyn D L Wilson, 'The Transmission and Use of the Collected Legal Decisions of Sir Richard Maitland of Lethington in Sixteenth- and Seventeenth-Century Scotland' (2018) 19 (3) The Library 325; Adelyn D L Wilson, 'The Elchies Manuscript and the Method of Sir Richard Maitland of Lethington' (2018) 62 (1) Manuscripta: A Journal for Manuscript Research 95.

Stair wrote his manuscript in the late 1650s and early 1660s is suggestive that he felt he could add to or improve upon this existing literature. As Ford noted, Stair was not alone in writing or arranging legal material about customary law in the late 1650s. Others too were interested, like Stair, though for a variety of reasons, in recording the customary law of Scotland or determining a common law in Scotland. In terms of contemporary writing about Scots law in the 1650s, Ford has noted that Stair was part of a specific group of writers who sought to write about the practice of law in Scotland in a more comprehensive manner, rather than explain how Scots law fitted around Roman law or write specifically about an area of law, such as feudal law. These authors did not merely copy a single decision practick or digest practick or compile Acts of Parliament; they attempted to pull together different sources of Scots law into one text. Ford has demonstrated that the 'period between around 1656 and 1666 formed a cohesive and distinctive phase in the development of the legal literature in Scotland'.[38] He has concluded that '[t]he obvious purpose of the writers was to improve the accessibility and hence the awareness of earlier books and sources, especially those that had not been available previously—above all Gibson's reports and also Spotiswoode's practicks—or that had not circulated freely—such as Hope's major and minor practicks'.[39]

Although varying in length and style, it is possible to find within this legal literature authors addressing the law applying to contracting behaviour and in some cases the addition of a commentary or structure.[40] On the whole, this literature can be divided for present purposes into three very general groups:[41] first, those who merely copied what they found in one of Balfour, Craig, Spotiswoode, Hope, or Durie, possibly for their own purposes and in abbreviated form; second, those who copied from one of these authors or from several of them, organizing their notes in alphabetical order or around the order they found in Hope's practicks or general substantive but unconnected titles; and, third, those who offered a more innovative method of organization and included some limited commentary. Even in this last group, however, it cannot be said that these authors broke new ground or wrote anything which was significantly distinctive or new about the law applying to contracting behaviour when compared to Stair. Nonetheless, it is important to survey these works in order to see the context within which Stair's unique structure, style, and use of sources emerged. First, therefore, mid-seventeenth-century commentaries or compilations on Scots customary law must be investigated. This involves, however, understanding how Scots lawyers were engaging with previous works on Scots customary law in the 1650s, as well as examining their own legal writing or texts they compiled about contract law.

---

[38] Ford *Law and Opinion* (n 1) 83.

[39] Ford *Law and Opinion* (n 1) 83.

[40] Ford identifies numerous texts written around the mid-seventeenth century, the authorship of which is not always entirely clear, which have been examined for the purposes of this chapter: NLS Ms 8490 (John Nisbett?); Adv Ms 24.4.14 (George Lockhart?); Ad Ms 24.3.9 (George Lockhart?); Adv Ms 25.4.2 (John Nisbet?); Adv Ms 24.2.3 (John Thomson?); Adv Ms 24.3.2 (Thomas Wallace?); Ad Ms 24.1.3 (Thomas Wallace?); NLS Ms 3171 (Thomas Wallace?); NLS Ms 943 (Thomas Wallace?) Adv Ms 24.1.3 (Peter Wedderburn?); NLS MS 5435 (Robert Ker?).

[41] cf Simpson and Wilson *Scottish Legal History* (n 3) 276–88.

Copying, Compiling, or Writing Commentaries upon Customary Law

Balfour

The practicks of Sir James Balfour (1525–83) are a collection of judicial notes collated in the mid-sixteenth century, but which continued to have relevance for Scots advocates in the mid-seventeenth century.[42] On the whole, however, Balfour's practicks are, in terms of contract law, unorganized and somewhat unconnected. As McNeill notes, 'the [Balfour's] *Practicks* is not concerned primarily with principles but rather with a series of isolated propositions roughly organized in a loose scheme.'[43] The overarching structure of Balfour's *Practicks* as a book may be suggestive of some organizational thought,[44] but in terms of contractual taxonomy it demonstrates little to no method.[45] Although his comments on the general law of contract are limited and his structure lacking in comparison to Stair's early manuscripts, there are aspects of Balfour which appear to have retained a continued significance in the mid-seventeenth century. For example, Balfour's entry on bonds was frequently copied or referenced by Stair's peer group.[46] Indeed, in Balfour you find a relatively detailed treatment of the law applying to bonds, which were, arguably, the most common way by which parties would formalize simple monetary loans in early modern Scotland.[47] Bonds appear frequently in seventeenth-century litigation, generally in relation to monetary obligations but sometimes also to non-monetary obligations.[48] Of course, there were numerous other ways by which a party may incur legal liability which were not formalized in the early modern period, but bonds nevertheless remained very important.[49] It is no

---

[42] Scots lawyers often referred to Balfour's *Practicks* in their own manuscripts, and, specifically for present purposes, they cited expressly Balfour's comments about bonds and the requirement for an express *causa* within bonds: Adv Ms 24.3.2 f81; Adv Ms 24.2.3 f173; NLS Ms 943 f26; Adv Ms 24.1.3 f67. You find the same account but not expressly mentioned in Adv Ms 24.3.2 f260. For reference to Balfour, see also Robert Burnett, *Ad Lectorem* in Craig *Jus Feudale* (n 35) xxxi.

[43] Peter G B McNeill, 'Introduction' in Peter G B McNeill (ed), *The Practicks of Sir James Balfour of Pittendreich, vol 2* (Stair Society 1963) xli.

[44] McNeill, 'Introduction' (n 43) xlii.

[45] For discussion of Balfour's *Practicks*, see Gero Dolezalek, 'The Court of Session as a Ius Commune Court—Witnessed by "Sinclair's Practicks", 1540–1549' in Hector L MacQueen, *Miscellany IV*, vol 49 (Stair Society 2002) 51–84; Simpson and Wilson *Scottish Legal History* (n 3) 211–13.

[46] Ad Ms 24.2.3 f173 (Thomson); Ad Ms 24.1.3 (Wallace); NLS MS 8490 (Nisbet) ff144–54; Ad Ms 24.3.2 (Wallace) f81.

[47] James J Brown, 'The Social, Political and Economic Influences of the Edinburgh Merchant Elite, 1600–1638' (DPhil, University of Edinburgh 1985); Lorna A Ewan, 'Debt and Credit in Early Modern Scotland: The Grandtully Estates 1650–1765' (DPhil, University of Edinburgh 1988); Douglas Watt, '"The Laberinth of Thir Difficulties": the Influence of Debt on the Highland Elite c.1500–1700' (2006) 85 (219) Scottish Historical Review 28; Cathryn Spence, *Women, Credit, and Debt in Early Modern Scotland* (Manchester University Press 2016). For details as to the form and structure of early modern bonds, see Peter Gouldesbrough (ed), *Formulary of Old Scots Legal Documents*, vol 36 (Stair Society 1985).

[48] Durie *Practicks*; Spotiswoode *Practicks*; Anonymous *The Decisions of the English Judges* (n 18); Dalrymple, *The Decisions of the Lords of Council* (n 18).

[49] Sometimes there is reference to 'tickets' in Durie's *Practicks*, which appears to be a form of informal promissory note which the Lords appear to have required to be proved by oath, witnesses, or writ (which was subscribed; see Durie *Practicks* 592). Walter Ross also refers to this informal practice in his

surprise therefore that Balfour's explanation of bonds and *causa* is frequently referenced in legal texts of the mid-seventeenth century, given their importance as a legal instrument.[50] Specifically, Balfour's requirement that the *causa* of a bond should be expressed in the bond is noteworthy: according to Balfour, if it was not stipulated in the bond itself, then it was void. Generally, however, bonds would not be characterized in this manner in the early modern period; the focus was upon satisfying formalities, not the underlying transaction or reason for creating the obligation.[51] In that sense, by requiring reference to *causa* within a bond, Balfour's *Practicks* is suggestive of a less formalistic and constitutive mode of contractual thought. It is indicative of a more developed understanding of the liability based on more than formality. Importantly, it is this section of Balfour's *Practicks* which is repeated in the manuscripts of several mid-seventeenth-century advocates.[52] Further, the idea that a bond must contain express mention of a *causa* is repeated in several cases reported by Durie, which remained an important text in the mid-seventeenth century.[53]

Balfour's discussion of 'pactioun' is also worth commenting upon. Although it is not directly mentioned in any of the manuscripts examined for this chapter,[54] it does demonstrate how pacts and *causa* were discussed in an important text which was used by Scots lawyers in the mid-seventeenth century. Balfour is explicit that the consent of two persons does not generally create an obligation, but he does speak of one exception.[55] For Balfour, *nuda pacta* are unenforceable, but pacts can become legally relevant when they relate to a specific legal claim.[56] Thus, he is speaking about a pact not to pursue a debt and a pact not to sue. According to Balfour, there are two types of enforceable *pacta*: one personal and one real. Real pacts are an agreement relating to a thing, and in the case of personal pacts it is an agreement relating to a thing from a person (presumably a service or debt). This reflects the discussion of pacts found in the *Digest* at D 2.14.7.4. That is, 'if you agree to give up any claim you may have against the other, I [the Praetor] will bar any action to enforce the claim'.[57] Balfour, however, goes further. He divides these pacts into 'profitable' and 'unprofitable'. In relation to the latter, the implication is that these pacts are unenforceable because they demonstrate an imbalance or inequality between the parties, and by implication the other party must have lacked consent. He explains that unprofitable pacts lack consent because the party was 'mad and furious' or 'surie and diseased', or the party was without 'richt

eighteenth-century lectures: Walter Ross, *Lectures on the History and Practice of the Law of Scotland Relative to Conveyancing and Legal Diligence* (Bell & Bradfute 1822) 45ff.

[50] Adv Ms 24.3.2 f81 (copy of Wallace); Adv Ms 24.2.3 f173 (copy of Thomson); NLS Ms 943 f26 (copy of Wallace); Adv Ms 24.1.3 f67 (copy of Wallace). Same account, but not expressly mentioned in Adv Ms 24.3.2 f260.

[51] Alfred W B Simpson, *A History of the Common Law of Contract: The Rise of the Action of Assumpsit* (OUP 1975) 88–115.

[52] See n 50.

[53] Durie, *Practicks* 39, 115, 150, 416, 553, 576, 627, 634, and 827.

[54] A copy of Nisbet's practicks—'A Treatise anent Scotts Law in Civills 1666'—dating from 1681 contains a discussion in similar terms: NLS MS 8490 ff144–54.

[55] Balfour *Practicks* 188–89 (emphasis added).

[56] For example, J A C Thomas, *Textbook on Roman Law* (first published 1976, North-Holland 2012) 334–36.

[57] *Digest* 14.7.4.

wit and judgment'.[58] Balfour also lists the types of 'pactioun' which are 'unprofitable'; these include pactions made with pupils, between wives and husbands, or to do things that are 'impossible' or 'dishonest'.[59] Balfour's practicks suggest here that there was a complexity to Scots practice with regard to pacts and that, despite the general formality of formation during this period, there were nonetheless exceptions.

Furthermore, in discussing the lack of consent, Balfour's *Practicks* are suggestive of a relatively developed system which was in place to deal with pactions. He alludes to a set of rules which presume that certain transactions are made without consent because (a) of the nature of the transaction itself and/or (b) the status or relationship of the parties involved on creates a presumption that there was no consent on behalf of one of the parties. The treatment of pacts found in Balfour reveals that although *nuda pacta* are not enforceable, there is a narrow conception of a pact, based on consent, which is enforceable. Further, this obligation, a profitable pact, appears to be based not just on consent but on the idea of 'richt' consent, that is, coming from someone who is exercising proper judgement and is neither vulnerable to manipulation nor 'mad and furious'. This seems to indicate some relatively developed thinking about the concept of consent and its implication in a legal context, even if it is restricted to a relatively narrow species of *pacta* and is very much relevant to the *nuda pacta* context within which Stair wrote when he spoke about the enforceability of a *nudum pactum*.

Nevertheless, these issues concerning *causa*, pacts, and consent are somewhat buried in Balfour. He is not systematic and does not attempt to bring out any particular discussion about why obligations are enforceable or what is exactly the source of contractual obligations. Prima facie, he does not evidence any general notion of contract. Thus, given that Balfour's *Practicks* does not attempt to analytically organize obligations or contractual behaviour, his contractual thought based on the *Practicks* is underdeveloped in comparison to Stair. Nor does he comment upon how the practice of law in Scotland differs from the *ius commune* or learned sources of law when he is discussing the law relating to contracting behaviour. However, if viewed on the basis of Dolezalek's interpretation, then Balfour's *Practicks* should be understood as being set against the backdrop of the *ius commune*. For example, Balfour's discussion of pacts and bonds is redolent of the conception of *causa* found in the early *ius commune* writings of Baldus, namely a hybrid of Roman law and canon law's conception of *causa*.[60] Indeed, reading Balfour alongside Baldus's discussion of *causa*[61] may in fact fill some gaps left from the otherwise sparse commentary on the *Practicks* and gives some insight into how mid-seventeenth-century legal minds in Scotland may have understood Balfour. Therefore, it could be said that using Balfour and copying from his manuscripts in the mid-seventeenth century would have presented the customary law of Scotland, and the law applying to contracting, as intricately linked to the *ius commune*, and in many ways dependent upon learned sources of law such as Baldus. Balfour may have recorded local variances of the *ius commune* in Scotland, but he in

---

[58] Balfour *Practicks* 189.

[59] Balfour also adds that pacts are binding upon successors as well as those making them.

[60] Reinhard Zimmermann, *The Law of Obligations: Roman Foundations of the Civilian Tradition* (OUP 1990) 551–53.

[61] Zimmermann *Obligations* (n 60).

no way presents a cohesive independent Scottish system of thought relating to contracts, and was therefore only useful to advocates if read against a much wider legal context and broader literature.

Craig

For an advocate in the 1650s, the *Jus Feudale* of Thomas Craig (1538?–1608) was a central text. Arguably, even for Scots lawyers before and after the mid-seventeenth century, Craig's *Jus Feudale* is an important text in the development of Scottish legal thinking. Often epitomized by advocates in the mid-seventeenth century,[62] Craig was used as a means by which to learn the law of Scotland and to understanding the authority of the various sources of law. Stair's contemporaries would often cite passages from Craig in their compendiums or reports.[63] Craig is also cited in the Court of Session by mid-seventeenth-century advocates; indeed, his work was cited before the Commissioners during the Interregnum,[64] and in the years following the Restoration he was frequently cited in the Court of Session into the early eighteenth century.[65] Moreover, his *Jus Feudale* was brought to print by Robert Burnett in 1655, which, as Ford demonstrates, was a significant event in terms of mid-seventeenth-century legal literature.[66] Organizing it around substantive issues, Craig makes far greater use of other jurists' works; as well as offering an account of the different authorities used in Scotland, he also gives a history of the law in Scotland. It is a classic example of late sixteenth-century legal humanism.[67] In terms of mid-seventeenth-century manuscripts, Craig is routinely cited with reference to the law applying to contracting,[68] which may be somewhat surprising given that in general the *Jus Feudale* has very little to say about the law applying to contracting. Nonetheless, what he does say is noteworthy and offers a key insight into mid-seventeenth-century attitudes to the law applying to contracts.

Craig equates the feus paid by a feuar to their feudal superior as being akin to a mutual contract. For Craig, this necessitates some discussion of what a mutual contract is. A mutual contract according to Craig is one of reciprocity. A feuar cannot expect performance from the superior if he has not fulfilled his obligations, and vice versa. Craig extrapolates general propositions based on the rudiments of civil law to apply to the contemporary practice of feu contracts. He says: '(although some people argue

---

[62] Ford *Law and Opinion* (n 1) 73–83.

[63] Ad Ms 24.1.3 (b) (abridgment of Wedderburn's *Practicks*) f62; Ad Ms 24.1.3 (Wallace) f67; Ad Ms 24.3.2 (Wallace) f89; NLS MS 5437 (Nisbet) f11.

[64] Anonymous *The Decisions of the English Judges* (n 18) 18, 85.

[65] James Dalrymple, *The Decisions of the Lords of Council & Session, in the Most Important Cases Debate before Them with the Acts of Sederunt* (Anderson 1681) 76, 89, 458, 743; John Lauder, *The Decisions of the Lords of Council and Session, from June 6th, 1678, to July 30th, 1712*, vols 1 and 2 (Hamilton & Balfour 1759–61).

[66] Ford *Law and Opinion* (n 1) 45ff.

[67] John W Cairns, T D Fergus, and Hector L MacQueen, 'Legal Humanism in Renaissance Scotland' (1990) 11 Journal of Legal History 40, 56.

[68] Adv Ms 24.3.2 f100; Adv Ms 25.4.2 f12; Adv Ms 24.1.3 ff63–64, 67. Although no express mention is made of Craig, Adv Ms 24.2.3 f172 makes the same *stricti iuris* bona fidei distinction found in Craig *Jus Feudale* 1.9.31.

otherwise) a feu is a form of reciprocal contract between lord and vassal, in which each is obligated to the other'.[69] His liberal approach to the Roman law of contract is evident when he says that 'this is characteristic of reciprocal and innominate contracts'.[70] For Craig, anyone familiar with a feu contract would say that a feuar must 'observe the same obligations which are customarily part of other contracts; specifically, he must demonstrate that all things which had been agreed have been fulfilled on his part or, at the least, that he has offered the completion of all things to which he is bound'.[71] Nevertheless, Craig is not content to define matters in this classical fashion, namely as an innominate contract. Citing prominent fourteenth century-jurist Bartolus de Saxoferrato, he notes that although with regard to feus 'its name is not found among the nominate contracts in law', it should be. 'Bartolus rightly thinks', says Craig, that all contracts which are created law or statute, whether they be named or not named, 'should properly be termed nominate, even if they are of a new format or type'.[72] From the perspective of contractual thought, this evidences that lawyers, such as Craig, were prepared to engage critically with the Roman law and to manipulate such sources for contemporary purposes.[73] Moreover, it demonstrates a synthetic application of Roman law to the law applying to contracting behaviour in the period before Stair.

Craig also considers whether feu contracts are *stricti iuris* or *bonæ* fidei, which is repeated several times by mid-seventeenth-century advocates when they offer a definition of a contract.[74] According to Craig, *bonæ* fidei contracts should be 'construed according to what is fair and right, even though nothing is mentioned in the contracts themselves'.[75] He goes on: 'It thus looks more to the intent of the contracting parties than to what was expressly agreed between them.'[76] Returning to the *Institutes*, he says that *bonæ* fidei contracts are those enumerated by Justinian, such as those involving sale, lease, and hire. He considers whether contracts of marriage are *bonæ* fidei or *stricti iuris* contracts, because 'In all such contracts, where we are often forced to rely on the faith of other people, one must consider whether what has been done is in accordance with the fairness and goodness which is customary in similar kinds of dealings.'[77] By virtue of the fact that reliance is placed upon the sincerity of parties' intentions in a contract of marriage, it should be classified as a *bonæ* fidei contract. This allows the contract to be interpreted according to what is 'fair and right' in the minds of the parties. On the other hand, 'actions are called *stricti juris* because faith is strictly curtailed and because goodness and fairness are, in a sense, constrained by the contract's limits'.[78] It is not 'admissible to depart from the express terms of such a contract nor to add to them'. Hence, engagements that are *stricti iuris*, such as caution and bail, are essentially formal engagements where 'specific mention of it has been made within the contract'. Craig tells the reader that although feus often originate from a

---

[69] Craig *Jus Feudale*, 1.9.31.
[70] Craig *Jus Feudale*, 1.9.31.
[71] Craig *Jus Feudale*, 1.9.31.
[72] Craig *Jus Feudale*, 1.9.32.
[73] Cairns 'Legal Humanism' (n 67).
[74] Adv Ms 24.2.3 f172; Adv Ms 24.3.2 f100; Ad Ms 24.1.3 f63.
[75] Craig *Jus Feudale* 1.9.33.
[76] Craig *Jus Feudale* 1.9.33.
[77] Craig *Jus Feudale* 1.9.33.
[78] Craig *Jus Feudale* 1.9.33.

pre-contract that is bonæ fidei, 'We affirm that the feudal contract is *stricti juris*'.[79] In the same way, 'all leases, sales, redemptions (which we call reversions) are considered to be completely *stricti juris*, as are similar contracts which frequently arise in the country over feus and immoveables'.[80] Craig offers two reasons why feus are *stricti iuris*; the first is that it is the custom in Scotland to do so. However, Craig warns that:

> since the feudal law which we employ has coalesced in its entirety out of customary law, it must not be followed to its logical conclusion (as scholars say). Customary law is *stricti juris*, even if it is set down in writing (something which does not make it any less customary, despite written law ranking above customary), and cannot exceed its defined limits.[81]

He is cautious about admitting Scots custom as a rule of law. The second reason is that 'by its very nature, a feu is a form of donation; and, as Baldus says, it is fair that all donations should be *stricti juris*'.[82] The reason for this is because 'no-one is presumed to have donated more than he expressly stated'.[83] Although Craig's discussion of bonæ fidei and *stricti iuris* is technically directed towards specific questions relating to feu contracts, it nevertheless offers an example of juristic writing about contracting behaviour before the time of Stair (which is systematic, coherent, and concerned with substantive questions rather than merely focusing on procedural or formulaic accounts of contracting).

Moreover, and importantly, Craig is clear about why Roman law is used in Scotland and to what extent it is used:[84]

> So it is that we follow the decisions and rules of the civil law, especially in the management of moveables, although each and every nation has retained its own individual forms of legal process. We employ our own forms of action which are not entirely inconsistent with the civil law, while we closely follow the civil arbitraments, servitudes, contracts both *bona fidei* and *stricti iuris*, and both nominate and innominate, evictions. Pledges, tutory, legacies, actions, exceptions, obligations, and finally in punishing delicts. In fact, I would say that civil law is so diffused through all our affairs and around all our concerns that practically no inquiry and no sort of case occurs in which its singular force and function are not manifestly apparent. Whenever something difficult arises in court or judgements, the solution is to be sought therein.

This is the most significant thing that Craig said with regard to contracting, and would have been well known to mid-seventeenth-century advocates by the time Burnett printed the *Jus Feudale* in 1655. It should be noted that Craig's statement above does not relate to the authority of Roman law but is a statement of practice. From it we can glean: first, and unsurprisingly, that Scots legal writing about customary law or Acts of

---

[79] Craig *Jus Feudale* 1.9.33.
[80] Craig *Jus Feudale* 1.9.33.
[81] Craig *Jus Feudale* 1.9.33.
[82] Craig *Jus Feudale* 1.9.33.
[83] Craig *Jus Feudale* 1.9.33.
[84] Craig *Jus Feudale* 1.2.14.

Parliament operated against the backdrop of how the law of contract was expressed in the Roman law sources available to Scots lawyers; second, that Roman law was already widely dispersed throughout the law applying to contracting in Scotland, suggesting it was already part of the customary law of Scotland; and third, it suggests that a *nudum pactum* was unenforceable at the start of the seventeenth century.

In terms of what Scots lawyers should do when faced with a novel situation of contract, Craig is also noteworthy. For it is one thing to say that Scots have in the past used Roman law in such situations, but it was another to justify why it should continue to be used in such cases. In the *Jus Feudale*, Craig demonstrated a way by which sources of Roman law (but, also, importantly, feudal law) could be used in contemporary legal reasoning.[85] He says in the *Jus Feudale*: 'We, in this kingdom, are bound by the laws of the Romans to the extent that they agree with the laws of nature and correct reasoning.'[86] Yet the difficulty here is determining how this should be done. No reasonable lawyer in the seventeenth century would object to the general tenor of Craig's explanation, but they might question, who then is to judge if Roman law is within the bounds of natural law? They could dispute the methods thereby adopted to determine its expression of natural law. In Craig's mind it was the opinion of learned jurists that mattered; it was their recognition of a solution and its inherent equity that should determine the answer to a novel issue; he says:[87]

> there is scarcely any wider tract of natural equity nor any more fertile field of meticulous judgments and arguments drawn from the very principles of nature than the books of the jurisconsults, from which should be drawn off, as from a fountain, what is fair and unfair according to nature, what agrees completely with correct reasoning and what disagrees.

Craig explains that Scots revert to Roman law because the laws and customs of Scotland are not written down. Thus, if there was no written law, established custom, or decision of the Court of Session applicable then legal experts' opinion should be consulted on the applicability of a Roman law.[88] Indeed the implication from Craig is that although Scotland has never had such experts as they— do elsewhere, such as France—the original lords of session are the closest Scotland has had to a jurisconsult. They were 'extremely well trained in civil and canon law' who were 'men learned and practised in both kinds of law, who followed the civil law in making judgment and commended it to their successors'.[89] This left the question of whether there were any contemporary legal experts in mid-seventeenth-century Scotland.[90] Craig's approach is sophisticated both as to who should be understood as a legal expert and how this process of reasoning should be done; it remained a difficult question for Scots lawyers

---

[85] Cairns 'The Civil Law Tradition' (n 15).

[86] Craig *Jus Feudale* 1.2.14.

[87] Craig *Jus Feudale* 1.2.14.

[88] Ford *Law and Opinion* (n 1) 215–40 and 556–67; Simpson and Wilson *Scottish Legal History* (n 3) 214–15.

[89] Craig *Jus Feudale* 1.2.14.

[90] Wilson and Simpson *Scottish Legal History* (n 3) 293–312.

in the mid-seventeenth century.[91] Nevertheless, in terms of contractual thought several points can be made about Craig's *Jus Feudale*.

It was not intended to be a comprehensive manual of Scots law nor to cover contracting in any detail; indeed, as Stair said in the *Institutions*, feudal law 'doth not extend to the half of our rights'.[92] So other texts would have to be used by Scots lawyers. Yet in Craig's *Jus Feudale* they found a systematic treatise of law that sought to order the sources of law in Scotland. It offered a written record of aspects Scots customary law, along with a history as well as a comparison of the Scots approach with the opinion of jurisconsults or contemporary legal experts. Significantly, Scots lawyers found an attempt, in Craig's work itself, to justify the use of feudal law and Roman law in the form of a learned lawyer's opinion. However, Craig offered little in the way of native taxonomy or detailed consideration of contracting. There is no reflection on the nature of contract. Nor a discussion of difficult current issues in the law of contract apart from those that related to feus. None of this should be expected, it was a treatise on feudal law, a status-based system of land law. Arguably, it did not speak directly to the needs to the emerging commercial society of the mid- to late seventeenth century.

Hope

The *Major Practicks* of Sir Thomas Hope (1573–1646) cover the period between 1608 and 1633 but were not published until 1936–37.[93] In the past, the authorship has sometimes been questioned yet the text available, and published, is generally accepted to be at the very least based on Hope's own manuscripts.[94]Advocates, however, referred to manuscript copies of a text produced by Hope from the mid-seventeenth to the late eighteenth century.[95] For example, in 1655, Burnett said they were 'the most valuable [Practicks]'.[96] Ford also highlights a letter from 1661, written by John Nisbet, Lord Ordinary, saying: 'As to our Scottish law … it will be fit to have a read often as a

---

[91] Ford *Law and Opinion* 228–40.

[92] Stair *Inst* 2.3.1.

[93] In 1937, Lord Clyde published the first printed edition of the *Major Practicks* based on a manuscript dating c.1656 (NS. Ad. Ms. 24.3.10): James A Clyde (ed), *Hope's Major Practicks, 1608–1633*, vol 2 (Stair Society 1937).

[94] In his introduction (ibid xxviii), Clyde deals with the question of authorship. There was some confusion in the eighteenth and nineteenth centuries as to whether the author of the *Practicks* was Sir Thomas Hope of Craighall (1573–1646) or (in truth) his son, Sir Thomas Hope of Kerse (1606–43). Clyde has convincingly asserted that the *Practicks* were in fact the product of the father, Lord Craighall, and not the son, Lord Kerse. However, Clyde does acknowledge that (ibid xiiv): 'Lord Kerse no doubt had access to the original of his father's "Major Practicks" during his father's lifetime, for he predeceased his father by three years. Besides interpolating his own notes, and others drawn from such of his father's papers as were available to him, he may even have contributed something to the form and arrangement of the materials, which his father had collected and placed at his disposal.'

[95] There is some doubt about whether Burnett was referring to Hope's *Major Practicks* or his *Minor Practicks*; see Ford *Law and Opinion* (n 1) 250. Clyde states that Hope's *Major Practicks* had circulated in the Faculty since 1641, whereas Ford says it is uncertain whether Hope's *Major Practicks* or his *Minor Practicks* had circulated: Ford, *Law and Opinion* (n 1) 45–46. Yet, even if Hope's *Major Practicks* did not circulate in the Faculty, it is still an important point of reference for legal thought in the mid-seventeenth century. Hope's *Minor Practicks* were eventually printed in 1726: Alexander Bayne (ed), *Minor Practicks, or, a Treatise of the Scottish Law* (Thomas Ruddiman 1726).

[96] Burnett, *Ad Lectorem* in Craig *Jus Feudale* (n 35) lxxxvii.

vade mecum a short manual written be Sir Thomas Hope, King's advocate, and Craig's de feudis ... [it is advisable to read] ... Duries practiques and any other practiques they can have, and acts of parliament.'[97] However, it should be noted that Burnett also said that Hope's *Practicks*, along with others, 'were either in the hands of a small number of people or badly and ineptly copied,'[98] which suggests that advocates' use of Hope's *Major Practicks* in the mid-seventeenth century may have been aimed at making them available or their contents known rather than influential or widely used. Whatever the case, it was a text advocates engaged with and drew from in the mid-seventeenth century.

Hope's *Major Practicks* demonstrate an attempt to organize contract law based on substantive and coherent rules.[99] Hope commences each title in the *Major Practicks* with a definition or a general proposition of law, which he often takes from Craig. Following his definition or proposition, he then proceeds to record the applicable Act of Parliament if there is one that is relevant. Hope invariably follows up his opening passages with some observations on the practice of law in Scotland. In terms of taxonomy, the structure of the *Major Practicks* is redolent of Justinian's *Institutes*. There are, however, important differences: in Book II, Hope addresses personal rights, and in Book III he addresses real rights. When he discusses personal rights, he is speaking about contracts. This contrasts with Justinian, who deals with property in Book II and contracts in Book III. Hope is moving the Justinian structure around—something Stair also did some thirty years later. Moreover, Hope arranges his discussion of contracts in an interesting way. He speaks about contracts, pacts, and obligations in the first three titles of Book II, and then in the following titles he discusses sale, loan, and hire, namely consensual contracts. He offers a general discussion of contracts before going on to speak about particular contracts. An exposition of the real contracts then follows his discussion of consensual contracts, with a short discussion of assignation and payment and discharge. In Justinian's *Institutes*, real contracts were dealt with before consensual contracts, and there was no discussion of consensual contracts in conjunction with pacts. This indicates that although Hope worked within the idiom of the *Corpus iuris* and the language of Roman law, he was nevertheless organizing matters in his *Major Practicks* in a manner contrary to Justinian, and he worked with the idea that consent was what linked together contracts. You could say he was working with the resources of the *Corpus iuris* and utilizing them for contemporary purposes.

Hope's particular title on contracts follows the pattern of proposition, legislation, and then observation. Despite the lack of narrative, his title on contracts gives some indication of Hope's contractual thought. Three particular points are worth highlighting here. First, he cites Craig's discussion of feu contracts in his opening paragraph. In contrast to Craig, he relates it not to feus but to contracts more generally. Therefore, Hope commences with the proposition that 'No one is permitted the return of performance in a contract unless the person proves to have fulfilled all the things on his

---

[97] Ford *Law and Opinion* (n 1) 285, quoting NAS, GD 6/2172 and EUL, La II 89, f147.

[98] Burnett, *Ad Lectorem* in Craig *Jus Feudale* (n 35) lxxxvii.

[99] For discussion of Hope's *Major Practicks* from the perspective of legal literature, see Simpson and Wilson *Scottish Legal History* (n 3) 284–85 and 300–10.

contract=mutual
obligation

part, or at least shows that he is prepared to the fulfilment of theirs.'[100] This indicates a notion that <u>contracts are essentially mutual obligations</u>. Second, this is followed by a further quotation from Craig which has already been given above.[101] As discussed earlier, in the *Jus Feudale* Craig spoke of the division between *stricti iuris* and bonae fidei contracts. In placing this division at the beginning of his title on contracts, he is implying that this distinction is applicable to all contracts in Scots law. Third, Hope paraphrases Balfour by saying: 'All contracts, bands, dispositions or assignations containing no tytle onerous or lucrative ar null be way of exceptione'.[102] As discussed before, Balfour said that when the obligation was unilateral and contained no express *causa*, then it was null and void. Hope, like Balfour, holds that the *causa* of a contract is important to the very existence of the obligation. In contrast to Balfour, Hope is more systematic in how he places this statement by putting it within the opening titles on contract—something which was repeated in several mid-seventeenth-century manuscripts.

In terms of Scottish legal writing, Ford makes the important observation that Hope had 'started to develop an understanding of the common law of Scotland that would depend neither on the belief that the old books and acts consisted of written law nor on the belief that the books of the feus contained proper law'.[103] Therefore, when Scots advocates in the 1650s turned to Hope's manuscripts to learn something about the practice of contract law and the approach taken in Scotland, they would have found a presentation of the law which was suggestive of a common law of contract in Scotland: a collection of propositions relating to contracting which were developed locally. In Hope, there is the emergence of the idea that the common law of Scotland included a system of contract law, which was more than Roman law plus Acts of the Scottish Parliament that addressed contracting. That said, Hope was merely presenting a snapshot of areas where there may be a customary law of Scotland, which applied to contracts. By and large, Hope appears to have shared Craig's viewpoint that <u>where statutes and custom were silent and analogous interpretation could not yield an answer then Scots lawyers should turn to Roman law</u>. He adopted the same caveat as Craig, however, saying, 'we are bound by Roman law so far as it appears to us to be consonant with natural equity and reason.'[104] And noted that Roman law offers 'our own courts … the key to the solution of many a difficulty'.[105] Nonetheless, Hope's *Major Practicks* are a notable attempt to write about the customary law in Scotland in a structured manner.

It must be stressed, however, that what stands out in Hope's *Major Practicks* in comparison to Stair is that he offers <u>little by way of synthesis or narrative</u>. There is no discussion about the sources of liability or about why obligations are arranged in a certain manner. There is no dialogue concerning morality or natural law in Hope's *Major Practicks*. Nor is there any attempt to justify why he is arranging matters in the

---

[100] 'Nemini agere licet ex contractu reciproco nisi probet Omnia quae convenerant ex sua parte impleta esse, aut saltem ad eorum impletionem se paratum ostendit' (Craig *de feudis*, I. 9. 31).

[101] Craig *Jus Feudale* 1.9.31.

[102] Hope *Major Practicks* 2.1.3.

[103] Ford *Law and Opinion* (n 1) 281.

[104] Hope *Major practicks* 1.8.17.

[105] Hope *Major practicks* 1.8.17.

way he does. He does not attempt to engage with other jurists other than by reference. In this sense, it appears more akin to a jurist's notes on the rules of contract, which, although organized with a system or method in mind, have the author's narrative redacted or omitted. However, the organization of matters into four books, and particularly the arrangement internally within the book on personal rights, is suggestive but not conclusive that Hope had some substantive ideas about the law applying to contracting behaviour. The *Major Practicks* shares therefore the somewhat sparse nature of Balfour's practicks. It could be suggested that Balfour's *Practicks* were supposed to supplement the pre-existing literature of the *ius commune* with a record of Scots customary law.[106] Nevertheless, Hope's practicks signal a noteworthy development in Scots legal thinking and the development of Scots contract law.

Durie

Sir Alexander Gibson, Lord Durie (?–1644), kept a detailed account of Court of Session decisions dating between 11 July 1621 and 16 July 1642. Eventually published in 1690 by his grandson Sir Alexander Gibson (?–1693), a manuscript copy of Durie's practicks was, however, available to advocates from the late 1650s.[107] Numerous manuscript copies of Durie's practicks have survived and appear to have been popular with mid-seventeenth-century advocates; such copies were generally abbreviated[108] and arranged into alphabetical order using substantive legal categories[109]—which, it should be noted, contrasts with the published edition that is arranged by date and indexed according to the parties' names.[110] Ford has shown that the compendium by George Lockhart (c. 1630–89) of what was to become Durie's *Practicks*, 'Ane Compend of Duries Practiques Ordine Alphabetico or Ane Alphabetical Compend and Index of Duries Ano Volumes of Practiques and Decisions', was particularly popular in the mid-seventeenth century.[111] Lockhart's compendium uses the category of marriage contract, but it does not have a singular category for contract, nor does it say anything directly about contract. At the very least, this suggests that if an advocate were looking for a proposition of law relating to contracting behaviour, then Lockhart's

---

[106] Peter Stein said much the same:

> The disjointed and fragmentary collections of maxims and practical hints [in Hope, Balfour, and Durie] provided no framework of principles within which the law could be developed. They were designed to provide a quick authority to assist a busy practitioner in preparing his argument. In 1609, John Skene produced an edition of the Regiam Majestatem and the Auld Lawes, in the preface of which he complained that his contemporaries found the old Scottish laws obscure and their language distasteful (*stylo horrido et aspero scriptas*). The Civil law books and the analytical summaries of the latest Continental commentators were easily accessible.
>
> (Stein 'The Influence of Roman Law' (n 16) 217)

[107] Ford *Law and Opinion* (n 1) 78, n 348. A Gibson (ed), *The Decision of the Lords of Council and Session in Most Cases of Importance, Debated, and Brought before Them; from July 1621 to July 1642* (Andrew Anderson 1690).

[108] Ad Ms 24.2.3 (vol 3) (by John Thomson).

[109] NLS MS 5435 ('Duries Pretickes Compendized Alphabetically, the 23 Jarri 1659').

[110] Ad Ms 24.4.14 ('Ane Compend of Duries Practiques Ordine Alphabetico or Ane Alphabetical Compend and Index of Duries Ano Volumes of Practiques and Decisions').

[111] Ford *Law and Opinion* (n 1) 78.

compendium would indicate that there was very little material of use to be found in Durie's report of decisions of the Court of Session; advocates would need to look elsewhere for the relevant law.

Thomson

John Thomson was relatively unknown to Scottish legal history until Ford drew attention to his legal texts produced sometime towards the end of the 1650s and in the 1660s. Ford tells us that Thomson studied at Glasgow University in the 1630s and subsequently established a legal practice in Dumfries in the 1650s. In contrast to Lockhart's compendium of Durie's *Practicks*, Thomson's notes on Durie's *Practicks* are more comprehensive, bringing together various sources to present a customary practice in Scotland with regard to contracting.[112] Dated from 1657, Thomson's notes on Durie are combined with references to Hope's *Practicks* and Acts of the Scottish Parliament; hence the full title given by Thomson:

> Sir Alexander Gibson—His Practiques and Observationes of the Decisions of the Lords of Sessione, from the Year of God 1621 to 1642, with Sir Thomas Hope His Observationes and Practiques, with ane Compend of the Acts of Parliament, all which are Redacted to the Ordinary Heads and Titles of the Scottish Law and Digested and Disposed in ane Alphabeticall Methode and Ordour and Contained in Three Tomes.

Under the heading 'Off contracts and bands', Thomson refers to several cases from Durie's *Practicks*, including *Forbesses v Muckall*[113] and *Douglas v Belshes*,[114] which consider the interpretation and enforcement of bonds. He cites Craig's distinction between contracts (they are either *stricti iuris* or bonæ fidei); says that all contracts are reciprocal; and quotes from Balfour regarding the importance of stipulating a *causa* within a bond, adding a further gloss, however, by saying 'all contracts, bonds, dispositions or assignations not containing ane title onerous or lucrative are null'.[115] He also noted the impression that these were customary rules of the Court of Session, but without reference to any specific case or authority, and that confessions of monetary obligations are 'sufficient probation of the writ', and that a 'contract or other obident is not gotten to be perfect until the time the parties' subscribe.[116] Nonetheless, he does also cite numerous acts of either the Scottish Parliament or the Court of Session which related to contracts and bonds, including the 1592 Act of Sederunt, which Hope also cites in relation to the enforceability of *pacta* within the Court of Session.[117]

---

[112] Ad Ms 24.2.3 (vol 3).
[113] Durie's *Practicks* 35.
[114] Durie's *Practicks* 90.
[115] Ms Ad 24.2.3 (vol 3) f173.
[116] Ms Ad 24.2.3 (vol 3) f173.
[117] Ms Ad 24.2.3 (vol 3) f175.

Wallace

As well as drawing attention to Thomson, Ford has highlighted Thomas Wallace's practicks as relatively distinctive in comparison to other mid-seventeenth-century legal literature.[118] Ford notes that Wallace's practicks circulated 'widely among practitioners in the College of Justice' in the 1660s and identifies around nine surviving copies.[119] At first appearance, his practicks appear to be a compendium of Durie's practicks, with additional references to Hope, Craig, and Acts of the Scottish Parliament. However, Ford comments that 'at many places [in the practicks] the author expressed his own views on how the law was then developing, often with reference to the opinions of others'.[120] On the whole, his comments upon the law of contract are very similar to those of Thomson and other compendiums produced by Stair's contemporaries: he says that a 'lucrative' causa is viewed with 'suspicion' whereas onerous causes are sufficient probation of a good *causa*;[121] citing Craig, he says that 'contracts be sunt bona fidei be striciti jurisis';[122] that 'all peoples enclosing in contracts on the narrative page as ye cause ane' are lawful contracts;[123] and subscription of a contract is not always necessary where there has been performance or other evidence offered, such as the payment of money.[124]

Of note, however, are two particular sections of Wallace's practicks which do not appear in other compendiums or practicks. First, he says, under the heading 'consent' and with reference to a specific passage in Craig,[125] that consent does not constitute an obligation without possession, but only possession can constitute an obligation. In using the term 'obligation', it is uncertain whether he is speaking more generally or specifically about a bond, nor is it clear if he is referring to the particular detail of Craig's passage, which concerns the creation of a feu contract, or something more general. But the presentation, within his practicks, suggests that he is wishing to say something more general and generic but is using Craig's specific discussion about feu contracts as a basis to extrapolate a broader conclusion about the necessity of possession, that is delivery, of the bond, before it is legally binding.[126] Second, he says with reference to Durie: 'A [third] party albeit they be not a contractor will get summons executione upon the contract if once it was right for implement of any clause that contained condition in favour of said party'.[127] He also says, again referencing Durie: 'in mutual contract […] the one party contradicting does not liberal the other fae the contract but only give him action with the contradicting party qua mutual contract not dissolution without consent of the injured party'.[128] In a similar manner to his general comments

---

[118] Ford *Law and Opinion* (n 1) 81.
[119] Ford *Law and Opinion* (n 1) 81.
[120] Ford *Law and Opinion* 82.
[121] Ad Ms 24.3.2 f81.
[122] Ad Ms 24.3.2 f100.
[123] Ad Ms 24.3.2 f100.
[124] Ad Ms 24.3.2 f100–01.
[125] Craig *Jus Feudale* 142ff.
[126] Ad Ms 24.3.2 ff98–99.
[127] Ad Ms 24.3.2 f102.
[128] Ad Ms 24.3.2 f102.

about bonds, these propositions which Wallace formulates are generalizations and are not found in other practicks. Moreover, although these passages appear to foreshadow the familiar modern doctrines of retention and third-party rights, Wallace's formulation is very much concerned with what actions were open to pursuers and what was procedurally possible when faced with these circumstances. Therefore, Wallace makes generalized comments which are not found in other practicks, but he is nevertheless very practical and procedurally focused; he certainly does offer any theoretical or philosophical commentary. It is tempting to say that, for Wallace, customary law was related to procedures of the Court of Session rather than anything substantive relating to the manifestation of equity or natural law within the specific circumstances of Scotland.

Legislative Acts Applying to Contracting

Before concluding, it is important to say something about Acts of the Scottish Parliament which applied to contracting. Generally, if there was an appropriate Act of Parliament, then early modern Scots lawyers treated such acts as their principal source of private law.[129] It could be said that the respective ranking and relationship between other sources of law, including Roman law, practicks, decisions of the Court of Session, and legal learning, caused disagreement or divergent approaches in the mid-seventeenth century.[130] Yet on the whole if there were any acts applicable then those acts would trump any contradictory sources of private law during the seventeenth century.[131] Lawyers may have questioned an act's scope, how it should be interpreted, or its authenticity or continued relevance, and disagreed about what filled the gap when there was no pertinent Act of Parliament; but, with the exception of Stair, when Scots wrote about the law of Scotland they placed statutory law as the primary source of law.[132] Additionally, the scarcity and reliability of statutory records was a common concern of Scots lawyers during this period; that is, whether practising lawyers had access to the most accurate written records of an old Act of the Scottish Parliament.[133] Moreover, the existing modes of creating law in Scotland were significantly undermined in the 1650s by the Commonwealth and the Interregnum, which suspended the lawmaking functions of the Scottish Parliament and the Court of Session.[134] Ford, Simpson, and Wilson have explained the importance of this period

---

[129] Of course, things are more complicated than this summary might suggest. Stair's approach to statutes, for example, is particularly complex and somewhat out of step with his contemporaries. For further discussion, see Wilson and Simpson *Scottish Legal History* (n 3) 292–327.

[130] For a summary, see Wilson and Simpson *Scottish Legal History* (n 3) 292–327

[131] For discussion, see Ford *Law and Opinion* (n 1), specifically 37ff (on Burnett), 211ff (on Wallace), 230ff (on Craig), 247ff (on Nisbet), and 248ff (on Hope). Also see Cairns, 'Historical Introduction' 104–05; John W Cairns, 'Attitudes to Codification and the Scottish Science of Legislation 1600–1830' (2007) 22 Tulane European and Civil Law Forum 1, 14ff.

[132] John Skene (ed), *Regiam Majestatem Scotiae, Veteres Leges et Constitutiones* (London 1613) iii; Craig *Jus Feudale* 1.8.6–17; Hope *Major Practicks* 1.1.2; Stair *Inst* 1.1.16–20; George Mackenzie, *The Institutions of the Law of Scotland* (John Reid 1684) 1.1.6; Cairns 'Attitudes to Codification' (n 123) 14ff; Cairns 'Historical Introduction' (n 16) 98ff; Ford *Law and Opinion* (n 1).

[133] Burnett, *Ad Lectorem* in Craig *Jus Feudale* (n 35).

[134] Ford *Law and Opinion* (n 1) 91–151.

for legal writing in Scotland and the development of legal attitudes with regard to the law of Scotland.[135] However, it is notable that despite this significant upheaval and challenge to legal and political institutions in Scotland, legal writing produced in Scotland during this period continued to reference the 1579 Act.[136]

From the perspective of contractual thought, it is of note that there was very little statutory law which would apply to contracting behaviour, which may speak directly to the place and necessity of other sources of law, whether they be *ius commune* or learned law.[137] Despite this, mid-seventeenth-century legal texts often refer to one particular Act of Parliament which has a direct bearing upon contracting behaviour:[138] the 1579 Act,[139] along with its related 1584 Act,[140] and 1593 Act.[141] John Skene's collation and reproduction of Acts of the Scottish Parliament published in 1597 made these statutes readily accessible to Scots lawyers in the mid-seventeenth century, without concern for their accuracy.[142] It is also possible that Scots lawyers became familiar with the 1579 Act through the practicks of Hope, Durie, and Spotiswoode as well as Craig's *Jus Feudale*, which all make reference to the 1579 Act.[143] Along with the 1584 and 1593 Acts, the 1579 Act suggests two things about mid-seventeenth-century contractual thought:[144] first, that there was an uncertainty with regard to informal agreements under the value of 100 pounds Scots; and second, that there was strict formality required for most other transactions, although mercantile exceptions applied.[145]

---

[135] Ford *Law and Opinion* (n 1) 91–151; Simpson and Wilson *Scottish Legal History* (n 3) 258–72.

[136] Ms Ad 24.2.3 f179; Ms Ad 24.3.2 f101; Ms Ad 24.1.3 f63ff.

[137] It could be argued that other significant Acts of this period which apply to contracting include the 1587 Act (RPS 1587/7/45), which set the rate of legal interest at 10%, and the 1661 Act (RPS/1661/300), which made bonds and contracts containing annual rents moveable and, importantly, only binding on successors if expressly stipulated. However, these Acts are not discussed in the manuscripts examined for this chapter.

[138] Ms Ad 24.2.3 f179; Ms Ad 24.3.2 f101; Ms Ad 24.1.3 f63ff.

[139] RPS 1579/10/33.

[140] RPS 1584/5/85. (Here the scope of the 1579 Act was clarified by the 1584: writs registered in the books of council and session or lord ordinary—that is, with the Court of Session—did not need to satisfy the formalities set out in the 1579 Act because registration was 'a greater solemn act than selling [sealing]' and even if not sealed it was still sufficient because both parties had consented to the registration.)

[141] 1593/4/44. (Here the formalities required of a writ falling within the scope of the 1579 Act were extended: the drafter's 'name, surname and particular remaining place, diocese and other denomination' was now required to be narrated within the writ.)

[142] John Skene, *The Lawes and Actes of Parliament, Maid be King Iames the First, and his Successours Kinges of Scotland Visied, Collected and Extracted Furth of the Register. The Contentes of this Buik, are Expremed in the Leafe Following* (Robert Walde 1597; republished Edinburgh 1682).

[143] Craig *Jus Feudale* (n 35) passim; Hope *Major Practicks* 2.1.7; Durie *Practicks* 43, 70, 292, 324, 358, 422, 458, 493, 522, 680, 723, and 832; Spotiswoode *Practicks* 359. In fact, this was an Act which continued to be cited by jurists into the eighteenth century. Stair *Inst* 1.10.9; George Mackenzie, *Observations on the Acts of Parliament* (Printed by the heir of A Anderson, Printer to His most Sacred Majesty, and are to be sold by T Brown and other book-sellers 1687) 192–93; Forbes *Institutes* (n 70) II.III.I.VI; Erskine *Institutes* III.II.

[144] For a useful analysis of the 1579 Act and its ambiguities, see Ilya A Kotlyar, 'The Influence of European Ius Commune on the Scots Law of Succession to Moveables, 1560–1700' (DPhil thesis, University of Edinburgh 2017) 35–41.

[145] It is worth noting that the 1579 Act came a year after the establishment of the 1578 Law Commission, which was asked 'to visit, review and consider the said laws [of Scotland] and to reason and confer thereupon'. Three weeks after the conclusion of the Commission, the 1579 Act was passed by the Scottish Parliament. It could be suggested that the Scots approach here was influenced by the 1566 Edict of Moulins, which introduced similar requirements but specifically starting the value of £100; Robert J Pothier, *A Treatise on the Law of Obligations, Or Contracts*, vol 1 (Robert H Small 1853) 538ff. For discussion of this period in France, see Marie Seong-Hak Kim, 'Custom, Community, and the Crown: Lawyers and the Reordering

At first appearance, it may seem that the 1579 Act only relates to heritable property—but the subsequent phrase 'and obligations of great importance' indicates a broader scope in terms of applying to bonds and contracts more generally. It required that obligations which related to heritable titles and those obligations of 'great importance' be executed in a written deed, witnessed and sealed by the respective parties— the alternative to this being that parties agree to the obligation before four witnesses and two reputable notaries. In Mackenzie's *Observations*[146] and Stair's *Institutions*,[147] the Act is understood to generate a category of voluntary obligation in Scots law which cannot be created, enforced, or acknowledged by a court unless it is executed in accordance with the strict formality of the Act (viz. *obligatio literis*).[148] Moreover, Stair and Mackenzie agreed that by custom 'obligations of importance' meant obligations of a value of 100 pounds Scots or more.[149] However, the Act did not say how obligations under the value of 100 pounds Scots were to be created and did not specifically reference mercantile obligations.

In terms of what the Act did express clearly, it required a category of obligation to follow strict rules of formation, which represents a constitutive mode of contractual thought. The idea that the writ itself created the obligation rather than being mere evidence of the obligation was a familiar mode of contractual thought in early modern Europe. It is no surprise, then, that the 1579 Act demonstrates a constitutive mode of thinking in the sixteenth and seventeenth centuries.[150] Although this type of contractual thought is unremarkable, it could be said, nonetheless, that constitutive thinking about contract formation is a significant signpost as to attitudes towards contracts and the creation of an obligation. That is, in contract theory there is a meaningful but subtle difference between saying no obligation exists because it was not executed in a writ, and saying you cannot prove the existence of this obligation because a writ is the only reliable means of proving the existence of the obligation. The first is a more basic, primitive, and material means by which to create an obligation, whereas the second represents a more complex, intangible, and abstract approach to contract formation.

of French Customary Law' in Charles H Parker and Jerry H Bentley (eds), *Between the Middle Ages and Modernity: Individual and Community in the Early Modern World* (Rowman & Littlefield 2007) 169–86. It would have surely been known to those on the Commission who had studied in France, including Thomas Craig (1538?–1608). Craig had by this point received an education in France. Spotiswoode, *Practicks* (n 34) 337.

[146] Mackenzie *Observations on the Acts of Parliament* (n 143) 192–93.

[147] Stair *Inst* 1.10.9.

[148] Kotlyar argues that money bonds were not understood as *obligatio litterarum* until the mid-eighteenth century. However, if used to designate a legal understanding of the instrument rather than a contemporaneous term, it can describe how some transactions, such as a money bond, were conceived. Kotlyar 'Scots Law of Succession' (n 136) 38.

[149] Several cases recorded in Durie's *Practicks* suggest this understanding and are collated in William M Morison (ed), *Decisions of the Court of Session, from its First Institutions to the Present Time* (2nd edn, Archibald Constable 1811): *Russell v Paterson* (1926) Mor 12383; *John Power v The Customers* (1626) Mor 83999; *Lord Gray v Graham* (1628) Mor 12382; *Oliphant v Monorgan* (1628) 8400; *Keith v Dick and Gray* (1629) 12383; *A v B* (1629) Mor 8400; *Ernock v Preston* (1636) Mor 12383; *Lillie v Laird of Innerleith* (1636) Mor 12383; *Keith v Johnston's Tenanats* (1636) Mor 8400; *Lillie v Laird of Innerleith* (1636) Mor 12383; *Skeen v ?* (1637) Mor 8401; *Craw v Culbertson* (1663) Mor 12384.

[150] See, for example, Spotiswoode *Practicks* 359.

Whatever the case, as will be suggested in the following chapter the legal status of non-heritable transactions under 100 pounds Scots was not expressly addressed in the 1579 Act and therefore left the possibility that these types of transaction were enforceable or could become enforceable in early modern Scotland without the same level of formality.[151] Additionally, the Act did not expressly address mercantile transactions, which again is suggestive of another category of obligation in early modern Scots law.[152] Arguably, it was within this legislative gap or through a restrictive interpretation of the 1579 Act that promises and verbal contracts (mercantile or not) could gain legal recognition in the Court of Session. However, as the previous discussion suggests, Balfour and Craig filled this gap with an appeal to Roman law in their practicks; and this is repeated in various other manuscripts from the mid-seventeenth century. It is important, however, that such an approach runs counter to the general approach of Roman law, which was a central source of law relating to contracting in mid-seventeenth-century Scotland and will be explored further in the next chapter. For now, however, it is important to note three things: that in the mid-seventeenth century, Acts of Parliament trumped all other sources of positive law but were very scarce; that Scots lawyers frequently referred to the 1579 Act; and that it generally demonstrates a constitutive mode of contractual thought in relation to particular category of contracting behaviour and leaves open the possibility for a different approach to be taken to other categories of contracting.

Causa, Pacts, and Contracts

Overall, the impression taken from the practicks examined here is that there were meaningful attempts made to bring together various sources used in Scotland into one text, and that this included a desire to record the law applying to contracting behaviour. Three reoccurring points of customary Scots contract law can be found in these texts: the idea that contracts should be divided into *stricti iuris* or bonæ fidei for the purposes of interpretation and enforcement; that contracts should be understood as mutual or reciprocal obligations; and, if there is a lack of mutuality in a contract or no express *causa* as to why it is gratuitous rather than onerous, then it was void or viewed with suspicion. Moreover, a *nudum pactum* was unenforceable but could gain legal significance in several specified ways. Along with discussions of *nudum pactum*, these practicks often noted evidential means by which an otherwise unwritten agreement could become an enforceable obligation. This should not be characterized as 'legal nationalism', but rather emanating from a practical need to record the practice of the Court of Session. As has been demonstrated in this chapter, these practicks provide an important context within which to understand Stair's own writing on conventional

---

[151] Several cases dating before Stair's *Institutions* could be read in this light: *Drummond v Bisset* (1551) Mor 12381; *Lord Monteith v Tenants* (1582) Mor 8397; *A v B* (1629) Mor 8400; *Wood v Moncur* (1591) Mor 7719; *Kintore v Sinclair* (1623) Mor 9425; *Laird of Clackmannan v Sir William Nisbet* (1624) Spotiswoode *Practicks* 247; *William Auld v Patrick Jack* (1627) Spotiswoode *Practicks* 247; *Lillie v Laird of Innerleith* (1636) Mor 12383.

[152] In 1632, the Lords of Session rejected the idea that the 1579 Act applied to obligations between two merchants: Durie *Practicks* 644ff.

obligations. As with Stair, this literature demonstrates that in the mid-seventeenth-century literature there was a renewed emphasis upon native customary law, including the law applying to contracting, and a concern with its origin from within Scottish institutions. It could be said that this literature was created in comparison to and in relation to transnational sources of law, such as Roman law, which otherwise provided Scots lawyers with a respected legal literature which they often understood as embodying equity. Yet one overriding point needs to be emphasized: the sources of the *Corpus iuris civilis* undoubtedly provided a rich and extensive backdrop against which Scots lawyers could write about a Scots customary practice. On that point, Craig's description should be underscored: 'I would say that civil law is so diffused through all our affairs and around all our concerns that practically no inquiry and no sort of case occurs in which its singular force and function are not manifestly apparent.'[153] Why, to what extent, and in what manner Roman law should be used is another question, but it unmistakably formed the lens as well as the material through which the majority of the law of contracting in Scotland was practiced. Thus, the status of Roman law as a source of contract law is a key aspect of mid-seventeenth-century contractual thought, something which the following chapter will examine.

Conclusion

When it comes to exploring Scots law before Stair, you can find two broad interpretations. First, there are those who stress the remarkable and relatively quick change which occurred in Scots law around the mid-seventeenth century. For example, Alan Watson remarked that 'few things seem more obvious than that the fundamental transition to the modern law [in Scotland] happened swiftly, between 1633—the last date of material in Lord Advocate Hope's *Major Practicks*—and about 1655 when Lord Stair's *Institutions of the Law of Scotland* were written.'[154] Lord Clyde suggested that Hope's *Major Practicks* 'does but a little to help bridge the yawning gulf which separates the scholarship and learning of Balfour and Craig from the astonishing produce of Stair's architectural genius'.[155] In a similar manner, Irvine Smith commented that the development of law in Scotland does compare to the 'steady march of the English law' when you consider the 'revolutionary change between the work of Hope ... and Stair, whose *Institutions* were published in 1681'. For him, such a change was 'inexplicable other than by the sheer genius of Stair'.[156] Second, some stress continuity within Scottish legal development during this period. For example, James Gow and Gerhard Lubbe have established separately some broad doctrines and rules of contract formation in the period before Stair that continue to resonate in the period after Stair wrote his *Institutions*, particularly in terms of formalities.[157] Sellar has done something

---

[153] Craig *Jus Feudale* 1.2.14.

[154] Alan Watson, 'The Rise of Modern Scots Law' (1977) La Formazione Storica de Diritto Moderno Europa 1167, 1167.

[155] Clyde *Hope's Major Practicks* (n 98) xvi.

[156] James Irvine Smith, 'The Transition to the Modern Law 1532–1660' in *An Introduction to Scottish Legal History*, vol 20 (Stair Society 1958) 22.

[157] James J Gow, 'The Constitution and Proof of Voluntary Obligations' (1961) Juridical Review 1 and 21; Lubbe 'Formation of Contract' (n 12).

similar with regard to promising,[158] and Alexander Mackenzie Stuart has done the same with relation to central doctrines of contract law as a whole, but notably with regard to the role of *causa*.[159] But what the first interpretation identifies and what the second interpretation does not dispute is that in terms of legal thought, including contractual thought, Stair represents a significant change. This chapter has also served to demonstrate that Stair's contract theory is remarkable in terms of its length, depth, and ambition. To explain this, however, it is not possible to rely solely upon legal sources. It is the theological, philosophical, and political context of the mid-seventeenth century which helps us to explain the distinctiveness of Stair's approach to contractual obligations.

[158] Sellar 'Promise' (n 13).
[159] Mackenzie Stuart 'Contract and Quasi Contract' (n 12).

2
Roman Law as a Source of Contract Law

If Stair is said to have transformed contractual thought in Scotland, then his approach to Roman law is significant. As the previous chapter concluded, in the seventeenth-century Roman law was frequently utilized by mid-seventeenth-century Scots lawyers particularly regarding novel questions of contract law. Yet it is of note that Roman law plays a different role in Stair's account of contracting when compared to his contemporaries.[1] Of course, the *Institutions of the Laws of Scotland's* ('*Institutions*') account of contracting is undoubtedly Romanistic.[2] It would have been hard for Stair to give an adequate description of the reality of Parliament House if his account did not adopt the nomenclature of Roman law and acknowledge the many places where Scots courts followed a particular Roman law solution. Nevertheless, Stair's approach signals a less deferential attitude. Not only is there a distinct willingness to innovate within this tradition, there is also a demonstrable examination of its value as a source of contract law throughout titles 10 to 18 of Book I.

Although Stair's approach to Roman law has been studied extensively within the secondary literature,[3] and indeed some have examined his approach to propositions of law taken from Roman law,[4] this chapter seeks to understand how Stair's theoretical aims affected his engagement with what was otherwise a mainstay of contracting in Scotland.[5] By incorporating an examination of Stair's theoretical aims, this chapter seeks to explain why the philosophical and political impulses of Stair motivated him to find a new theoretical model for the customary law of Scotland—one that innovated

---

[1] See Chapter 1 for an account of how Stair's contemporaries in Scotland engaged with Roman law sources of the law applying to contracting.

[2] Wilson argues Stair's fourth version of the *Institutions*, published in 1693, is 'heavily Romanised' in comparison to previous iterations. Adelyn L M Wilson, 'The Sources and Method of the *Institutions of the Law of Scotland* by Sir James Dalrymple, 1st Viscount Stair, with Specific Reference to the Law of Obligations' (DPhil thesis, University of Edinburgh 2011) 265.

[3] Peter Stein, 'The Influence of Roman Law' (1963) 8 Juridical Review 205; William M Gordon, 'Roman Law in Scotland' in Robin Evans-Jones (ed), *The Civil Law Tradition in Scotland* (The Stair Society 1995) 13–40.

[4] Peter Stein, *Fault in the Formation of Contract in Roman Law and Scots Law* (University of Aberdeen Press 1958) 175 ff; Gerhard Lubbe, 'Formation of Contract' in Kenneth Reid and Reinhard Zimmermann (eds), *A History of Private Law in Scotland*, vol 2 (OUP 2000) 1–46; William M Gordon, 'Risk in Sale—From Roman to Scots Law' in William M Gordon (ed), *Roman Law, Scots Law and Legal History* (Edinburgh University Press 2007) 164–76; Adelyn L M Wilson, 'Stair, Mackenzie and Risk in Sale in Seventeenth Century Scotland' (2009) 15 (1) Fundamina 168–80; Wilson 'The Sources and Method' (n 2); Paul McClelland, 'The Seller's Liability for Sale of Fault Goods in Scots Law' (LLM thesis, University of Glasgow 2015) 14–28.

[5] Taking this approach is not to discount Wilson's suggestion that Stair's knowledge of Roman law developed and deepened between the 1660s and 1690s, particularly given that he attended lectures in Leiden during his exile in the 1680s. This is certainly a plausible explanation, as Stair did not formally study law before becoming an advocate. The aim here, however, is to explain how Stair justified his approach to Roman law sources in theoretical terms, regardless of more practical considerations. See Wilson, 'Sources and Method' (n 2) 265.

Contract before the Enlightenment. Stephen Bogle, Oxford University Press. © Stephen Bogle 2023.
DOI: 10.1093/oso/9780192884961.003.0003

on its Roman law foundations—including the law of contract. Although John Ford has painstakingly shown that several alternative theories of legal authority were extant within seventeenth-century Scotland—principally the notion that expert legal learning, using juristic methods, could provide a source of law[6]—Stair's approach remains distinctive. As the first jurist to set out expressly a theory of law which could justify the law of Scotland, including the law of contract, he undertook a task whose necessity is not immediately apparent. Why alongside an account of private law in Scotland, did he offer a sophisticated natural law explanation of contracting, employing an account of foundational principles, rights, liberty, human action, and commerce?

Terminology: Roman Law, Civil Law, and the *Ius Commune*

Before answering these questions about Stair's contractual thought, it is vital to set out what Stair meant by 'Roman law', attending to the distinction between 'Roman law' and 'Civil law' of which much modern legal history is mindful. As William Gordon explains, to a historian Roman law 'means the law of Rome, up to and including the restatement of the law carried out under Justinian I in the sixth century AD'.[7] Civil law, however, has a less precise meaning. It can be used to refer to the Justinianic compilation or to the tradition or traditions of scholarship which followed the re-emergence of this code in the thirteenth century. Importantly, Civil law in either of these senses does not mean the law applying to interpersonal relationships in contrast to the law applicable to the state or public authority.[8] Although this distinction stems from Justinian's *Institutes*, it should be held apart from the two other senses sketched out here. While none of these modern definitions map easily on to how Stair used the term 'Roman law', it could be said that he used the term in a rough approximation of how it is used nowadays, ie to refer to the law of the people of Rome codified by Justinian in the sixth century. Yet this needs further explanation.

Stair himself was aware of the possibility of confusion. For example, when describing the laws of nations which are 'the customs owned and acknowledged by all, or at least the most civil nations' Stair says that some refer to this as the 'common law'.[9] Alive to the risk of misunderstanding, Stair draws the important distinction between use of the term 'common law' to describe the 'ancient and unquestionable customs' of English lawyers and use of the term to refer to the law of nations, which are customs shared between countries, ie the *ius commune*. He adds that Scots would refer to Roman law as the 'common law' of Scotland in a similar way to English lawyers referring to their common law.[10] Of note, however, is that a few paragraphs later, Stair tries to bring the English law and *ius commune* senses of 'common law' together saying:[11]

---

[6] John Ford, *Law and Opinion in Scotland during the Seventeenth Century* (Hart 2007).

[7] William M Gordon, 'The Civil Law in Scotland' in William M Gordon (ed), *Roman Law, Scots Law and Legal History* (Edinburgh University Press 2007) 327.

[8] Peter G Stein, 'Roman Law, Common Law, and Civil Law' (1991–92) 66 Tulane Law Review 1591–604.

[9] Stair *Inst* 1.1.11.

[10] Stair *Inst* 1.1.16.

[11] Stair *Inst* 1.1.16.

The English, also by their common law, in opposition to statute and recent customs, mean their ancient and unquestionable customs. In a like manner, we are ruled in the first place by our ancient and immemorial customs, which may be called our common law; though sometimes by that name is understood equity, which is common to all nations or the civil Roman law, which in some sort is common to very many.

As will be shown, Stair had a very specific sense of what equity was, effectively seeing it as a means of reasoning which revealed the natural law solution in particular circumstances. But for now, it is important to note that Stair is suggesting that at the root of the common law, whether this is the law common to nations, the Roman law which is common to many, or the long-established customs of particular nations, is equity. In doing so, Stair is not suggesting here that Roman law held similar legal status and authority in Scotland as the common law of England held in that nation. His point is instead that Scots lawyers referred to Roman law as the common law to designate what *might* be the applicable law when there was no pertinent statute. Sometimes Roman law would have authority but this was because it would often but not always constitute an example of equity, just as custom might.[12]

This distinctive perspective on Roman law also comes through in the way Stair spoke about 'civil law' as a term signifying the 'the law of each society of people under the same sovereign authority, or the law of the citizen of that commonwealth'.[13] As Stair explained, this definition would apply, of course, to 'the civil law of the Roman commonwealth or empire', 'the most excellent' of civil laws. Though the perceived affinity between Scots law and Roman law meant that this 'civil law' of Rome was valuable to Scots lawyers, its authority was not binding; instead, 'as a rule' it was followed for its equity.[14]

As Alan Watson has noted, by 'as a rule' Stair meant a commonly followed custom. He did not mean that Roman law was formally recognized as a source of law.[15] It is telling also that Stair speaks of 'civil law' and 'Roman law' interchangeably in title 10 of Book 1 in a way that suggests he is speaking about the law of the society of ancient Rome, which was compiled by Justinian in the *Corpus iuris civilis*. By recounting a history of Roman law in this manner, Stair was implying to his reader that when he discussed Roman law, he was ultimately dealing with the law of an ancient society that was no longer alive as a direct source of law. As such, though Roman law was the 'most excellent' of civil laws it should not be followed automatically; it was something which could be used comparatively, as an example, examined to evaluate its equity.

how Stair defines Roman law

---

[12] This is not necessarily how his contemporaries understood things. Indeed, one of the overarching conclusions of John Ford's *Law and Opinion in Scotland during the Seventeenth Century* (Hart 2007) is that in taking this approach Stair was out of step with his contemporaries who were far more likely to see Roman law as the embodiment of equity and demonstrating a way of reasoning and handling law which could be emulated by Scots lawyers.

[13] Stair *Inst* 1.1.12.

[14] Stair *Inst* 1.1.12.

[15] Alan Watson, 'The Rise of Modern Scots Law' (1977) 3 La Formazione Storica de Diritto Moderno Europa 1167, 1167.

Two Objectives

Stair's *Institutions* was an impressive attempt to shift the focus away from the *ius commune* tradition towards the local customary law of Scotland. In doing this, Stair minimized the role of Roman law by arguing that it was not the common law of Scotland and by offering an alternative methodology for handling Roman law sources of contract law. In fact, he cast some doubt on Roman law as a source when there was already a great deal of ambiguity about the authority of various sources of law in Scotland. So, this raises a question, why, in the context of contract law, where Roman law was otherwise the leading alternative source within Scotland, did Stair adopt a less deferential attitude? Surely, when you are lacking sources of law it is unhelpful to devalue a vital source in an area where its authority was relatively settled?

In starting to answer this question is best to begin with Stair's two express objectives. His first is to present 'a Summary of the Laws and Customs' of Scotland.[16] He explains in his 1681 dedication to Charles II that 'our law is most part consuetudinary' which gives Scotland the most expedient of laws but is also 'obliterated and forgot'.[17] Thomas Craig, of course, noted in his *Jus Feudale*, which was reprinted by Burnett's 1655, that 'Roman laws and civilian system are not much used in France, Germany, Spain and England' but that it must be remembered that 'in those places, the laws and customs of the country are almost entirely set down in writing' whereas 'in our country, there is a great dearth of written laws and so we naturally follow the civil law in most matters'.[18] In writing the *Institutions*, therefore, Stair was directly responding to this need for a written account of the customary law. A consequence of this first objective was a reconfiguration of the place of Roman law within Scottish legal practice. Not only this, but Stair expresses a preference for customary law over legislation. He notes that 'we are not involved in the labyrinth of many and large statues, whereof the posterior do ordinarily so abrogate and derogate from the prior, that it requires a great part of life to be prompt in all these winding'. Such as state of affairs would result, according to Stair, in the subjects of a nation giving 'more implicit faith to their judges and lawyers than they need, or ought'.[19] As will be discussed further below, Stair says later in the *Institutions*, that nations are the most happy when their laws are based on long-established customs 'wrung out from their debates upon particular cases, until it comes to the consistence of fixed and known custom'.[20] For him, customary law is what comes closest to equity which is central to his second objective: to explain the common and equitable principles of law regardless of its locality and demonstrate that law was a rational discipline.

Prima facie, Stair's first objective appears parochial and contrasts with the pan-European *ius commune* tradition most Scots lawyers would have been familiar with in the seventeenth century. Yet Stair has an opposing universalist impulse which

---

[16] Dedication to the first edition of the *Institutions*, published in 1681, and repeated in the second edition in 1693.

[17] Dedication (n 16).

[18] Craig *Jus Feudale* 1.2.14.

[19] Dedication (n 16).

[20] Stair *Inst* 1.1.15.

transcends the notion of local customary law.[21] In his dedication, he tells Charles II that the laws and customs of 'your ancient Kingdom of Scotland ... can be nowhere so fitly placed, as under the rays of your royal protection'. It will 'tend to the honour and renown of your Majesty', he says, 'that you have governed this nation so long and so happily, by such just and convenient laws, which are here offered to the view of the world, in a plain, rational and natural method'.[22] In fact, Stair concludes in the *Institutions* that he has shown to the world that:

> The Law of Scotland in its nearness to Equity, plainness and facility in its Customes, Tenors and Forms, and in its celerity and dispatch in the Administration and Execution of it, may be well paralleled with the best Law in Christendom, which will more plainly appear, when the proportion and propinquity of it to Equity shall be seen.

To demonstrate this, Stair starts his account of the laws of Scotland from a universal point of view. He says that no man 'can be a knowing lawyer in any nation, who hath not well pondered and digested in his mind the common law of the world'.[23] So, Stair wanted to illustrate the 'material justice' of the 'common law of the world' and show that these laws derived from 'self-evident principles, through all several private rights thence arising'[24] and, importantly, to exhibit that Scots law was an eminent example of this material justice.

In attempting this sort of project, Stair was not alone. He was emulating the new legal science of nation states, which emerged in mid- to late seventeenth century.[25] Scores of jurists across Northern Europe sought to enrich the study of municipal laws of nation states through the study of natural law. Of particular note is Grotius's *Introduction to the Jurisprudence of Holland*,[26] written in 1619–20.[27] Although this sort of literature could be viewed as inward-looking, insofar as it took the nation state as its starting point, it nonetheless generated a new genre of legal theory which sought to show how natural law and customary law could be melded together.[28] Importantly, this did not necessarily require jettisoning the study of Roman law. It did, however, introduce a parallel legal science of the nation state which drew upon Roman law

---

[21] Klaus Luig, 'Stair from a Foreign Standpoint' in David M Walker (ed), *Stair Tercentenary Studies*, vol 33 (Stair Society 1981) 239–52. Klaus Luig, 'The Institutes of National Law in the Seventeenth and Eighteenth Centuries' (1972) Juridical Review 193–226, 225–26.

[22] Dedication (n 16).

[23] Stair *Inst* 1.1.

[24] Dedication (n 16).

[25] Quentin Skinner, *The Foundations of Modern Political Thought, vol 1: The Renaissance* (CUP 1978) 207–08; Laurent Waelkens, *Amne Adverso: Roman Legal Heritage in European Culture* (2015) 135. Gianfranco Poggi, *The Development of the Modern State* (1978); John W Cairns, 'Institutional Writings in Scotland Reconsidered' (1984) 4 (3) The Journal of Legal History 76–117, 77.

[26] Hugo Grotius, *The Introduction to Dutch Jurisprudence* (first published 1631, Charles Herbert tr, John van Voorst 1903).

[27] It is likely that Stair was aware of the *Introduction to Dutch Jurisprudence* (or *Inleydinge*) in the 1680s, if not before. See Adelyn L M Wilson, 'Stair and the Inleydinge of Grotius' (2010) 14 (2) Edinburgh Law Review 239–68.

[28] Luig 'Stair from a Foreign Standpoint' (n 21). Here Luig mentions writers such as Hugo Grotius, Guy Coquille, Georg Adam Struve, and Gottfried Wilhem Liebniz.

concepts, extending beyond these to incorporate Bodin's notions of sovereignty and Grotian natural law.[29] Furthermore, Grotius also established a new model and method for the laws of nations, which understood such laws as being built upon reworked natural law foundations. This had a marked impact on Scots law into the eighteenth century.[30] In truth, Grotius' *De Jure Belli ac Pacis* is a central text for Stair both as a source of natural law propositions[31] but also as a method, particularly *The Preliminary Discourse*. Stair notes in the opening passages of the *Institutions* that it was a 'Learned Treatise', which demonstrated how law is a rational discipline.

Detaching law from the notion that it was the mere result of a lawmaker's whims was key to Stair's second objective and evidently influenced by Grotius. Moreover, Stair's engagement with Grotius, and the *De Jure Belli ac Pacis'* continued relevance to eighteenth-century legal thought is significant to how the legacy of Stair's theory is framed. That is, Stair's own iteration of natural law may have lost its relevance to Scots lawyers in the eighteenth century, as it no longer served as a meaningful justification for Scots customary law but, arguably, the style, methods, and approach of Stair, ie using natural law in a juristic manner, continued to be popular amongst moral philosophers in Scotland who remained, as Stair was, engaged with Grotius's new model for natural law. As the concluding chapter will argue, it is this which Stair holds in common with eighteenth-century moral philosophy, particularly Gershom Carmichael. For now, however, our purpose is to understand the relationship between Stair's own natural law theory, the customary law of Scotland and Roman law.

Common Law Principles

Stair begins his account of the common principles of 'the peculiar laws of all nations' with a definition of law itself: 'law is the dictate of reason, determining every rational being to that which is congruous and convenient for the nature and condition thereof.'[32] Even God, according to Stair, as a rational being 'unchangeably determines himself by his goodness, righteousness, and truth' to follow divine law. Stair's focus, however, is to sort out what is natural law, ie the will of God, and what is not. He wants to ensure the relationship between these two sources of law, natural and human law, is properly understood to explain the development and application of law by legislators, judges, and jurists.

 equating divine + natural law?

On this basis, it is useful to understand the various ways by which Stair thought that natural law became manifest in the world through the innate knowledge of man. Hence, it could be said that reason is a faculty of man's cognition,[33] the will is an

---

[29] Benjamin Straumann, *Roman Law in the State of Nature: The Classical Foundations of Hugo Grotius' Natural Law* (CUP 2015).

[30] John W Cairns, 'The First Edinburgh Chair in Law: Grotius and the Scottish Enlightenment' in John W Cairns (ed), *Enlightenment, Legal Education, and Critique: Selected Essays on the History of Scots Law, Volume 2* (Edinburgh University Press 2015) 82–110.

[31] William Gordon, 'Stair, Grotius and the Sources of Stair's *Institutions*' in William Gordon (ed), *Roman Law, Scots Law and Legal History: Selected Essays* (Edinburgh University Press 2007) 255, 263; Wilson, 'Sources and Method' (n 2) 131–71.

[32] Stair *Inst* 1.1.1.

[33] Stair *Inst* 1.1.1.

instinct,[34] Divine law is written on his heart,[35] conscience acts as a witness in man's deliberations,[36] equity is a mode of reasoning through which man can determine equality amongst persons,[37] and moral law is the 'rule of manners of men' found in 'all times, places and persons'.[38] As the paragraphs below will explain, by elucidating how each of these expressions of natural law comes to be known, Stair can illustrate the means by which natural law and human law interact and relate to each other. Stair's understanding of man's direct access to natural law has important consequences for how he approaches what would otherwise be the traditional sources of law which applied to contracting in Scotland, such as Roman law. But before explaining this in more detail it is vital to unpack Stair's understanding of equity; of all expressions of natural law, equity is most central to Stair's explanation of the interaction between positive law and natural law.

Equity, Utility, and Roman Law

According to Stair, equity derives from the moral principle, *quod tibi fieri non vis, alteri ne feceris* (do unto others as you would have others do unto you). Once this frame of reasoning has been adopted, Stair explains that men are forced to see matters from the perspective of their adversaries. If undertaken in good faith, this axiom works to readdress an otherwise unfair balance of perspective, ensuring that equality between parties is reached. Stair offers the example of parents who should place themselves in the shoes of their children, and *vice versa*. Stair argues that out of such a process of reasoning each would understand the demands of the other, ensuring that parents and children do unto each other what they would have done to them. In addition to this first sense of equity, Stair introduces a second. Here he writes that when equity is applied 'nothing is to be done, which is not congruous to human nature' which for Stair means that the 'common interest of mankind is preferred to the interest of any part of men'. This being so, equity does not moderate 'the extremity of human laws' as much as it 'comprehends the whole law of rational nature'. If equity did not comprise the whole law, it would be unable to remedy the 'rigour and extremity of positive law in all cases'.[39] Equity is not, therefore, something that contrasts with law: it is the law. Thus, equity is either embodied in positive laws or comes to the fore when the positive law fails to give adequate expression of it. As he explains, although positive laws are useful and necessary many '*casus incogitati*' or unanticipated cases arise. Given that positive laws are 'inventions of frail men' this is to be expected,[40] but should not lead us to assume that positive laws and equity are separate. They are one.

'Human law', says Stair, 'is that which, for utility's sake, is introduced by men.'[41] It is initiated 'by tacit consent, by consuetude or custom, or by express will or command of

---

[34] Stair *Inst* 1.1.2.
[35] Stair *Inst* 1.1.3.
[36] Stair *Inst* 1.1.5.
[37] Stair *Inst* 1.1.6.
[38] Stair *Inst* 1.1.7.
[39] Stair *Inst* 1.1.6.
[40] Stair *Inst* 1.1.6.
[41] Stair *Inst* 1.1.10.

these in authority, having legislative power'.[42] He explains that the law of Scotland 'at first could be no other than *æquum et bonum*, equity and expediency'.[43] According to Stair, no historical evidence suggests that any nation did at first create positive laws. Upon the creation of government, however, 'it is necessarily implied that they [peoples] must submit to, and be governed by a law, which could be understood no other than what their sovereign authority should find just and convenient'.[44] Just as parties submit themselves to the final decision of arbitrators, so peoples at the formation of states submitted to the authority of a sovereign. Second, he says, submission to a sovereign authority is recognized as preferable to every individual judging their own interests against another. Stair makes an evident reference to Thomas Hobbes by noting that the alternative is individuals 'take and hold by force, what he conceived to be his right, without any superior to himself to be judge to appeal to, and thereby live in perpetual war'. Hence 'government necessarily implied in the very being thereof a yielding and submitting to the determination of the sovereign authority in the differences of the people'. Otherwise, he says, society would revert to a state of private judgement where force rather than law would determine rights.[45] Yet Stair does not wish to say that it is ultimately fear that forces a community to hand power to a ruler with absolute power to create law. In contrast, Stair offers five reasons as to why positive law is useful explaining how the customary law of Scotland can be understood as equitable, albeit man-made.

First, it is often difficult for men to agree on the specific application of equity: 'though equity be clear in its principles and *in thesi*, yet the deduction of reason further from the fountain, through the bias and corruption of interest, may make it much dubious *in hypothesi*, when it comes to the decision of particular cases'.[46] Second, it is necessary to make clear what obligations should be enforceable by positive law and those which, although owed, would be troublesome to enforce. To illustrate the point, Stair says 'you cannot poind for unkindness' as this is something which is often only known internally.[47] Third, it prevents error or fraud in specific situations, such as specific rules about the formalities of a contract or the transfer of property. Fourth, there may be instances where the positive law is able to help individuals realize an outcome in a more effective manner than a literal application of equity. He offers the example of inheritance, saying that although by the law of nature the right of succession belongs to all the children, most nations 'for the flourishing of families do otherwise' giving to the eldest son and assuming that the rest of the family will be provided for. Fifth, according to the different sensibilities and character of people in different nations, there may be a willingness to punish more strictly or more leniently specific types of wrong.[48]

On the last point, Stair remarks that although the 'humours and inclinations of people' may lead to 'heavier penalties' in different countries, it is surely the case that 'they are most happy, whose laws are nearest to equity, and most declaratory of it, and

---

[42] Stair *Inst* 1.1.10.
[43] Stair *Inst* 1.1.16.
[44] Stair *Inst* 1.1.16.
[45] Stair *Inst* 1.1.16.
[46] Stair *Inst* 1.1.15.
[47] Stair *Inst* 1.1.15.
[48] Stair *Inst* 1.1.15.

least altering of the effects thereof.'[49] Although there are exceptions where it is necessary to alter what might otherwise naturally follow from equity, this should be done
with caution. Indeed, 'the nations are more happy, whose laws have entered by long
custom, wrung out from their debates upon particular cases, until it come to the consistence of a fixed and know custom.'[50] Rules can be tested and, if necessary, discarded
if they fail to embody equity or demonstrate utility. From here Stair turns his attention to legislation, contrasting wisdom of custom with statutes' immaturity. He says,
'in statutes the lawgiver must at once balance the conveniences and inconveniences;
wherein he may and often doth fall short' as, contrary to customs, legislation cannot
be tested over time and is passed in a moment. Yet there are countless hard cases or
unforeseen circumstances which are unanticipated, which equity must then resolve.
He goes on to say:[51]

> But these are best which are approbatory, or correctory of experienced Customs,
> and in a customary Law, though the people run some hazard at first of their Judges
> Arbitrament: Yet when that Law is come to a fulness and consistence, they have by
> much the advantage in this, that what custom hath changed, is thrown away, and ob-
> literate without memory, or mention of it; but in Statutory Written Law, the Vestige of
> all the alterations remain, and ordinarily increase to such a Mass, that they cease to be
> Evidences, and Securities to the people, and become Labyrinths, wherein they are fair
> to lose their Rights, if not themselves, and must have an implicate Faith, in these who
> cannot comprehend them without making it the work of their life.

This raises the question which sources might disclose the customs of Scotland. The
way that Stair established the relationship between natural law in all its manifestations
and positive law makes this a significant question. Crucially, the way he set up the relationship between natural and positive law, and the way he understood common law
had implications for what kinds of sources would be appropriate in determining law
of Scotland.

Unsurprisingly, bearing in mind Stair's notions of common law, Stair says 'Our
customs have arisen mainly from Equity, so they are also from the civil, canon and
feudal laws' but he stresses 'none of these have with us the authority of Law, and therefore are only received, according to their Equity and Expediency, *Secundum bonum
& æquum*.'[52] Though Scots customary law had taken a great deal of terminology,
definitions, and forms of Roman, canon, and feudal law, none of these bodies of law
were immune from being rejected if they did not accord with equity. Though some
thought otherwise, Stair was clear that 'these Laws are an example' and not a rule.[53]
On that basis, Roman law should not be treated as a default source of law when legislation and custom were silent: recourse is to be made directly to equity. When it comes
to the law of contract, therefore, there is a great deal to suggest that the Roman law

---

[49] Stair *Inst* 1.1.15.
[50] Stair *Inst* 1.1.15.
[51] Stair *Inst* 1.1.15.
[52] Stair *Inst* 1.1.16.
[53] Stair *Inst* 1.1.16.

sources, terminology, and taxonomy made a firm footprint on the law of Scotland. Importantly, however, according to Stair's theory, it is Roman law's equity and utility that demonstrates its applicability. According to Stair, its authority derived neither from a transplantation into Scots law by learned jurists nor an endorsement by an act of the Scottish Parliament.

Roman Law, Sovereignty, and Equity

It was common for Scots lawyers to account for the authority of Roman law by extolling its equity, but Stair's approach was unusual.[54] What troubled Stair's contemporaries, therefore, at least in theoretical terms if not in practice, was offering an account of how it related to other sources of law used in Scotland and, vitally, when it was appropriate to use Roman law in pleadings.[55] As has been explained, Stair used equity in a very particular way, as a mode of reasoning but also as the foundation of all positive laws. This meant, in a hierarchy of sources, Stair placed customary law first, followed by legislation, and where these were silent, equity itself. He also preferred the development of law overtime and through the slow progress of customary law. What is more, the *Institutions* makes evident that he trusted the Court of Session as a main driver for the cultivation of customary law, through individual decisions, it would develop and test the equity of a solution. Hence, he wanted judges not jurists to be the judge of Roman law's applicability. In a novel contract case, however, a judge was able to appeal direct to equity, Roman law was only a comparative example. In taking this approach, Stair placed the Court of Session at the forefront of developing the customary law of contract in Scotland. In doing this, he tried to reframe the role of Roman law and, importantly, jurists.

To explain this further, it is helpful to consider Stair's near contemporary, Sir George Mackenzie, took a different approach. For example, Mackenzie argued when there is no statute or custom, judges should not turn directly to equity.[56] For him, equity was embodied in 'the writing of learned lawyers who give their judgment in abstract cases wherein none are concerned but their souls, reputation and posterity'.[57] By learned lawyers, Mackenzie had in mind the authors collected in the *Digest*, fifteenth- and sixteenth-century commentaries on Roman, feudal, and customary law, along with jurists who had written about local laws, including Scotland, with the aim of transferring the learning of Roman law into their regional system of law.[58] Although Mackenzie held that man had direct knowledge of moral law in a similar manner to Stair, he did not think that this could be a guide to novel legal situations. For him, judges were not legislators and had no authority to turn directly to equity for

---

[54] Andrew R C Simpson and Adelyn L M Wilson, *Scottish Legal History, vol 1* (Edinburgh University Press 2017) 293–315.
[55] Ford *Law and Opinion* (n 6) 37–51 (on Robert Burnett); 209–10 (on Robert Spotiswoode); 211–12 (on Thomas Wallace); 213–47 (on John Nisbet); 231–32 (on Thomas Craig); 251–81 (on Sir Thomas Hope); and 491–99 (on George Mackenzie). Simpson and Wilson, *Scottish Legal History* (n 54) 293–315.
[56] British Library, Add MS 18236, f108–09. Ford *Law and Opinion* (n 6) 484.
[57] British Library, Add MS 18236, f108–09.
[58] Ford *Law and Opinion* (n 6) 492–99.

they were too prone to mistakes, arbitrariness, or worse. Moreover, judges were often too detained by the specifics of the case to see the wider picture. Only when the legal issue was considered in abstraction could a learned jurist find the equitable outcome. Hence, equity embodied in Roman law and illuminated by learned authors was how Scots law should solve hard cases.[59]

So, Stair put his faith in the judiciary not jurists to develop the law of contract. John Ford has demonstrated that Stair believed the sovereign in Scotland had devolved their judicial functions to the Court of Session.[60] Hence, the Court of Session was both a court of equity and law with, in some instances, the power to make law. It could appeal directly to equity without the fear of arbitrariness. This was a key point for Stair. In an epistle to the Lords of Session, which prefaced volume 1 of his *Decisions*, Stair stressed the importance of impartiality and judicial independence, saying '[i]t is the great interest of Mankind, that every man should not be Judge in his own Cause, but that there should be indifferent Judges … who might hear and determine the Controversies of Parties' and that 'either party should acquiesce in the publick judgment of Authority'. Moreover, he says '[i]t is amongst the greatest interest of Mankind, that they many securely enjoy their Rights and Possessions, being free from fear to be over-reached, or oppressed, without remedy; which can not be attained, unless their Right be lodged in the hands of just and judicious Judges'.[61] However, he stressed that without printed and published decisions parties need to rely on the good reputation of judges. Yet this may make parties suspicious that judges make decisions like the 'Delphick Sword, bowing or bending to the several Parties'. Furthermore, judges without printed decisions need to rely on 'bonum & equum' and therefore 'differ like from Abriters' until they have 'fixed Customs and Statutes'.[62]

Stair, however, is keen to show that judges' decisions are 'a firm and stable Rule' and that there 'can be no way better known' to ensure consistency, equity, and trust in judges than 'by publishing and comparing Decisions, whereby it may be seen, that like Case have like events, and there is no respect of persons in Judgement'.[63] He goes on, 'all men cannot be Lawyers, nor can the most part have discretion enough to understand equum & bonum; yet few will be found to want capacity to compare Decisions, and so perceive if they be congruous and uniform, and if they find them such, they may easily be perwaded, that their uniformity could be by no other Rule than Law, and Justice'.[64] Hence, Stair argues that printing decisions will not only aid judges but also assure parties, lawyers, and the public that the Lords of Session are applying the law justly, consistently, and impartially. Yet as the *Institutions* demonstrate, Stair did not feel confident that printing the decisions and urging his judicial colleagues to read

---

[59] John W Cairns, 'Attitudes to Codification and the Scottish Science of Legislation 1600–1830' (2007) 22 Tulane European & Civil Law Forum 1, 14–20; John W Cairns, 'Natural Law, National Laws, Parliaments, and Multiple Monarchies: 1707 and Beyond' in John W Cairns (ed), *Law, Lawyers, and Humanism: Selected Essays on the History of Scots Law, vol 1* (Edinburgh University Press 2015) 115.

[60] Ford *Law and Opinion* (n 6) 524.

[61] James Dalrymple, *The Decisions of the Lords of Council and Session in the Most Important Cases Debate before Them, with Acts of Sederunt* (Anno Dom, Andrew Anderson, 1683) iv.

[62] Dalrymple *The Decisions of the Lords of Council* (1683) (n 61) iv.

[63] Dalrymple *The Decisions of the Lords of Council* (1683) (n 61) iv.

[64] Dalrymple *The Decisions of the Lords of Council* (1683) (n 61) iv.

them was enough. If Stair wanted to ensure, for example, that a novel solution to a contractual problem could be found he had to exhibit how that could be done.

Kings, Jurists, and Judges?

If Stair was to be successful, he needed to demonstrate an alternative model of legal reasoning; one which showed that judges not jurists can find the equitable solution to a contractual problem. That is, as was traditional in Scotland, a jurist would, for the most part, if there was no statutory law or customary solution, appeal to Roman law. It was against this tradition that Stair offered his new philosophical basis for private law in Scotland, including the law of contract. Indeed, as Ford has concluded in writing the *Institutions*, Stair himself did not want to be taken as a learned source of law nor did he see his *Institutions* as a record of advocates' collective wisdom about equity, ie a collection of learned opinion. Stair, per Ford, 'tried to promote the idea that all laws must be derived from the exercise of sovereignty by a lawgiver, so that no amount of reasoning by any corps of experts could itself result in the introduction of law'.[65] Ford goes on to say that Stair 'detached the law of Scotland from the philosophical basis on which it been placed by other jurists'.[66]

Thus, Stair consciously wrote against the idea that learned sources of law were in some way a better guide to equity than reason. On Stair's account, learned lawyers, erudite advocates, or ancient sources are highly esteemed but their interpretation of law is not a shortcut towards a just and equitable resolution. Nor could moral philosophers or theologians offer easy answers to the specifics of day-to-day ethical questions. In the *Institutions*, however, he tried to offer a demonstration of how such an evaluation could be done. On Stair's account, the introducing or reforming laws should be done when there was an evident utility and in keeping with natural law. Stair replaced the idea that jurists could develop the law in line with learned opinion with the idea that judges had the sovereign authority to do this. Yet past decisions of the Court of Session were not enough for a judge. Nor potentially was it enough for his wider seventeenth-century audience merely to invoke sovereignty and lionize the Lords of Session. It was therefore necessary to provide a fuller account of the common principles of law, which underpinned the law of Scotland.

Indeed, as Luig noted, a close examination of Stair's handling of individual questions of law, particularly where Scots customary law did not have an established answer, demonstrates that Stair was not dogmatic in the *Institutions* (as if judging the matters as a lord of session).[67] However, Luig rightly suggests Stair would have surely intended that his reader observe closely how he reasoned in the *Institutions* when the law was uncertain; that is, from principle, to various sources which have touched upon the question at hand, to an evaluation of a solution's equity and expediency. In doing so, 'he knew very well that by this sort of reasoning his doctrine became not only a controlling instance over the judiciary but even more a guide-line for forthcoming

---

[65] Ford *Law and Opinion* (n 6) 572.
[66] Ford *Law and Opinion* (n 6) 572.
[67] Luig 'Stair from a Foreign Standpoint' (n 21) 239–52.

decisions'. Thus, the *Institutions* offered an example of how reason could be placed before authority. Yet why would he wish to place reason before authority in his account of the customary law of Scotland?

Revolution, Restoration, and the Claim of Right

As noted in the Introduction, Stair entered the Faculty of Advocates on 17 February 1648. Following the execution of Charles I on 30 January 1649, he was called upon by the 1649 Parliament to serve as both an Ambassador and a Law Commissioner. 'Politically exclusive in outlook' the 1649 Parliament 'sought to create a Covenanted godly state in Scotland'.[68] On the agenda of the Parliament in 1649 was 'the great harm, oppression, burning, plundering and pitiful devastation suffered by' tenants during the recent troubles;[69] the oppression, violence, and corruption of soldiers, baillies, and judicatories;[70] and the conditions of the poor in towns and Burghs around Scotland. This Parliament was also concerned with drunkenness,[71] swearing,[72] fornication,[73] witchcraft, and those who 'consult with the devil'.[74] Thus a law commission was appointed on 15 March 1649 to 'revise and consider all laws' of Scotland where godly rule was being pursued with urgency and fervour.[75] The Act says that the 1649 Parliament was 'zealously desirous' to ensure that the laws were 'for the glory of God, the good of his people and for the furtherance of the administration of justice within this kingdom'.[76] Ford has noted that Stair's direct involvement with the Commission may have been limited.[77] Soon after his appointment, he departed for The Hague as secretary to the Parliamentary Commission sent to negotiate with (the soon to be) Charles II.[78] Yet, as Cairns tells us, nothing much came of this Commission or many of the other commissions established during this period.[79] Nevertheless it did pose a question for Stair at the beginning of his legal career: is the law of Scotland just and how could it be shown to bring glory to God?

It was explained in the Introduction that in comparison to several of his peers, Stair did well under the Commonwealth. For instance, on 1 July 1657 he was appointed to act as a commissioner within Cromwell's Commission for the Administration of Justice which had supplanted the Court of Session; that is, he was effectively appointed to a position akin to a Lord Ordinary.[80] Stair's appointment was against a backdrop of

---

[68] Michael Lynch, 'The Wars of Covenant' in Michael Lynch (ed), *The Oxford Companion to Scottish Legal History* (OUP 2007) 112.

[69] RPS 1649/1/32; 1649/1/67; 1649/1/77; 1649/1/329; 1649/1/329; 1649/1/409.

[70] RPS 1649/1/101; 1649/1/96; A1649/1/81.

[71] RPS 1649/1/119.

[72] RPS 1649/1/119.

[73] RPS 1649/1/62.

[74] RPS 1649/1/63.

[75] RPS, 1649/1/306.

[76] RPS 1649/1/119.

[77] John D Ford, 'Dalrymple, James, first Viscount Stair (1619–1695)' *Oxford Dictionary of National Biography* (OUP 2004) <https://www.oxforddnb.com/> accessed 8 April 2021.

[78] Ford 'Dalrymple' (n 77).

[79] Cairns 'Attitudes to Codification' (n 59) 13.

[80] George Brunton and David Haig, *An Historical Account of the Senators of the College of Justice: From its Institution in 1532* (1832) 346 ff.

Cromwellian dominance in Scotland, following the Cromwellian Act of Union, which was passed on 26 June 1657. The business of the Court of Session had stopped in 1650 during this disruption.[81] As part of George Monck's governance of Scotland, he appointed new judges to the Court of Session; most of these judges were from the English bar; Monck had hoped this would anglicize Scots law.[82] With the death of Cromwell in 1659 the political and religious culture of Scotland changed again. The Court of Session closed its doors on 26 February 1659, as the Cromwellian regime came to an end and more chaos loomed ahead. It is reported that on the eve of taking his army south in October 1659, Monck' consulted Stair,[83] who urged Monck to re-establish the administration of justice by 'ordinary channels'.[84] During this period, Stair would have been faced with the question of whether the law of Scotland and that of England and Wales could be effectively assimilated and on what basis should this be decided. Moreover, he would have witnessed the great disruption which this period had caused to the administration of justice, and so he would have been very keen to understand how the law of Scotland could be applied under these circumstances.[85]

Of course, Stair circulated the first drafts of the *Institutions* to lawyers, not the public. And although the text remained in manuscript until 1681, Stair evidently wanted to establish knowledge of the law in Scotland, along with a system and method which did not revert to politically contentious theories of law and authority. Yet as Jackson has argued, during this period, lawyers played an 'increasingly significant role'. She suggests that 'with an established church that was both institutionally impotent and ideologically bankrupt, it was the members of Scotland's legal profession that gradually came to exert the greatest influence over the theory and practice of monarchy in late seventeenth-century Scotland.'[86] She notes that though Stair and Sir George Mackenzie held different theories of law, they sought the same end: 'to establish the ultimate sources of political sovereignty in order to deduce the rights and duties mutually incumbent on monarchs and subjects alike'.[87] Stair's project—of clarifying the law, including the law applying to contracting behaviour—therefore had important, if not subtle, political aims. Along with asserting the Godly and natural law origins of the law in Scotland, he aimed to demonstrate how private law rights, including the right to contract, were fundamental rights which the sovereign enforced through the positive laws of Scotland.

Despite writing the *Institutions* in late 1659 and early 1660, Stair chose to publish his *Institutions* in 1681. Publishing a full account of the private rights in Scotland, not long

---

[81] Brunton *An Historical Account* (n 80) 346.

[82] Ronald Hutton, 'Monck [Monk], George, First Duke of Albemarle (1608–1670), Army Officer and Naval Officer' in *Oxford Dictionary of National Biography* (OUP 2004) <https://www.oxforddnb.com/> accessed 8 April 2021.

[83] John M Graham (ed), *Annals and Correspondence of the Viscount and the First and Second Earls of Stair* (William Blackwood & Sons 1875) 16.

[84] Graham *Annuals and Correspondence* (n 83) 16.

[85] William L Mathieson, *Politics and Religion: A Study in Scottish History from the Reformation to the Revolution*, vol 2 (James MacLehose and Sons 1902) 175; Rosalind Mitchison, *Lordship to Patronage Scotland 1603–1745* (Edinburgh University Press 1983) 68; Julia M Buckroyd, 'Bridging the Gap: Scotland 1659–1660' (1987) 66 (181) The Scottish Historical Review 1–25; Gillian H MacIntosh, 'The Scottish Parliament under Charles II 1660–1685' (2007) International Review of Scottish Studies 1–35.

[86] Clare Jackson, *Restoration Scotland: Politics, Religion and Ideas* (Boydell 2003) 220.

[87] Jackson *Restoration Scotland* (n 86) 220.

after Lauderdale had been accused of abusing the rights and liberties of Scots, and following the exclusion crisis, where the Duke of York sought to assert Royal authority in
Scotland,[88] is evidently a political statement. In comparison to the fiery treatises and
pamphlets often associated with the 1670s and 1680s it is far less direct but is nevertheless an effective way for a moderate, like Stair, to assert the authority of law against
a political regime who sought to assert the absolute authority of the Crown.[89] And so
republishing the *Institutions* in 1693 is also notable.

In the 1693 edition Stair added the fourth book, which asserted that the 'authority
of the Lords of Session was requisite to be known at all time, and never more than
now'.[90] To make this statement then was to make a political point about the legitimacy
of the Court of Session within Scotland's constitutional structure and the authority
of the King and Parliament.[91] Against the background of the 1689 Claim of Right,
which had apparently, according to Stair, confirmed that decisions of the Court of
Session were final and not subject to Parliamentary review—unless overturned by
legislation—there is evident political intention to the 1693 *Institutions*. That is, publishing a treatise on private rights and asserting that the Court of Session had complete
authority in the 'decision of private right, and making the same effectual by legal execution'[92] Stair tried to ensure a constitutional settlement during the reign of William
and Mary, which gave the judiciary a prominent role in determining what the private
law of Scotland was.

most convincing to situate this in historical context.

but what about godly law / theological impulses?

Law as a Rational Discipline

In putting forward an account of the common principles of law and demonstrating that
equity was the foundation of Scots customary law, Stair had only partially achieved
his second objective. For what was also important to him was to ensure that law was
not taken to be a mere implement of power or arbitrariness. In the *Institutions*, Stair's
theory had the consequence of detaching the law of Scotland from the fads of power
and politics. By returning to his original notion that law is the dictate of reason he tries
to demonstrate that it is not the arbitrary will of legislators. After giving an account of
the role of sovereignty in the creation of laws in Scotland, he asks whether law be handled as a rational discipline. He acknowledges that most 'lawyers are for the negative
part, commonly esteeming law, especially the positive and proper laws of any nation,
incapable of such a deduction, as being dependent upon the will and pleasure of law-
givers, and introduced for utilities sake . . .'.[93] On this basis, he says, most lawyers conclude there are no common principles upon which human law rests.[94] Stair comments

---

[88] Jackson *Restoration Politics* (n 86) 48–53.
[89] MacIntosh *Scottish Parliament under Charles II* (n 85) 179–211.
[90] Stair *Inst* 4.1.1.
[91] See Ford *Law and Opinion* (n 6) 520; John Ford, 'Protestations to Parliament for Remeid of Law' (2009)
85 (225) The Scottish Historical Review 57–107.
[92] Stair *Inst* 4.1.1.
[93] Stair *Inst* 1.1.17.
[94] Stair *Inst* 1.1.17.

that those who take this approach use 'the artificial method of rational Disciplines' and find themselves satisfied with 'any order'.[95]

He blames, primarily, 'the confused Order of Civil Law [read Roman law] (which is the greatest blemish in it)' but adds that such confusion is perpetuated by learned authors who, out of respect for past authors, tolerate errors and are insensitive to the disorder. He adds that 'there is little to be found among the Commentars and Treatise upon the Civil Law' who might start from 'known Principles of Right' but whom through their debates make a 'Congestion of the Context of the Law, which exceedingly nauseates delicate engines, finding much more work for their memory, than judgment in taking up and retain the Lawgivers Will', Stair wishes that those who write about the law would search into the reason behind the law and argues that both Hugo Grotius and François Douaren have demonstrated that this possible. How can reason find the equity of a particular legal problem which does not have an evident solution?

Stair starts answering this question with a Pauline notion, saying that the common principles of law are 'created in and with the soul of man' and arise without 'reasoning or debate, as naturally as heat doth from fire, or the light from the sun'. From these 'rules of righteousness' are thereafter deduced by reason.[96] Hence, according to Stair, 'the law is reason itself, as to its principles about the rights of men, and therefore called the law of reason'.[97] God, he explains, gave man more 'radiant Rays of Reason, and preserved it more after his Fall' in order that he will know his 'Rights of meum & tuum'. In comparison to other sciences, he says, what is ours and what is yours is known easily and is not 'dubious and conjectural, and attainable only with great pains'. So long as a man is not blinded by self-interest or statutes and customs which are to the contrary, he is able to 'discern right from wrong'. Importantly, Stair qualifies this by saying that although it is simple to know right from wrong it is not possible for an individual man on the basis of his own knowledge to determine 'matters of Intricacy or Difficulty which require more eminent Judgment and long Experience'. On this point, Stair adds that 'God doth Expostulat and Argue with men … from these common Principles of Righteousness' through the conscience of individual men. Having established the origins of the common principles, Stair acknowledges that it is not enough merely to declare that the positive laws of whatever country are based on and originate from equity. But the approach to demonstrate the equity of laws should not be to take the various laws and examine them in the hope of determining their equity. There are too many individual human laws and too many variations made to laws for utility's sake to enable the equity of those laws to be immediately evident. Rather, what Stair suggests is to return first to the principles and then work from those principles towards the individual rules, which will them enable him to demonstrate their equity.[98] Importantly, these principles are evident, to the judicious, within the positive law itself and so it is possible to reason from existing propositions of law back towards the common principles. But equally, as Stair demonstrates, you can reason from foundational principles towards the rules of positive law.

[95] Stair *Inst* 1.1.17.
[96] Stair *Inst* 1.1.17.
[97] Stair *Inst* 1.1.17.
[98] Stair *Inst* 1.1.17.

God, Obedience, and Freedom

As later chapters will explore in more depth, Stair starts from foundational principles drawn from mainstream Christian morality. To adopt this approach, is unique in comparison to his legal colleagues in Scotland. Of course, it's hard to imagine anyone in Parliament House denying the general thrust of Stair's overarching theological account of the common principles of natural law, morality, and the place of God within the hierarchy of laws. Yet arguably, they might have queried its need given that Justinian's *Institutes* offered an acceptable account of the relationship between the divinity and positive law.[99] It would have also been evident to his mid-seventeenth-century readers particularly, that Stair's first principles account contrast greatly with Craig's long and elegant historical account of law's origins, starting with the 'the great flood' and then weaving through a Biblical history of law which was interweaved with classical histories of Athens, Rome, and other ancient civilizations.[100] After this, Craig comes to Roman law. He offers a careful history of the development of Roman law and concludes:[101]

> The worth and pre-eminence of the civil law [read Roman law] is apparent to anyone who sees the grace of its speech or its status as the purest font of equity or the weighty and incisive reasoning of its decisions and pronouncements. Nothing better or more seemly could be written; nothing could be devised that better sheds light on doubtful matters; nothing can explain more effectively what ought to be done.

If Craig's history was not enough to explain the value and authority of Roman law, Stair's legal colleagues may have taken the perspective of Mackenzie: the equity of Roman law is evident, tested, and trustworthy, it has often received sovereign confirmation. On this view, it might be asking why is Stair's new theory necessary? We know the authority of law is ultimately based on the Crown's sovereignty. Nevertheless, Stair takes a new perspective and starting point. He provides an underpinning for his account of the common principles of law, including the law of contracting. Evidently, and unlike his contemporaries, Stair did not want to rely on the laws of an ancient civilization as a guide to equity. He wanted to show that at its core law is a rational discipline and capable of being determined by deduction from first principles. He sought to demonstrate how positive law interacts with higher level principles of Christian morality. In contrast to Craig and Mackenzie, he places reason before antiquity and theological philosophy before tradition and history.

So, he says that the first principles of equity are that God is to be obeyed, that men are free, and that this freedom can be used to enter voluntary obligations.[102] These

---

[99] For example, see Clare Jackson's account of Stair's contemporary Francis Grant and his description of Roman law's divine origins: Clare Jackson, 'Revolution Principles, Ius Naturae and Ius Gentium in Early Enlightenment Scotland: The Contribution of Sir Francis Grant, Lord Cullen (c.1660–1726)' in Tim Hochstrasser and Peter Schröder (eds), *Early Modern Natural Law Theories: Contexts and Strategies in the Early Enlightenment* (Kluwer 2003) 107–40.

[100] Craig *Jus Feudale* 1.1.1–16.

[101] Craig *Jus Feudale* 1.1.12.

[102] Stair *Inst* 1.1.18.

principles are otherwise known as obedience, freedom, and engagement and they are considered by Stair to serve as the foundation of human law. These principles are not, however, directly transposed into positive law. Since human laws are introduced for 'profit and utility', the positive Law is, *in bono*, or *utili*. If man was not corrupted by sin, Stair explains, there would be no difference between what is equitable and what is good, and man would live by natural law alone. But in a postlapsarian state, it is not possible to trust each individual's own sense of natural law nor does every man have a willingness to live by it. Therefore, it is necessary, according to Stair, to create societies, which introduce peace and quietness. By setting up societies, men aim to 'mutually defend one another and procure to one another their Rights, and also to set clear limited to ever man's Property, & to maintain Traffick & Commerce among themselves and others'. Rooted in the first principles of equity but amended because of the postlapsarian conditions of man, Stair believes it is possible to show that varying human laws of Scotland can be explained and understood to be connected to and originating from equity.[103]

After making his case, Stair says that if the principles of equity are obedience, freedom, and engagement then the principles of human law or positive law are society, property, and commerce, each of which imposes a duty upon individuals and results in interpersonal obligations as well as obligations of individuals to God. The outcome, 'the final ends', of these principles are 'the maintenance, flourishing and Peace of Society, the security of Property, and the freedom of Commerce', which animate the positive or human law of nations, including Scotland.[104] The 'efficient cause' are the original principles of equity, which through their implementation in society and translation into human laws become, in some places, adapted because of utility and requirements of expedience. But, nonetheless, they are *in bono*, good laws, albeit not bringing about perfect balance between what each person is entitled to *in æquo*.

Obedience is a principle of equity and of human law; it is the 'submission of and sequacity of the mind and will of man to the Authority and Will of his Maker', which binds a man to the law of nature, the reason, and his conscience.[105] All of these are means by which man knows what is right and wrong and create a duty upon man to do that which is right, which creates an obediential obligation known in both equity and the positive, human law of nations. Freedom, which is again found in equity and the positive man-made laws of Scotland, begins where obedience ends; it allows man to create his own obligations upon himself through engagements, known as conventional obligations.[106] Importantly, he says that man has this freedom provided it, 'be ordered and directed to the glory of God'.[107] He likens this to the freedom given to ambassadors who are obliged to carry out the orders of a King but to do so in the manner they see fit or to marriage whereby a man can decide whether and who to marry but not determine the terms or nature of that marriage. Freedom therefore comes with both obligation and latitude, which Stair sees as a great gift which God has given to

---

[103] Stair *Inst* 1.1.18.
[104] Stair *Inst* 1.1.18
[105] Stair *Inst* 1.1.19.
[106] Stair *Inst* 1.1.20.
[107] Stair *Inst* 1.1.20.

man. Engagement is the last principle, which is created by men and owed towards both God and whoever is the counterparty. It creates an obligation of performance, because there is nothing more natural than 'to stand by the Faith of our Pactions'.[108]

Following his account of the principles of human law and their origin, which creates obligations upon individual men, Stair changes the lens of analysis from the duty to the right. He says, 'the Object therefore, the formal and proper Object of Law, are the Rights of men'.[109] Rather than viewing matters from the perspective of what we owe to others, Stair demonstrates that you can also view matters from the perspective of what is owed to us.[110] On this account, you have the principles of human law—society, property, and engagement—which provide a guide to the common good of society, and a test of the utility for specific rules of law. These principles of human law can be shown to relate to Christian morality's core principles: to obey God, to love thy neighbour, and to bring glory to God through our use of freedom. Yet positive law is the realization of duties in the form of individual rights: the right of personal liberty, obligations owed to us, and our dominion over our property. He explains, 'Personal liberty, is the power to dispose of our Persons, and to live where, and as we please, except in so far, as by Obedience or Ingagement, we are bound', whereas Dominion is the 'the power of disposal of the Creatures in their substances, fruits and use'.[111] For most obligations there is correspondent 'personal Right, which hath no proper Name, as it is in the Creditor, but hath the Name of Obligation, as it is in the Debitor' which entitles the creditor to obtain, compel, and demand what they are due from the debtor.

At this point, Stair criticizes the order of Roman law because it structures private law around persons, things, and actions rather than around obligations and rights. Later chapters will examine in detail the implications of this move by Stair. For now, it is helpful to remark that for Stair focusing on rights entails that you will ask first about their creation, then about their content and then about their enforcement. Stair structures his *Institutions* upon this insight. It is on this basis that you can order and arrange the law demonstrating that it is a rational discipline and connected to common principles of equity.[112] To take this approach is also to reject the feudal notion of status whereby the law was structured around your place within a hierarchy of preconfigured roles relating to land. Stair places the protection of individuals, liberty, and contract at the heart of his account of private law.

Conclusion

Although Stair used a philosophical methodology placing the law of Scotland upon a new theoretical basis, he made direct appeals to equity. In doing this, he both

---

[108] Stair *Inst* 1.1.21.
[109] Stair *Inst* 1.1.22.
[110] As the final chapter will show, this is a move which is also made by Gershom Carmichael. He shared Stair's project of translating the obedience of Christian morality into a juristic language of interpersonal dual relationships, ie right and duty are correlated and described as the realization of natural law within society.
[111] Stair *Inst* 1.1.22.
[112] Stair *Inst* 1.1.23.

minimized the authoritative value of Roman law as a source of law over equity while remaining largely within a Roman law framework. Alongside his philosophical language, Stair continued to use Roman law terminology. His environment was dominated by the *ius commune* tradition that shaped the mindset of Scots lawyers. Like other Scots lawyers, he applied this mindset when thinking about the law of contracts. Indeed, it could be said that title 10 of Book 1 of the *Institutions* is a seventeenth-century Calvinist iteration of the Roman law of contracts. Beside principles of natural law formulated in a Calvinist manner, he narrates numerous rules of contracting taken from Roman law. He supplements Roman law commentaries with references to Scripture, Classical literature, and decisions of the Court of Session.[113] By weaving these sources and traditions in this way, Stair creates an innovative taxonomy but under the shadow of the Justinianic approach. Since Stair was operating within an environment in which it was difficult to conceive of a legal system, and indeed laws of contract, without recourse to the *Institutes* and *Digest*, the *Institutions* bare this footprint clearly. Yet the *Institutions* is an account that reaches far beyond a juristic description of legal propositions; it provides a theory to legitimate the political and theological status of the law of Scotland, including its approach to the law of contract. A project of this ambition was unique in comparison to Stair's contemporaries and arguably has never attempted again by a Scots jurist. But as the final chapter will argue, it was the moral philosophers in Scotland who continued to seek out an explanation of law and society from first principles.

---

[113] Stair *Inst* 1.10.7

3

A New Basis for Contract Law

Title 10 of Book I of the *Institutions of the Law of Scotland* (*Institutions*) is where Stair offers an overview of conventional obligations which is followed by several other titles dealing with specific types of contract. In comparison to texts used by Scots lawyers during the mid-seventeenth century, such as Balfour's *Practicks*, Craig's *Jus Feudale*, Hope's *Major Practicks*, Durie's *Practicks* or Thomson or Wallace's *Practicks*, Stair's coverage of contract law is extensive. In terms of scope and detail, it is more comparable to Arnold Vinnius' *Institutionum Imperialium Commentaries*[1] or Petrus Gudelinus' *Commentariorum de Jure*[2] which were also available to Scots advocates, including Stair. Yet Stair differs from these texts too. He gives an account which is exclusively of the customary law of Scotland, deploys a rich philosophical and theological language, and weighs up propositions of law according to both their equity and utility. In the opening title, Stair covers: the origins of convention obligations; the right of man to use his freedom to bind himself; the acts which trigger the creation of a conventional obligation; the different types of conventional obligations; whether promises and pactions are morally as well as legally obligatory; the differences between Roman and Scots law; and the common features of contracts. It is these concepts, ideas, and explanations of conventional obligations that are the focus of the following chapters. Before going into detail about his approach to *nuda pacta*, the will, freedom, or commerce, this chapter gives an overview of Stair's treatment of the law of contracts, demonstrating particularly his methodology of weighing up the value of a rule of contract according to either its equity or utility.

Equity and Utility

[handwritten: balance between equity + utility]

Stair's account of contractual obligations is shaped by an underlying evaluative system. As he explains the law, Stair assesses how it relates to equity and utility. It is this method that materializes his new philosophical basis for the law of contract in Scotland. Indeed, discussing both the equity and utility of a rule of Scots law is central to Stair's account of private law, allowing him to explain human law's relationship to natural law. The success of his project relies on his ability to demonstrate that the rules of private law in Scotland are the result of a balance between what equity requires, ie do unto others what you would have done unto you, and what utility necessitates, ie what is overall profitable to society, considering the need for certainty, stability, and the common good. As Stair explains in the opening passages of the *Institutions*, upon

---

[1] Arnold Vinnius, *Institutionum Imperialium Commentaries Academicus & Forensis* (Amsterdam 1659).

[2] Petrus Gudelinus, *Commentariorum de Jure Novissimo Libri Sex: Optimia Methodo, Accurateac Erudite Conscripti, Additis Harum Vicinarumque Region Moribus* (Ex Officina Hieronymi Verdus 1620).

Contract before the Enlightenment. Stephen Bogle, Oxford University Press. © Stephen Bogle 2023.
DOI: 10.1093/oso/9780192884961.003.0004

entering society and creating laws based on equity but nevertheless man-made, man should be prepared 'to quit something of that which by equity is his due' in order to avoid quarrelling.[3] Throughout his account of private law, including contract law, Stair is guided by a sense that human law is the result of this process. Thus, Stair may have agreed with the idealized system of natural law which Grotius expounded but the law of Scotland could not guarantee such a principle in practice, and it was not reasonable of individuals to expect that. The common good of society often outweighed the benefits due to an individual under equity. As Stair says, 'There be many points of right competent to men in equity, as it may be more profitable for the people to forbear the pursuance of them, than to be at the trouble and the expenses of the pursuit, as when human laws do cut off matters of less concernment.' Positive law thereby cuts off commutative justice's requirement of equality. In his account of contract law particularly you see Stair balancing the need for honesty and fairness and for parties to do what their conscience requires against the needs of commerce, which overall profited benefits to society. Indeed, Stair's account of contracting which seeks a balance between equity and utility is often tipped in favour of the principle of commerce/utility. Before highlighting some examples of this, it is important explain how Stair arranged his discussion of conventional obligations in the *Institutions*, particularly how it corresponds to the classic structure of Justinian's *Institutes*.

Stair's Division of Contracts and Method

The relationship between the structure of the *Institutions* to that of Justinian's *Institutes* is complex; Stair utilized the *Institutes* but equally took great liberties with it. For now, it is important to note that in *Institutes* students of Roman law are told that obligations can be divided in one of three ways. The first way refers to the mode by which the obligation is created, the second refers to the event, and the other third refers to the obligation's source. Scots lawyers would have been intimately familiar with these taxonomical divisions; indeed, from Hope to Mackenzie these classifications were utilized in Scots legal writing about the law of contract.[4] If organized by mode, then contracts are divided into those created by conduct, words, writing, and consent. Yet if contracts are divided by event, then you proceed on the basis that there are obligations arising from a contract, as if by contract, from a wrong, or as if from a wrong.[5] The final way of dividing contracts is between praetorian and legal obligations. According to this way of distinguishing contrast, there are obligations created either by statute or by a decision of the praetor. The part of Book III of Justinian's *Institutes* that deals with obligations is divided into seventeen subheadings, each addressing a different type of contract or quasi-contract and ending with a title on the discharge of obligations. Although Stair borrows from this schema, his approach differs in several meaningful ways.

---

[3] Stair *Inst* 1.1.18.
[4] Craig *Jus Feudale* 1.9.31; Hope *Major Practicks* 2.1.3; Mackenzie *Institutions* 3.1.5.
[5] Justinian *Inst* 3.14.

First, in contrast to the three ways of dividing contracts, Stair starts with his own classification based on a singular explanation: obligations stem from the will. On this basis, Stair's first division is between obedential and conventional obligations which each originate in the will. 'From Obediential Obligations, flowing from the Will of God', Stair says, 'Order leads us next to Conventional Obligations' which arise from 'the Will of Man'.[6] He explains a conventional obligation in contrast to freedom. First, he says that God has left man free to create obligations using his own will but that when such an obligation is created 'God obliges us to performance, by mediation of our own Will'. He clarifies, however, that 'yet such Obligations, as to their Original, are Conventional and not Obediential'.[7] In keeping with Stair's conception of contracts arising from will alone, Stair explains that conventional obligations 'do arise from our Will and Consent ... the will is the only Faculty constituting Rights, whether Real or Personal'. In creating a conventional obligation, Stair tells his reader that there is a 'diminuation of Freedom' because such an obligation gives the power to restrain or constrain and the power of extraction to another.

In spite of Stair's idiosyncratic scheme of classification, the layout of his text resembles the *Institutes*. For example, after his general discussion of 'Obligations Conventional, by Promise, Paction and Contract' in title 10 of Book I, Stair discusses ten contracts[8] taken from Justinian's *Institutes*.[9] Furthermore, the closing title in Book I of the *Institutions* which considers 'Liberation from Obligations', which resembles the *Institutes* insofar as describing contracts according to their type[10] Yet upon close inspection, this layout does not suggest that the content of Stair's and Justinian's works are the same. Far from it. Within the *Institutions*, each contract, loan, mandate, custody, sale, hire, society, and accessory obligation is considered as a form or type of contract which provides a format within which to discuss the customary law of Scotland. Throughout, there are numerous references to decisions of the Court of Session, classical writers, modern commentators on Roman law, natural law theorists like Grotius, as well as statutes of the Scottish Parliament. Paying particular regard to how these contracts applied in Scotland, Stair carefully examines whether the approach taken in Scotland is either the most equitable and, if not, whether it is justifiable on the grounds of utility.[11] The standard manner in which Stair undertakes this exercise is to give: (i) an initial definition of legal terminology, often taken from the *Institutes*, which is followed by (ii) a discussion of Roman law, and then (iii) a discussion of practice

---

[6] James Dalrymple, Viscount Stair, *Institutions of the Law of Scotland* (Andrew Anderson 1693) 1.10.1.

[7] Stair *Inst* 1.10.1.

[8] [1] Mutuum and [2] Commodatum (Stair *Inst* 1.11) (cf Just *Inst* III.xiii); [3] Mandat (Stair *Inst* 1.12) (cf Just *Inst* III.xxvi); [4] Despotitum and [5] Pledge (Stair *Inst* 1.13) (cf Just *Inst* III.xiii); [6] Emption and [7] Permutation (Stair *Inst* 1.14) (cf Just, *Inst* III.xiii); [8] Location and [9] Conduction (Stair *Inst* 1.15) (ie Just *Inst* III.xxiv); [10] Society (Stair *Inst* 1.15) (cf. Just *Inst* III.xxv).

[9] Of obligation by consent title (Just *Inst* III.xxii); Of purchase and sale (Just *Inst* III.xxiii); Of letting and hiring (Just *Inst* III.xxiv); Of partnership (Just *Inst* III.xxv); Of agency (Just *Inst* III.xxvi).

[10] Stair *Inst* 1.1.18.

[11] Loan, or Mutuum & Commodatum, where Bills of Exchange (Stair *Institutions* 1.11); Mandat, or Commission, where of Trust, &c. (Stair *Inst* 1.12); Custody, or Depositum, where also of Pledge and Hypothecation (Stair *Inst* 1.13); Permutation and Sale, or Emption and Vendition (Stair *Inst* 1.14); Location and Conduction, where of Annualrent and Usury (Stair *Inst* 1.15); Society, where of Co-partnery (Stair *Inst* 1.15); Accessory Obligations, where of Transaction, Caution, Oaths and other Accessories (Stair *Inst* 1.16) and Liberation from Obligations (Stair, *Inst* 1.17).

in Scotland and how this practice relates to both Roman and natural law. As such, while there are many references to Roman law throughout, it is evident that Roman law is being used as an example, amongst several, of approaches to addressing a legal problem.

Acts of the Will

As mentioned in the previous section, one of the main points of departure from the Justinian account of the contract law is that Stair offers the will as the central trigger for the creation of an obligation. Thus, throughout his account of conventional obligations he repeatedly notes how this approach differs from that taken in Roman law.[12] As will be discussed in Chapter 4, this difference affects his assessment of *nuda pacta* but also how he frames the necessary requirements of various contracts as formalities rather than constitutive actions. It also means that he offers an elaborate account of the will and how it comes to form an obligation. Importantly, Stair considers that 'not every act of the will … creates an obligation' and this leads to his description of acts of the will.[13] There are three acts of the will, according to Stair: desire, resolution, and engagement. Desire is when you have a 'tendency or inclination' towards an object, but this is not sufficient to create an obligation. Resolution is 'a determinate purpose to do that which is desired', but again this is not sufficient to create an obligation; this resolution can be relinquished without 'fault'. Stair gives some examples, however, of exceptions where a change of resolution is blameworthy. First, he says, somewhat opaquely, that the resolution cannot be changed without fault, even if there has been an accident because it is necessary to hold such a person responsible for their resolution. Second, he writes that it is blameworthy to abandon a resolution when it has been expressed to another to assure them that you will act accordingly, thereby inducing reliance. The third kind of blameworthy inconstancy is when altering a resolution signals culpable unpredictability or a failure to appreciate the seriousness of the circumstances and the effects of changing one's mind. Nonetheless, in general, Stair says that a resolution of the will cannot bind a man because it is not the final action of the will. It cannot, in general, give grounds to compel performance even if the resolution is for the good of another until it is 'so fully cleared, or confirmed by Word or Writ'.[14]

Types of Conventional Obligation

Before speaking about specific contracts in the titles that follow, Stair offers fresh concepts and ideas by which to examine and describe the law of contract. He draws out of the Roman law sources ideas and concepts which help to construct his will-based account of the customary law of Scotland. Thus, along with his account of the will as the singular ultimate cause of an obligation he underpins the customary law

---

[12] Stair *Inst* 1.10.6; 1.10.11; 1.10.12.
[13] Stair *Inst* 1.10.1.
[14] Stair *Inst* 1.10.2.

of contracting in Scotland with a new analytical framework using Roman law concepts but in an innovative manner. In using these concepts in this manner, Stair was evidently influenced by what he found in Chapters 11 and 12 of Book I of *The Rights of War and Peace*. Grotius provided there an analytical discussion of the natural law applying to promising and contracting, but as will be argued in later chapters Stair's discussion of the will is more central to Stair than it is in *The Rights of War and Peace*.

To start, Stair distinguishes between different types of conventional obligation, holding that the will can create a pollicitation offer, a promise, a paction, or contract, and a *jus quaesitum tertio* or third-party right. It should also be added that Stair understands an acceptance of an offer to be an act of the will, which creates a conventional obligation. Although he does not make this expressly clear, it is nevertheless evident that if an offer is an act of the will, which carries with it an (implied) condition of acceptance, then the act of acceptance should be considered to satisfy that condition and be an act of the will which creates a conventional obligation.[15] This does raise the question of whether acceptance of an offer is binding immediately upon acceptance or whether it is binding upon the offeree receiving the acceptance.[16] Stair is unfortunately unclear on this point; but if his approach to acceptance is compared to his treatment of promises and third-party rights then, theoretically, the offeror does not need to know of the acceptance in order for an obligation to exist. It is the moment of acceptance when the formation of the obligation is completed, not necessarily receipt of acceptance. For now, what should be noted is that Stair's analytical organization of conventional obligations shows his willingness to go beyond the traditional structures and notions of Roman law. It is worth saying a little more about the concepts which Stair brought to the customary law of Scotland.

Common Requisites of Contracts

Stair speaks of the 'common requisites' of a contract.[17] From the perspective of Stair's methods, these passages show how he used both Roman law and other native legal sources to demonstrate his points. In four paragraphs, he refers to decisions of Court of Session, the *Digest*, the *Institutes*, and the *Codex*. Each validates his central claim: <u>the will is the source of an obligation</u>. Therefore, although he mentions four common requisites, they are all based on the notion of a 'rational will' binding parties to a contract. The requisites are in effect capacity, incapacity, impossibility and unlawfulness, and error. In the first instance, incapacity and capacity ultimately concern the lack of the ability to reason. What is noteworthy about Stair's discussion of capacity is that he explains the deviation from his principal position, ie that only those who have reached the age of majority have a rational will, using the concept of utility. It is for utility's sake that the positive law of Scotland requires that curators receive consent from their minors before contracting on their behalf. Though minors were not considered to have a

---

[15] Stair *Institutions* 1.10.3; 1.3.9.
[16] In years to come, both the Outer House and Inner House in *Thomson v James* (1855) 18 D 1 considered this question.
[17] Stair *Institutions* 1.10.13.

rational will, utility dictated that they be consulted in order that .... In the second instance, Stair describes impossibility and unlawfulness as relating to what is within the
power of the will to do. In the third instance, where an error has occurred, he quotes
from the *Digest*: 'err in the substantials of what is done, contract not, *l.9. ff de cont.
empt'.*[18] This particular common requisite requires further explanation.

Macleod argues that Stair's approach to error can be interpreted in two ways,
adopting either an objective approach to error or a subjective approach.[19] In very general terms, Macleod suggests that you can divide these two approaches into two separate traditions of legal thought within European legal history: one relating to error in
the Thomist tradition, which he associates with objectivism, and the other being the
ius commune tradition, which he associates with subjectivism.[20] For him, Stair opted
not to follow Grotius, who had departed from the *ius commune* approach himself.
Hence, according to Macleod, Stair followed the *ius commune* 'subjective consensus'
understanding of contract formation.[21] Macleod concludes that Stair's account of
error places him 'firmly in the *ius commune* tradition, treating error in the substantials
as merely the real-world trigger for other rules of contract law'.[22]

Macleod is right to draw attention to Stair's *ius commune* approach; it is evident and
plain on the face of the text. Yet this should not necessarily preclude the possibility
that behind Stair's endorsement of the simple statement of D 18.1.9 there was not a
more nuanced understanding which had an affinity with the Aristotelian-Thomistic
tradition. Indeed, the passages Macleod cites can equally be read as examples of what
Aquinas termed antecedent ignorance.[23] On that basis, the use of *ius commune* texts
and expressions does not preclude a Thomist understanding of error. For example,
there are other passages where Stair's treatment of error suggests that he adopted other
categories of ignorance, which relate to the Thomist tradition.[24] Later chapters will return to this, however.

The important point for present purposes is that this is an example of how Stair
tried to bring together the Roman law sources and propositions of law, which were familiar to Scots lawyers, and his overarching aim to demonstrate the equity of Scots law.
Stair drew upon medieval theological and philosophical literature when he drafted the
Institutions and particularly in formulating his theory of human action. For him, it
offered a strong and robust philosophical basis upon which to explain human action
and, vitally, it helped him demonstrate that the various rules of contract law he handled in the *Institutions* amounted to an equitable appropriation of mainstream explanations of human action found in the conventional accounts of moral reasoning.

---

[18] *Digest* 18.1.9.
[19] John Macleod, 'Error Before Bell: The Roots of Error in the Scots Law of Contract' (2010) 14 (3)
Edinburgh Law Review 385–417.
[20] For discussion, see James Gordley, *The Philosophical Origins of Modern Contract Doctrine* (OUP 1991)
10–69; Catharine MacMillan, *Mistakes in Contract Law* (Hart 2010) 10–26; Wim Decock, *Theologians and
Contract Law: The Moral Transformation of the Ius Commune (Ca. 1500–1650)* (Brill 2013) 274–97.
[21] Macleod 'Error Before Bell' (n 19) 401.
[22] Stair *Institutions* 1.10.2.
[23] Stair *Institutions* 1.10.13; 1.10.2; 4.40.24.
[24] Stair *Inst* 1.9.9; 1.10.6; 1.10.2; 1.17.14.

Promises

Promises are foundational to Stair's project. They held a deep moral and theological significance in the seventeenth century. According to Stair, a promise is an act of the will that is pure and simple with no implied condition that the promisee accepts the promise.[25] Stair debates with Grotius in the passages of his text concerning promises and ultimately disagrees with him. By bringing this sort of debate into a text primarily concerned with a description of Scots customary law, Stair again demonstrates to his reader that he is throughout his *Institutions* evaluating the equity of the Scots' approach. Unlike other aspects of his account of contracting, Stair appears to brush aside concerns of utility and practicality opting for the most demanding of options: promises are binding without acceptance and merely upon the will resolving to be bound. He notes that Grotius says acceptance is necessary for every conventional obligation, and so promises made to infants, idiots, absents, or persons who are not yet born are revocable and not wholly binding when made.[26] The promise only becomes obligatory once accepted, on Grotius's account. For Grotius, Roman law attenuated natural law in that it said promises could not be revoked until acceptance.[27] Stair says that Grotius is right to hold a promise which is not accepted is not binding, this is because non-acceptance should be interpreted as a rejection. Rejection nullifies the obligatory effect of the promise upon the promisee. Stair says that a right and power to demand performance of the promise can exist so long as the beneficiary has not rejected the right and even if the beneficiary has no knowledge of that right.[28] In this regard, Stair was opting for what was possibly the most equitable interpretation of the law of Scotland, which was, otherwise, often balanced by his concerns of utility.

Third-Party Rights

Stair approach to promising has a direct impact on how he accounts for third-party rights. However, the passages where Stair considers third-party rights have received a great deal of attention over the years, in large part because they are opaque.[29] Interpretation of these passages has revolved around three interrelated issues: Stair's use of 'pollicitation', his discussion of third-party rights, and his (second-hand) reference to the Jesuit theologian-cum-jurist, Luis de Molina (1535–1600). Amongst the many contributions to this debate, Rodger's analysis is the most compelling interpretation of Stair's intentions (showing why Molina's supposed position was appealing to Stair), while Richter's research is the most instructive about what material was actually

---

[25] Stair *Inst* 1.10.4.
[26] Stair *Inst* 1.10.4.
[27] Stair *Inst* 1.10.4.
[28] Stair *Inst* 1.10.4.
[29] The most famous consideration was in the Inner House and House of Lords in the case of *Carmichael v Carmichael's Executrix* (1919) SC (IH) 363 rev (1920) SC (HL) 195, a decision now reversed by Contract (Third Party Rights) (Scotland) Act 2017.

available to Stair (demonstrating that Stair directly consulted Molina).[30] For present purposes, it is Rodger's interpretation which explains the rationale behind Stair's approach to third-party rights and so helps elaborate upon Stair's contractual thought.

Firstly, Rodger investigates what Stair's original intentions were when he drafted these paragraphs in the 1660s.[31] Rodger established that in the early manuscripts, and indeed the first edition of 1681, there was no comma between 'promise' and 'pollicitation' and that in some later manuscripts the sentence read: 'promise pollicitation or offer, paction and contract'. Further, Rodger highlighted how Stair later added to these sections several extra references and extrapolations—and, importantly, these three paragraphs, which encompass 1.10.3 to 1.10.5 of the printed editions, were originally one paragraph. Rodger's interpretation establishes that when Stair used the term 'pollicitation' he had the traditional Roman law meaning in mind—a promise, which does not need acceptance to be binding—but, crucially, he did not mean to say that it was an obligation owed to the municipality. Accordingly, when Stair says, 'we must distinguish betwixt Promise [,] pollicitation or offer and paction and contract', his intention is to distinguish between two types of promises and two types of agreement.[32] Therefore, Stair's meaning is that there are some promises that do not need acceptance to be binding, namely pollicitation, and there are some promises that do, namely offers. Recalling Stair's analysis at the start of his treatment of conventional obligations, and indeed his earlier account of obligations generally,[33] it makes perfect sense to say that there are some acts of the will which are immediately binding, namely pollicitation, whereas there are some which are conditionally binding, namely offers.

If one takes the manuscripts from 1662 as the original layout of the text, then Stair's discussion of *jus quaesitum tertio* immediately followed his discussion of promising. Consequently, the discussion preceding Stair's analysis of *jus quaesitum tertio* should be set against his remark that a person can have a right even though he is unaware of the promise or offer he has been made. Thus, bearing in mind Rodger's insights, it is clear that when Stair moves on to discuss *jus quaesitum tertio* he is presenting this as an act of the will, the creation of a third-party right. This is a right which can be created without the beneficiaries' knowledge. Upon this revised understanding of these paragraphs, one can argue, as Rodger does, that Stair's use of Molina was not erroneous but was a purposeful reference; even though, importantly, it has now been shown by Richter that he most probably took his reference to Molina from Grotius, who in fact, may have misinterpreted Molina in the first place.

---

[30] Thomas Richter, 'Molina, Grotius, Stair and the Jus Quaesitum Tertio' (2001) Juridical Review 219. See also Wilson's discussion: Adelyn L M Wilson, 'The Sources and Method of the *Institutions of the Law of Scotland* by Sir James Dalrymple, 1st Viscount Stair, with Specific Reference to the Law of Obligations' (DPhil thesis, Edinburgh 2011) 148–53. For a brief but helpful explication of Molina's position, see Decock *Theologians and Contract Law* (n 20) 202.

[31] Alan F Rodger, 'Molina, Stair and the Jus Quaesitum Tertio' (1969) Juridical Review 34–44, 128–51. Of interest, is that Astorri describes a very similar approach to pollictatio is taken by the Lutheran theologian, Valentin Alberti (1635–97): Paolo Astorri, *Lutheran Theology and Contract Law in Early Modern Germany (ca. 1520—1720)* (Brill 2019) 205–07.

[32] Stair does not think there is any meaningful distinction between paction and contract, but he does acknowledge some sort of distinction here by saying 'paction *and* contract'.

[33] Stair *Inst* 1.3.

Whatever the case, Molina's discussion under Disputatio 262 and 263 contains a debate about whether promises without acceptance are binding in natural law and, if so, according to either honesty or justice. In his discussion, Molina argues that it is the will of the promisor which determines if the promise is binding legally or morally. A promise without acceptance is always binding but the question is whether the will of the promisor intended it to be legally or morally binding (both of which, of course, had important consequences for the promisor). On this basis, Grotius may have been somewhat impressionistic with his use of Molina, but it was probably the Grotian interpretation that Stair took to be Molina's. That being so, there is good reason to understand Stair's use of Molina as apposite to his purpose, ie to demonstrate that promises without acceptance were binding morally, and indeed his overall aim, ie to show that Scots law is as close as possible to the realization of natural law. The fact that Stair was prepared to acknowledge promises as binding without acceptance therefore has a bearing upon how one understands his treatment of *jus quaesitum tertio*. It also demonstrates that underneath his account of the customary law of Scotland he was introducing relatively current debates within natural law alongside a doctrinal account of the law.

Pacta and *Nuda Pacta*

Much of the chapters that follow is dedicated to contextualizing Stair's approach to *nuda pacta*. Importantly, in the *Institutions* Stair says that *nuda pacta* are enforceable in Scotland, explaining that the reason Roman law did not enforce *nuda pacta* was merely to do with the necessity of 'clear proof of Pactions and Agreement'.[34] This is an example of where Stair opts for the equitable explanation of the Scots law approach rather than the utility-based justification. He says that in Scots law it is not necessary 'insist on these [requirements of proof], because the common custom of nations hath resiled therefrom, following rather the canon law, by which every paction produceth action, *et omne verbum de ore fideli cadit in debitum*'.[35] He says: 'pactions, contracts, covenants, and agreements, are synonymous terms both in themselves, and according to the recent customs of this and other nations'. He adds that it is 'unnecessary to trace the main subtilties and differences amongst pactions and contracts in Roman law'.[36] Whether the lords of session were enforcing *nuda pacta* in the early 1600s to the mid-seventeenth century is a debatable point. This means that Stair's statement should, as a report of the practice of Scots law, be treated with caution. Whatever the case, Stair does not expressly define a *nuda pacta*, but it is evident that he has in mind the notion of an informal agreement which is not clothed in a nominate contract or yet to be performed. It is through his discussion of *nuda pacta* that Stair attempts to explain the strict formality required in the law of Scotland for the creation of a conventional obligation.

---

[34] Stair *Inst* 1.10.7.
[35] Stair *Inst* 1.10.7.
[36] Stair *Inst* 1.10.10.

Formality

The difference between the ideal of equity, that the will creates conventional obligations, and the practicalities of positive law, namely the formalism of the law of Scotland, is an important illustration of how Stair explains the distance between equity and human law. It also demonstrates how Stair stylistically navigates the difference between his theoretical explanation of contracting and the reality of legal practice in seventeenth-century Scotland, demonstrating the need for law to be effective for the sake of utility. Before and after Stair the law in Scotland had strict rules of formality not only due to customary practice relating to bonds but also stemming from a series of Acts of Parliament, which addressed this question directly.[37] Scots generally treated Acts of Parliament as holding the utmost authority during the seventeenth century, and therefore in expressing that *nuda pacta* were enforceable Stair was saying something which would on the face of it contradict practice and therefore needed further explanation. The 1579 Act, as set out below, was important to the practice of law in Scotland in the seventeenth century,[38] and it continued to be cited by jurists into the eighteenth century.[39] Along with the 1584 and 1593 Acts, the 1579 Act and its application by the Court of Session is significant not only for what it reveals about the constitution and execution of contracts, but also because of what it did not say. The Act required that obligations which related to heritable titles and those obligations of 'great importance' be executed in a written deed, witnessed and sealed by the respective parties.

Therefore, when Stair said that *nuda pacta* were enforceable this was against the backdrop of the 1579 Act, which suggested that there was a category of contractual obligation that could only be created by an act rather than the will. In these cases, a constitutive external act was the trigger for the creation of the obligation. The idea that the writ itself created the obligation rather than being mere evidence of the obligation was a familiar mode of contractual thought in early modern Europe. It is no surprise, then, that the 1579 Act demonstrates a constitutive mode of thinking in the sixteenth and seventeenth centuries.[40] Stair, however, wished to demonstrate that all conventional

---

[37] RPS 1579/10/33; 1583/4/44; 1584/5/85.

[38] John Skene's collation and reproduction of Acts of the Scottish Parliament published in 1597 made these statutes readily accessible to Scots lawyers in the mid-seventeenth century without concern for their accuracy: John Skene, *The Lawes and Actes of Parliament, maid be King Iames the First, and his Successours Kinges of Scotland Visied, Collected and Extracted Furth of the Register. The Contentes of this Buik, are Expremed in the Leafe Following* (Robert Walde 1597). Republished in 1681. Several manuscripts produced in the mid-seventeenth century mention it: Ms Adv 24.2.3 f179; Ms Adv 24.3.2 f101; Ms Adv 24.1.3 f63ff. It is also possible that Scots lawyers became familiar with the 1579 Act through the *practicks* of Hope, Durie, and Spotiswoode as well as Craig's *Jus Feudale*, which all make reference to the 1579 Act: Craig *Jus Feudale* passim; Hope *Major Practicks* 2.1.7; Durie *Practicks* 43, 70, 292, 324, 358, 422, 458, 493, 522, 680, 723, and 832; Spotiswoode *Practicks* 359.

[39] Stair, *Inst* 1.10.9; George Mackenzie, *Observations on the Acts of Parliament* (Printed by the heir of A Anderson, Printer to His most Sacred Majesty, and are to be sold by T Brown and other book-sellers 1687) 192–93; William Forbes, *Institutes of the Law of Scotland* (first published 1722, Edinburgh Legal Education Trust 2012) II.III.I.IV; John Erskine, *An Institute of the Law of Scotland* (first published 1773, Edinburgh Legal Education Trust 2014) III.II.

[40] See, for example, Spotiswoode *Practicks* 359.

obligations were ultimately an act of the human will, but prima facie the 1579 Act of Parliament undermined the purity of this claim, setting out in legislation that in issues of importance the act of writing that formed the obligation. In this way, the practice challenged the ideal Stair paraphrases in the Institutions: that 'every paction produceth action'.[41] Clearly something more than consent was required in practice.[42] Stair's description of the 1579 Act, however, helps him to maintain that the law practised in Scotland was consistent with equity. Stair explains earlier in the *Institutions*:[43]

> [S]o naked pactions among the Romans were ineffectual, when they did not interpose stipulation. And with us, agreements requiring writs are ineffectual, and may be resiled from, unless writ be interposed. Yea, in most matters of importance, obligations with us are ineffectual, unless proven by oath of party, or by writ. Civil obligations are those, which have a civil effect and execution, though perhaps they be not naturally obliging; as with us an obligation in writ doth civilly oblige, and hath execution at the instance of the creditor's heir or assignee, thought the debt was paid to the cedent or defunct [assignee or deceased], because the debtor hath not been so cautious as to keep a discharge in writ. But most part of obligations are both natural and civil; and there are many such particular obligations, which will occur in their proper places.

To overcome the formalism represented by the 1579 Act, Stair pursues an explanation on the basis that some obligations are so important that the positive law requires more than what natural law requires. In this instance, he opts for a utility-based justification for the customary approach of Scots law. That is, positive law ostensibly departs from equity and natural law in some instances, but for good reason: to make the law effective in practice. Hence, Stair was maintaining that the will is the source of liability but offers an explanation as to why sometimes the positive law cuts off what equity requires by installing strict rules of formation.[44]

Gratuitous and Onerous

Stair passes over with almost no comment what was otherwise a common feature of native accounts of contracting in Scotland a key concept: *causa*. As will be explained, this is significant not just in terms of Scots legal practice but within the wider scope of the *ius commune* tradition. In Stair's account, *causa* is a way by which you determine the purpose of the contract, but it has no direct bearing on the enforceability of the transaction. On this, Stair is evidently following Grotius' discussion in Chapter 12 of Book I where these concepts are deployed as tools of natural law organization rather than as indicators of legal enforceability. Thus, like Grotius, he explains the different

---

[41] Stair *Inst* 1.1.9.
[42] The glossators and the commentators addressed this, and the late scholastics discussed it at length regarding obligations. See Gordley *Philosophical Origins* (n 20) 41–56.
[43] Stair *Inst* 1.3.5.
[44] Gerhard Lubbe, 'Formation of Contract' in Kenneth Reid and Reinhard Zimmermann (eds), *A History of Private Law in Scotland*, vol 2 (OUP 2000) 1–46 at 23–25; Wilson 'Sources and Method' (n 30) 193–97 and 199.

types of Roman law contract, namely the nominate and innominate contracts and the real and consensual contracts and also stipulations from a natural law position. 'All Pactions and Contracts, being now equally efficacious', he says, it is better to divide them according to the object of the contract rather than by the way they are perfected, that is, by thing, word, writ or sole consent.[45] If you divide contracts according to their object, they are, on Stair's account, either gratuitous or onerous. A gratuitous contract is where there is an obligation on one side but not the other, whereas an onerous contract is where there is an obligation on both sides. Stair therefore makes a threefold division, saying that an obligation is: (i) to give something, or (ii) for the use of something, or (iii) for services. He notes that some special consideration should be given to money, 'which is the common token of Exchange' given for things or for services; but importantly there are also transactions which relate only to money, such as bills of exchange. In making these various distinctions between the object of contracts and the type of uses that are made of contracts, Stair uses the conventional Roman law concepts of nominate and innominate contracts but not how they would have been used by either legal humanists or canonists. For Stair, as with Grotius, the *causa* of a contract is the purpose of its creation and not the reason for its enforcement or validity; it is only a means by which to categorize or organize different types of conventional obligation. Of course, he acknowledges that *causa* determines the appropriate means by which a contract should be executed (which is revealing of its practical significant for Scots lawyers), but it does not determine. according to Stair, whether the contract or promise should be enforced. That is, in offering his own discussion and division of contracts, Stair uses the common language of Roman law but takes his own approach recasting things from the view of his central idea that the will creates conventional obligations. Stair tries to offer in these paragraphs a new framework within which to view the different types of contract in contrast to the traditional Roman law scheme that had tended to be used in the law of Scotland until this point.

Laesio Enormis

Turning to consider questions of *laesio enormis*, Stair did not insist that the positive law in Scotland should seek to restore equality within a bargain, unless there had been some form of fraud.[46] He did have a rather expansive conceptualization of fraud that he discussed in previous titles of the *Institutions*,[47] but in terms of conventional obligations he rejected the ancient doctrine of *laesio enormis*.[48] Stair was very much

---

[45] Stair *Inst* 1.10.11.

[46] For a detailed exploration of fraud in Scots law, see Dot Reid, 'Fraud in Scots Law' (DPhil, University of Edinburgh 2013) Chapters 3–5. As Reid shows, for Stair, fraud encapsulated a far wider range of behaviour and instances than intentional fraud. Dot Reid, 'The Doctrine of Presumptive Fraud in Scots Law' (2013) 34 (3) Journal of Legal History 307–26.

[47] Reid 'Fraud in Scots Law' (n 46).

[48] Reid argues ('Doctrine of Presumptive Fraud' (n 46) 314) that commutative justice and the requirement of equality manifests in Stair's category of fraud, which included: (1) 'where the deeds alleged can have no fair construction, but do infer fraud' (Stair *Inst* 1.9.11); (2) collusion between family members to subvert the effect of diligence (Stair *Inst* (n 49) 1.9.11); (3) gratuitous alienations or fraudulent preferences to defeat the claims of creditors (Stair *Inst* 1.9.14–15); (4) latent defects (Stair *Inst* 1.10.14); (5) taking advantage of the ignorance and simplicity of a seller (Stair *Inst* 1.10.14); (6) holding on to goods 'till pinching necessity,

aware that in terms of commonplace conceptions of commutative justice used in the mid-seventeenth century and in Grotius' *The Rights of War and Peace*, an equitable approach, according to the law of nature, would allow one to argue that in an exchange one should receive a just price.[49] Stair, however, did not adopt this notion, saying rather: 'the Romans did not notice every inequality, but that which was enorm, above the half of the just value .... And the opinion of Grotius is for the affirmative upon this ground.' He expands upon Grotius's proposition 'that the purpose of the contracters is to give one thing for another of equal value, without purpose to gift on either hand'.[50] But, for Stair, 'the more probable in some cases, wherein, though it be the purpose of the parties to interchange things of equal value without donation, yet that equality hath no determinate or certain rule, but their own opinions'.[51] Martin Hogg has remarked that 'while one finds in Stair's writing a blend of natural law, reason, Scripture and Aristotelian virtues, the last of these is very muted: essentially the autonomy of parties and the will triumphs over the ideas of commutative justice (such as the just price) and liberality'.[52] Moreover, this is an example of Stair demonstrating that Scots law deviated from equity for reasons of practicality.

Hence, this rejection of equality as a proposition of the law of Scotland is not necessarily in contradiction with the stated aims of the *Institutions*, which was to show the equity and common principles of natural law which underlay the man-made law of Scotland[53] but to leave space for utility too. For Stair, it is debatable point whether the human law should restore exact equality and so he opts for what he thinks is the most probable and practical description of the law's working. It could be said that his use of the term 'probable' is suggestive of early modern casuistry literature, which in very general terms said that a doubtful matter of conscience should be determined according to whatever was the most likely answer.[54] A form of 'liberty-centred probabilism' can be found in the early modern period, which taught that 'doubtful precepts' of morality should not be taken to be binding upon one's conscience because 'moral precepts are restrictions on our freedom of action'.[55] If this is what Stair means by probable, he is not directly challenging the natural law commitment to equal exchange but instead suggesting that in doubtful cases a degree of latitude should be afforded to parties. Clearly, he thought the *laesio enormis* test too doubtful to propose that it was or should be part of the law of Scotland. Preferring the law to allow the enforcement of 'the rate parties agree on',[56] it is evident that Stair did not see any practical alternative.

---

which ariseth extreme dearth' (Stair *Inst* 1.10.14); and (7) inflating the price when the buyer has a special need that puts him at the mercy of the seller.

[49] Hugo Grotius, *The Rights of War and Peace* (first published 1625, Liberty Fund 2005) 2.12.11–14.
[50] Stair *Inst* 1.10.14.
[51] Stair *Inst* 1.10.14.
[52] Martin Hogg, *Promises and Contract Law: Comparative Perspectives* (CUP 2011) 136.
[53] Stair *Inst* 1.10.14.
[54] Ford alludes to an alternative analysis: John D Ford, *Law and Opinion in Scotland during the Seventeenth Century* (Hart 2007) 536 n 287.
[55] Rudolf Schüssler, 'On the Anatomy of Probabilism' in Jill Kraye and Risto Saarinen (eds), *Moral Philosophy on the Threshold of Modernity* (Springer 2005) 91–113 at 103.
[56] Schüssler 'On the Anatomy of Probabilism' (n 55) 103.

Second, Stair may have wished to demonstrate the equity of the law of contract in Scotland, but, when it came to equality within a bargain, Scots courts did not in practice rebalance bad bargains. Indeed, there is very little evidence (if any) of judicial control of prices in the immediate period before Stair wrote his *Institutions*. Despite a great deal of legislative control of prices during this period, it is difficult to find evidence of judicial oversight.[57] Evidence suggests that legislative price control was a familiar part of contracting as far back as the 1400s.[58] It appears, however, that this was an exception. That is, from a review of the sources, price control occurs within certain types of contract,[59] for very particular policy reasons,[60] and was always introduced by the king, parliament, or local authority. In modern parlance, this was public regulation of transactions, rather than judicial or doctrinal regulation of price. There is no record of a court readjusting the price in bargaining in the immediate period before Stair wrote his *Institutions*.[61] A low or high price may be indicative of circumvention, or force and fear, or exploitation of a minor; but the law prior to Stair does not appear to have permitted a general review of price.[62]

Thirdly, and importantly, Stair notes under his discussion of fraud in title 9 of Book I that in Roman law *actio redhibitoria et quanti minoris* in several instances, including when there was a great disparity between the value and the price of the goods. In such situations, Stair said Roman law presumed fraud allowing the action of *quanti minoris* but explains, 'they did not consider small differences betwixt the ware and price' as to do so would cause 'multitudes of debates hurtful to trade, the design whereof is to gain ...' Stair acknowledges that if too strict an approach was taken to determining the exact price, 'there would be nothing to induce a moderate gain' as merchants would be continually suited for fraud by unhappy buyers. He also recognizes that it is common for merchants to exaggerate how much an item costs them, to overstate how much other buyers are paying for things and to embellish how 'fashionable or good' their wares are. He says it is neither unlawful nor against any civil law for a seller to take such an approach and it is the approach of Roman law to only allow remedies when

---

[57] The economy during the seventeenth century was extremely unstable and often regulated. Prices would vary greatly, affecting the bargains of both the poor and wealthy: S G E Lythe, *The Economy of Scotland in its European Setting 1550–1625* (Oliver and Boyd 1960); Keith M Brown, 'Aristocratic Finances and the Origins of the Scottish Revolution' (1989) 104 (410) English Historical Review 46–87; Douglas Watt, '"The Labernith of Thir Difficulties": The Influence of Debt on the Highland Elite c.1550–1700' (2006) 85 (219) Scottish Historical Review 25–51.

[58] RPS 1425/3/11 ('Of victuals not to be made more expensive').

[59] RPS 1592/4/78 ('Against unlawful conditions in contracts or obligations').

[60] Some examples: RPS 1540/12/70 ('For eschewing of dearth of victuals, meat and fish'); RPS A1567/12/24 ('A commission to certain lords of the estates to consider such articles as are committed to them and to report the same again in the next parliament'); RPS A1573/4/3 ('Concerning the importation of wine and prices thereof'); RPS 1581/10/47 ('Concerning the setting of order and price on all stuff'); RPS A1605/6/5 ('Convention of the estates, 7 June 1605'); RPS A1609/1/11 ('Regarding the prices of writs and seals'); various Acts passed by Parliament on 16 November 1641; RPS 1645/11/289 ('Order: concerning chamber rents for members of parliament').

[61] This is based upon a survey of the following sources: Sinclair's *Practicks* (1540s?), Balfour's *Practicks* (1570s?), Craig's *Jus Feudale* (1600?), Spotiswoode's *Practicks* (1640s?), and George Mackenzie, *The Institutions of the Law of Scotland* (John Reid 1684).

[62] Joe Thomson makes some cursory remarks about the law that applied before Stair, but in reality his history does not go further back than Stair's *Institutions*: Joe Thomson, 'Judicial Control of Unfair Contract Terms' in Kenneth Reid and Reinhard Zimmermann (eds), *A History of Private Law in Scotland*, vol 2 (OUP 2000) 157–74.

the difference between the price and value are great. Explaining that he has examined Roman law's approach in detail because on this issue it is the 'most equitable and expedient', Stair continues to explain 'we [in Scotland] allow not the quarrelling of bargains upon presumed fraud *ex re ipsa*'. Assessing the consequences of this, Stair considers 'the not inconsiderable damages in traffic' if an alternative approach was taken, noting that trade requires that it be 'current and secure' to prosper. 'For there is nothing more prejudicial to trade, than to be easily involved in pleas' observes Stair. To be drawn into litigation, Stair notes, 'diverts merchants from their trade, and frequently marrs their gain, and sometimes their credit'.[63]

Again, this demonstrates both Stair's technique of evaluation but also the balance he often tries to strike between utility and equity. That is, Stair rejected the requirement of strict equality, and was able to explain why Scots law did this, ie because parties would use it to quarrel over trivial differences. Utility, practicality, and the common good of society require that something of equity is given up. Hence, the departure from equity is justified by his explanation of how equity and utility work together within the law of Scotland. Yet interesting, Stair was prepared to speak of an obligation of commerce which although not fully developed in the *Institutions* is suggestive that there was duty upon parties to ensure each other's needs were met within a contract even if exact equality was not required. It alludes to the notion that even if the law did not require it, our conscience did.

Obligation of Commerce

Stair mentions an obligation of commerce in two distinct places, first in title 14 of Book I where he considers sale and barter and then in Book II when he describes the creation of property. In the context of sale, he says it is necessary to distinguish it from barter but explains that it is common for these to be conflated because they relate to the 'mutual obligation of mankind to exchange, what they may spare from their own necessary use, with what other are willing to give in exchange'.[64] He goes on to suggest civil authorities should encourage and support trade, reminding his readers that 'commerce and free trade is by the law of nations' and should be 'urged and compelled' for the mutual benefit of nations and people.[65] Barter, however, is ineffective when it comes to international trade and so he explains 'common tokens of exchange have been invented and allowed over all the civil nations of the world, as comprehending the value of everything venal'.[66] Although Stair does not say this obligation materializes any right to demand the sale of goods, it does give further context to his favourable approach to commerce and his foregrounding of it when he says it is one of the three principles of positive law.[67] It also illuminates what Stair often meant when he said that

---

[63] Stair *Inst* 1.9.10.
[64] Stair *Inst* 1.14.
[65] Stair *Inst* 1.14.
[66] Stair *Inst* 1.14.
[67] Stair *Inst* 1.1.18.

utility required or necessitated a departure from the equitable solution: the traffic of commerce required security, certainty, and a willingness to exchange.

A far more Biblical and arguably political explanation is offered of the obligation of commerce in Stair's passages describing the creation of property. Nonetheless it is still an account which emphasizes the need for the circulation of goods within society, which in some instances requires force. Stair says there is 'in Property implied an Obligation of Commerce, or Exchange in case of necessity'.[68] He explains, that 'when God created man, he gave him dominion or lordship over all creatures of the earth, in the air and in the sea'.[69] He is quick to correct those who infer from this 'that Adam was not only the governor of this whole inferior world, but that he was proprietor of it, and that all rights of government or property, behoved to be derived from his disposal, or by succession to him'.[70] Stair says that Genesis 28 is to the contrary, making clear that dominion was a gift from God 'to mankind, when there was in their persons only; and did not import a present right of property, but only a right or power to appropriate by possession, or *jus ad rem*, not *jus in re*'. There was only a right of possession, according to Stair, which meant that 'when possessors removed from these parts, they ceased to be theirs'. Stair also pours scorn on the idea that 'man by his fall hath lost his right to the creatures, until by grace he be restored, and that the sole dominion of them belongs to the saints'.[71] After clearing the ground, he says 'that by the law of nature, the birth and fruit of both sea and land were acquirable by all mankind, who had equal interest therein, and every one might take and make use thereof, for his necessity, utility, and delight'. These interests which man has in common otherwise become 'proper', that is, real rights, for several reasons, including: (i) to prevent a man who possesses something the injury of losing it; (ii) to protect against the wrong that a man should lose something which he has made through his industry or art; (iii) to avert any interference in the transfer of possession; and (iv) to allow the creation of a security.[72]

After explaining the need for a distinction between moveable and heritable property and explaining what type of thing falls into each category, he discusses common property.[73] As noted above, Stair says there is an implied obligation of commerce within property in times of necessity. He explains that 'property could not consist, seeing by the division inferred therethrough, every man cannot have actually all necessaries without exchange'.[74] He says that where there is no authority who will take from an owner and give to those in need, 'it may be taken by force'.[75] Stair goes on to

---

[68] Stair *Inst* 2.1.6.

[69] Stair *Inst* 2.1.2. cf Grotius *The Rights of War* (n 49) 2.2.1–5.

[70] Stair *Inst* 2.1.2. cf Robert Filmer, *Patriarcha: Or the Natural Power of Kings* (Walter Davis 1680).

[71] cf Richard Fitzralph of Armagh (1300–1360), discussed in Richard Tuck, *Natural Rights Theories* (CUP 1979) 24–31.

[72] Stair *Inst* 2.1.2; cf Samuel Pufendorf, *The Whole Duty of Man, According to the Law of Nature* (first printed (in English) 1735, Liberty Fund 2003) 4.4.1–15.

[73] Stair, *Inst* 2.1.3–5.

[74] Stair, *Inst* 2.1.6. cf Lutheran theologians who took an interest in understanding contract law built their explanations on a similar idea that God permitted private property but only on the understanding that it would be exchanged, given and distributed generously by individuals, ie as a means for charity. Although this notion is nascent in these passages of Stair, the Lutheran's explication of this idea is far more extensive and central to their description of contract law in comparison to Stair. For in-depth discussion of the Lutheran approach, see Astorri *Lutheran Theology and Contract Law* (n 31) 150–51.

[75] Stair *Inst* 2.1.5.

say that there is an obligation to give in times of need or necessity to those who cannot offer anything in exchange and 'cannot otherwise preserve their life, but with the obligation of recompense when they are able'. Importantly, the necessity according to Stair must be real and serious, and he distinguishes this situation from that of charity and aliment, which are obligations with 'no determinate bounds, but left to the discretion of the giver, not of the demander, and so can be no warrant for taking by force, and without the proprietor's consent'.[76] Stair deals with the question of necessity and ownership by introducing an obligation which binds the owner to provide for the person in need. Legally speaking, therefore, if the owner does not perform their obligation and there is no authority to enforce it on behalf of the person in need, then it is legitimate according to the law of nature for man to take such things by force. Justification for such action is based on an interpersonal obligation and not a property right or claim to common ownership. It is therefore an account which stresses the need for mutual exchange, commerce, and the willingness to trade.

Loan, Mandate, Custody, Sale, Hire, and Society

The pattern discussed above—definition, description of Roman law, discussion of practice in Scotland, and an evaluation of the equitable approach—is repeated in Stair's treatment of specific contracts. As has already been shown with regard to structure, *nuda pacta, causa*, and formalities, either expressly rejects the Roman law approach or implies it is no longer relevant by minimizing its place within his discussion.[77] In at least twenty instances, Stair explains why customary law of Scotland departs from Roman law, and each time he explains it is due to either the equity or utility of the Scottish solution.[78] As is common with his method, he often states what

---

[76] Stair *Inst* 2.1.6.

[77] ie (1) Stair *Inst* 1.10.7 ('... the Canon law having taken off the exception of civil law, *ex nudo pacto*'); (2) Stair *Inst* 1.10.10 ('... *unnecessary* to trace the subtilties [of the Roman law of contracts] ...'); (3) Stair *Inst* 1.10.14 ('In this the Romans did not notice every inequality, but that which was enorm, above the half of the just value, *but that which our custom alloweth not*, ...'); (4) Stair *Inst* 1.17.16 ('In obligations which are not in dando but in faciendo, the common opinion of the doctors is, that there can be no pursuit for performance, but only for interest; for before the delay there is no pursuit, and after, the creditor cannot pursue for performance, but for interest, l.13.in fine ff.de re judicata; but it seems more suitable to equity, that it should be in the creditor's option even after the delay, either to suit for performance or interest, as he pleaseth, if both be prestable'); (5) Stair *Inst* 12.13.7 ('Here there ariseth a Question, whether a Mandatar may instruct another person, or sub-commit his Mandat, wherein the Civil Law, and most of the Doctors are in the Affirmative. But the nature of the Contract inferreth the contrary, which ought to take place, unless Law or Custom were opposite, *which is not with us*'); (6) Stair *Inst* 1.13.13 ('We shall not insist in the manner of the sale of pledges prescribed by the Roman law, and the intimations or denunications requisite to be made to the debtor, that being wholly changed by our customs').

[78] ie Stair *Inst* 1.10.7 (*nudum pactum* are enforceable); 1.10.8 (*pactum corvinum de hæreditate viventis* are allowable); 1.10.14 (*laesio enormis* is not followed); 1.10.15 (in cases of latent insufficiency, Scots custom, contrary to Roman law, was to offer the return of goods before seeking rebate); 1.11.13 (loans made to prodigals are allowable); 1.11.3 (lending to sons *in partia potestas* is allowable); 1.11.3 (no restrictions on unmarried woman acting as cautioners); 1.11.5 (argues that *mutuum* is underpinned by restitution, ie an obediential obligation or reparation); 1.12.7 (sub-contraction of a mandate is allowable); 1.12.10 (no strict liability regarding mandator); 1.12.15 (mandates entering an heir party to an action are allowed); 1.13.2 (depositors are not liable for 'light faults' during period of custody); 1.13.10 (goods lost by depositor due to calamity are not liability to pay double value by way of compensation); 1.13.14 (pactum *legis commisoriae* is allowable); 1.14.3 (earnest in sales contracts is not required); 1.14.7 (risk in the contract of sale does not rest

equity requires by comparing it to what Roman law did. Often his discussion is framed within the context of a historical account of why Roman law took one approach rather than another. The implication is that the Roman law approach was suitable for that society, but that Scotland might require to take a different approach. In the case of utility, his conclusion is often that the standards which Roman law expected are too demanding to carry out in practice. Yet what sets Stair's account apart from his contemporaries is how he shaped his account of the law of contract around the core concepts of the will, liberty, and equity, which means the primary focus of this book is upon the opening passages of title 10 of book I. It is here where Stair's distinctive contractual thought is laid out.

Conclusion

The footprint of Roman law upon Stair's account of conventional obligations is evident. His layout itself indicates this. Moreover, his pattern of citation is telling of the weighty influence Roman law had over the Scots' legal mind.[79] One of the most notable evolutions within the manuscripts of the *Institutions* is the type and volume of citations, which Stair added. In title 10 alone, the citation of Roman law sources doubled from 1661 to 1693.[80] Several authors have noted the Romanization of Stair's *Institutions*.[81] Therefore, although the following chapters stress the place of theology and philosophy within Stair's account of contracting, they make this argument in full cognizance of the fact that he often made use of Roman law in composing this account. That Stair, like many of his contemporaries, relied on Roman law should not overshadow how he placed the law of Scotland, including the law applying to contracting, on to a new philosophical basis. He used a philosophical methodology and made direct appeals to equity, thereby minimized the authoritative value of Roman law as a source of law per se, whilst at the same time accomplishing the feat from within a Roman law framework. The task of the following chapters is to explain and understand the role that Stair's philosophical and theological impulses played in his handling of Scots contract law.

---

exclusively with buyer); 1.15.8 (annual rents are allowed to be paid beyond the price of the principal); and 1.17.5 (cautioners cannot be pursued before principal debt has been discussed).

[79] See Wilson 'The Sources and Method' (n 30) 251–69.

[80] Wilson says it increased from 161/2 in the 1662 version to 353 in the 1693 version: Wilson, 'Sources and Method' (n 30) 66–67.

[81] William Gordon, 'Roman Law in Scotland' in Robin Evans-Jones (ed), *The Civil Law Tradition in Scotland*, vol 2, supplementary series (The Stair Society 1995) 13–40; Grant McLeod, 'The Romanization of Property Law' in Kenneth Reid and Reinhard Zimmermann (eds), *A History of Private Law in Scotland*, vol 1 (2000) 220–42; Wilson, 'Sources and Method' (n 30) 66–130.

4

Standing by the Faith of Pactions and Promises

The enforcement of *nuda pacta* is, prima facie, a departure from the traditional approach of Roman law and is redolent of canon law's approach to contracting.[1] Therefore, in terms of legal history, Stair's statement that *nuda pacta* are enforceable in the Court of Session, namely a secular court, is a significant break from centuries of legal practice and is representative of a shift in legal thought.[2] More generally, the recognition of the enforceability of a *nudum pactum* within a secular court is a significant development of contractual thought within European legal history which signals the emergence of modern notions of contract, including the secularization of contracting and the unification of different systems of law otherwise applicable to contracting behaviour. It also diminishes the authority of the learned law of Roman law found in the *Digest* and commentaries upon the *Corpus iuris civilis*, which appeared to say otherwise.[3] Arguably, by the time Stair said *nuda pacta* were enforceable within a Scots secular court, it was something that was already being practised in various jurisdictions and geographical locations across Europe. The aim of this chapter is to explain Stair's role and motivations as the first jurist in Scotland to proudly proclaim that *nuda pacta* were now enforceable in Scotland.

Stair here brought philosophical and theological perspectives to bear on his legal point of view. Stair's choice of legal rule was not simply a privileging of canon law over Roman law, but also, and importantly, it demonstrated a direct connection between the positive law of Scotland and God's Moral Law, written on the heart of man and communicated through his conscience. As we have seen, Stair's contemporaries who wrote practicks or compiled commentaries on the law of Scotland were not prepared or able to take the step towards declaring *nuda pacta*'s enforceability, whereas Stair around the same time did so with little hesitancy, driven by coherent theological and philosophical positions. Although this chapter does not try to resolve continuing

---

[1] Richard Hyland, 'Pacta Sunt Servanda: A Meditation' (1993–94) 34 Virginia Journal of International Law 405.

[2] William W McBryde, 'Promises in Scots Law' (1993) 41 International Comparative Law Quarterly 48; Martin Hogg, 'Promises: The Neglected Obligation in European Private Law' (2010) 59 International Comparative Law Quarterly 461; Warren Swain, 'Contract as Promise: The Role of Promising in the Law of Contract. An Historical Account' (2013) 17 (1) Edinburgh Law Review 1–21. More generally, see Charles Fried, *Contract as Promise: A Theory of Contractual Obligations* (first published 1981, OUP 2015); Martin Hogg, *Promises and Contract Law: Comparative Perspectives* (CUP 2011).

[3] For discussion of Scotland, see generally John D Ford, *Law and Opinion in Scotland during the Seventeenth Century* (Hart 2007), whereas for a discussion of Roman law in Europe more widely, see Klaus Luig, 'The Institutes of National Law in the Seventeenth and Eighteenth Centuries' (1972) 17 Juridical Review 193; Quentin Skinner, *The Foundations of Modern Political Thought, vol 1: The Renaissance* (CUP 1978) 207–08; Peter Stein, *Roman Law in European History* (CUP 1999) 71–94; Randall Lesaffer, *European Legal History: A Cultural and Political Perspective* (CUP 2009) 309–17, 320–38, 340–45, 350–67.

Contract before the Enlightenment. Stephen Bogle, Oxford University Press. © Stephen Bogle 2023.
DOI: 10.1093/oso/9780192884961.003.0005

discussions within Scottish legal history about whether or to what extent the Court of Session was enforcing *nuda pacta* in the period before Stair, it does try to offer something new to such discussions by taking this approach. It draws attention to the deeper motivations of Stair as he took the bold step of upturning centuries of legal thought.

Stair's technique, distinguishing him from his legal contemporaries, was to apply natural law theory to the law of Scotland directly, and, if necessary, in contradiction to positive Roman law and traditional notions of the Court of Session's temporal jurisdiction. When Stair viewed the practice of Scots law, no matter whether it expressed itself as enforcing *nuda pacta* or not, he looked for the correct application of a natural law principle. Of course, Roman law could be viewed by lawyers and theologians in the early modern period as near-embodiment of natural law; but, given Stair's theory of natural law, he did not take this approach. Stair drew from a Calvinist notion that basic principles of natural law, that is, the Moral Law, were known to man without reasoning, observation, the wisdom of antiquity or Roman law, and even Scripture. Simply by the innate sense of the basic principles of morality imprinted on man's heart, namely conscience, which included standing by the faith of his pactions, man knew what he should do, at least in very basic terms. If Stair was to demonstrate the law of Scotland related to the nature of man and the Moral Law of God, it was imperative that *nuda pacta* were, at least in theory, enforceable—and, given his particular type of natural law theory, he could minimize the otherwise received wisdom and equity of Roman law which dominated a great deal of Scottish legal thinking in the mid-seventeenth century. It will also be suggested that this strong sense of the moral imperative of standing by the faith of your pactions, influenced by Stair's Calvinist understanding of human nature, meant that he differed from Grotius and others by suggesting that promises, even without acceptance, were, theoretically, enforceable in Scots law.

Stair and *Nuda Pacta*

During the opening passages of the *Institutions of the Law of Scotland* (*Institutions*), Stair explains some of the common principles of the Moral Law, which he sees manifest within the positive law of nations and, importantly, Scots customary law. He tells his readers that 'when we come to the Obligations by Paction, Promise, or Contract, all which do arise from the Principle of Ingagement, ... it shall be sufficient here, to conclude with the Law, that there is nothing more Natural, than to stand to the Faith of our Pactions'.[4] At the root of promises, pacts, and contracts, according to Stair, is a common principle, meaning that unlike Roman law, Stair's account of the ways by which you can create an obligation starts from a generalized, singular proposition. Speaking of conventional obligations in more detail under title 10, he goes on to say that 'The Romans [required] solemnity of words, by way of Stipulation ... unless there were the intervention of some Deed, or thing beside the consent, or that it were a Contract allowed of Law, or such other Paction as it specially confirmeth, without all

---

[4] Stair *Inst* 1.1.21.

which, it was called *nudum pactum inefficax de agendum*.[5] However, he went on to say: '[w]e shall not insist in these, because the common Custom of Nations hath re-siled therefrom, following rather the Canon Law, by which every Paction produceth Action, *omne verbum de ore fideli cadit in debitum*'.[6] In support, Stair cited the *Liber Extra* from the *Corpus iuris canonici*,[7] the Leuven jurist Petrus Gudelinus (1550–1619)[8] and the canonist Arnold Corvinus (?–1680).[9] In terms of Scots customary law, he cited a 'special Statute of Session'[10] and the 1631 Court of Session case, *Sharp v Sharp*, which is reported in Durie's *Practicks*.[11] Some take Stair at face value: in the mid-seventeenth century, Scots courts were enforcing *nuda pacta*.[12] Others, however, have questioned his summary on the basis of documentary evidence suggesting that Stair's description is misleading, at least in terms of the Act of Sederunt he cites in sup-port of Scots customary law.[13] As will be explained, this is a tricky issue to resolve if you approach the question as black and white: it was enforceable or not enforceable. As will be shown, whatever position you might take, it could be reasonably suggested that the law was in flux during the mid-seventeenth century and that Stair opted for the affirmative. Additionally, whether there was an Act of Sederunt or not, it is clear that Stair's contemporaries did not make such statements in their practicks or compil-ations, that it contradicted what Craig said in the *Jus Feudale*, and that it overturned centuries of juristic writing which said otherwise. It was a bold juristic step. But it was also unsurprising given the developments in related jurisdictions in Europe at this time in parts of France, the Low Countries, and Germany. In contrast, the theo-logical and philosophical motivations which prompted Stair to take this decisive step, as will be explained, may distinguish this development in Scotland from that of other

---

[5] Stair *Inst* 1.10.7.

[6] Stair *Inst* 1.10.7.

[7] Stair *Inst* 1.10.7. Specially, *Liber extra* 1.35.1 and 3—for discussion, see William M Gordon, 'Stair, Grotius and the Sources of Stair's *Institutions*' in William M Gordon (ed), *Roman Law, Scots Law and Legal History: Selected Essays* (Edinburgh University Press 2007) 255, 263; Adelyn L M Wilson, 'The Sources and Method of the *Institutions of the Law of Scotland* by Sir James Dalrymple, 1st Viscount Stair, with Specific Reference to the Law of Obligations' (DPhil, thesis University of Edinburgh 2011) 247–49.

[8] Gordon 'Stair, Grotius and the Sources' (n 7) 263–65; Wilson 'Sources and Method' (n 7) 247–49. Stair could have consulted either Petrus Gudelinus, *Commentariorum de Jure Novissimo Libri Sex: Optimia Methodo, Accurateac Erudite Conscripti, Additis Harum Vicinarumque Region Moribus* (printed in Antwerp, Ex Officina Hieronymi Verdus 1620) (1643 edition printed in Arnhem).

[9] Petrus Guideline's, *Commentariorum de Jure Noisome Libri Sex: Optimia Methodo, Accurateac Erudite Conscripti, Additis Harum Vicinarumque Region Moribus* (Ex Officina Hieronymi Verdus 1620). Johann Arnold Corvinus, *Digesta per Aphorism's Strictim Explicate* (Elzvir 1636) (Stair was probably consulted for the Amsterdam edition).

[10] Arguably, no extant copy or official record of a 1592 Act of Sederunt relating specifically to *nuda pacta* is available. See *The Acts of Sederunt of the Lords of Council and Session, from the 15th of January 1553, to the 11th of July 1790* (Elphingston Balfour 1790).

[11] Alexander Gibson (ed), *The Decision of the Lords of Council and Session in Most Cases of Importance, Debated, and Brought before Them; from July 1621 to July 1642* (Andrew Anderson 1690) 553–54. Various manuscript copies of Durie's *Practicks* would have been available to Stair in the early 1660s. Numerous ver-sions are available in the Advocates' Library: Adv Ms 6.1.3; 24.2.2.; 24.4.8–13; 24.5.7; 25.1.13; 25.5.14.

[12] Alexander J Mackenzie Stuart, 'Contract and Quasi Contract' in *An Introduction to Scottish Legal History*, vol 20 (Stair Society 1958) 241; McBryde 'Promises in Scots Law' (n 2); William D H Sellar, 'Promise' in Kenneth Reid and Reinhard Zimmermann (eds), *A History of Private Law in Scotland*, vol 2 (OUP 2000) 251, 261ff; Swain 'Contract as Promise' (n 2).

[13] Wilson 'Sources and Method' (n 7) 200–01.

jurisdictions. It is important, however, before examining Stair's approach, to context-ualize his statement that *nuda pacta* are enforceable in a Scots secular court.

Nuda Pacta in Legal History

Corpus iuris civilis

The *Digest* of the *Corpus iuris civilis* offers the paradigmatic statement of a pact,[14] and Craig was most likely referencing this in *Jus Feudale*.[15] In D 2.14.1, Ulpian says: '1. Moreover, pact is derived from agreement (the word peace comes from the same origin). 2. An agreement is the agreement and consent of two or more persons about the same thing'. Stipulation is, according to Ulpian, 'void unless there is agree-ment'.[16] However, he goes on to say that '[b]y universal law some agreement gave rise to actions, some to defences'.[17] If the pact is not clothed by a recognized contract, such as hire, partnership, loan, or deposit, there is no ground for action: 'it is settled that no obligation arises from the agreement. Therefore, a naked agreement gives rise not to an obligation but to a defence'.[18] In terms of a defence, a pact would, for ex-ample, have legal significance if it related to the resolution of an existing action or confirmed that one party will not sue the other. Many other pacts were also recog-nized in the *Digest* as having legal effect, such as those which gained recognition on the basis of *bona fides*, for example, a supplement or alteration of a recognized nom-inate contract (for instance, in a sale contract, namely *lex commissoria*[19]), or the sub-stitution of agreed-performance with something else (*pacta ex intervallo*[20]). Other pacts mentioned in the *Digest* were simply recognized by the Praetor as enforceable, such as a pact to pay a debt of another (*constitutum debiti*[21]), or a pact made with a ship's captain guaranteeing the safety of goods transported (*receptum nautae cauponis stabularii*[22]). Medieval jurists, such as Accursius, upon discovering these rules and ex-ceptions, suggested that nominate contracts, innominate contracts, and pacts were in essence agreements.[23] On this basis, the difference for them was between enforceable agreements, such as *pacta vestita*, and unenforceable agreements, or *pacta nuda*.[24] As Zimmermann notes, upon introducing this idea and distinction, '*pacta vestita* were now very much the rule; the few remaining unenforceable *pacta nuda* appeared as something of an anomaly; and seeing that vestments were available so liberally, they were bound, sooner or later, to find a charitable champion who was prepared to save

---

[14] Reinhard Zimmermann, *The Law of Obligations: Roman Foundations of the Civilian Tradition* (OUP 1996) 538.

[15] Craig *Jus Feudale* 1.2.14.

[16] *Digest* 2.14.1, 1.

[17] *Digest* 2.14.1, 3.

[18] *Digest* 2.14.7, 1–4.

[19] *Digest* 18.3.

[20] *Digest* 2.14.7, 5.

[21] *Digest* 13.5.

[22] *Digest* 4.9.

[23] Zimmermann *The Law of Obligations* (n 14) 538–39.

[24] Zimmermann *The Law of Obligations* (n 14) 538–39.

them too from the chill of death'.[25] Importantly, however, these jurists did not go further when making these observations, and certainly did not suggest that Roman law was wrong in terms of how it approached *nuda pacta*, or that jurists and judges should move beyond Roman law and formulate a general rule.

As Chapter 1 demonstrated, Balfour's practicks, which were used by Scots during the mid-seventeenth century, indicate that Scots made distinctions between different types of pacts or pactions, which were enforceable or unenforceable, depending on various factors. Balfour's practicks demonstrate that, in the sixteenth century, jurists like him were trying to find more substantive ways by which to organize or differentiate between enforceable and unenforceable pacts within the customary practice of the Court of Session. Therefore, when Craig says in the *Jus Feudale* that Scots follow the Roman law when it comes to pacts, he was not merely indicating that the basic rule of D 2.14.1 was followed but also alluding to this more complicated and intricate system of enforceable and unenforceable pacts, which jurists were, over the centuries, trying to organize or explain. Zimmermann suggests it was in the sixteenth century that jurists started to consider that in actual fact *nuda pacta* were no longer an anomaly but rather equally enforceable, and with this collapsed the medieval distinction between *vestita pacta* and *nuda pacta*. Feenstra has also drawn attention to a mid-seventeenth-century controversy between two prominent Dutch jurists, who debated whether *nuda pacta* were enforceable in Roman law—a debate Scots lawyers would have encountered as students,[26] which again demonstrates the complexity of not only the practice but also the interpretation of Roman law texts relating to *nuda pacta*. Importantly, however, what Balfour, Craig, and many of these Dutch jurists represent is a continued engagement with Roman law within the paradigm of *nuda pacta*, whereas Stair abandoned, at least in theory, this entire approach to the creation of an obligation. However, before exploring why Stair felt confident enough to leave behind the known way of Roman law, it is important to grasp the practice and evolution of canon law.

Corpus iuris canonici

The jurisdiction of canon law courts was established early in Scotland, possibly around the eleventh century, and arguably only disappeared in practical terms in the seventeenth century.[27] Indeed, following the Reformation, contractual disputes were still heard in the newly formed commissary courts which, in effect, continued the canon law tradition of enforcing agreements or promises fortified with an oath in the post-Reformation period.[28] The approach of canon law to *nuda pacta*, in contrast to the

[25] Zimmermann *The Law of Obligations* (n 14) 539.

[26] Robert Feenstra, 'Pact and Contract in the Low Countries from the 16th to the 18th Century' in John Barton (ed), *Towards a General Law of Contract* (Duncker & Humblot 1990) 197.

[27] Research suggests that it might have been established and accepted as a legitimate forum from as early as the eleventh century: see David Baird Smith, 'Canon Law' in *An Introductory Survey of the Sources and Literature of Scots Law*, vol 1 (Stair Society 1936) 185.

[28] David B Smith, 'The Spiritual Jurisdiction 1560–64' (1993) 25 Records of the Scottish Church History Society 1–18; Simon Ollivant, *The Court of the Official in Pre-Reformation Scotland, based on the Surviving Records of the Officials of St Andrews and Edinburgh*, vol 34 (Stair Society 1982); John W Cairns, 'Historical

Digest, was based on the Biblical principle: 'But let your speech be yea, yea: no, no: and that which is over and above these, is of evil.'[29] In the *Book of Numbers,* it says: 'If any man makes a vow to the Lord, or bind himself by an oath: he shall not make his word void but shall fulfil all that he promised.' Unsurprisingly, canon law transplanted these Biblical norms into practical rules, primarily in relation to agreements and promises.[30] Accordingly, in the *Decretum*[31] one finds the Church's practical application of these norms to disputes about promises and agreements. In the thirteenth century, a gloss to 1.35.1 of the *Decretals of Gregory IX* emerged: 'pacta quantumcumque nuda servanda' (pacts, however naked, must be kept/*pacta sunt servanda*).[32] The source of this now famous maxim is a little unclear, but it is commonly attributed to the thirteenth-century canonist Hostiensis.[33] What is for sure is that it did not appear in the original *Decretals* or the *Decretum.*[34] However, it was to appear in the *Corpus iuris canonici* and to mark a distinct line between secular and religious norms with regard to contracting behaviour.[35] This gloss was an ethical and legal restatement of Biblical teaching[36] recast in canon law to mean that a person should do what he said he would do (whether that is a promise or an agreement). Canonists and theologians who were mindful that they should not extend the Church's jurisdiction into temporal matters had concerns about the potential scope of this rule.[37] To allay these fears, the Church developed a procedural requirement.[38] The Church would concern itself with agreements or promises registered with the church court. Otherwise, it would only consider those promises or agreements fortified with an oath. The requirement of an oath explains why an action in the church court is as a breach of faith. In raising an action in a church court, one was not in pursuit of payment or performance, but reporting

[margin, handwritten] biblical teaching informs canon law approach to nuda pacta

Introduction' in Kenneth Reid and Reinhard Zimmermann (eds), *A History of Private Law in Scotland* (OUP 2000) 14, 83–84; Sellar 'Promise' (n 12) 262–65; Thomas Green, *The Spiritual Jurisdiction in Reformation Scotland: A Legal History* (Edinburgh University Press 2019).

[29] Matthew, Chapter 5, verse 17, Douay-Rheims edition (first published 1546, John Murphy Company 1899).

[30] Examples include: Numbers 30:5; James 5:12; Proverbs 19:5; Matthew 5:17. Also see Richard H Helmholz, *The Spirit of Classical Canon Law* (The University of Georgia Press 1996) 145.

[31] Not officially endorsed by the papacy, but influential, Gratian's *Decretum* was published sometime between 1139 and 1142. This is the first clear expression of canon law's application to what we might now call contracts. Ecclesiastical decision-makers across medieval Europe would have known Gratian's *Decretum*; if there was no copy in the local cathedral or church, the priests, lawyers, and clergy would have learned many of its maxims in the seminaries and universities of continental Europe. For more detail regarding the development of canon law and a general notion of contract, see Helmholz *The Spirit of Classical Canon Law* (n 30); Hogg *Promises and Contract Law* (n 2) Ch 3; Wim Decock, *Theologians and Contract Law: The Moral Transformation of the Ius Commune (ca. 1500–1650)* (Brill 2013) 122.

[32] *Decretals of Gregorii IX 1.35.1* in *Corpus Iuris Canonici* (In aedibus Populi Romani 1582) <http://digital.library.ucla.edu/canonlaw> accessed 5 April 2021.

[33] Hyland 'Pacta Sunt Servanda: A Meditation' (n 1) 416.

[34] Hyland 'Pacta Sunt Servanda: A Meditation' (n 1) 416.

[35] *Decretales Gregorii P.IX 1.35.1* (n 32).

[36] Jan Hallebeek, 'Medieval Legal Scholarship' in Jan Hallebeek and Harry Dondorp (eds), *Contract for a Third-Party Beneficiary* (Brill 2008) 22.

[37] For further discussion, see Richard H Helmholz, *The Oxford History of the Laws of England, Vol I: The Canon Law and Ecclesiastical Jurisdiction from 597 to the 1640s* (OUP 2004) 355–57.

[38] For detailed discussion of the development of these ideas, as well as the theological debate behind the jurisdictional scope of ecclesiastical courts, see Decock, *Theologians* (n 31) 122; Helmut Coing, 'English Equity and the Denunciatio Evangelica of the Canon Law' (1955) 71 Law Quarterly Review 223.

a sin.[39] In theory, it remained a sin to break a promise according to canon law, but it was only the clergy who were held to this standard in a church court. Thus, an action against a layman was on the basis that an oath had been made to God, which was now broken.[40] Green has demonstrated that with the *de facto* abolition of canon law courts in Scotland in 1560 and the eventual creation of commissary courts in 1563, the Court of Session in effect assumed jurisdiction, although not expressly, over spiritual matters, including oaths, as it acted as a court of appeal during this period.[41] In theory, this brought the enforceability of *nuda pacta* within the remit of the temporal Lords of Session and suggests, on one analysis, that a customary practice and law therefore emerged.[42] Whether this is the case or not, as Chapter 1 demonstrated, juristic writing does not state clearly that there was such practice. Indeed, the first written statement that there was such a change and that *nuda pacta* were enforceable, and therefore the practice of canon law courts was followed by the law of Scotland, is within early drafts of Stair's *Institutions* which circulated the Faculty in the 1660s.

Nuda pacta and the ius commune

Before examining why Stair took this step in the 1660s, it is important to grasp, in outline, how Scots lawyers understood the concept of *causa* in the mid-seventeenth century. In both canon law and Roman law, the concept of *causa* became significant as medieval jurists' and canonists' understanding of *nuda pacta* developed.[43] In the *Digest*, the lack of *causa* was used to explain why a *nudum pactum* was unenforceable, which became important to how lawyers conceptualized the enforceability of pacts in the medieval and early modern period. Ulpian said: 'but where there is no cause for the agreement, it is settled that no obligation can be created. And so a bare *pactum* gives rise to no action but does give rise to a defence'.[44] Therefore, if a pact was to be enforceable, what was an acceptable *causa*? By the late sixteenth and the seventeenth century, there were two principal ways of thinking about *causa* with regard to

---

[39] Hay offers a useful sixteenth-century account of how oaths and promise-keeping were viewed by the Church in Scotland. In his lectures on marriage, he said:

> He [Augustine] says elsewhere that 'To swear is to give God His right to the truth', and this is done when God is invoked as a witness to the truth. According to Raymund an oath is an affirmation or denial, supported by the witness of a sacred thing. By 'witness of a sacred thing' is meant God, the Holy of Holies, as well as creatures, in which God's perfection is mirrored, for God's image is in man's soul and at least a trace of Him is visible in other creatures.

See John C Barry (ed), *William Hay's Lectures on Marriage*, vol 24 (Stair Society 1967) 323.

[40] As Decoct narrates, there continued to be a discussion into the sixteenth century amongst canonists as to whether an *actio* could be raised against a layman who broke a promise: Decock, *Theologians* (n 31) 127–30.

[41] Green, *The Spiritual Jurisdiction in Reformation Scotland* (n 28) 10–27; see also, Sellar, 'Promise' (n 12) 260.

[42] Sellar, 'Promise' (n 12) 260.

[43] Ernest G Lorenzen, 'Causa and Consideration in the Law of Contracts' (1919) 28 (7) Yale Law Journal 621–46; John L Barton, 'Causa Promissionis Again' (1966) 34 Tijdschrift voor Rechtsgeschiedenis 41–73; Italo Birocchi, *Causa e Categoria General del Contratto* (G Giappichelli 1997); Laurent Waelkens, 'La Cause de D. 44,4,2,3 par' (2007) 75 Tijdschrift voor Rechtsgeschiedenis 199–212; J A C Thomas, *A Textbook on Roman Law* (2013 reprint, North-Holland Publishing Company 1976) 260–65.

[44] *Digest* 2.14.7, 4.

nuda pacta.[45] The first emerged from the medieval *ius commune* under the influence of scholasticism and canon law, often associated with the *mos italicus* approach to Roman law sources.[46] The second came from legal humanists, who sought to revive the 'true meaning' of the *Digest* whilst also using the *Corpus iuris civilis* as an exemplar for contemporary law.[47] This is often associated with the *mos gallicus* approach to Roman law. The *ius commune* sense of the term, inter alia, focused on determining the intention of parties, whereas legal humanists generally associated the term with some form of legal recognition of a transaction's enforceability. Scots lawyers would have been familiar with both approaches, although they may not have expressed things in terms of different schools of thought.

Put broadly, the *ius commune* conception of *causa* focuses, inter alia, upon the intention of parties, whereas the legal humanist conception of *causa* designates the legal enforceability of transactions.[48] Legal humanists were far more matter of fact about the *causa* of a transaction in comparison to those jurists from the *ius commune*. It was shorthand for a state-sanctioned contract.[49] Therefore, if the contract matched one of Justinian's contracts, or it was clothed in a recognized *vestitus*, it had a sufficient *causa*. For instance, Petrus Gudelinus, whose commentaries on Roman law were known and used by Scots lawyers during the mid-seventeenth century, provides a good example of what might be characterized as a legal humanist conception of *causa*.[50] He spoke of the *causae* of obligations but did not analyze *causa* in terms of intention. He stayed within the closed list of contracts and remarked upon customary law's innovations. In contrast, another jurist known to Scots, Arnold Vinnius, spoke of a division between obligations based on voluntary and involuntary *causa*.[51] He also spoke of *nuda pacta* as being enforceable, but tried to explain the link between *nuda pacta* and nominate contracts based on intention, namely *animo obligandi*.[52] In comparison, Gudelinus presented the enforceability of *nuda pacta* as an exception of customary law and thereafter proceeded to speak about the closed list of contracts and recognized *vestitus*.[53] The legal humanist approach is sometimes characterized as invoking a procedural or legalistic conception of *causa*, whereas the *ius commune* conception of *causa* is described as being elaborate, flexible, and Aristotelian.[54] As will be indicated, it appears

---

[45] Put broadly, it is possible to describe early modern legal thought in Europe as being divided into two camps: the *mos italicus* and the *mos gallicus*. The former encapsulated a medieval understanding of civil law, typified by the commentators and glossators, whereas the latter was a sixteenth-century movement known as legal humanism, which was typified by the approach of French jurists and later Roman-Dutch jurists.

[46] James Gordley, *The Philosophical Origins of Modern Contract Doctrine* (OUP 1991) 49–57, 77–79.

[47] Decock *Theologians* (n 31) 115.

[48] See Decock *Theologians* (n 31) 108.

[49] eg Decock quotes Hugo Doneau: 'Duorum pluriumve consensus in hoc ut unus alteri quid det aut faciat, jure ad eam rem et praestationem comprobatus' (Decock *Theologians* (n 31) 130).

[50] Petrus Gudelinus, *Commentariorum De Jure Novissimo Libri Sex: Optimia Methodo, Accurateac Erudite Conscripti, Additis Harum Vicinarumque Region Moribus* (Ex Officina Hieronymi Verdus 1620) III.I ('In quo de obligationibus, nec non de actionibus & execeptibus & jure in integrum restitutum quaetertia pars est juris priuati').

[51] Arnold Vinnius, *Institutionum Imperialium Commentaries Academicus & Forensis* (Apud Ludovicum & Danielem Elzevirios 1659) III.XIV (p 576).

[52] Vinnius *Institutionum* (n 51) III.XVI (p 579).

[53] Gudelinus *Commentariorum* (n 50) III.I.

[54] Gordley *Philosophical Origins* (n 46) 49–57.

that in the period before Stair the Court of Session was influenced more by a *ius commune* concept of *causa* in comparison to a legal humanist conception.

Nuda pacta and customary law

For centuries, under the jurisdiction of conscience and the rules of canon law, ecclesiastical courts enforced, in Scotland as well as across Europe, what would otherwise be considered *nuda pacta*. In contrast, secular courts and juristic writing throughout the medieval period maintained that a *nudum pactum* was unenforceable, at least by a secular power. It was in the sixteenth century, however, that things changed. Across various jurisdictions, geographical locations, confessional divides and academic traditions, *nuda pacta* gained recognition as legally enforceable in non-ecclesiastical forums. In terms of timelines, Wim Decock observes that 'the Iberian Peninsula seems to have been the first place where the civilian tradition definitively managed to recreate itself in the image of the twin traditions of moral theology and canon law'[55] through its recognition of *nuda pacta* in secular courts and juristic writing. For example, in Navarra, the judge and jurist Fortunius Garcia (1494–1534) argued in a treatise published in Bologna in 1514[56] that an action can be raised in both civil and secular courts to enforce *nuda pacta*.[57] Or, for instance, Luis de Molina (1535–1600), working in Coimbra in the mid-sixteenth century, referred to the statutory rule of the *Ley Paresciendo* of Castile (c. 1484) as an example of secular enforcement of *nuda pacta*.[58] In the Southern Netherlands, Nicolas Everaerts (1461–1532), Matthaeus Wesenbecius (1531–86), and Petrus Gudelinus (1550–1619) are important figures too. As jurists, judges, and advocates, they offered a theoretical justification for a *nudum pactum*'s secular relevance, but also recorded the enforcement of *nuda pacta* in secular courts as a form of customary law.[59] Renowned for his practical approach to law, Everaerts was a jurist as well as the president of the *Grand Conseil of Malines*, the supreme court of the Southern Netherlands,[60] which assumed the jurisdiction of canon law along with civil matters and which is said to have enforced *nuda pacta*.[61] For instance, Gudelinus,

---

[55] Decock *Theologians* (n 31) 158.

[56] Decock *Theologians* (n 31) 158.

[57] Garcia repeated this in several places, including a treatise republished in 1585 in Cologne: Fortunius Garcia, *Tractus de Ultimo Fin Iuris Civilis et Canonici* (Apud Joannem Gymincum 1585) 164.

[58] Decock *Theologians* (n 31) 160–61.

[59] Klaus P Nanz, *Die Entstehung des allgemeinen Verstagsbegriffs im 16. bis 18. Jahrhundert* (Schweitzer 1985) 135–48; Feenstra 'Pact and Contract in the Low Countries' (n 26) 199; Decock *Theologians* (n 31) 155–56. Of note is that generally Lutheran theologians, when they considered contracting, strictly maintained the division between a pactum and a contract: Paolo Astorri, *Luther Theology and Contract Law in Early Modern Germany (ca. 1520—1720)* (Brill 2019) 118–19.

[60] Laurent Waelkens, *Amne Adverso: Roman Legal Heritage in European Culture* (Leuven University Press 2015) 114.

[61] See Paul van Christinaeus, *Practicarum Quaestionom Rerumque in Supremis Belgarum curiis Iudicatarum Observatarumque Volume II et III*, vol II (Hieronymus Verdussius 1626) decision 91. Paulus Christinaeus (1543–1631) was practising advocate of the Grand Conseil of Malines. It is highly likely that Scots lawyers, including Stair, would have been familiar with Gudelinus' and Christinaeus' method and the practice of the Grand Conseil: a 1671 edition of Christinaeus's text, along with another Christinaeus text, was held by the Advocates' Library in 1692 (Anon, *Catalogus Librorum Bibliothecae Juris Utriusque, tam Civilis Quam Canonici, Publici Quam Privati, Feudalis Quam Municipalis Variorum Regnorum, cum Historicis Graecis & Latinis, Literatis & Philosophis Plerisque Celebrioribus* (George Mosman 1692) 7). If

who was an advocate of the *Grand Conseil of Malines*, and also a jurist, remarked in his *Commentariorum* that 'today we are realistic about verbal obligations and do not need stipulation. For, although the verbal obligations agreed upon today are proposed bare, yet the obligation is effective, according to our customs for producing action; this comes from the Pontifical right and is transplanted into customs'.[62] Some years before, in 1568, Wesenbecius said much the same in his *Paratitla in Pandectarum iuris civilis libros quinquaginta*:[63] 'Still, it is common opinion and so it is observed in practice that today all agreements are indiscriminately actionable, even in the civil courts. I think this opinion is true and must be followed'.[64] In addition, Robert Feenstra stresses that the commentary by the French jurist and advocate of the Paris Parlement, Charles Du Moulin (1500–66), should not be overlooked.[65] After describing the approach of Roman law to pacts and stipulations, in his commentary on D 45 he said that 'today, in practice all these laws and theories are superfluous, because [...] the striking of an agreement and conclusion is allowable and not prohibited and no agreement is forbidden or deemed unfit as contract because it arises by an ineffective implementation of a stipulation, [...] so many long and painstaking Commentaries may be superfluous'.[66] Albeit slowly and somewhat unevenly, numerous secular courts in Europe began to enforce *nuda pacta* in the sixteenth and seventeenth centuries. Yet, despite this, no Scots lawyer before Stair had expressed or suggested that such a change had taken place or was practised by the customary law of Scotland.

Before Stair

Several secondary sources suggest that *nuda pacta* were enforceable, in practice if not juristically acknowledged, in Scotland before Stair, implying that in the late sixteenth century the only bar to enforcement was procedural rules relating to proof.[67] However, there is no definitive statement relating to *nuda pacta* in these cases until

---

Wesenbecius and Gudelinus represent a theoretical reflection on the practice of courts in the Southern Netherlands, Christinaeus represents the recording of it. His work and statement about the enforceability of a *nudum pactum* is often cited by later jurists; but, as Feenstra stresses, 'it is only a statement of Christinaeus' personal opinion on the subject'. He published several works recording the practice and decisions of the Grand Conseil of Mechlin and other local courts. See Feenstra, 'Pact and Contract in the Low Countries' (n 26) 203.

[62] Gudelinus, *Commentariorum* (n 50) III.V.

[63] Matthaeus Wesenbecius, *Paratitla in Pandectarum Iuris Civilis Libros Quinquaginta* (Basile 1568) 110. The 1665 Amsterdam edition of this was recorded in the 1692 catalogue of the Advocates' Library (Anon, *Catalogus* (n 61) 58). Lord Fountainhall's diary also records that he held a copy of this or an earlier edition in 1675 (Donald Crawford, *Journals of Sir John Lauder Lord Fountainhall with His Observations on Public Affairs and Other Memoranda 1665–1676* (Scottish History Society 1900), 291.

[64] I have used Decock's translation: Decock, *Theologians* 156–57.

[65] Feenstra, 'Pact and Contract in the Low Countries' (n 26) 203. The first edition of this title was published in 1562, quoted here: Charles Du Moulin, 'Nova et Analytica Explicatio Rvbr. et Leg. ...' in *Opera Quae Extant Omnia, Ex Variis Librorum Apothecis* (Apud viduam Mathvrini dv Pvis, via Iacobæ sub singno Coronae Aureæ 1658) IV, col 127–287.

[66] Du Molin 'Nova et Analytic' (n 65) col 134.

[67] Mackenzie Stuart 'Contract and Quasi-Contract' (n 12) 249; McBryde 'Promises in Scots Law' (n 2); Sellar 'Promise' (n 12) 261; Swain 'Contract as Promise' (n 2).

at least 1672, when Stair was directly involved in the decision.[68] That is significant in and of itself: no-one writing or commenting upon the law applying in Scotland, before Stair, had said that *nuda pacta per se* were enforceable in Scotland. However, the first place to start is the early 1630s case of *Sharp v Sharp*,[69] which is reported by Lord Durie in his practicks and referenced by Stair in his *Institutions* to support his statement regarding *nuda pacta*. Interestingly, this case demonstrates the influence of *ius commune* thinking with regard to *causa* but also that *nuda pacta*, if conceived as described above, were considered unenforceable at this time. *Sharp* confirms that, at this stage in Scotland, the mere consent of a party was not enough to create a legally recognizable obligation in Scotland, and that one needed to have a demonstrable *causa*.[70] The fact that the court said that Scotland no longer follows the 'doctors' with regard to innominate contracts only means to say that it was now the practice to focus upon the *causa* of the contract rather than the form. From this, one would think it is fair to generalize that *causa* was necessary to create an enforceable obligation in Scotland whether it be a bond, a contract or any other legal instrument.[71] Balfour and Hope confirm the concept's relevance in their respective treatises,[72] which is often repeated in the manuscripts produced by Scots lawyers in the mid-seventeenth century.[73]

Mackenzie Stuart, Sellar, and Lubbe also agree that based on *Sharp* and other cases from this period[74] it was the *ius commune* conception of *causa* which the Lords of Session drew from, rather than that of the legal humanist. *Sharp* would also suggest that concluding an onerous agreement in a written contract—signed and witnessed— was sufficient to satisfy the requirement to have a sufficient *causa*, which also fits with how mid-seventeenth-century lawyers wrote about *causa* in their manuscripts.[75] On this basis, the enforceability of an onerous executory contract in the early seventeenth century seems certain, so long as the contract was executed in a writ. Otherwise, most onerous transactions would have a demonstrable *causa*, such as sale, loan, hire, or part-performance of an obligation, and not necessarily require a writ. However, what *Sharp* does indicate is that the Court of Session was considering, albeit indirectly, the reason or basis of liability, rather than rejecting, on the basis of D 2.14.1, that *nuda pacta* were unenforceable: they wanted to know the cause of the liability, which for

---

[68] James Dalrymple, Viscount Stair, *Decisions of the Lords of Council and Session, in the Most Important Cases Debate before Them, from July 1671, to July 1681*, vol II (Andrew Anderson 1687) 51–52.

[69] Durie's *Practicks* 553–54 (Mor 4299 (1632)).

[70] Lubbe and Mackenzie Stuart share this conclusion: Gerhard Lubbe, 'Formation of Contract' in Kenneth Reid and Reinhard Zimmermann (eds), *A History of Private Law in Scotland* (OUP 2000) 13 and Mackenzie Stuart 'Contract and Quasi-Contract' (n 12) 250. Walker and Normand disagree: David M Walker, *A Legal History of Scotland, IV* (Tottel 2001) 704; Wilfrid G Normand, 'Consideration in the Law of Scotland' (1939) 55 Law Quarterly Review 359.

[71] See also: *Craw v Culbertson* Mor 12384 (1663); *Cheyne v Keith* Mor 12385 (1664).

[72] The understanding that a *nudum pactum* is an agreement without *causa* fits with what has already been noted with regard to both Hope (Hope *Major Practicks* 2.1.3) and Balfour (Balfour *Practicks* 149), who both mention *causa* in relation to contracts and also the argument made by Haddington in *Kintore* (*Kintore v Sinclair* (1623) Mor 9425). Hope's *Minor Practicks* (Alexander Bayne (ed), *Minor Practicks, or, a Treatise of the Scottish Law* (Thomas Ruddiman 1726) 142) offers further support for this understanding of *Sharp* (n 11).

[73] Adv Ms 24.3.2 f81; Adv Ms 24.2.3 f173; NLS Ms 943 f26; Adv Ms 24.1.3 f67.

[74] Mackenzie Stuart 'Contract and Quasi-Contract' (n 12) 250; Lubbe 'Formation' (n 70) 11; Sellar 'Promise' (n 12) 265.

[75] Adv Ms 24.3.2 f81; Adv Ms 24.2.3 f173; NLS Ms 943 f26; Adv Ms 24.1.3 f67.

Stair, of course, was the will of a party.[76] It appears, however, that, unlike Stair, they still drew upon the *ius commune* concept of *causa*, rather than the approach found in Stair whereby the will is said to be the *causa*.

Although no Scots lawyer would directly state that *nuda pacta* were enforceable, they would acknowledge numerous exceptions: for example, promises and informal agreements concluded in a commercial context between two merchants, and under the value of 100 pounds Scots, were enforceable in the period before Stair;[77] until 1639, promises or agreements fortified with an oath and not more than 40 pounds Scots could be brought to the commissary courts in Scotland;[78] and, importantly, promises or informal agreements could be legally relevant in instances of *rei interventus* and homologation.[79] In terms of the former, witness evidence was taken, if the value was under 100 pounds Scots, but in all other instances a writ was required in order to establish the existence of a legally binding promise or agreement. This raises the question as to whether a Scottish legal mind in the mid-seventeenth century would have seen these promises and informal agreements as creating an obligation or merely barring the other party from withdrawing from the promise or agreement. Although there are several examples of this recorded in various practicks, the fact that there is no reasoning and that these cases are procedural hearings about proof means it is difficult to draw too much from these cases. More generally, against the backdrop of juristic texts used by Scots lawyers in the mid-seventeenth century, such as Balfour, Hope, and Craig, who said that *nuda pacta* were unenforceable, and the decision in *Sharp*, a cautious lawyer would most probably have categorized these as exceptions to the general rule or would not necessarily have conceived of these decisions as demonstrating a customary practice. The status of *nuda pacta* during this period was in transition and that Scots would have been aware of the approach of other jurisdictions and the jurisdictional gap left by the closure of canon law courts. This leads to the question as to why Stair took the step he did and what motivated him to take this step.

Stair took the decisive step in two notable places. The first was in his early manuscripts of the *Institutions*, which circulated within the Faculty of Advocates in the 1660s. In these manuscripts, he announced that *nuda pacta* were now enforceable in a secular Scots court. The second step was in his report of the 1672 Court of Session decision in *Deuchar v Brown*, published by Stair in 1687. There Stair made the first clear indication in print that the Lords of Session considered *nuda pacta* to be enforceable.[80] Importantly, the report comes from Stair himself in the second volume of his *Decisions of the Lords of Council and Session* published in 1687.[81] There are several ways to explain why Stair took the decisive step and declared *nuda pacta* enforceable.

---

[76] Stair explains this conception of *causa* clearly in his report of *Deuchar v Brown*: Stair *Decisions of the Lords of Council and Session* (n 68) vol II, 51–52. Also see (1672) Mor 12386.

[77] James J Gow, 'Constitution and Proof of Voluntary Obligations' (1961) Juridical Review 1.

[78] Sellar, 'Promise' (n 12) 262–67.

[79] *Russell v Paterson* (1626) Mor 12383; *John Power v The Customers* (1626) Mor 83999; *Lord Gray v Graham* (1628) Mor 12382; *Oliphant v Monorgan* (1628) Mor 8400; *Keith v Dick and Gray* (1629) Mor 12383; *A v B* (1629) Mor 8400; *Ernock v Preston* (1636) Mor 12383; *Lillie v Laird of Innerleith* (1636) Mor 12383; *Keith v Johnston's Tenants* (1636) Mor 8400; *Lillie v Laird of Innerleith* (1636) Mor 12383; *Skeen v???* (1637) Mor 8401; *Craw v Culbertson* (1663) Mor 12384.

[80] Stair, *Decisions of the Lords of Council and Session* (n 68) vol II, 51–52. Also see (1672) Mor 12386.

[81] (1672) Mor 12386; Stair, *Decisions of the Lords of Council and Session* (n 68) 51–52.

On first appearances, it would be tempting to say that Stair was Lord President of the Court of Session in 1672 and simply decided the case contrary to existing law and the understanding of most advocates in Parliament House. Another possibility is that Stair framed matters the way he wanted them to be understood and contrary to how it was actually argued in *Deuchar*.[82] Consequently, on such a reading, Stair was involved more directly with the development of Scots law, putting into practice the ideas and interpretation of conventional obligations which he had written about in the early 1660s and managing the reception and reporting of this case himself. In that sense, Stair's method of innovation was that of a jurist who became a law-reforming judge. Alternatively, it could be argued that Stair's manuscript of the *Institutions* circulated around the Faculty of Advocates from 1662 and that it initiated a change in contractual thought within the Faculty and the College of Justice, subsequently influencing the arguments made in *Deuchar* and the eventual decision in that case. Of course, it is not possible to prove this with any certainty, but what is known is that Stair's manuscript was part of a body of literature, including, for example, Gudelinus's *Commentariorum*, Vinnius's *Commentary*, and Grotius's *The Rights of War and Peace*, which circulated within the legal profession in Scotland, suggesting that *nuda pacta* and promises were now enforceable according to the customs of most nations. On this analysis, Stair's method is that of a learned jurist articulating the law, which is then received into the practice of customary law. However, Stair would not have described what happened in *Deuchar* in these terms, nor would he have understood his role as a jurist and judge in this manner.

Calvinist Natural Law Theory

Standing to the faith of our pactions

Although the foregoing may offer some possible legal explanations, it does not fully capture the theological motivations and philosophical disposition which Stair displays in the *Institutions* or the *Divine Perfections*, nor for that matter the high-minded religious and moral context of mid- to late seventeenth-century Scotland. In the *Institutions*, Stair said he wished to demonstrate the equity inherent within the positive law in Scotland and its nearness to the natural law, which for him was the Moral Law of God and the principles that have been written on the hearts of men.[83] He set out to trace the law practised in Scotland back to common principles shared amongst nations. But, also, he wanted to demonstrate how the individual rules of law in

---

[82] He says in the epistle to the first volume of his *Decisions* that 'Neither have I recorded any decisions but what was determined while I was present, being resolved to take nothing at the second hand': James Dalrymple, Viscount Stair, *Decisions of the Lords of Council and Session, in the Most Important Cases Debate before Them, from July 1671, to July 1681*, vol I (Andrew Anderson 1683). And he also says there: 'I had the best opportunity to make these observations, being scarce a day absent in any of these Session wherein I have marked them from the first of June 1661 until the first of August 1681. And I was not one day absent from the thirteenth of January 1671 ... ': Stair *Decisions*. James Dalrymple, Viscount Stair, *The Decisions of the Lords of Council & Session, in the Most Important Cases Debate before Them with the Acts of Sederunt*, vol I (Andrew Anderson 1681) vii.

[83] Stair *Inst* 1.1.3–7.

Scotland related to these fundamental principles of natural law. Although his audience may have been primarily legal, in his printed editions he makes clear that he wishes to show to 'persons of honour and discretion' the 'fountains and principles of the peculiar laws of all nations, which reason makes intelligible to the judicious'.[84] He wished to reveal that the law of Scotland, like that of other nations, was based upon common principles, and that these were Christian principles.[85] For him, Roman law could be improved upon and should not be looked upon with undue reverence.[86] Rather, Stair approved of Roman law only when it was equitable. Conscience and reason, directed by the Moral Law, would guide a decision-maker as to whether Roman law should be followed or not. There was, for Stair, 'nothing more natural, than to stand to the faith of our pactions'[87]—and this was the common principle upon which the law of conventional obligations in Scotland was based, as also the common law of nations.[88] Importantly, he wished to demonstrate that the law of Scotland followed, in this regard, the canon law. Stair makes minimal reference to canon law in the *Institutions*, and it is significant, therefore, that when he does it is an aspect of canon law which is evidently based on a Scriptural reference and a rudimentary moral principle or virtue. Grounding the law of conventional obligations upon a basic moral principle, recognizable in terms of Scripture, church doctrine and mid-seventeenth-century notions of virtue, is a central aim for Stair, and this is shaped by his Calvinist-influenced theory of natural law.

Pactions and promises in the *Divine Perfections*

The theological significance of this basic principle, which Stair places at the root of his account of obligations, is demonstrated by the fact that Stair discusses promise-keeping and standing by pactions in the *Divine Perfections*. Opening mediation XIV 'Upon the Justice of God', Stair says there is a special instance of God's goodness which is manifested within man, namely justice. He says: 'I know the Justice of God by the Light of Nature, from an inbred Principle of the naturel Conscience, shewing me that I ought to be just: Justice is implied in the Conception of a Deity'.[89] After discussing man's natural knowledge of justice, he says: 'man could not live in the World, or converse with Men, if he had not the natural knowledge of Justice; he could neither know what he ought to give, nor what he ought to crave, what he should encourage, nor what he should discourage'.[90] Stair then speaks of three types of justice: attributive, distributive, and judicial. He explains: 'Attributive Justice is the giving to every rational Being that which is their own, by allowing them to enjoy whatsoever they have that is their own, not enjoyed and possessed by them; under which are comprehended all

---

[84] Stair *Inst* 1.1.

[85] James Dalrymple, Viscount Stair, *Institutions of the Law of Scotland* (Andrew Anderson, 1st edn, 1681) 15.

[86] Stair *Inst* 1.1.16.

[87] Stair *Inst* 1.1.18.

[88] Stair *Inst* 1.1.

[89] Stair *Divine Perfections* 181.

[90] Stair *Divine Perfections* 182.

Obligations to do or perform, whether by Paction or Promise, or by law of a Superior Power.'[91] Explaining why he uses the term 'attributive' rather than the more familiar term 'commutative' justice, he says it is 'chiefly exercised in exchanging of Deeds and Things; but the Term is too narrow to express the Thing'. He describes this as 'a chief Branch whereof is the allowing others to enjoy their own without Molestation; which is properly expressed by Innocence, that is, doing them no Hurt, neither in this nor in the performance of Promises, when there is no other Cause; or even in the restoring the Goods of others, is there anything of Commutation'.[92] It is notable that Stair says man knows he should perform his promises and pactions due to justice, which is an innate principle, and something man knows without reasoning. Stair describes justice as an attribute of God, which is reflected in man and is necessary for man to live in community.

Calvin's approach to natural law

The epistemological idea that natural law, including principles that we should perform our contracts and promises, is innate within man's nature and known without reasoning can be found in Calvin. In his *Commentaries on the Epistle of Paul the Apostle to the Romans*,[93] which would have been well known to Scots in the mid-seventeenth century, Calvin gives his clearest exposition of his approach to natural law. In reference to Romans 2:14–15, Calvin says that God did not think it was enough to 'condemn [man] by mere assertion and only to pronounce on us the just judgment of God; but he proceeds to prove this by reasons, in order to excite us to a greater desire for Christ, and to a greater love towards him'.[94] He goes on to claim that 'ignorance is in vain pretended as an excuse by the Gentiles, since they prove by their own deeds that they have some role of righteousness: for there is no nation so lost to everything human, that it does not keep within the limits of some laws'.[95] Speaking of nations' laws, he says 'it is beyond evident that they [nations] have some justice and rectitude, which the Greeks called preconceptions ... and which are implanted by nature in the hearts of men'.[96] Calvin then alludes to what has been implanted, saying all 'the Gentiles alike instituted religious rites, they made laws to punish adultery, and theft, and murder, they commended good faith in bargains and contracts'. He explains the role of conscience, saying that whether someone is a Jew or Gentile, God 'could not have more forcibly urged them than by the testimony of their own conscience, which is equal to a thousand witnesses'. For Calvin, it does not matter whether you are a pagan or Christian or otherwise: provided you are a human, you will have implanted

---

[91] Stair *Divine Perfections* 183.

[92] Stair *Divine Perfections* 183.

[93] John Owen (ed), *Commentaries on the Epistle of Paul the Apostle to the Romans* (Calvin Translation Society 1849).

[94] Owen *Commentaries on the Epistle of Paul* (n 93) 96.

[95] Owen *Commentaries on the Epistle of Paul* (n 93) 96.

[96] Owen *Commentaries on the Epistle of Paul* (n 93) 96–97. N.B. Contrast the Calvinist quasi-physiological or anthropological description of morality with the Biblical and rational approach taken by Lutherans. For an account of Lutheran approaches, see Paolo Asttori, *Lutheran Theology and Contract Law in Early Modern Germany (ca. 1520—1720)* (Brill 2019) 186–207.

basic principles according to which you can determine the basics of right conduct. In offering this account of natural law, Calvin separates the Moral Law of God from the Biblical precepts and makes man's conscience a direct means by which man's behaviour is judged. In reference to the latter position, Backus suggests that it is this which distinguishes a Calvinist approach to natural law from that of a Thomist approach, where conscience is conceived in terms of *conscientia* and *synderesis*. In this regard, Stair's account of the origins of the basic principles of natural law, which underpin justice, and which form the foundation of civil laws in both the *Institutions* and the *Divine Perfections*, is Calvinist. Arguably, this approach is also what separates Stair's approach to Roman law sources in comparison to Lutherans, who would otherwise suppose Roman law was God-given[97] or an embodiment of equity and learning.[98] It is also this attitude which helps explain why Stair's approach to conventional obligations differs from that of Grotius and other natural law writers of the early modern period.

Stair, Grotius, and virtue

If the enforcement of a *nudum pactum* is based upon an innate principle of man's nature, what is the basis of its obligatoriness: God or man's nature? Is it virtue or utility? Law or morality? Stair addresses this question in the *Institutions*, saying: 'let us inquire whether promises or naked paction are morally obligatory by the law of Nature.'[99] The opinion of François de Connan or Franciscus Connanus (1508–51), he notes, is to the contrary: 'where there is not equivalent cause onerous intervening', there is no moral obligation arising. Grotius addressed this question in *The Rights of War and Peace* in 1625,[100] and Wilson suggests that Stair took his knowledge of Connanus from that discussion.[101] Grotius's argument with Connanus begins on the basis that treaties between nations would be unenforceable if they were only binding after performance or transfer of a thing. This, of course, is a crucial tenet of Grotius's overall aim to establish a law of nations, but he develops this political angle by arguing that society itself is a common covenant of people. He asks how this covenant could be binding if performance or the transfer of a thing was necessary first.

After making these broader political points, Grotius uses a property law analogy in much the same way as the late scholastics,[102] and in a fashion similar to that of Stair.[103]

---

[97] For example, see Martin Bucer's commentary on Romans: Irena Backus, 'Bucer's View of the Roman and Canon Law in his Exegetical Writings and in his Patristic Florilegium' in Christoph Strohm and Henning P Jürgens (eds), *Martin Bucer und das Recht* (Droz 2002) 83–100.

[98] For example, see Philip Melanchthon's various orations and commentaries: James Q Whitman, *The Legacy of Roman Law in the German Romantic Era* (Princeton University Press 1990) 1–40. For a fuller discussion of the Lutheran theological approach to contract, and particularly their conceptualization of contracts, see Astorri *Lutheran Theology and Contract Law* (n 96) 113–51.

[99] Stair *Inst* 1.10.10.

[100] Stair *Inst* 1.10 ('For it is the will of the owner, that naturally transferreth right from him to the acquirer; so in person rights, that freedom we have of disposal of ourselves, our actions and things, which naturally is in us, is by our engagement placed in another, and so engagement is a diminution of freedom …').

[101] Wilson 'Sources and Method' (n 7).

[102] cf Wim Decock, Wim Decock, 'Jesuit Freedom of Contract' (2009) 77 Tijdschrift voor Rechtsgeschiedenis 423, 436.

[103] Stair *Inst* 1.10.

He says it is of course possible in property law to transfer a thing by 'the bare will' of a man; if the bare will of a man is sufficient to transfer property, then why, asks Grotius, is the will not sufficient to transfer the power over our actions? However, it is here that one finds the crucial difference between Stair and Grotius. Nothing is more 'agreeable', according to Grotius, 'to human Fidelity, as to observe whatsoever has been mutually agreed upon'.[104] He thereafter quotes classical sources, such as Paulus and Cicero, who both acknowledge the value of adhering to one's word.[105] This approach is important because Grotius's theory of natural law differs from Stair through its emphasis upon the rational and social nature of man. Thus, when man performs his promise, he is acting in accordance with natural law and he is doing so according to his own will. In the same manner that Aristotle called a virtuous action—such as promise-keeping—an action whereby the desire and reason of man act together, Grotius too was ascribing right action to man based on his own free will.

Stair's approach is different. He responds to Connanus, firstly, by citing canon law, saying that it 'insinuates an anterior reason to its own position', and suggesting that it is evidently based on natural law, but also quoting from the *Digest*, where it says 'there is nothing ... so congruous to humane trust, as to perform what is agreed among them'. Stair wants to demonstrate that it is not because of some sense of *quid pro quo* that men perform their obligations, but due to God's design and its innateness in man's nature. Secondly, through citation of several Biblical passages, the *Digest*, canon law, and other sources, Stair wishes to show that this moral principle is acknowledged across different nations and at different times because, again, it is inherent in the nature of men to know this proposition. As Hogg points out, the citation of these Biblical verses is more than window-dressing. Both of these references stress that, in making a promise, one is making a promise to God.[106] Stair thereafter repeats Grotius's argument, which might be categorized as latently endorsing a utility-based justification: that is, if promises and agreements were not morally binding, 'then all pactions and agreements among nations would be ineffectual, and all commerce and society among men should be destroyed'.[107] However, in comparing Grotius and Stair and considering their respective engagement with notions of virtue, Hogg has made the important observation that Stair did not place the moral obligatoriness of a promise or contract upon the virtue of commutative justice or promise-keeping. Nor, as argued above, does Stair wish to say that our natural instincts alone, without God, tell us that we should perform promises, contracts, pacts, and so on. As Hogg has pointed out, Stair says that by creating a conventional obligation one gives the 'liberty in our power, that we may give it up to others, or restrain and ingage it, whereby God obliges us to performance, by mediation of our own will; yet such Obligations, as to their Original, are conventional, not obediential'.[108] In no place does Stair suggest that man acts virtuously or rightly when he performs a paction or promise. Aristotle did, however, and Grotius did too. Man does it according to his nature, which God has written on his

---

[104] Hugo Grotius, *The Rights of War and Peace* (first published 1625, Liberty Fund 2005) 2.11.4.
[105] Grotius *The Rights of War* (n 104) 2.11.4.
[106] Hogg *Promises and Contract Law* (n 2) 142.
[107] This is also, one might add, reminiscent of Hobbes and latterly Locke. See Neil MacCormick, *Legal Right and Social Democracy: Essays in Legal and Political Philosophy* (OUP 1984) Ch 4.
[108] Stair *Inst* 1.10.

heart and through obedience. That is, because Stair's approach is shaped by a Calvinist understanding of virtue and human nature, credit could not be given to man himself, as glory was due to God. Performing a promise or virtue was adhering to the law written on man's heart and carrying out the justice which God has willed, and therefore the performance is an act of obedience.

Calvin said that it is 'beyond dispute, that free will does not enable any man to perform good works, unless he is assisted by grace',[109] and he goes on to say 'no will is free which has not been made so by divine grace ... that the righteousness of God is not fulfilled when the law orders, and man acts, as it were, by his own strength, but when the Spirit assists, and the will (not the free will of man, but the will freed by God) obeys'.[110] It will be recalled that Aristotelian ethics placed value upon choosing rightly. This is what is virtuous, the decision to act virtuously without hesitation or compulsion. According to Aristotle, when someone performs a virtuous action, they should receive praise; the man who chooses rightly should be praised. However, in the context of Calvinism, a virtuous action is not something which man is capable of. Man is 'devoid of all uprightness', and he 'cannot arrogate anything, however minute, to himself without robbing God of his honour'.[111] Calvin corrects the 'Philosophers' who 'set it down as beyond dispute, that virtue and vice are in our own power. For (say they), If it is in our choice to do this thing or that, it must also be in our choice not to do it ... if we do good when we please, we can also refrain from doing it; if we commit evil, we can also shun the commission of it (Aristot. lib. iii. c.5).'[112]

Performing a promise or a contract could not be deemed a virtuous act if Stair were to offer a theory in line with Calvinist orthodoxy. Man could only act virtuously through God's grace. In this light, Stair's statement at the beginning of title 10 becomes less obscure. Stair said that God has given man liberty so that 'we may give it up to other, or restrain and engage it, whereby God obliges us to performance, by mediation of our own will; yet such obligations, as to their original, are conventional'.[113] It follows, then, that when man performs a conventional obligation it is not only out of an obligation to God, but also because God tells man to perform this obligation. No praise or credit should be given to man for doing so. Man performed his conventional obligations because of God's natural law, his Biblical teaching and his direct instructions to man. It was this philosophical understanding of man's moral apparatus and a theological interpretation of the law applying to contracting behaviour which contributed to Stair's confidence that the approach of Roman law should no longer be followed in Scotland. There is, however, an additional social context to Stair's statement that *nuda pacta* are enforceable. That is, Stair's philosophical and theological understanding of

---

[109] Calvin *Inst* 2.2.6.

[110] Calvin *Inst* 2.2.8.

[111] Calvin *Inst* 2.2.1.

[112] Calvin *Inst* 2.2.3.

[113] Stair *Inst* 1.10. A very similar approach was taken by Melanchthon and other Lutheran theologians, as described by Astorri: performance was mediated through or orchestrated by the Holy spirit. Yet it appears that Stair was, in contrast to Lutherans, far more prepared to acknowledge a Grotian natural law basis rather than solely scriptural basis of contractual fidelity. For Astorri's description of Lutheran approaches, see Astorri *Lutheran Theology and Contract Law* (n 96) 188–94.

promise-keeping and *nuda pacta* could also be explained by motivations arising from the context of the National Covenant of 1638.

The National Covenant of 1638

It might be worth making clear that, in the mid-seventeenth century, a great deal of moral, political, and theological literature which circulated in Scotland stressed the fundamental importance of promise-keeping and performing one's contracts.[114] Firstly, as Chapter 7 explains, Scots theologians, ministers, and the Church gave very clear and direct guidance to the laity with regard to an individual's personal ethics, including to stand by the faith of their pactions. Indeed, one of the most important expressions of Church of Scotland doctrine in the mid-seventeenth century, *The Larger Catechism of the Westminster Confession of Faith*, was designed to instruct the laity. It said: 'The duties required in the eighth commandment, are truth, faithfulness, and justice in contract, and commerce between man and man.'[115] Another example is commentaries upon Scripture. Thus, James Fergusson (1621–67),[116] a contemporary of Stair whilst a student, who was later appointed Professor of Divinity in 1660,[117] extrapolated upon verse 8 of Paul's letter to the Philippians, saying:[118]

> Christians ought to consider, and accordingly to perform what things are just, that is, whatever we are bound to do unto others, whether to God or man, Matth. 22.21. whether by the Law of Nature 1 Tim. 5.8. or of Nations, Ruth 3.13. by reason of our place or station, Heb. 6.11. whether things we owe be determined by action, as such a sum of money, or so much grain, Col. 4.1, or onely to be determined according to the rules of prudence, equity, or charity, Col. 4.1. whether it be fear or honour, Rom. 13.7. good will, Rom. 13.8 or somewhat further; so as none be defraud of that which he willeth them to think upon.

This spiritual teaching about the morality of contracting was often mixed with political and theological aims. From a political perspective, Samuel Rutherford (1600–61) discusses whether a king is bound by his promises or covenants to 'defend true Protestant Religion'. Rutherford does so by appealing to Scripture, saying that Proverbs 6:1 is clear: 'faith it is by a word and striking of hands, by a word of promise

---

[114] Indeed, there is a good example of the high moral status that both promise-keeping and adhering to agreements had for seventeenth-century Scots found within the unpublished moral treatise of Stair's friend James Dundas, Lord Arniton (c1619–79). Although unpublished and presently held within a private collection, Broadie gives an insightful overview, particularly of Dundas's reflections on Regulus's return to Carthage: Alexander Broadie, 'James Dundas on the Hobbesian State of Nature' (2013) 11 (1) The Journal of Scottish Philosophy 1–13. See also, Giovanna Gellera, *The Philosophy of James Dundas* (Edinburgh University Press forthcoming).

[115] (London 1655) 135.

[116] William G Blaikie, 'Ferguson, James (1621–1667)' in *Oxford Dictionary of National Biography*, vol 18 (Smith, Elder & Co 1885–1900).

[117] Although, following Restoration, he never actually took up the post at Glasgow.

[118] James Fergusson, *A Brief Exposition of the Epistles of Paul to the Philippians and Colossians* (Christopher Higgins 1656) 109.

and covenant. Now the Creditor hath coactive power, though he be an equall or an inferior to the man who is surety, even by law to force him to pay, and the Judge is obliged to give his coactive power to the Creditor, that he may force the surety to pay.'[119] In a similar vein, in 1649, George Gillespie considered the legitimacy of the Solemn League and Covenant entered into between the Scottish and English Parliaments in 1643. Reflecting on the Engagement crisis, when Scotland became divided between anti-Engagers and Engagers, his consideration of promise-keeping had very practical political consequences. Asking the general question of 'whether a confederacy and association with wicked men, or such as are of another Religion be lawfull', Gillespie makes clear that he is against the Engagement.[120] Thus he answers 'no' but does add the qualification if they are civil Covenants 'for commerce or peace ... they are allowed according to the Scriptures, Gen. 14.13., Gen. 31.44.1., Kings 5.12., Jer. 29.7., and Rom. 12.18. Such Covenants also Christian Emperors of old, had sometimes with pagans.'[121] Later, he explains: 'And here is the Reason why Covenants of peace and commerce, even with infidels and wicked persons are allowed, yet military associations with such, disallowed: for the former keeps them, and still divided as two: the latter unites us and them, as one and imbodieth us together with them.'[122]

Much has been written about the creation, significance, and importance of the National Covenant of 1638 to Scottish national identity, the subsequent Civil Wars, and the development of Scottish Protestant culture.[123] Stair would have certainly signed it himself. Moreover, the religious and political culture within which Stair wrote the *Institutions* was animated by discussions about the significance and nature of the National Covenant. Two things may be noted for present purposes. First, the theology surrounding the National Covenant placed a profound importance on the justice and morality of promise-keeping and covenanting or contracting. Moreover, covenant or federal theology, which dominated Scottish theological writing throughout the seventeenth century, not only used the language and notion of promises, covenants, and pactions, but did so in a legalistic manner. Such theology explored the idea that God had entered into a personal covenant with individuals, promising salvation.[124] Indeed, later theologians have argued that mid-seventeenth-century theologians misused the

---

[119] Samuel Rutherford, *A Treatise of Civil Policy: Being a Resolution of Forth three Questions Concerning Prerogative, Right and Privilege* (Simon Miller at the Star in St Paul's Church-yard near the West End 1656) 400.

[120] George Gillespie, *A Treatise of Miscellany Questions wherein Many Useful Questions and Cases of Conscience are Discussed and Resolved* (Thomas Whitaker 1649) 169.

[121] Gillespie *Questiones* (n 120) 169.

[122] Gillespie *Questiones* (n 120) 182.

[123] For example, see Arthur H Williamson, *Scottish National Consciousness in the Age of James VI* (John Donald 1979); Jenny Wormald, *Lords and Men in Scotland: Bonds of Manrent* (John Donald 1985) 1442–603; Jane E A Dawson, 'Bonding, Religious Allegiance and Covenanting' in Julian Goodare and Steve I Boardman (eds), *Lords and Men in Scotland, 1300–1625* (Edinburgh University Press 2014) 155–72; Laura A M Stewart, *Rethinking the Scottish Revolution* (OUP 2016).

[124] For example, see James Durham and David Dickson, *The Sum of Saving Knowledge* (Anon 1605); Samuel Rutherford, *The Covenant of Life: or A Treatise of the Covenant of Grace* (Andrew Anderson 1654); Patrick Gillespie, *The Ark of the Testament Opened, or ... a Treatise of the Covenant of Grace* (Anon 1655); Patrick Gillespie, *The Ark of the Covenant Opened; or, A Treatise of the Covenant of Redemption* (Anon 1677); James Durham, *A Commentarie upon the Book of Revelation* (Christopher Higgins 1658).

legal language and ideas of contracting and promising, which in turn undermined their theological aims.[125] Whatever the case, a second point should be emphasized. Covenant theology represented, in theory, the revitalization of a direct relationship between the individual parishioner and God. Furthermore, the promulgation of the National Covenant around the country in the years that followed, with many swearing to its terms or signing it, involved a practical act undertaken by not just clergy, nobility, and lairds, but also the rank-and-file laity of Scotland. In the 1640s, every parishioner was expected to either sign a copy of the National Covenant or promise to adhere to its terms.[126] The theology of the National Covenant stressed an individual relationship between God and any man, woman, and child in Scotland, which was not filtered through priest, bishop, pope, or the king. In practice, it was represented by a renewal of faith—and, importantly, this was expressed in the language of promise, oath, vow, or covenant.[127] Stewart has explained how the National Covenant was part of a political strategy to involve men and women from outside the governing elite in the larger power struggle between the Church of Scotland, the Scots nobility, and Charles I. She has shown how many Scots' encounters with the Covenant would have been auricular during private or public meetings, rather than in written form. But also, 'the exhaustive forms of media in which the Covenant circulated during the 1640s gave it a ubiquity that was probably unmatched by any other text in the Reformation century except catechisms and New Testaments. Covenants were everywhere in 1638.'[128] Many Scots did sign it, perhaps thousands. Throughout the seventeenth century, the obligations of the Covenant were debated. For many, the interpretation, effectiveness, and meaning of the National Covenant determined whether they could engage with the church and state. Despite the vagueness and continuing debates about the National Covenant, it is clear that most Scots were encouraged to see their relationship with God as being shaped in some way by an individual contract. Against this background, Stair's confidence to take the final step and declare the enforceability of *nuda pacta* could be said to correlate with the wider political, religious, and social context of mid-seventeenth-century Scotland.[129]

---

[125] James B Torrance, 'The Contribution of McLeod Campbell to Scottish Theology' (1973) 26 (3) Scottish Journal of Theology 295–311. Torrance, however, as Stair's *Institutions* demonstrate, and this chapter shows, is probably wrong about the meaning of promise and covenant within Scots law during the mid-seventeenth century.

[126] David Stevenson, 'The National Covenant: A List of Known Copies' (1988) 23 Records of the Scottish Church History Society 255–99; Laura A M Stewart, *Urban Politics and the British Civil Wars: Edinburgh, 1617–53* (Brill 2006) 236; Laura A M Stewart, 'Authority, Agency and the Reception of the Scottish National Covenant of 1638' in Robert Armstrong and Tadhg Ó hAnnracháin (eds), *Insular Christianity: Alternative Models of the Church in Britain and Ireland, c.1570–1700* (OUP 2013) 88.

[127] David G Mullan, *Scottish Puritanism, 1590–1638* (OUP 2000) 171–207.

[128] Stewart *Rethinking the Scottish Revolution* (n 123) 116–17.

[129] In the *Divine Perfections*, Stair discusses man's covenant with God stating that the covenant is created by an act of the will of man, albeit generated by God. See James Dalrymple, Viscount Stair, *A Vindication of the Divine Perfections: Illustrating the Glory of God in Them by Reason and Revelation: Methodically Digested Into Several Mediations* (Brabazon Aylmer 1695) 323–25.

Conclusion

Taking the step of declaring a *nudum pactum* to be enforceable was a significant development both historically and theoretically. Promises, verbal agreements or informal written agreements are natural ways by which people interact, build relationships, coordinate actions, and exchange services or goods. Often, however, in legal history these types of interaction are understood to be instances of *nuda pacta* due, in part, to some lack of written or external formality. Additionally, those who make a verbal or informal agreement envisage this to be binding, at least socially and morally, from the moment of formation even if performance or fulfilment of the promise or agreement is potentially delayed until a future date. However, this sort of transaction is known to a lawyer as an executionary obligation, and the agreement or promise about future performance or fulfilment of the agreement or promise is no more than a *nudum pactum*.[130] Further, in comparison to a *quid pro quo* sense of liability found in the common law conception of consideration or the preconfigured modes of liability found in Roman law, the enforcement of a *nudum pactum* does not require an exchange of things or services or an externalization in a physical transfer of a thing or money. Largely, therefore, the enforcement of a *nudum pactum* can evidence a more abstract—in the sense of non-corporeal—and generalized understanding of liability, namely that a mental element, such as consent or the will of parties, is the source of liability. Conversely, defining liability in terms of a promise or the will of parties may also mean that a wider range of factors or *indicia* are acknowledged as legally relevant, in contrast to, for instance, some prefigured legal act, such as a stipulation.[131] Moreover, from a practical point of view, if a system enforces *nuda pacta*, this leads to vital questions: how does one prove a verbal promise if the promisor recants? Or how do you substantiate the agreement of parties? What is the significance of legal formalities? How does one ensure that parties' intentions and consent are not misconstrued or misrepresented? In other words, it can require the introduction of new evidentiary procedures or a relaxation of existing rules premised on the idea that *nuda pacta* are unenforceable. The enforcement of *nuda pacta* can also be indicative of a moralization of the law of contracting, with ethical or religious notions of proper behaviour being read into or transposed into legal rules or doctrine.[132] Therefore, it is a significant development not only historically but also from the perspective of contractual thought.

Shifts in the Scottish legal thinking regarding enforcement of the *nuda pacta*, is first noticeable in the early manuscripts of Stair's *Institutions* and then in his 1683 report of the case of *Deuchar*. Although it is possible to suggest that *nuda pacta* were in effect enforced in Scotland before Stair wrote, this chapter has sought to explain why it was Stair who made the initial step. Taking Stair's philosophical understanding of man's innate moral faculties, namely his conscience, alongside his theological understanding

---

[130] That is, a voluntary obligation which is enforceable before either party has performed: Patrick Atiyah, *The Rise and Fall of the Freedom of Contract* (OUP 1979) 2–7.

[131] In regard to the early modern period, this is generally associated with the emergence of natural law theories: David Ibbetson, 'Natural Law and Common Law' (2001) 5 Edinburgh Law Review 4, 6.

[132] Patrick Atiyah, *Promises, Morals and Law* (OUP 1983) 4–5; Hogg 'Promises: The Neglected Obligation' (n 2) 461–79.

that performing pactions, promises, and contracts is an act of obedience, it becomes possible to offer an explanation within the intellectual context of mid-seventeenth-century Scotland, showing in addition that aspects of Stair's thought are unique in contrast to his contemporaries and transcend his milieu. Particularly of note is the strong sense that performing promises is unrelated to the acceptance or the reliance of another party. It is this context which helps frame the theoretical and historical significance of Stair's statement and its importance to his overall project, whereby he could demonstrate the connection between the law practised in Scotland and the Moral Law found in man's conscience. It could therefore be suggested that the Calvinist context of Scotland and Stair's philosophical background contributed to this juristic development and to the contractual thought of Scotland more generally. A Calvinist understanding of the virtue and the morality of promise-keeping helped shape Stair's original approach and so laid the ground for a key doctrine of contemporary Scots contract law that comparative lawyers often remark upon: namely, that a promise is enforceable with the knowledge or acceptance of the other party. It has also been shown to aptly fit with the wider social, political, and religious context of Scotland following the creation of the National Covenant. Stating that a *nuda pacta* is enforceable emerged from Stair's strong sense of man's natural moral duty, to stand by the faith of pactions, including, for him, promises, which was uttered against the intellectual and social background of Scotland's religious and political revolution. The consequence of this statement was that even if the other party did not know you had promised to benefit them, or had necessarily accepted the promise, you were still bound by your combined moral and legal duty to perform that promise. This rule, shorn of its seventeenth-century philosophy, is still recognized in modern Scots law.[133]

---

[133] *Regus (Maxim) Ltd v Bank of Scotland Plc* 2013 SC 331, 338; *Carlyle v Royal Bank of Scotland Plc* [2015] UKSC 13, paras 25, 29. Martin Hogg, 'Perspectives on Contract Theory from a Mixed Jurisdiction' (2009) 29 (3) Oxford Journal of Legal Studies 643.

5

Stair's 'Plain Method' and Structure

In writing the *Institutions of the Law of Scotland* (*Institutions*), Stair was very much aware of his style and method.[1] Additionally, he demonstrates a very keen desire for an apt structure or system around which the private law of Scotland, including the law applicable to contracting behaviour, could be arranged.[2] Self-consciously, he explained in several places that the organization, presentation, and structure of his description of the law in Scotland was important.[3] In contrast to contemporary legal writing in Scotland, this self-consciousness is notable and makes clear that Stair had a deliberate purpose when it came to his structure and the arrangement of material.[4] Of course, for centuries, lawyers were aware of the significance of structure and the invariable tendency of law to become or appear unorganized,[5] but what is particularly noticeable is that Stair does not follow the established patterns found in mid-seventeenth century legal writing. This has a marked effect on how he explains, understands, and arranges the law of conventional obligations; and, importantly, it continues to inform modern-day taxonomical discussions in Scotland.[6] Although the structure and style of Stair's *Institutions* is something which has been commented upon within the secondary literature,[7] it is the intention of this chapter to suggest some other possible sources of inspiration for Stair's style and to pursue further the philosophical and theological

---

[1] eg Stair, *Inst* Dedication (2nd edn, 1693) 1.1; 1.1.17; 1.1.23. Additionally, Ford has noted that some near-contemporaries of Stair referred to early manuscripts of the *Institutions*, which contained Stair's account of voluntary obligations, as '*System iuris*' or 'Stair's Systeme', demonstrating that it was not just Stair who was conscious of his style. Ford remarks that two—not necessarily exclusive—senses were given to the term 'system' in the seventeenth century, one referring to things connected together and the other being a design of principles and conclusions: John D Ford, *Law and Opinion in Scotland during the Seventeenth Century* (Hart 2007) 87. See John Lauder, Lord Fountainhall, who refers to 'Stair's system' in 1677: David Laing (ed), *Historical Notices of Scottish Affairs, Selected from the Manuscripts of Sir John Lauder of Fountainhall, Bart.*, vol 1 (Bannatyne Club 1848) 134.

[2] Stair *Inst* 1.1.23.

[3] Stair *Inst* 1.1; 1.1.17; 1.1.23.

[4] There are no similar comments found in Craig, Balfour, or Hope, for example.

[5] Alan Watson, *The Making of the Civil Law* (Harvard University Press 1981); Peter Stein, 'Legal Humanism and Legal Science' (1986) 54 (2) The Legal History Review 297–306; Peter Stein, 'The Quest for a Systematic Civil Law' (1995) 90 Proceedings of the British Academy 147–64; Peter Birks, 'Definition and Divisions: A Meditation on Institutes 3.13' in Peter Birks (ed), *The Classification of Obligations* (OUP 1997) 1–36.

[6] eg Martin Hogg, 'Perspectives on Contract Theory from a Mixed Legal System' (2009) 29 (4) Oxford Journal of Legal Studies 643–73.

[7] Archibald H Campbell, *The Structure of Stair's Institutions* (Jackson, Son & Co 1954); Peter Stein, 'The Fate of the Institutional System' in Johann van de Westhuizen and Johann Van der Westhuizen (eds), *Huldigingsbundle Paul van Warmelo* (Universiteit van Suid-Afrika 1984) 218–27; David M Walker, 'The Structure and Arrangement of the *Institutions*' in David M Walker (ed), *Stair Tercentenary Studies*, vol 33 (Stair Society 1981) 100–06; John D Ford, 'Stair's Title "Of Liberty and Servitude"' in Andrew D E Lewis and David J Ibbetson (eds), *The Roman Law Tradition* (CUP 1994) 135–58; Danie Visser and Niall Whitty, 'The Structure of the Law of Delict in Historical Perspective' in Kenneth Reid and Reinhard Zimmermann (eds), *A History of Private Law in Scotland*, vol 2 (OUP 2000) 422–76; Ford *Law and Opinion* (n 1) 20, 25, 176–77.

Contract before the Enlightenment. Stephen Bogle, Oxford University Press. © Stephen Bogle 2023.
DOI: 10.1093/oso/9780192884961.003.0006

roots of his approach. Therefore, this chapter will explain why Stair was impressed by Grotius's demonstration of a universal and methodical approach in *The Preliminary Discourse* of *The Rights of War and Peace* and will suggest why he was receptive to François Douaren's criticism of traditional methods otherwise used to arrange Roman law: these authors emboldened Stair to leave behind the known way of Roman law and to innovate, but did not appear to give him a structure or an arrangement. It will be suggested that he most likely took the term 'conventional obligation' from Hugo Donellus, who also offered an innovative account of the law of contract, albeit a commentary upon Roman law. But again, Donellus does not appear to have been the direct inspiration for Stair's arrangement of material.[8] After showing some reasons why Stair chose not to follow the established path of Justinian's *Institutes*, it will be suggested that, in developing a new organization of the law of Scotland, Stair drew upon a loose application of Aristotle's physics and logic in determining how to structure things, which connected with his Calvinist-influenced understanding of the Moral Law and its relationship to man's decision-making. On that basis, it will discuss how Stair arranged the *Institutions* on the basis of mid-seventeenth century epistemic understandings of the Moral Law, which stressed primacy of obligations owed to God, then to others, and then to oneself.

Before Stair

No overarching system or synthesis of sources

Before Stair's attempt to synthesize 'the law of Scotland', the legal system in Scotland, and its sources, were multi-faceted, generally unconnected with one another, and, if arranged, often done so alphabetically or using the structure of Justinian's *Institutes*.[9] As Dolezalek has explained, in the sixteenth century compliers of legal texts 'considered it a waste of time to explain the principles and rules of the Jus Commune' as such things were so easily accessible.[10] In comparison, sources and rules of domestic law were difficult to find, verify, and interpret. By consequence, treaties on domestic law would often bring together single propositions of law, which were often compared to *ius commune* position. And so, if there was such a thing as 'the law of Scotland' to be gleaned from these domestic sources, it was, from the point of view of organization, unsystematic and sparse without its *ius commune* underpinning. Again, as Dolezalek rightly underlines, it was not until the 1650s when printing became much cheaper that Scots authors attempted to provide 'amalgmations of the Jus Commune with Scottish

---

[8] Italo Birocchi, *Causa e Categoria General del Contratto* (G Giappichelli 1997); Wim Decock, *Theologians and Contract Law: The Moral Transformation of the Ius Commune (ca. 1500–1650)* (Martinus Nijhoff Publishers 2013) 133–35; Niels de Bruijn, '"No One is a Better Jurist than Accursius": Medieval Legal Scholarship as the Fountainhead of Inspiration for Jacques Cujas and Huges Doneau?' (2014) 82 Legal History Review 72–99; Dmitry Poldnikov, 'Origins of General Concept of Contract in Western European Legal Science' (2016) 2 Journal on European History of Law 53–59.

[9] eg Hope's practicks in the style of the *Institutes*, and Spotiswoode's practicks in alphabetical order. Durie's practices were also arranged in alphabetical order.

[10] Gero Dolezalek, *Scotland under Jus Commune*, vol 55 (Stair Society 2010) 3.

domestic law'.[11] And it was this which provided the opportunity for taxonomical innovation.

The lack of systematic writing was acknowledged by Scots writers in the early modern period and into the seventeenth century. Indeed, Stair often noted, in the *Institutions*, the confused order of the sources of law that applied in Scotland.[12] Although legal sources in Scotland were wide-ranging, they were often of uncertain authoritative value and not always written or printed. It is no surprise then, that in terms of written material, Scots advocates were resourceful and open to different sources. Hence, seventeenth century Scots lawyers would take their legal propositions from a range of texts, including the *Corpus iuris civilis*, the *Corpus iuris canonici*, commentaries upon Roman law, practicks about customary law in Scotland, from the relatively rare-printed compilations of Scots legislation.[13]

In addition to the unsystematic nature of sources of law in Scotland, contractual practice was just as complex. Numerous ways to create an obligation exited. There was registration of oaths and there was registration of writs;[14] there were bonds of many different sorts; there were charters entered into between feudal superiors and vassals; and there were verbal agreements which, in some circumstances, could become binding.[15] If anything general can be said about contractual practice and the law of Scotland in the seventeenth century, it is that legal doctrine focused upon external actions and did very little, if any, theorizing about the nature of consent.[16] Obligations could be created in a variety of different ways, but Scots legal writing did not attempt to pull these otherwise discrete practices of contracting into a general category, such as conventional obligations.[17] There was no overarching genus, just many different instances.

Corpus iuris civilis

Despite these various sources, the most influential system of taxonomical thought about private law and contracting in the mid-seventeenth century was the *Corpus iuris civilis*.[18] From the perspective of contractual thought in the seventeenth century, there

---

[11] Dolezalek, *Scotland under the Jus Commune* (n 10) 4.

[12] Stair *Inst* 1.1.17; 1.1.16; 1.1.22; 1.3.2.

[13] Andrew R C Simpson and Adelyn L M Wilson, *Scottish Legal History: Volume 1, 1000–1707* (Edinburgh University Press 2017) 257–316.

[14] Walter Ross, *Lectures on the History and Practice of the Law of Scotland*, vol 1 (2nd edn, Bell & Bradfute 1822) 92–120; Peter G B McNeill (ed), *The Practicks of Sir James Balfour of Pittendreich*, vol 2/vol 22 (Stair Society 1963) 658; *Guide to the National Archives of Scotland* (The Stationery Office 1996) 206–10.

[15] Peter Gouldesbrough (ed), *Formulary of Old Scots Legal Documents*, vol 36 (Stair Society 1985). Also see discussion in Chapter 4 about the practice in Scots customary law with relation to *nuda pacta*.

[16] See Gerhard Lubbe, 'Formation of Contract' in Kenneth Reid and Reinhard Zimmermann (eds), *A History of Private Law in Scotland*, vol 2 (OUP 2000) 18–33.

[17] See discussion in Chapter 1.

[18] It was probably Denis Godefroy (1549–1622) who first used the term *Corpus iuris civilis* in 1583 to refer to the *Codex*, *Digest*, *Institutes*, and *Novels* of Justinian: Olivia Robinson, *The Sources of Roman Law: Problems and Methods for Ancient Historians* (Routledge 1996) 57; Jan Hallebeek, 'Medieval Legal Scholarship' in Jan Hallebeek and Harry Dondorp (eds), *Contract for a Third-Party Beneficiary* (Brill 2008); Michael H Hoeflich, 'A Seventeenth-Century Roman Law Bibliography: Jacques Godefroy and his "Bibliotheca Juris Civilis Romani"' (1982) 75 Law Library Journal 514–52; Peter Stein, *Roman Law in European History* (CUP 1999) 71–85; Randall Lesaffer, *European Legal History: A Cultural and Political Perspective* (CUP 2009)

are four basic points which could be made about what advocates would have found in *Corpus iuris*. First, in the *Corpus iuris* the law of contract was not unified: it is a law of *contracts*, not contract. Justinian's *Institutes* offers a clear example of the un-unified nature of Roman contract law: '[contracts] fall into four species, for contract is concluded either by delivery, by a form of words, by writing, or by consent'.[19] Of course, 'species' alludes to a generalized conception, but this was never explained or accounted for in the *Institutes*. Nonetheless, the *Digest* alludes to a more generalized understanding of contract law, namely the idea of *contractus* (meaning the contraction of a liability),[20] *conventio* (to come together),[21] *consensus in idem* (a meeting of the minds),[22] and *pactum* (which came to mean an informal agreement).[23] In the fourteenth century, jurists began to bring these component parts together into a more generalized notion of contract.[24] However, it is important to stress that when Godefroy came to compile the *Corpus iuris* in the sixteenth century, he wished to present Roman law without the interpolations of the glossators or commentators. Accordingly, the Roman law, which mid-seventeenth century Scots lawyers encountered in the *Corpus iuris*, was probably presented without the kind of extensive gloss or commentary found in medieval editions of the *Corpus iuris*.[25]

Second, in theory this was a closed system of recognized types. There is a prefigured list of basic types of contract, with pre-set triggers for formation and predetermined terms. That is, the general rule found in the *Corpus iuris* is that an agreement is only legally enforceable if it conforms to the pre-defined category of a consensual contract (*emptio venditio, locatio conductio, societas*, and *mandatum*) or a real contract (*mutuum, commodatum, depositum*, and *pignus*). In terms of real contracts, the key prompt was the delivery of a thing, but with each different type of real contract carrying its own fixed terms. There were some general features, however: real contracts, for example, were unilateral and gratuitous, and accordingly no payment was required. Whereas with consensual contracts the trigger for creation was consent, although not necessary in terms of the *Institutes*, it would be evidenced by external acts, such as writing or *arra*. However, consent did not mean the terms of the contract could be created *ex nihilo*; again, the consequences of the contract and the basic terms were pre-set according to the *Corpus iuris*.

Third, one of the main consequences of being a closed system is that any other means by which one could create an obligation is generally excluded or acknowledged

---

351–52. A 1670 edition was held by the Advocates' Library: Ad MS 25.7.12 (*Summary of Catalogue of the Advocates' Manuscripts* (National Library of Scotland 1971) 67).

[19] *Justinian Inst* 2.13.2.

[20] *Gaius Inst* 3.88. Also see Paul Collinet, 'The Evolution of Contract as Illustrating the General Evolution of Roman Law' (1932) Law Quarterly Review 488.

[21] *Digest* 2.14.1.3.

[22] *Digest* 2.14.1.1.

[23] *Digest* 2.14.7.4. Barry Nicholas, *An Introduction to Roman Law* (OUP 1962) 192.

[24] James Gordley, *The Philosophical Origins of Modern Contract Doctrine* (OUP 1991) 30–69.

[25] Lawyers in Scotland were, nonetheless, also aware of the glossators and commentators. Indeed, they made good use of them: Stein, 'The Influence of Roman Law'; David M Walker, *A Legal History of Scotland*, vol IV (Bloomsbury Professional 1996) 700–01; Gero Dolezalek, 'The Court of Session as a Ius Commune Court—Witnessed by "Sinclair's Practicks", 1540-1549' in H L MacQueen (ed), *Miscellany IV*, vol 49 (Stair Society 2002) 51; John W Cairns, 'Jus Civile in Scotland, ca. 1600' (2004) 2 Roman Legal Tradition 136.

by means of an exception to the closed list. For instance, Roman law did not theoretically acknowledge the enforceability of promises.[26] The basic response found in the *Digest* was that a promise or verbal agreement was beyond the list of recognized contracts. It gave rise to a natural obligation, but not a legally actionable obligation.[27] The *Digest* and the *Institutes* did recognize situations where an innominate contract could become enforceable: through the transfer of a thing or performance on one side of the bargain, a transaction could become an innominate contract.[28] Additionally, as discussed in Chapter 4, a pact could become 'clothed' or a *vestitum pactum* when it related to a recognized contract or a situation where it became legally relevant.[29] The rigidity of this closed system was counterbalanced by the relative flexibility of a stipulation, which would allow for promises and other agreements to be transformed into legally recognized obligations.[30] Indeed, stipulations enjoyed a great deal of flexibility in comparison to consensual and real contracts, because the content of the obligation was not predetermined.[31] However, the formation of the obligation was pre-set and required, in theory, strict compliance in order to create the obligation. Thus, according to the *Institutes*, a stipulation was an obligation, which was contracted by question and answer: '"Do you engage yourself to do so and so?", "I do engage myself"; "Do you promise?", "I do promise"; "Do you pledge your credit?", "I pledge my credit"; "Do you guarantee?", "I guarantee"; "Will you convey?", "I will convey"; "Will you do?", "I will do". A stipulation may be a flexible thing, but it required strict formality.[32] The question and answer must match, and the correct formulation of words must be used.

---

[26] *Digest* 2.14.7.4.

[27] Gordley *Philosophical Origins* (n 24) 41–45.

[28] *Justinian Inst* 3.24.1:

> Consequently, if a man gives clothes to a fuller to clean or finish, or to a tailor to mend, and the amount of hire is not fixed at the time, but left to subsequent agreement between the parties, a contract of hire cannot properly be said to have been concluded, but an action is given on the circumstances, as amounting to an innominate contract.

Also see *Digest* 19.5.22.

[29] In general, today we may say that *pacta vestita* can be into three broad categories: subsidiary pacts, which were ancillary to a recognized contract (for example, *Digest*, 14.7.5; *Digest* 14.7.6); praetorian pacts, which were specific and granted overtime by praetorian edict; and statutory pacts or *pacta legitima*, which were recognized by some sort of statute. Nevertheless, technically, a *pactum vestitum* was utilized as a defence. It was only once a pact was clothed, on the basis of one of these grounds, that it would become legally relevant in an action.

[30] Alan Watson, 'The Evolution of Law: The Roman System of Contracts' (1984) 2 (1) Law and History Review 1–20.

[31] See Alan Watson, *The Spirit of Roman Law* (University of Georgia Press 2008) 73. Watson also suggests that the flexibility of a stipulation and the traditionalism in Roman law meant that a move towards a general notion of contract was slow and never deemed necessary. See Watson 'The Evolution of Law' (n 30) 1–20.

[32] However, see Martin Hogg, *Promises and Contract Law: Comparative Perspectives* (Cambridge University Press 2011) 113. Hogg argues that the form of stipulation found in the *Digest* is an extremely flexible one, which is not inhibited by strict formality; he describes it as a 'promissory action'. He remarks:

> It has been said of the stipulation that 'its usefulness and flexibility made it the cornerstone of the Roman contractual system'. The prominence of this promissory action assured it a continuing role in later European legal thinking through the reception of Roman law into the later European *Ius Commune*. However, despite the relaxation of its attendant formalities, it did not develop into the general contractual action of the later law; for that, recourse was had to Roman law's consensual contracts.

Fourth, there is generally no moralizing or theoretical explication about motive or intention in these sources aside from the opening passages of the *Digest*.[33] This is not to say that there was not an understanding or implied consideration of intention or motive; but this was not discussed or analyzed in detail within these sources. For example, the *Corpus iuris* presents a system of contracting which focuses upon external acts, which are pertinent to the creation of an obligation rather than any internally relevant factors such as consent or intention.[34] Of course, the lack of consent was relevant to whether or not some contracts where enforceable or not, such as a contract of sale. But there is no great consideration of why some acts incur liability whereas others do not. Roman jurists, praetors, and lawyers did not express abstract grounds of liability within their decision-making, which is reflected in the *Corpus iuris*.[35] Of course, the seeds of a general notion of contract were present in Roman law, but the sum of these parts was never analyzed into a theoretical structure. Buckland argues that, in reality, a contract did not mean a concurrence of internal wills, but the concurrence of two external acts.[36] Abstract notions such as binding oneself and the morality of promise-keeping, although acknowledged as moral duties,[37] were not fused with the positive law as part of any grand moralization of the law.[38] Watson explains that although 'jurists were rigorously positivist in their approach to law' and 'almost totally disinterested in natural law', it should not be forgotten that 'in their day, vibrant philosophical traditions of natural law were supplemented by Christian theorists such as St Augustine'. Watson's point is that to take the *Digest* as a sole summation of Roman legal thought around AD 300 or AD 600 is mistaken, as Justinian's codification and subsequently the *Corpus iuris civilis* give a very 'lopsided view of the law in early Byzantium'.[39] However, the present point is that the texts of the *Corpus iuris* used by early modern Scots lawyers did not use normative ideas or unificatory ideas, such as the will, when discussing the law of contract.[40]

[33] Alan Watson, *Law Out of Context* (University of Georgia Press 2000) xii–xiii.
[34] In contrast, Collinet suggests that, by the sixth century, Roman law had developed an understanding that contract was the result of the concurrence of the wills, but he acknowledges that it was under canon law's developments in the thirteenth century that this idea was clearly articulated (Collinet 'The Evolution of Contract' (n 20)); cf Roberto Fiori, 'The Roman Concept of Contract' in Thomas A J McGinn (ed), *Obligations in Roman Law* (The University of Michigan Press 2013) 40–75.
[35] Watson *The Spirit of Roman Law* (n 31) 73; James Gordley, 'Why Look Backward' (2002) 50 (4) The American Journal of Comparative Law 657–70; James Gordley, 'The Method of the Roman Jurists' (2013) 87 (4) Tulane Law Review 933–54.
[36] William W Buckland, *A Textbook of Roman Law* (CUP 1921) 410–11.
[37] The formalism of Roman law can sometimes be mistaken for bluntness or a disregard for morality. Arguably, this emerges from the difficulties of establishing invariably moral notions like consent, will, or intention; without reliance of external action, these moral notions are beyond the realm of a court. The internal psychological state of a party is a perennial problem for the evidential procedures of any legal system, old or new. For an early legal system like Roman law, it would be surprising to find anything less than a pragmatic uncompromising approach to evidence and formation. For discussion, see Buckland *A Textbook of Roman Law* (n 36) 410–11; Tony Weir, 'Contracts in Rome and England' (1996) 66 Tulane Law Review 1616, 1617; Calum Carmichael (ed), *The Deed and the Doer in the Bible: David Daube's Gifford Lectures*, vol 1 (Templeton Press 2008) Ch 2.
[38] Fritz Shulz, *Principles of Roman Law* (Marguerite Wolff tr, OUP 1936) 164–237; Marcus T Cicero, *De Officiis* (Walter Miller tr, Harvard 1913) 1.7.
[39] Watson *Law Out of Context* (n 33) xii–xiii.
[40] As Watson says, the jurists of Roman law did not see the purpose of law to make Roman citizens more virtuous: 'in a large part the jurists were not interested in the law as social engineering'. See Watson *The Spirit of Roman Law* (n 31) 73.

Stair's System

Arguably, for a modern lawyer, matters become much more familiar when you turn to Stair's *Institutions*. He writes in the local vernacular of Scotland, not in Latin, which was otherwise the universal language of lawyers within Europe in the seventeenth century. Additionally, Stair tries to summarize, in one place, the laws that were applied in Scotland which related to private rights or commutative justice. He avoids the use of copious footnotes and attempts to explain the law from first principles, which he believes will be recognizable to not just lawyers but also 'persons of honour and discretion'.[41] He divides his book, initially, into three, but eventually into four parts, which represents a simple organization of the law around interpersonal obligations and their triggers for justifying legal enforcement. That is: first, the creation and protection of rights and obligations relating to people; second, the creation and protection of rights and obligations in relation to property; third, the transfer or extinguishing of these rights; and fourth, the right to and process of enforcement of these rights. In terms of contractual obligations, he offers a basic division which is able to accommodate and organize, under two headings, a large number of propositions and rules that were otherwise unconnected. That is, there were two main types of obligation: conventional obligations and obediential. Conventional obligations encompassed a huge variety of transactions, including promises, pacts, bonds, sales, leases, loans, and oaths. These transactions were linked; there were 'common requisites' amongst these types of transaction.[42] The Justinian fourfold division of contracts, along with the many details regarding innominate contracts and stipulations, is jettisoned by Stair's principle-based approach.[43] For Stair, it was no longer necessary 'to trace the many subtilties and differences amongst pactions and contracts in the Roman law'.[44] For example, '[p]actions, contracts, covenants, and agreements, are synonymous terms'.[45] As already demonstrated, he places the moral principle of standing by your pactions at the root of his account; but, as will be shown, Stair connects this to basic notions of human action, namely the will. Stair attempts to connect c1ontractual remedies too, saying that non-performance of any of these transactions would naturally lead to specific implement if not damages.[46] The intricacies of determining a contract's *causa* were no longer used to describe a contract's enforceability but rather to categorize the type of transaction, onerous or gratuitous. It was a general rule of contract that courts should not intervene in the terms of the contract.[47] At this point, it might be useful to give an overview of the structure of the first three books of the *Institutions*.

---

[41] Stair *Inst* 1.1.
[42] Stair *Inst* 1.10.13.
[43] Stair *Inst* 1.10.7.
[44] Stair *Inst* 1.10.10.
[45] Stair *Inst* 1.10.10.
[46] Stair *Inst* 1.17.16; 1.10.16.
[47] Stair *Inst* 1.10.14.

Table of contents: The arrangement

II.   Dispositions, where of, Resignations in favorem, Apprisings and Adjudications of Real Rights, &c.

III. Confiscations, where of, Single Escheat, Liferent Escheat, Shipwreck, Waith Goods, Treasure, Forefaulture, Bastardy and Last Heir

IV.   Succession, by the Civil and Feudal Law, and our Law, where of, Deathbed, Annus deliberandi, and Kinds of Heirs in Scotland

V.   Heirs, where of, Heirs, Heirs-male, Heirs-portioners, Heirs of Conquest, Tailzie and Provision, and their Brieves and Services, &c.

VI.   Behaving as Heir, where of, Gestio pro Hærede, and the Exceptions against this Passive Title

VII. Lucrative Successors, how this Passive Title is Extended, and how Limited, by our Practice

VIII. Executry, where of, Testaments, Codicils, Legacies, Relict's part, Bairns' part, Dead's part, Confirmations, and Office of Executry

IX.   Vitious Intromission

Consistent structure from the 1660s to the 1690s

Stair stuck to this overall structure throughout numerous versions of the *Institutions*. Over thirty years, as different versions of the *Institutions* emerged, several changes can be identified; but his structure, nonetheless, remained consistent.[48] On the face of it, however, an important structural change appeared to have been made in 1693, as Book IV was added. Stair explained in the preface to the 1693 edition that:

> finding it would be acceptable to divide the institutions of our law into four books, as the Institutions of the Civil Law are divided, and especially, because there is a more eminent distinction in our law betwixt heritable rights of the ground, and moveable rights; I have divided this edition into four parts: The first, being the original personal rights: The second, of original real rights; The Third, of the conveyance of both: And the fourth, of the cognition and execution of the whole.[49]

It would, however, be wrong to assume that, because Stair added the fourth book and said it was in part because he felt the law of Scotland could be presented in a similar manner to *Institutes* of civil law, he was following the Justinian model. It is clear, upon a survey of the topics and content of Book IV of Stair's *Institutions* and that of Justinian, that Stair was very much focused on the rules and terms upon which the substantive rights described in Books I to III could be enforced in the

---

[48] Arguably, Stair's changes were minor: the titles of individual chapters changed slightly, more titles were added, a table of contents was inserted, an index was included, and his references to different sources grew, including decisions of the Court of Session and civil law.

[49] See the advertisement attached to the second edition in 1693.

Court of Session. In contrast with Book IV of Justinian's *Institutes*, which covered actions or the triggers upon which you could raise an action, Stair's Book IV is concerned with the law applying to the process. Obligations, which would otherwise be found in Book IV of the *Institutes*, were placed through Books I to III of the *Institutions*. In contrast to the *Institutes*, Stair did not speak of a separate law of persons, opting rather—it would appear—for a title on liberty, where no distinction is made between different types of legal status. It should also not be overlooked that when Stair published the *Institutions* as three books in 1681, he did publish a version of what was to become Book IV of the *Institutions* under the title *Modus Litigandi* in the same year, which suggests that he intended his presentation of the substantial law to be read in conjunction with his description of process and procedure.[50]

Philosophical and theological roots of the system

The distinctiveness of Stair's approach has been noted previously within the literature; however, generally the focus has been upon the legal influences and precursors to Stair rather than the philosophical or theological drivers behind Stair's structure. It is well established in the literature that he was a legal humanist of some sorts. For example, Cairns, Fergus, and MacQueen[51] have noted the influence of legal humanism upon Scots lawyers before the seventeenth century; and in *Law and Opinion*, Ford explained its influence upon not just Stair, but also many of his contemporaries.[52] In her detailed examination of Stair's sources, Wilson has demonstrated that Stair drew widely during the drafting and subsequent revisions he made on title 10 from the work of what we might deem to be 'legal humanists'.[53] But, as Ford demonstrates in his explanation of Scots lawyers' engagement with legal humanism in the mid-seventeenth century, what it means is not always certain, as there are many different approaches to the law which are captured by this label. Therefore, it is important to understand what it means to say that Stair was influenced by legal humanism, although, as will be suggested, this does not offer a completely satisfactory explanation as to why Stair adopted the particular structure he applied to the law of Scotland. Nonetheless, it is first useful to establish what kind of legal humanism might be attached to Stair, because it evidently contributed to his method and to his approach to the law of contract.

---

[50] James Dalrymple, *Modus Litigandi or Form of Process observed before the Lords of Council and Session in Scotland* (Andrew Anderson 1681).

[51] John W Cairns, T D Fergus, and Hector MacQueen, 'Legal Humanism in Renaissance Scotland' (1990) 11 (1) Journal of Legal History 40–69.

[52] Ford *Law and Opinion* (n 1) 48, 89.

[53] Adelyn L M Wilson, 'The Sources and Methods of the Institutions of Scotland, by Sir James Dalrymple 1st Viscount Stair, with Specific Reference to the Law of Obligations' (DPhil thesis, University of Edinburgh 2011).

Stair and Legal Humanism

Two phases of legal humanism

Stein has argued that legal humanism should be understood as divided into two broadly defined phases. The first phase dates from around the mid-fifteenth century, whereas the second dates from around the mid-sixteenth century. The first phase 'directed [its] attention to the state of the authoritative texts', namely the *Digest* and the *Code*. It 'sought to discard all the glosses and commentaries that stood between the reader and the texts—to discover directly the meaning of the texts'.[54] Osler explains that legal humanism was 'the investigation of Roman law, using philological and historical methods', with a broader interest in the history of antiquity, which 'may be contrasted with the pragmatic, unhistorical application of Roman law to the conditions of contemporary Europe'.[55] On the basis of the *Institutions*, it is possible to see an interest in history and to a lesser extent philology, but it would be bold to say that this first phase of legal humanism is what we see in Stair's *Institutions* and his approach to conventional obligations.

However, it is the second phase of legal humanism which is more easily identifiable with Stair. This phase is typified by a growing sense of admiration for classical learning but also, crucially, of the difference between the politics and culture of Roman society and sixteenth century Europe. Often you will find a critical assessment of Roman law within this genre of legal writing, questioning whether it is 'the best exemplar' for modern law.[56] Of particular note is this phase of legal humanism's critique of the order and arrangement of the *Corpus iuris*. This criticism contributed to humanist interest in reorganizing the *Corpus iuris* and numerous different models and organization of law appearing in legal textbooks and other summaries of local law.[57] As Ford explains, the 'humanist interest in systematic arrangement arose from the revival of classical rhetoric among scholars who believe that they might at least be on their way to satisfying Cicero's desire for *ius civile ad artem redactum*'.[58] A very good example of this is François Douaren (1509–59), whom Stair cites in the *Institutions*.[59]

---

[54] Stein 'Legal Humanism and Legal Science' (n 5).

[55] Douglas Osler, 'Legal Humanism' in European and Comparative European History, Max Planck Institute for Legal History and Theory <http://www.rg.mpg.de/research-project/legal-humanism> accessed 7 April 2021.

[56] Osler 'Legal Humanism' (n 55).

[57] Peter Stein, 'Donellus and the Origins of the Modern Civil Law' in Johan A Ankum and Felix B J Wubbe (eds), *Mélanges Felix Wubbe* (Editions Universitares 1993) 439–52.

[58] Ford *Law and Opinion* (n 1) 48.

[59] Stein says: 'the centre of legal humanism was the University of Bourges, where the whole law faculty was caught up in the ferment of deconstructing Justinian's texts, and the manifesto of the group was written in Bourges in 1544, namely Duarenus' *Epistula de ratione docendi discendi iuris* [Franciscus Duarenus, *Omni Opera*, Aureliae Allobrogum (1608)]'. Stein 'Donellus' (n 57) 443.

Clarity over tradition

In 1544, Douaren published his *Epistula de ratione docendi discendi iuris*, where he argued that jurists and lawyers have neglected clarity for tradition. Too often, according to Douaren, lawyers have disregarded lucidity and order because of ignorance or sometimes failing to follow basic principles.[60] 'Because of their folly', lawyers have tried to learn the law through knowledge of each individual particular rather than from general statements.[61] He says: 'like Lucian, sitting on the sea shore, trying to count the waves, until they eventually engulf him', lawyers try to memorize and learn law by learning each individual rule.[62] According to Douaren, you cannot 'perfect' your knowledge of law through the study of each individual command found in Bartolus or the *Corpus iuris*.[63] Douaren tells his reader that students should commence with a study 'of certain precepts, and the theorems of universals, which prepare them to judge the good and be informed about individual matters, so far as can be hoped for'.[64] As Stein surmises, 'Duarenus [Douaren] argued that law should be capable of being expounded by the same method as other scientific disciplines, namely, by proceeding from what is universal and more familiar to us, to what is particular'.[65] As Wim Decock notes, Douaren's letter of 1544 'consecrated the legal humanist movement',[66] and '[i]t would stimulate generations of jurists to get a deeper historical understanding of pristine Roman contract law without preventing them from being creative in systematizing the Roman legacy in new ways'.[67] In adopting a plain and rational method, it would be fair to say that Stair consciously emulated the legal humanism of which Douaren's *Epistula de ratione docendi discendi iuris* created a 'manifesto'.[68] However, this does not explain why he chose the order he adopted.

Rationalizing the discipline

The most evident example of legal humanism for Stair was Craig's *Jus Feudale*, which was historical, demonstrating not just feudal law's contingency and context but also human law's changing nature more generally. Stair may have been inspired by Douaren and emboldened by Craig's explanation and account of the sources of the law in Scotland, but he did not follow Craig in developing his structure and arrangement of the laws of Scotland. But it is noteworthy that Stair cites Grotius as an example of someone who demonstrated that law could be 'handled as a rational discipline'.[69] It

---

[60] Franciscus Duareni, *Epistula de Ratione Docendi Discendi Iuris* (1544) in *Francisci Duareni Jurisconsulti Celeberrimi: Opera Omnia. Diligenter Emendate & Aucta Opportunis Notis. Volumen Quartum* (Typis Josephi Rocchii 1768) 364–65.

[61] Duareni 'Epistula' (n 60) 369.

[62] Duareni 'Epistula' (n 60) 369.

[63] Duareni 'Epistula' (n 60) 369.

[64] Duareni 'Epistula' (n 60) 369.

[65] Stein 'Donellus' (n 57) 443.

[66] Decock *Theologians and Contract Law* (n 8) 121.

[67] Decock *Theologians and Contract Law* (n 8) 121.

[68] Wilson 'Sources and Method' (n 53) 100–01.

[69] Stair *Inst* 1.1.17.

was this which gave Stair an example of how the law could be organized on the basis of foundational principles. Grotius's *Preliminary Discourse* was philosophically richer in its approach than that of Craig, and far more universal in scope. As Grotius himself explained, you can begin your study of what is right, and what others owe to you, by studying the *Corpus iuris civilis*, or by producing your own commentary or abridgment of it, but few have considered, according to him, the universal foundations of law and the best method for such a task. In Book I of *The Rights of War and Peace*, Stair would have found Grotius's explanation of how man comes to know natural law: 'the Law of Nature is generally provided either *à priori*, that is, by Arguments drawn from the very nature of the Thing; or *à posteriori*, that is by Reasons taken from something external'.[70] For Grotius, you could establish whether something is a priori by 'shewing the necessary Fitness or Unfitness of any Thing, with a reasonable and sociable nature', while a posteriori is 'when, we cannot with absolute Certainty, yet with very great Probability, conclude that to be by the Law of Nature, which is generally believed to be so by all, or at least the most civilized, Nations'. The idea of organizing things on the basis of first principles would have appealed to Stair, and it prompted him to consider not only how to demonstrate how rules of Scots law related to reason but also how he might organize the law of Scotland relating to contracting obligations on a rational basis which did not derive from the *Corpus iuris civilis*.

Searching for the genus of contracts

Although Stair criticized Roman law sources and traditional juristic methods, this should not suggest that, before Stair, jurists did not consider organizing concepts for what we might now call the law of contract. Indeed, for centuries, jurists mused about what linked together the different types of contracts and actions they found in the *Corpus iuris civilis*.[71] In the *Digest*, Ulpian appears to suggest that consent is what connects contracts: 'there is no contract, no obligation that does not consist of consent whether it is formed by the handing over of something, or by the use of certain words'.[72] Indeed, Gordley supposes 'the Romans might not have found these ideas [about consent] particularly novel'.[73] Famously, commentators such as Bartolus and Baldus considered this question and said that the root of all contracts was consent.[74] Jesuit and Dominican theologians-cum-jurists did much the same in the sixteenth and early seventeenth centuries, drawing upon the work of medieval glossators and commentators.[75] It may therefore be unsurprising that ideas of contract can be found in a collection of medieval laws applied in Scotland known as *Regiam Majestatem*,[76]

---

[70] Hugo Grotius, *The Rights of War and Peace* (first published 1625, Liberty Fund 2005) 1.1.10.

[71] Gordley *Philosophical Origins* (n 24) 41–44.

[72] *Digest* 2.14.3. Gordley quotes this passage: 'Ius Quaerens Intellectum: The Method of the Medieval Civilians' in John W Cairns and Paul J du Plessis (eds), *The Creation of the Ius Commune: From Casus to Regula* (Edinburgh University Press 2010) 96.

[73] Gordley *Philosophical Origins* (n 24) 45.

[74] Gordley *Philosophical Origins* (n 24) 41–44.

[75] Gordley *Philosophical Origins* (n 24) Ch 4.

[76] Peter Stein, 'The Source of the Romano-Canonical Part of Regiam Majestatem' (1969) 48 (14) Scottish Historical Review 107–23.

which was, to some extent, used or understood as a source of law in Scotland in the mid-seventeenth century.[77]

In fact, it would probably be fair to say that it was commonplace, within the *Corpus iuris* commentary literature used by Scots lawyers in the mid-seventeenth century, to find discussion of the genus of contracts.[78] For example, the *Commentariorum de jure novissimo libri sex*[79] by Petrus Gudelinus (1550–1619), first published in 1620 and used by Scots lawyers, includes a fairly lengthy, albeit somewhat superficial discussion of a general category of contract, which he defines as an agreement or covenant.[80] In contrast, the *Institutionum imperialium commentaries academicus & forensis*[81] of Arnold Vinnius (1588–1657) demonstrates more extensive consideration of contract. In his discussion of the roots of obligations, he says that, although in Justinian you find four types of cause—contract, quasi-contract, delict, and quasi-delict—in Aristotle's *Ethics* you find 'one way to comprehend everything. There are two types of exchange, volitional & non-volitional, voluntary and involuntary. Volitional appeals to commerce, agreements, contracts, non-volitional, ill-advised acts & delict.'[82] It is significant that Vinnius considered a twofold division between obligations and is expressly using Aristotle as a source of inspiration, revealing a willingness to go beyond legal literature in order to find organizing ideas. Such an approach can be found in both the *Inleydinge* and *The Rights of War and Peace*, where Grotius also attempted to find principles or concepts to organize the laws of nature as well as, importantly, the laws applied in Holland in the early seventeenth century. However, unlike Vinnius, he did not connect it to human action or Aristotle, but to principles and virtues; that is, for him, contracts arise by either the duty of good faith[83] or the reciprocal nature of the exchange.[84] The approach taken by Hugo Doneau (1527–91) is similar to Gudelinus and Vinnius: he offers fairly lengthy discussion about obligations and contracts in general before proceeding to individual contracts.[85] It is particularly interesting to see frequent use of 'conventio' in the description and titles of Oswald Hilliger's *Donellus Enucleatus*,[86] which suggests that Stair may have taken some degree of inspiration from this compendium of Doneau when it came to conceiving of the term 'conventional obligation'.[87]

---

[77] Hector L MacQueen, '"Regiam Majestatem", Scots Law, and National Identity' (1995) 74 (197) Scottish Historical Review 1–25; Ford, *Law and Opinion* (n 1) 37–49, 251–65 passim.

[78] For a discussion of many of the texts, which Stair is known to have had access to, see Robert Feenstra, 'Pact and Contract in the Low Countries' in John Barton, *Towards a General Law of Contract* (Duncker & Humblot 1990) 197–213; cf Wilson 'Sources and Method' (n 53) and the books recorded in *Catalogus Librorum Bibliothecae Juris Utriusque, ...* (George Mosman 1692).

[79] Petrus Gudelinus, *Commentariorum de Jure Novissimo Libri Sex: Optimia Methodo, Accurateac Erudite Conscripti, Additis Harum Vicinarumque Region Moribus* (Ex Officina Hieronymi Verdus 1620).

[80] Gudelinus *Commentariorum* (n 79) III.I.

[81] Arnold Vinnius, *Commentarius Locupletissimus, Academicus & Forensis, In Quatuor Libros Institutionum Imperialium* (Ex officina Joannes Maire 1642).

[82] Vinnius, *Institutionum* (n 81) 3.14 (576).

[83] Hugo Grotius, *The Introduction to Dutch Jurisprudence* (first published 1631, Charles Herbert tr, John van Voorst 1903) 3.1.1–2.

[84] Grotius *The Rights of War* (n 70) 2.12.

[85] Hugues Doneau, *Commentarii de Iure Civilii*, vols 2 (Apud heredes Andreæ Wecheli 1589–90).

[86] Oswald Hilliger, *Donellus Enucleatus siue Commentarii* (Peter Bellerum 1642) 12.11–17 (281–93).

[87] Stair *Inst* 1.10.1.

Several points need to be noted, however. First, prior to these early modern writers, such as Doneau, you generally do not find criticism of the existing patterns, methods, or ways of doing things which is connected to a project of reform or rejection of the structure of the *Corpus Iuris Civilis*. Of course, you will find consideration of deficiencies, suggestions of what Roman jurists might have intended, and side-comments upon what might link together contracts and why. Emphasis, however, was placed not upon innovation but rather upon interpretation. Second, although jurists such as Vinnius, Gudelinus, and Doneau did consider organizing concepts in their commentaries, the central point is that this is presented as marginal or as a commentary upon the Justinian structure of contracts. They may criticize it, but they do not transcend it or jettison the structure. Additionally, these commentaries do not show in comparison to Stair a significant or extensive philosophical underpinning. Rather, they demonstrate a sensibility and appreciation for order, clarity and accuracy but do not examine or draw upon other disciplines, at least not evidently, in how they discuss potential organizing concepts. Third, Grotius may have abandoned the practice of producing commentaries on the *Corpus Iuris*: in the *Inleydinge*, he offered a sophisticated account of Dutch customary law and in places offered new ideas and concepts. But, as Lee and Feenstra suggest, Grotius had not 'thrown off the shackles of the Roman law', and so, for example, his concept of *promissio* was still in effect a stipulation, and his concept of an *implied promissio* was another way to describe the Roman law categories of real and personal contracts.[88] Grotius, you could say, therefore took the Roman categories with him. Fourth, Grotius, in *The Rights of War and Peace*, does demonstrate a far deeper engagement with the foundations of the laws of nature and how they should be structured, which is a watershed moment in terms of natural law methodology—but it is on these points where he is distinct from Stair: Grotius tried to demonstrate that you can establish and build a system of natural law based on an understanding of an individual's rights, which can be done through a process of rationalization and examination of human nature. From this process, you come to the conclusion that man has a right to liberty, a right to property and a right to justice upon injury. On this basis, it is difficult to say that Stair found a structure in Grotius from which he built his taxonomical structure but he did find in Grotius an example of how to write about law's foundations.

Using principles

Stair is therefore notable in comparison to the medieval and early modern texts which considered the genus of contracts, because he implemented a taxonomical structure based around a genus, jettisoning the approach he found in Justinian's *Institutes*— and he did this using a theory of human action. In contrast to the glossators, the

---

[88] Robert W Lee, *An Introduction to Roman-Dutch Law* (5th edn, OUP 1953) 432. Feenstra expressly endorses the quotation: Feenstra 'Pact and Contract' (n 78) 208. For the particular sections of the *Inleydinge*, see Grotius *The Introduction* (n 83) 3.1.1–22 and 3.1.52–53.

commentators, the ancient statutes of Scots law and the late scholastics, Stair was far more comprehensive in developing this idea. The way he uses and describes principles is different and far more theologically and philosophically rich. Indeed, with the exception of Grotius (if classified as a jurist), it is difficult to find jurists using principles as organizing concepts or tools, despite their popularity in other disciplines.[89] Stair draws on the philosophical or conceptual sense of principles as a starting point for deduction. Using principles, Stair brings together under the heading of conventional obligations the Roman categories of contracts, along with different sources of law, such as customary law, feudal law, and canon law, and tries to accommodate many different types of legal instrument, such as bonds. He demonstrates that these transactions emanate from the will, which he underpins with a principle; and then he proves how these particular rules of Scots law fit under a generalized notion, and explains why they sometimes do not. If Craig and Douaren embolden Stair to leave established patterns of organization behind, and Grotius gave an example of how a new order could be found and justified, there was much he could have also taken from the traditional discussion of the genus of contracts found in the *Digest*, Bartolus, Baldus, and indeed contemporary commentaries on the *Corpus iuris civilis*. But Stair's approach, although inspired by what he found within existing legal literature, remains notably different—which, it is suggested, can be explained by exploring his philosophical and theological standpoint, and how he brought that to bear upon his juristic work.

Stair and Aristotelianism

If the legal literature in the mid-seventeenth century demonstrates new ideas and styles of legal writing, then it appears that Stair's theological and philosophical disposition, which was broadly influenced by an Aristotelian philosophy and Reformed theology, offered him a means by which to find his own way. In other words, it may be suggested that Stair drew upon his own philosophical and theological viewpoint when he came to find a way by which to organize the law in Scotland applying to contracts. In order to develop this suggestion that Stair combined his philosophical learning with his juristic organization of rules applying to contracting, the context of Glasgow University in the mid- to late seventeenth century, and particularly the relationship between Aristotelianism and Ramism, will be examined. It is first necessary to give an explanation of the curriculum at the university before explaining the philosophical roots of Stair's taxonomical structure and his organization of the law applying to contractual obligations.

---

[89] See Neal W Gilbert, *Renaissance Concepts of Method* (Columbia University Press 1960); Sarah Hutton, *British Philosophy in the Seventeenth Century* (OUP 2015) 7–26; Peter R Anstey, *The Idea of Principles in Early Modern Thought* (Routledge 2017). See, however, Astorri's discussion of Lutheran theologians who explored, in depth, the notions of pact, promise and contract connected it to Biblical passages. Such an approach, as will be demonstrated, is very similar to that adopted by Stair, albeit his approach is more philosophical. Paolo Astorri, *Lutheran Theology and Contract Law in Early Modern Germany (ca. 1520—1720)* (Brill 2019) 143–51.

Aristotelianism

Stair spent ten formative years at Glasgow University. As a student, he attended between 1633 and 1637[90] and returned as a regent, teaching from 1641 until he left in the summer of 1647 to join the Faculty of Advocates.[91] The curriculum from 1633 to 1647 was dominated by Aristotelian philosophy.[92] Glasgow's adherence to Aristotelianism is very much in keeping with post-Reformation universities and is particularly evident from two sources.[93] Firstly, the university was subject to two General Assembly visitations during this period (1639–40 and 1642).[94] One of those involved in the visitation, Robert Baillie, explained that students would start their Master of Arts degree with Latin language classes, and then move on to Greek. At this time, they would also study the *Organon* of Aristotle, which included the categories, interpretation, prior analytics, posterior analytics, and the topics. The 1642 visitation stated that it was required that students should possess their own copy of the Bible as well as 'Paræus', which presumably referred to David Pareus's commentary on the Heidelberg Catechism.[95] It is also notable that students were required to read Aristotle in Greek rather than Latin. As students progressed, they would be subject to public examinations which consisted of, inter alia, disputations and declamations. Towards the end of the degree, students would encounter Aristotle's moral philosophy, which consisted of his ethics, politics, and economics. As students advanced, they would be lectured on Aristotle's physics and metaphysics.[96] Secondly, Christine Shepherd's study of theses, lecture notes, and other material from this period demonstrates the footprint of Aristotle upon the

---

[90] For Glasgow University records referring to Stair, see Cosmo Innes (ed), *Munimenta Alme Universitatis Glasguensis. Records of the University of Glasgow, from its foundation till 1727* (Maitland Club 1854) xi, 99.

[91] John Ford and Dot Reid have also stressed this point: John D Ford, 'James Dalrymple, First Viscount Stair (1619–1695)' in *Oxford Dictionary of National Biography* (OUP 2004) <https://doi.org/10.1093/ref:odnb/7050> accessed 8 April 2021; Dot Reid, 'Thomas Aquinas and Viscount Stair: The Influence of Scholastic Moral Theology on Stair's Account of Restitution and Recompense' (2008) 29 Journal of Legal History 189–214.

[92] This is no surprise, given the huge influence Aristotelianism had in Europe at this time: Heinrich Kuhn, 'Aristotelianism in the Renaissance' in Edward N Zalta (ed), *The Stanford Encyclopedia of Philosophy* (first published 2005, Spring 2018 edition) <https://plato.stanford.edu/archives/spr2018/entries/aristotelianism-renaissance/>> accessed 8 April 2021. For a detailed commentary, see Manfred Svensson, 'Aristotelian Practical Philosophy from Melanchthon to Eisenhart: Protestant Commentaries on the Nicomachean Ethics 1529—1682' (2019) 21 (3) Reformation & Renaissance Review 218–38.

[93] See George H R Parkinson (ed), *The Renaissance and Seventeenth-century Rationalism: Routledge History of Philosophy*, vol IV (Routledge 1993); Joseph S Freedman, 'Aristotle and the Content of Philosophy Instruction at Central European Schools and Universities during the Reformation Era' (1993) 137 (2) Proceedings of the American Philosophical Society 213–53; Richard A Muller, 'Reformation, Orthodoxy, "Christian Aristotelianism", and the Eclecticism of Early Modern Philosophy' (2001) 81 (3) Dutch Review of Church History 306–25. See too Manfred Svensson and David S Sytsma, *A Bibliography of Early Modern Protestant Ethics* (ca. 1520—1750) (2020) <(PDF) A Bibliography of Early Modern Protestant Ethics, ca. 1520-1750 (updated Aug. 27, 2020) | Manfred Svensson and David S. Sytsma - Academia.edu> accessed 15 April 2021.

[94] For Robert Baillie's firsthand account of the 1642 visitation: David Laing (ed), *The Letters and Journals of Robert Baillie 1632-1642*, vol 2 (Bannatyne Club 1842) 463–65. Also see James Coutts, *A History of the University of Glasgow, from its Foundation in 1451 to 1909* (James Maclehose and Sons 1909) 106–07.

[95] David Pareus and Zacharias Ursinus, *Corpus Doctrinae Christinae, Ecclesiarum a Papatu Reformation, Contenens Explicationes Catcheticas D Zachariae Ursini* (Iona Rosa 1621).

[96] Coutts *A History* (n 94) 167.

syllabus.[97] She also highlights regents' use of medieval ideas and arguments found in the works of, for example, St Thomas Aquinas and John Duns Scotus, which were presumably used during lectures to illuminate Aristotle. Regents, however, also used the relatively modern commentaries of, inter alia, Peter Martyr Vermigli (1499–1562), Girolamo Zanchi (1516–90), and Giacomo Zabarella (1533–89).[98] Of particular note is that Coimbra commentaries from the sixteenth century, known as *Conimbricensis Collegii Societatis Jesu commentarii*,[99] were also used. This shows that Scots were not too fussy about the religious denomination of their physicists or logisticians.[100]

As Stair's students moved through Aristotle's *Organon*, he would have introduced his class to a fundamental proposition of Aristotelian logic: knowledge is either discursive or non-discursive. Some things we know by argument, and some things we know without argument. This distinction was a self-evident truth for Aristotle. Once logic was established on the basis of self-evident truths or axioms, argument could commence. Importantly, all scientific knowledge, according to Aristotle, was discursive, that is, based upon argument.[101] Discursive knowledge derives from dialectical reasoning, syllogisms, and induction, and is therefore a form of knowledge which is derived from argument.[102] Importantly, according to Aristotle, 'All instruction given or received by way of argument proceeds from pre-existent knowledge.'[103] Therefore, in order to commence with argumentation, one needs non-discursive knowledge. It is non-discursive knowledge which provides the premise or first principle upon which an argument commences. These first principles are recognized by the *nous* of man (roughly translated as 'intuition'). This is knowledge which comes immediately to man without argument, namely non-discursive knowledge. According to Aristotle, non-discursive knowledge consists of fundamental things such as the rules of logic, knowledge of concepts, definitions, and virtues. Man knows these things without any need for further argument, demonstration, or proof. In his *Metaphysics*, Aristotle says: 'It is impossible that there should be demonstration of absolutely everything; there would be an infinite regress, so that there would still be no demonstration.'[104]

This forms part of the background to Stair's discussion of his method, and particularly how he differed from Grotius's rational method: they generally agree on what the law of nature is but disagree on the question of how you come to have knowledge of the law of nature. Or it could be that the disagreement is about the *ordo essendi* rather

---

[97] Christine Shepherd, 'Philosophy and Science in the Arts Curriculum of the Scottish Universities in the 17th Century' (DPhil thesis, University of Edinburgh 1975).

[98] See Shepherd, 'Philosophy and Science' (n 97) 63.

[99] Jill Kraye (ed), *Cambridge Translations of Renaissance Philosophical Texts: Moral and Political Philosophy*, vol 2 (CUP 1997) 80.

[100] Dogmatic orthodoxy, however, was never far away. For instance, Aristotle's *Nicomachean Ethics* would be supplemented with Christian commentaries by trustworthy Presbyterian theologians such as the university principal John Strang: Shepherd 'Philosophy and Science' (n 97) 166. For a mature account of his thought, see John Strang, *De Voluntate et Actionibus Dei circa Peccatum* (Apud Ludovicum & Danielem Elzevirios 1657); John Strang, *De Interpretatione et Perfectione Scripturae, una cum Opusculis de Sabbato* (Ex Officina Arnoldi Leers 1663).

[101] Aristotle, *Posterior Analytics* (Geoffrey R G Mure tr, Clarendon Press 1928) II.19.

[102] Aristotle, *Posterior* (n 101) I.1.

[103] Aristotle, *Posterior* (n 101) I.1.

[104] Aristotle, *Metaphysics* (William Ross and John A Smith trs, Clarendon Press 1908) IV.4; cf Stair *Divine Perfections* 155.

than the *ordo cognoscendi*.[105] Where Stair's Dutch counterpart would have said you can observe man to be sociable and know yourself to be sociable, and therefore deduce the foundational principles of the law of nature, Stair would say that there are some things which are axiomatic and known to man as self-truths without any reasoning or argument or observation, such as the basic principles imprinted on man's heart (which reason cannot tell him alone).[106] Stair and Grotius may have both thought man had innate knowledge of natural law and he was sociable, but Grotius understands man to have reasoning tools which will lead to a shared understanding of natural law, whereas Stair thought that man had access to innate propositional statements of morality or rules of conduct which informed him, without reasoning, of the basic natural law of God.[107] It is the description of how you gain knowledge of natural law which separates these two authors. That is, Grotius's moral epistemology is within the compass of man's own reflection upon his nature, whereas Stair's differs in offering a more anthropological account of the law of nature, which needs to be enlivened by Scripture, revelation, grace, and rational deduction from innate principles.

Equally, another point where Stair and Grotius would most likely depart is with regard to Aristotle's *Metaphysics*, in that Grotius put his faith in classical sources of wisdom, whereas Stair put his faith in Aristotelian methods. Hence, Grotius appears to have little use for Aristotle's *Organon* or his *Metaphysics*,[108] whereas Stair appears to have continually drawn from *Metaphysics*. One of the major Aristotelian ideas students would have taken from Aristotle's *Metaphysics* was that to *know* something is to know the *cause* of something. This cornerstone of Aristotelian philosophy was developed in Aristotle's *Physics*. In the opening passage of the *Physics*, Aristotle said: 'The natural way of [enquiry] is to start from the things which are more knowable and obvious to us and proceed towards those which are clearer and more knowable by nature; for the same things are not "knowable relatively to us" and "knowable" without qualification.'[109] He continued: 'Now what is to us plain and obvious at first is rather confused masses, the elements and principles of which become known to us later by analysis.'[110] Aristotle says that in order to organize and analyze the confused masses of particulars 'we must advance from generalities to particulars; for it is a whole that is best known to sense-perception, and a generality is a kind of whole, comprehending many things within it, like parts.'[111] In *Physics*, Aristotle said that when one is confused with regard to the order of something, one should move, initially, from the general to particular. It is important, however, to note that the idea of moving from the

---

[105] I am grateful to Dr Giovanni Gellera for this observation.

[106] For discussion of Stair's approach, see Alasdair MacIntyre, *Whose Justice? Which Rationality?* (Duckworth 1988) 209–40; and, for discussion of Grotius, see Jon Miller, 'Innate ideas in Stoicism and Grotius' in Hans W Blom and Laurens C Winkel (eds), *Grotius and the Stoa* (Royal van Gorcum 2004) 157–76.

[107] Indeed, Stair himself explains the difference between him and Grotius with regard to why there is an obligation of restitution of property: Stair *Inst* 1.7.2.

[108] Richard Tuck, 'Grotius and Selden' in James H Burns and Mark Goldie (eds), *The Cambridge History of Political Thought 1450–1700* (CUP 1991) 499–529; Benjamin Straumann, *Roman Law in the State of Nature: The Classical Foundations of Hugo Grotius' Natural Law* (CUP 2015) 83–102.

[109] Aristotle, *Physics* (Robert P Hardie and RK Gaye trs, Clarendon Press 1930) I.1.

[110] Aristotle *Physics* (n 109) I.1.

[111] Aristotle *Physics* (n 109) I.1.

universal to the particular was something that Grotius endorsed, but this probably relates more to the influence of Ramism upon Grotius than it does to the influence of Aristotelianism.[112] However, this leads to the important question of Ramism and of how this could be said to relate to Stair's own philosophical viewpoint and taxonomy.

Ramism

So far, the prescribed curriculum of Glasgow has been discussed and the dominance of Aristotelian ideas has been shown. It could be argued, however, that regents, like Stair, taught Aristotelianism but they did not necessarily endorse it personally. Indeed, the early to mid-seventeenth century is often associated with a rejection of Aristotle and the reception of René Descartes's rationalism.[113] Even before Cartesian philosophy, it could be argued that the influence of Aristotelianism was waning during the time of Stair's own undergraduate studies, following the new methodology of Petrus Ramus (1515–72).[114] Simply put, Ramus wished to make education more accessible to his students and possibly to an audience beyond the formal bounds of a university. In making an argument for wholesale reform of university teaching, he drew from the work of Rodolphus Agricola (1443–85), who said that you do not need to start your study of logic by learning Aristotle's categories and his two analytical treatises, but rather you can start an argument and build knowledge from consideration as to whether an argument or proposition is reasonable and justified.[115] Agricola was in a sense continuing a major debate which accompanied Aristotle's logic throughout the medieval period and into the early modern period: was logic a means to acquire knowledge (*ordo*) or merely a way to arrange knowledge (*methodus*)?[116] In his *Dialecticae libri duo* published in 1556, he argued that logic was about *being* and the art of analyzing and examining something which related to being. He went to the extreme, in comparison to others, of saying that *methodus* was the only way to knowledge, and that the distinction between *methodus* and *ordo* was meaningless.[117] In effect, Ramus was arguing that there was no need to study the first books of Aristotle's logic, the categories, the analytics, but rather you

---

[112] Derek van der Merwe, 'Ramus, Mental Habits and Legal Science' in Danie Visser (ed), *Essays on the History of Law* (Juta & Co 1989) 32–59; Robert Feenstra, 'La Systématique du Droit dans l'œuvre de Grotius' in Lawrence M Friedman and Mauro Cappelletti (eds), *La Sistematica Giuridica: Storia, Teoria e Problem Attuali* (Istituto della Enciclopedia italiana 1991) 333–45; Visser and Whitty 'The Structure of the law of Delict in Historical Perspective' (n 7) 422–76.

[113] Desmond M Clarke, 'Descartes' Philosophy of Science and the Scientific Revolution' in John Cottingham (ed), *The Cambridge Companion to Descartes* (CUP 1992) 258–85.

[114] Walter J Ong, *Ramus, Method, and the Decay of Dialogue: From the Art of Discourse to the Art of Reason* (first published in 1958, Chicago University Press 2004) 295–310; Joseph S Freedman, *Philosophy and the Arts in Central Europe, 1500–1700: Teaching and Texts at Schools and Universities* (Taylor Francis 1999) 119; Erland Sellberg, 'Petrus Ramus' in Edward N Zalta (ed), *The Stanford Encyclopedia of Philosophy* (2014) <https://plato.stanford.edu/archives/win2020/entries/ramus/> accessed 8 April 2021.

[115] Gilbert *Renaissance Concepts of Method* (n 89) 70–131; Ong *Ramus, Method and the Decay of Dialogue* (n 114) 92–126.

[116] Sellberg 'Petrus Ramus' (n 114).

[117] Donald R Kelley, *The Beginning of Ideology: Consciousness and Society in the French Reformation* (CUP 1981) 142; Ong *Ramus, Method and the Decay of Dialogue* (n 114) 71–93.

should progress straight to the topics or the consideration of eloquence and methods of persuasion.[118] He was, however, importantly, in favour of Aristotle's method of starting from the familiar and moving towards the unfamiliar, but he rejected the epistemic and metaphysical grounds upon which that was based.

Whether Stair was impressed by Ramus is something which cannot be ruled out conclusively. Ramism was very popular amongst Lutherans and Calvinists during the mid- to late seventeenth century. However, there is some evidence to suggest that Stair did not adopt Ramism in his teaching and in his foundational understanding of human knowledge, including his moral epistemology. Stair's nineteenth century biographer, Mackay, mentions that a student of Stair, Robert Law, son of Thomas Law, a minister of Inchinnan, Inverclyde, preserved notes from Stair's lectures.[119] Although these do not appear to be available today for consultation, Mackay reported that 'between 29 October and 29 December 1643' Stair gave a course of lectures upon logic, which were 'cramped with technicalities which the Latin schoolmen had imposed on the *Organon* of Aristotle'.[120] Additionally, Stair published student theses in 1646 which are based upon Aristotle's *Organon*, physics and ethics and make frequent reference to various Aristotelian commentaries.[121] However, in Stair's mature work on natural philosophy, the *Physiologica nova experimentalis*,[122] he demonstrates an understandable respect for Aristotle, although his comments show that he is far from a dogmatic disciple.[123] It should be noted, however, that to depart in the seventeenth century from Aristotle's natural philosophy is different from departing from his logic, metaphysics, or ethics.[124] Indeed, it is probably when both the *Institutions* and the *Divine Perfections* are read in conjunction that a strong indication of Stair's fundamental ideas becomes evident. Grotius is far more Ramist than Stair. For, although Stair may have been sympathetic to the systematic, methodical, and clear presentation of Ramism, he retained the notion, particularly in terms of ethics and theology, that there are some things that man knows without argument, which are axiomatic. That is, knowledge of the law of

---

[118] Kelley *The Beginning of Ideology* (n 117) 142.

[119] Coutts *A History* (n 94) 106.

[120] Aeneas J G Mackay, *Memoir of Sir James Dalrymple, First Viscount Stair* (Edmonston & Douglas 1873) 17.

[121] Jacob Dalrimplio, *Theses Logicae, Metaphysicae, Physicae, Mathematicae, et Ethicae. Quas Adolescentes hac vice ex Collegio Glasguensi Publice Propugnabunt, ad diem 27 Julii 1646* (Georgius Andersonus 1646). See Sytsma's translation of Dalrymple's ethical theses: James Dalrymple of Stair, ' "Ethical Theses" in Theses Logicae, Metaphysicae, Physicae, Mathematicae, et Ethicae (George Anderson 1646)' (David S Sytsma tr, 2020) <(PDF) James Dalrymple of Stair: Ethical Theses (Glasgow, 1646) | David S. Sytsma - Academia. edu>) accessed 29 October 2022.

[122] James Dalrymple, Viscount Stair, *Physiologica nova Experimentalis in Qua, Generales Notiones Aristotelis, Epicuri, & Cartesii Supplentur* (Cornelium Boutesteyn 1686).

[123] eg Stair *Physiologia* (n 122) 7:

> Aristoteles principia & placita sua longe plenius & prudentins tractavit, etenim eruditionem in diversas disciplinas & methodos redgit, quod à nullio alio factum est, indcirco ipsius philosophia ut clarior & cohærentior cito prævaluit, & ubi clara ac distincta principia attingere non potuit, terminis generallbus quantum poctuit prximiorobus usus est, & prudenter satis eorum imbecillitatem abscondit.

[124] For discussion of Stair's innovation in terms of natural philosophy, see Giovanna Gellera, 'Natural Philosophy in the Graduation Theses of the Scottish Universities in the First Half of the Seventeenth Century' (DPhil thesis, University of Glasgow 2012) 66–71. Also see Hutton *British Philosophy in the Seventeenth Century* (n 89) 72–91.

nature is derived, inter alia, by reasoning from the first principles engraved on man's heart. In taking that approach, he remained very much influenced by Aristotelian logic and metaphysics. On this basis, it can then be suggested that this philosophical perspective provided Stair with a skeletal structure around which to organize the law of Scotland.

Aristotelianism gave Stair a structure for law of Scotland

Principles and the Structure of Obligations

The idea that there are axiomatic principles which man possesses is often stated by Stair in the *Institutions* with regard to his moral reasoning. For example, in the opening paragraph of the 1693 edition of the *Institutions*, Stair says when explaining his method: 'No man can be a knowing lawyer in any nation' if he has not 'well pondered and digested in his mind the common law of the world'.[125] He goes on to explain: 'I have therefore begun with the common principles of law'.[126] Consistently throughout the various versions of the *Institutions*, Stair says, within the opening few paragraphs, that 'the first principles of this Natural Law are known to men without Reasoning or experience, without Art, Industry or Education, & so are known to men every where through the World'.[127] He explains this, saying: 'It is said to be written in the Hearts of Men, because Law useth to be written on the Pillars or Table for certainty or Conservation: So this Law is written by the Finger of God upon Man's Heart, there to remain for ever.' Again, consistently since the original versions of the *Institutions* from the late 1650s, it is said by Stair that 'this Law is also called Conscience, … which relates more to the Principles of Religion, than Morality', but nevertheless he stresses that it gives a man some basic direction as to what he should and should not do, such as claiming back a debt which has already been paid but which he could legally claim.[128] Later on in the *Institutions*, Stair says the 'practical principles' of equity arise in man 'without reasoning or debate, as naturally as heat from fire'.[129] In arguing that law was a rational discipline, Stair said it was from these self-evident principles that law is deduced. These, of course, were obedience, freedom, and engagement. As already examined in Chapter 4, this led Stair to hold that the law applying to contracting behaviour derived from a basic principle: 'that there is nothing more natural than to stand by the faith of our pactions'.[130] This was a simple self-evident principle of natural law. This practical principle of natural law was also related to a principle of commerce, which was a principle of positive law, known to man due to its utility. But it was principle before utility for Stair.

The idea that aspects of man's knowledge are innate, and imprinted in his soul as first principles, is repeated in Stair's *Divine Perfections*.[131] There Stair says that by the

---

[125] Stair *Inst* 1.1.
[126] Stair *Inst* 1.1.
[127] Stair *Inst* 1.1.3. This is also consistent with the Stair *Divine Perfections* 139.
[128] Stair *Inst* 1.1.5.
[129] Stair *Inst* 1.1.17 (Ad Ms 25.3.3 ff14–15).
[130] Stair *Inst* 1.1.21 (Ad Ms 25.3.3 ff15–16).
[131] Stair *Divine Perfections* 154–55.

free Bounty of God did imprint upon the Soul of Man the first Principles of his Knowledge of Things that fall not under sense, without which he could never have had firm and clear Knowledge, albeit he had the Capacity to discern Implications and Consequences downwards from Causes to Effects, and upwards from Effects to Causes; for if there were not some Principles self-evident, the Chain of Consequences might run without end.[132]

Later in the *Divine Perfections*, Stair discusses the general innate principles and inclinations of man, saying that the goodness of God is mirrored in the soul of man, which includes principles such as:

to do that which is congruous to and becoming to his Nature, not only to what is essential to him, but to what is superadded by the Divine Benignity, which is more sensibly felt in the Aversion of things which are unbecoming Man, and which all judge to be vicious and vile.[133]

After citing common Christian virtues such as temperance, sobriety, modesty, meekness, and so on, he goes on to say that God[134]

hath imprinted on the Soul of Man special Principles for eminent cases, which operate like Instincts without necessity of reasoning, as the desire of Happiness, the care to preserve Life, the abhorrence of Cruelty, the desire to relieve the Innocent opprest, Gratitude to Benefactors, Faithfulness to those that do rationally rely and trust, Love to those in Society and Friendship, that especial which is most entire and absolutely by Marriage ...

On this basis, the natural law content of Stair's *Institutions* is based on simple axiomatic principles which derive, according to Stair, from knowledge of God's will, which is imprinted on man's soul. Therefore, the structure of Scots law, if based on principles known to all men and intrinsically rational and universal, should be organized and follow what is written on man's heart or soul.

Stair and the Structure of the *Institutions*

Principles, obligations, and rights

Before looking at how this philosophical and theological position informed the structure of the *Institutions* and how it would have been understood by Scots in the mid-seventeenth century, it is important to start with how Stair describes it. In the *Institutions*, Stair says the 'Law of Nature is also termed the Moral Law, being

---

[132] Stair *Divine Perfections* 115.
[133] Stair *Divine Perfections* 161.
[134] Stair *Divine Perfections* 161.

the absolute and adequate Rule of the Manners of men, for all times and places'.[135] He later gives some indication as to what the Moral Law consists of, saying first that its principles

> are such as are known without arguing, and to which the judgement upon apprehension thereof, will give its ready and full assent, [which are that] God is to be adored and obeyed, Parents to be obeyed and honoured, Children to be loved and entertained; and such are these common Precepts which are set forth in the Civil Law, to live honestly, to wrong no man, to give every man his right.[136]

At this point, Stair introduces the concept of a right, saying: 'here we shall speak of the most general Principles, which have influence upon all the Rights of men, leaving the more particular ones to the Rights flowing therefrom in their proper places'.[137] Before speaking about rights in more detail, Stair says that the

> first Principles of Equity are these, that God is to be obeyed by man. 2. That man is a free creature, having power to dispose of himself and of all things, in so far as by his obedience to God he is not restrained. 3. That this freedom of man is in his own power, and may be restrained by his voluntary engagements, which he is bound to fulfil, or take them up more summarily.[138]

He goes on to explain that these are 'also three prime Principles of the positive Law', but because man is now 'depraved & wanting Justice' he has decided not to insist upon the exact enforcement of the first principles of equity but rather to 'make up Societies of men' so that they 'may mutually defend one another, and procure to one another their Rights, and also to set clear limits to every man's Property, & to maintain Traffick & Commerce among themselves and with others'. On this basis, therefore, the principles of positive law are, according to Stair, society, freedom, property, and commerce.[139] He then explains that:

> formal and proper Object of Law, are the Rights of men; a Right is a Power given by the Law, of depositing of things, or exacting from persons that which they are due; this will be evident if we consider the several kinds of Rights, which are three, our Personal Liberty, Dominion and Obligation.[140]

In a few densely packed paragraphs, Stair offers a theory as well as several potent concepts upon which he can not only justify the law of Scotland but also organize and arrange it in a novel manner.

---

[135] Stair *Inst* 1.1.7.
[136] Stair *Inst* 1.1.18.
[137] Stair *Inst* 1.1.18.
[138] Stair *Inst* 1.1.18.
[139] Stair *Inst* 1.1.18.
[140] Stair *Inst* 1.1.21.

Liberty and obligation

Freedom and liberty appear central to Stair's account of law and the structure of the *Institutions*. The following two chapters will examine in detail his conception of liberty and compare Stair's approach to conceptions of liberty found in Grotius. For now, however, it should be noted that obligations should be seen not as contrasting with or describing a state of non-liberty but rather as either the enforcement of what one should do with one's liberty or the withdrawal of that liberty because one has failed to use that liberty correctly. Enforcement of an obligation is the denial of the opportunity to choose to do the right thing. What this means is that Stair presents the private law of Scotland in the opening titles of the *Institutions*, including the law applying to contracting, as legal obligations which encapsulate the Moral Law. On his account, legal obligations, importantly, remind men of their obligations to others, direct them as to what they should do, and at times prevent us from misusing our liberty. Such an understanding is consistent with Calvin's explanation of the uses of law,[141] namely *usus elechticus* (law as a mirror),[142] *usus politicus* (law maintaining external discipline),[143] and *usu in renatis* (law after regeneration).[144] There is no contrast in Stair between obligation and liberty in the sense found with Hobbes in the *Leviathan* and what is sometimes characterized as negative liberty. As will be discussed, under the title on liberty, Stair discussed legitimate and justified interferences with liberty which are thereafter explained under the following titles of the *Institutions*. Hence, when an obligation is enforced, man does, at one level, lose liberty in terms of his ability physically to choose another option, or the opportunity to carry out right action; but, at another level, the enforcement of the obligation ensures that a man does what the Moral Law requires of him and therefore that he acts with liberty, which could be roughly termed a positive conception of liberty. In terms of structure, however, there is more to be said at this point as to why the title is there, what use it has for Stair to contrast liberty with servitude, and how it relates to other options open to Stair.

Stair and Justinian

It is fairly clear that Stair had in mind Justinian's *Institutes* when he started to draft the opening titles of Book I—and so, prima facie, the inclusion of a title on liberty is not so surprising. Indeed, some early manuscript copies of Stair's *Institutions* start with variations of the opening sentence from the *Institutes*:[145] '*institia est constans et*

---

[141] To an extent, it is similar to Luther's legal philosophy also: Harold J Berman, *Law and Revolution, II: The Impact of the Protestant Reformations on the Western Legal Tradition* (Harvard University Press 2006) Ch 2, specifically regarding Philip Melanchthon. Also see Astorri, *Lutheran Theology and Contract Law* (n 89) Ch 2.

[142] Calvin *Inst* 2.7.6; 2.7.7; 3.18.9.

[143] Calvin *Inst* 2.7.10; 2.7.6–7.

[144] Calvin *Inst* 2.7.12.

[145] cf Ad Lib Ms 24.2.10 (1659–62): 'Jurisprudence is the knowledge of right, and justice is the inclination of the will to give every man his right and law is the command so that the best placing and action of the will be all the rights of men, and knowing from what law they arise.' Also, Ad Lib Ms 25.1.14 (1671?): 'Jurisprudence is the knowledge of right, and justice is the inclination (or will) to give every man his

perpetua voluntas ius snum cuique tribuens / Justice is an unswerving and perpetual determination to acknowledge all men's rights'.[146] Stair, however, is innovating within the Justinian structure, or using the traditional arrangement of the *Institutes*, where a discussion of a free man is placed first, but adopting a different understanding of an individual, liberty and private law. The first difference is that Stair does not speak about different types of status which a person can hold within a legal system, namely free born, freedman, independent and dependent persons, and so on, but rather starts from a position of a free person, *sui iuris*, who nevertheless is defined or appears within the legal system as someone with various obligations and duties owed towards others. Of course, you can see different aspects of the Justinian law of persons arising throughout the *Institutions*, which are mostly dispersed throughout Book I, but Stair does not see these categories as the starting point from which to arrange the private law of Scotland. The second difference is that Stair does not see the private law as being structured by descending hierarchical rules relating to each particular person's station in society, but rather he presents, through his taxonomy, private law as a system of rights and obligations which are owed to each other on an interpersonal and horizontal level.[147] Therefore, Stair's structure starts with the individual and what individuals owe to each other, in contrast to a system which starts with feudal law, or an account of legal institutions' authority over individuals, or a sovereign's right to govern and create law. However, what is of interest is that he does speak of servitude within this opening title; he says that servitude is diametrically opposite to liberty. This contrast Stair uses to explain liberty appears idiosyncratic in comparison to contemporary legal writing in the mid-seventeenth century.[148]

Copying Grotius? Puzzling servitude?

Ford has suggested it is somewhat puzzling that Stair does not just have a title describing liberty and the obligations placed upon it: why does Stair contrast liberty with servitude, and why does he include this in his legal treatise when servitude and slavery, according to Stair, were no longer in force in Scotland?[149] There is also another related question: how does Stair's treatment of liberty relate to Grotius? Is Stair positioning servitude and liberty in the same way that Grotius described the formation of civil government as an alienation of liberty?[150] Perhaps Stair is suggesting that to be under the civil law of Scotland you are under a form of servitude? Indeed, it may be

right, and law is the command or will of right holding forth accordance all rights of men, and knowing from what law they arise'. Further, Ad Lib Ms 25.3.2 (1666?): 'Jurisprudence is knowledge of will or rights and justice is the inclination to give every man his right. And is the rule or will by holding forthin over the rights of men and showing form the law that doth arise'.

[146] *Justinian Inst* 1.1.

[147] For comment upon this, see Neil MacCormick, 'Stair as Analytical Jurist' in David M Walker (ed), *Stair Tercentenary Studies*, vol 33 (Stair Society 1981) 187–99.

[148] MacCormick, 'Stair as Analytical Jurist' (n 147) 194.

[149] John D Ford, 'Stair's Title "Of Liberty and Servitude"' in Andrew D E Lewis and David J Ibbetson (eds), *The Roman Law Tradition* (CUP 1994) 135–58.

[150] Grotius *The Rights of War and Peace* (n 70) 1.3.2–8.

proposed that Stair took inspiration from Grotius's *The Rights of War and Peace* and is merely using servitude as a way by which to describe a state of government whereby man transfers his liberty to civil government or a sovereign in order to establish order, but sacrifices his liberty in the process. Certainly, in *The Rights of War and Peace* Stair would have found an example of how you can develop an account of not just private law but the law of nature by starting with an account of individuals and the rights they owe to each other. Therefore, it may be attributing too much to Stair to suggest that he was innovating, as he may have only been emulating or copying Grotius. In that sense, Stair's structure is a result of his reading of Grotius and is consequently an attempt to build a system of private law in Scotland based on the three natural rights found in *The Rights of War and Peace*: liberty, property, and commerce. This chapter, however, argues otherwise.

First, it should be noted that it would be wrong, on the basis of titles 1, 2, and 3 of the *Institutions*, to characterize Stair as a natural rights theorist akin to Grotius. As has already been explained, and will be developed further in the following chapters, there are important philosophical and theological differences between Stair and Grotius, which mean that Stair did not completely adopt or follow Grotius's natural rights model. Therefore, the inclusion of the title on liberty is not an articulation of a right in the sense that Grotius gives to it, nor does it have the same political implication. As Tuck has stressed, although Presbyterians may in the mid-seventeenth century appear very close to the natural rights theories associated with Grotius or Hobbes, and for that matter Locke, Presbyterians' project should be cast in a different light: 'they wished to combine a stress on the need for consent with a reluctance to construe the magisterial power as constituted by individuals promising not to exercise their natural rights'.[151] The danger of arguing the former, that civil government is constituted by individuals sacrificing their natural rights, including their liberty, was akin to what Calvinists would have said was an Arminian heresy, of which, ironically, John Maxwell, bishop of Ross (1586?–1647), had accused the Presbyterians: that is, overestimating man's abilities by suggesting that he could create a society, government, and laws without the aid of God.[152]

Second, in terms of how we understand the inclusion of servitude, Ford's interpretation is important. He indicates that Stair's title 'Of liberty and servitude' can be understood if read against Presbyterian political ideology of the mid-seventeenth century. In particular, contrasting liberty with servitude was a means by which to stress the difference between, on the one hand, the law of Scotland, which is based on the law of nature and applied by the sovereign without a transfer of liberty, and on the other hand, a state of affairs where the law and the liberty of a subject is said to be dependent upon the rule and laws of the sovereign. The latter would appear similar to absolute sovereignty, whereas the former is a far more limited sense of sovereignty which is bounded by the law of nature and is more agreeable to mid-seventeenth century Presbyterians. At several important points during the seventeenth century, leading Presbyterians in Scotland searched for a political language and ideas which could plot

---

[151] Richard Tuck, *Natural Rights Theories* (CUP 1979) 144.
[152] James Maxwell, *Sacro-Sancta Regum Majestas: Or; The Sacred and Royall Prerogative of Christian Kings* (first published 1644, Tho Dring 1680).

a course between the absolute right of kings and the natural rights associated with writers such as Grotius or the Jesuits.[153]

Ford provides a significant examination of Stair alongside Samuel Rutherford (1600–61), demonstrating that they both shared the understanding that civil government and positive laws were akin to a network of rights and duties, but that civil government was created by both divine appointment and consent of the people.[154] Ford explains that Stair separated his title on liberty and servitude from his consideration of persons because a master slave relationship cannot be analyzed in terms of Stair's interpersonal view of private law. Status could not provide the starting point for Stair's vision of Presbyterian legal order whereby everyone's use of their liberty was equally accountable to God and his peers. Adopting an interpersonal or horizontal description of private law, as an interplay between individual's rights and duties, provided a legal description which fitted with the Presbyterian ideal of a political order. If this explains why Stair's structure commences with an explanation of liberty and servitude, and why liberty is said to operate in harmony with obligations, how should Stair's selection of specific obligations be understood, namely titles 4 to 10 of Book I?

The Moral Law and canon law

In general outline, it could be suggested that Stair structures the layout of his account of obligations on the basis of his understanding of what the Moral Law is and its respective priorities. Indeed, to speak of the Moral Law in the mid- to late seventeenth century would have invoked in the minds of Stair's readers the *Decalogue* or the Ten Commandments. Question 98 of the *Larger Catechism*, which accompanied the *Westminster Confession of Faith*, asked: where is the Moral Law summarily comprehended? The answer is given: 'The moral law is summarily comprehended in the Ten Commandments, which were delivered by the voice of God upon Mount Sinai, and written by him in two tablets of stone; and are recorded in the twentieth chapter of Exodus; the four first commandments containing our duty to God, and the other six our duty to man.' Further on in the *Catechism*, it is said that 'The sum of the six commandments which contain our duty to man, is, to love our neighbour as ourselves, and to do to others what we would have them do to us.'[155] Additionally, to say man was by nature free and that this is a principle he knows without argument was in many ways to invoke Chapter 9 of the *Westminster Confession of Faith* (1647), which said: 'God hath endued the will of man with natural liberty, that it is neither forced, nor by any absolute necessary of nature determined to good or evil.' Stair's general iteration of the principles of the Moral Law are unsurprisingly closely connected and resemble the propositions found in the *Larger Catechism* and its summary of the *Decalogue*.

---

[153] John D Ford, 'Lex, Rex Iusto Posita: Samuel Rutherford on the Origins of Government' in Roger A Mason (ed), *Scots and Britons: Scottish Political Thought and the Union of 1603* (CUP 1994) 262–90.

[154] John D Ford, 'Stair's Title "Of Liberty and Servitude"' (n 149) 156.

[155] Over 100 editions were printed between 1650 and 1670 in London, Glasgow, and Edinburgh. The edition used here is the 1655: *The Confession of Faith, and the Larger and Short Catechism, Agreed upon by the Assembly of Divines at Westminster* (London 1655). Answer to question 122.

A good example of how the Moral Law might be understood in terms of duties placed upon men can be found in the mid-seventeenth century exposition by James Durham (1622–58) of the *Decalogue*, which was published posthumously.[156] Speaking of the ways by which a man may increase his estate and improve his lot, Durham says that there are three priorities which should guide a man's decision:[157]

1. For the end, 1. The chief and last is God's glory, that we may be serviceable to him with our substance, in our generation, and may be kept from stealing and lying. Prov. 30.8, 9.
2. Others good, that we may be helpful to them, for men may and should work for this end, although they had what were sufficient for themselves, see Ephes. 4.28.
3. Our selves are to be considered, and we are to look here, 1. to necessity, 2. to convenience, 3. to honesty.

Durham's summation of what a man can do with his liberty demonstrates how Stair's contemporaries may have formulated the priority of obligations placed upon a man. This priority of obligations may have given Stair the broad outline of how a positive law based on the Moral Law should be arranged, with conventional obligations, what man wished to do coming last in the hierarchy; that is, our obligations to God and then to others are anterior to our own individual voluntary obligations. On this basis, it appears that the basic principles of law, around which Stair orders the positive law of Scotland derive from seventeenth century theological accounts of Moral Law. Indeed, the analytical structure of these theological expositions may have provided a blueprint for Stair's taxonomy.[158] Therefore, the basic principles around which the *Institutions* are structured would have been fairly recognizable in the mid-seventeenth century as propositions of or related to statements found in the *Decalogue*, which were summarized in the *Shorter* and the *Larger Catechism of the Westminster Confession of Faith*.[159]

If each of the first six titles of the *Institutions* can be related to a Presbyterian description of the Moral Law, it is also evident that the opening titles—on conjugal, parental, restitution, reparation, and conventional obligations—are areas of human action or relationships which would traditionally, in the century before Stair wrote, have been regulated by canon law.[160] The practical importance of canon law and the integral part

---

[156] James Durham, *A Practical Exposition of the X Commandments* (Kings Armes 1675). cf Lutheran theologians and jurists: Astorri, *Lutheran Theology and Contract Law* (n 89) 118–51. Of interest is the way Stair and other Presbyterian's approach the practical implications of *Decalogue*, particularly relating to contracting. As Astorri makes clear, Lutheran's viewed matters through the lens of property and theft, which appears to contrast with the approach described in this chapter taken by Stair and others in Scotland.

[157] Durham *A Practical Exposition* (n 156) 413.

[158] For example, cf: conjugal obligations, described in Stair *Inst* 1.4 and *Larger Catechism* (n 155) 133–34; obligations relating to parents, children, tutors, and curators in *Inst* 1.6 and 1.7 and *Larger Catechism* (n 155) 128 ff; and restitution, recompense and remuneration, reparation, and conventional obligations and *Larger Catechism* (n 155) 135 ff.

[159] *Shorter Catechism* and *Larger Catechism* (n 155).

[160] For an account of the reach and scope of canon law into the private and interpersonal lives of individuals, see Simon Ollivant, *The Court of the Official in Pre-Reformation Scotland, based on the Surviving Records of the Officials of St Andrews and Edinburgh*, vol 34 (Stair Society 1982) 70–97; Richard H Helmholz, *The Spirit of Classical Canon Law* (The University of Georgia Press 1996) 88–166, 174–99, 229–56.

canon law courts played in Scottish society prior to 1560 is well known.[161] What might not always be evident, however, is that Stair, in the opening titles of the *Institutions*, is demonstrating and describing the jurisdictional competence of the Court of Session, that is, a secular court, in areas which clearly fell within the spiritual scope of the Roman Catholic Church and its network of courts. This is therefore an important summation of the law as applied in Scotland, including contractual obligations, as it demonstrates that these are civil matters rather than spiritual, or at least they can be handled and resolved by the positive law of Scotland. As a Calvinist, Stair would not have viewed, for example, marriage as a sacrament, but rather he would have understood it, from a theological perspective, as being a temporal affair.[162] It would have been important therefore, if he was describing the law of Scotland, that he placed this clearly within the jurisdiction of a temporal court. Indeed, the central placement of marriage and the family more generally within a Christian's life is a familiar move within Protestant theology and legal writing following the Reformation, and therefore it is unsurprising when viewed from a theological perspective that Stair places family as the primary obligations placed upon an individual.[163] From this perspective, it is possible to see the opening titles of the *Institutions* as not only a legal formulation of the second part of the *Decalogue* but also a clear articulation and declaration of the jurisdictional competence of the Court of Session and the law of Scotland in areas of human behaviour and relations which were previously within the domain of canon law and the Roman Catholic Church.

Obligations before property

If the first principles upon which the law of Scotland is derived mirror the second part of the *Decalogue*, this puts intrapersonal and interpersonal laws before any laws which relate to things or institutions. Unlike the principles of Moral Law, Stair also sees property rights as being created by men and emerging for the sake of utility. After speaking of liberty, Stair opens his title on obligations, saying: 'Rights [called] personal, or Obligations, being in Nature and Time, for the most part anterior to, and inductive of, Rights Real of Dominion and Property, do therefore come next unto Liberty.'[164] Under title 1 of Book III, Stair explains that property rights are an artificial creation of men emerging out of shared ownership and then possession and then the creation of rights. He says God gave man 'Dominion or Lordship over all the Creatures of the Earth in the Air, and in the sea', and that this dominion was 'given to Man without

---

[161] David Baird Smith, 'Canon Law' in *An Introductory Survey of the Sources and Literature of Scots Law*, vol 1 (Stair Society 1936) 183–92; William Gordon, 'A Comparison of the Influence of Roman Law in England and Scotland' in William Gordon (ed), *Roman Law, Scots Law and Legal History: Selected Essays* (CUP 2007) 309–23; Thomas M Green (ed), *The Consistorial Decisions of the Commissaries of Edinburgh, 1564–1576/7*, vol 61 (Stair Society 2014).

[162] Alexander Henderson, *The Government and Order of the Church of Scotland* (Anon. 1641) 26–27.

[163] Steven Ozment and John Witte, 'Luther', in J Witte Jr and Gary S Hauk (eds), *Christianity and Family Law* (CUP 2017) 179–94; Barbara Pitkin, 'John Calvin' in J Witte Jr and Gary S Hauk (eds), *Christianity and Family Law* (CUP 2017) 195–210.

[164] Stair *Inst* 1.1.3.

distinct proportions or bounds', allowing men to have an 'equal interest'.[165] He went on to explain:

> yet the use and fruit thereof must in some cases, and might in all cases become proper, and could not without injury be taken from him, much more the things which had received specification from his art or industry became proper, and all other might be debarred from any profit or use of it.[166]

One would expect Stair to adopt this type of historical explanation of property rights given the influence of legal humanism upon the *Institutions* and the general theological premises of seventeenth-century Protestantism, which denied the property rights theories they found in medieval theological literature and contemporary writers such as the Jesuits of the Counter-Reformation.[167]

Conventional and obediential obligations

This is where the division of obediential and conventional obligation originates. Stair understands that God has made laws for man, which are rational but also written on his heart. They are binding because they are rational, and man is commanded by God to follow them. It is not because man first determines their utility or because they are recorded in texts from antiquity or because reason binds God and man. This does not mean, however, that man cannot, from these basic principles written on his heart, deduce further conclusions; but fundamentally, the law which Stair articulates, his organizational starting point, is the axiomatic principles he says are known to all men. Although Stair is more philosophical than Calvin in his explanation of the innate principles in man, and demonstrates a greater eagerness to explain the internal workings of man's mind, his general approach and exposition, in the *Divine Perfections*, of what is imprinted in man's soul is very much in keeping with Book 2 Chapter 8 of Calvin's *Institutes*, where he offers an exposition of God's Moral Law.[168] Indeed, although the *Divine Perfections* is more optimistic in tone, saying that God requires such things for our happiness, when compared to mid-seventeenth century Scots theological literature, the idea that such things are imprinted on man's soul or heart is discussed in detail.[169] Importantly, therefore, for Stair, law does not start from the point of view of liberty, like Grotius, but from first basic principles of obedience of natural law, which we did not create due to reason, utility, or tradition, but which are known without reasoning.

---

[165] Stair *Inst* 2.1.1.

[166] Stair *Inst* 2.1.1.

[167] Tuck *Natural Rights Theories* (n 151) 32–57.

[168] This is far from exclusive to Calvinism: Merio Scattola, 'Before and After Natural' in Tim J Hochstrasser and P Schröder (eds), *Early Modern Natural Law Theories* (Kluwer 2003) 12–30. See also, Astorri, *Lutheran Theology and Contract Law* (n 149) 47–109.

[169] Scattola 'Before and After Natural Law' (n 168); Giovanna Gellara, 'Pride Aside: James Dundas as a Stoic Christina' (2019) 17 (2) Journal of Scottish Philosophy 157; Alexander Broadie, 'James Dundas, the First Lord Arniston, on the Idea of Moral Philosophy and the Concept of Will' in Alexander Broadie (ed), *Scottish Philosophy in the Seventeenth Century* (OUP 2020) 159.

As will be discussed with regard to Stair's conception of liberty, it is only after saying what man should do that he organizes the law of obligations around what man then does with his liberty, including the creation of obligations with other men. Conventional obligations are nonetheless binding not because of virtue, reason, or utility, but because, again, man knows, due to the law of nature imprinted on his heart, that he should perform his conventional obligations. That is, according to Stair, to stand by the faith of one's 'pactions' was a self-evident precept of natural law. This allowed him to start from axiomatic principles and deduce the implications of these principles into particular instances. He was able to show how the complex and disparate rules of contracting related to a foundational moral precept of natural law. Thereafter Stair highlighted, through reasoning, that man could recognize these axiomatic principles in practice. He saw their utility. However, importantly, the utility of the principle, for Stair, was merely a consequence of the principle that people should adhere to their pactions. It was profitable to adhere to promises because it emerged from this basic principle; it was not the profitability of promise-keeping which made it a principle. In summary, Stair's basic pattern of reasoning about moral principles exemplifies the general application of the principles of logic and metaphysics found in Aristotle's *Organon* but does so in a very Calvinist manner.

Conclusion

Legal humanism provided Stair with a critique of traditional Roman law sources, but this critique did not necessarily offer any specific template which Stair favoured. For instance, Douaren did not try to rearrange the *Corpus iuris*; he only criticized its order and called for a new approach. As Stein says, Douaren 'did not demonstrate how the new method should be applied in detail'.[170] When Donellus (1527–91) did attempt to reorder matters, he focused on particular aspects of the *Corpus Iuris*, such as Justinian's *Institutes*. That is, Donellus sought to draw together Justinian's books on obligations and actions, whereas Stair wanted a system to explain the law of Scotland as a whole, rather than rearrange the classic text of Justinian. Moreover, Grotius's *The Rights of War and Peace* would have certainly presented Stair with an example of humanist writing, but Stair's epistemology and logic is different from Grotius and leads him on a different path. Where Grotius was attempting to organize the idealized principles of natural law which each man could deduce, Stair was trying to organize the rules, decisions, and particular doctrines of positive law on the basis of inherent principles which man knew without reasoning. The suggestion made in this chapter, therefore, is that Stair's treatment of conventional obligations differs in comparison to his humanist counterparts because of his specific philosophical and theological standpoint. This is because Stair was employing a Calvinist anthropology along with Aristotelian methods. He therefore tried to structure the law of Scotland around basic principles of Moral Law found in Scripture, particularly the Ten Commandments, the *Westminster Confession of Faith* (1647), and what he asserted to be written on man's heart. Roman

---

[170] Stein 'Donellus' (n 57) 443.

law, for Stair, did not offer this philosophical, theological, or Scriptural grounding. Nor did the traditional Justinian structure explain, as required by Aristotelian philosophy, the causes of actions which was necessary for Stair.[171] In Aristotelianism, Stair found both a method and a teleological system upon which to shape the law and incorporate Calvinism. In describing Stair's Aristotelianism, this chapter is not attempting to reinterpret the humanism of Stair that is evident and express. The analysis provided here offers an account of Stair's method stressing his theological and philosophical impulses.[172] Indeed, intellectual histories of mid-seventeenth century scholars often uncover a complex relationship between humanism and Aristotelianism, and so it is no surprise that Stair demonstrates this complexity too.[173] Because the relationship in the early modern period between humanism and (say) scholasticism or Aristotelianism is not black and white, it may not always be helpful to use these genres when trying to explain a more general point: whether you can define Stair as a scholastic, Aristotelian, legal humanist, or otherwise, on the basis of the argument presented above, it is suggested that he drew directly from theological and philosophical ideas when developing his methods, structure, and organization of the law applying to contracting behaviour.

---

[171] Stair *Inst* 1.3.2.

[172] Margo Todd, *Christian Humanism and Puritan Social Order* (CUP 1987) Ch 5; Richard M Muller, 'Calvin and the "Calvinist": Assessing Continuities and Discontinuities between the Reformation and Orthodoxy' (1995) 30 Calvin Theological Journal 360–72; John Coffey, *Politics, Religion and the British Revolutions: The Mind of Samuel Rutherford* (CUP 1997) Ch 3.

[173] Todd *Christian Humanism* (n 172); Muller 'Calvin and the "Calvinist"' (n 172); Coffey, Politics Religion and the British Revolutions (n 172).

6

Human Action, the Will, and Freedom

As an aspect of human action, the will is an important concept within Stair's account of law and is critical to his description of conventional obligations and the idea that man has a freedom to contract. Prior to the 1660s, the term 'will' did not play a significant role either in contemporary legal writing about contracting in Scotland or within legal literature used by lawyers in Scotland. In terms of the history of contract law in Europe, James Gordley and Wim Decock[1] have argued that the will becomes a key legal concept in contractual thought from the early seventeenth century onwards via the juridical commentaries of the late scholastics.[2] In contrast, it does not appear to have played a role in English legal thought until the late eighteenth century.[3] It does appear in Grotius's *The Rights of War and Peace*[4] of 1625, but does not figure in his basic account of the law applying to contracting in the Dutch provinces, the *Introduction to Dutch Jurisprudence* published in 1631.[5] This raises some basic questions which link to the development of contractual thought during the early modern period. First, where did this term come from? Second, why did Stair use the term rather than 'consent' or 'consensus', which were more familiar to jurists? Third, how was the term used in other seventeenth-century Scots writing? Did Stair use the term 'will' in the same way as other Scots? Did he merely copy Grotius, or did he have a different meaning? Fourth, what did the term 'will' mean to Stair and other seventeenth-century writers or readers? It is easy for a modern reader of Stair to apply contemporary concepts of human psychology and decision-making to a seventeenth-century term like 'the will'. Because the term is so familiar, its philology, theological significance, and complexity can go unnoticed. Similarly, because terms like 'liberty' and 'freedom' are used

---

[1] James Gordley, *The Philosophical Origins of Modern Contract Doctrine* (OUP 1991) Ch 4; Wim Decock, *Theologians and Contract Law: The Moral Transformation of the Ius Commune (ca. 1500–1650)* (Brill 2012) 167–70.

[2] The term 'late scholastic' can mean several things. Generally, it is used to refer to writers or teachers who used the work of Thomas Aquinas to address the perceived intellectual ills of their day, including Lutheranism, nominalism, and humanist political theory. Roughly this period is said to run from the end of the sixteenth century and into the middle of the seventeenth century, with the early stages being associated with the writing or teaching of Pierre Crockaert (1465–1514), Francisco de Vitoria (1485–1546), and Domingo de Soto (1495–1560). The later stages of this movement are associated with Jesuits such as Luis de Molina (1535–1600), Francisco Suárez (1548–1617), Leonard Lessius (1554–1623), and Juan de Oñate (1597–1646). Crucially, it is these later writers who wrote about, inter alia, the law of contract. For discussion, see Decock *Theologians and Contract Law* (n 1) 15–16.

[3] David Ibbetson, *A Historical Introduction to the Law of Obligations* (OUP 2001) 221–45.

[4] Hugo Grotius, *The Rights of War and Peace* (first published 1625, Liberty Fund 2005) 2.11.1–4; 2.11.7; 2.11.11–17.

[5] For discussion, see Robert Feenstra and Margaret Ahsmann, *Contract: Aspecten van de Begrippen Contract en Contractsvrijheid in Historisch Perspectief* (Kluwer 1988) 17–20; Robert Feenstra, 'Pact and Contract in the Low Countries from the 16th to the 18th Century' in John Barton (ed), *Towards a General Law of Contract* (Duncker & Humblot 1990) 197–213; Martin Hogg, *Promises and Contract Law: Comparative Perspectives* (CUP 2011) 128–30.

Contract before the Enlightenment. Stephen Bogle, Oxford University Press. © Stephen Bogle 2023.
DOI: 10.1093/oso/9780192884961.003.0007

to describe human action in the seventeenth century, the different historical senses with which these terms were used to describe the will can be lost. The meaning of 'the will', 'liberty', or 'freedom' in the seventeenth century is far more complex than contemporary notions convey.[6]

Here it will be shown that in the seventeenth-century use of the term 'will' and its associated vocabulary of desire or inclination and reason or intellect was commonplace within philosophical theology despite confessional divergences.[7] It will be seen from the history of the concept of the will that this idea would have been familiar to Stair's contemporaries and as it was used extensively by theologians and philosophers in the seventeenth century. This common background acted as a shared library for writers as varied as Stair, Grotius, and the late scholastics,[8] suggesting intellectual connections which transcended divergences about church, state, or religion. There was a shared metaphysical and theological lexicon, even if used differently in the hands of particular writers. On that basis, Stair's use of the term 'will' and its related concepts is far more extensive and transformative in comparison to Grotius from the perspective of contractual thought, and reflects the sophistication of the late scholastic's accounts of human action.[9] However, in suggesting this shared heritage of concepts with scholastic writers, this does not go so far as to recharacterize Stair's account of the law of contract as scholastic. Rather, if Stair's account is to be defined as anything, it is best characterized as a Calvinist strain of the Protestant natural law theories which emerged in the seventeenth century,[10] an example of the transplantation of commonplace philosophical explanation into legal discourse.

Seventeenth-century conceptions of the will cannot fully be understood without also understanding how concepts such as liberty and freedom were used to describe the will of man. As this chapter demonstrates, there was a range of meanings given to terms such as 'freedom' or 'liberty' within seventeenth-century literature which could be used in conjunction with each other. This is in contrast to Thomas Hobbes (1588–1679), who reduced the concept of liberty or freedom to an absence of external

---

[6] See Albrecht Dihle, *The Theory of Will in Classical Antiquity* (California University Press 1982); Alasdair Macintyre, *Whose Justice? Which Rationality* (Duckworth 1988) 103–241; Thomas Pink, 'Freedom of the Will' in John Marenbon (ed), *The Oxford Handbook of Medieval Philosophy* (OUP 2012); Jean Porter, 'Action and Intention' in Robert Pasnau and Christina van Dyke (eds), *The Cambridge History of Medieval Philosophy*, vol 2 (CUP 2010) 506–16; Risto Saarinen, *Weakness of Will in Renaissance and Reformation Thought* (OUP 2011).

[7] For discussion of philosophical theology, see Diogenes Allen and Eric O Springsted, *Philosophy for Understanding Theology* (2nd edn, Westminster John Knox Press 2007); Thomas P Flint and Michael C Rea (eds), *The Oxford Handbook of Philosophical Theology* (OUP 2011); Michael J Murray and Michael Rea, 'Philosophy and Christian Theology' in Edward N Zalta (ed), *The Stanford Encyclopaedia of Philosophy* (Spring 2020 Edition, 2014), <https://plato.stanford.edu/archives/spr2020/entries/christiantheology-philosophy/> accessed 8 April 2021..

[8] Including Luis de Molina (1535–1600), Francisco Suárez (1548–1617), Leonard Lessius (1554–1623), and de Oñate (1597–1646). See Decock *Theologians and Contract Law* (n 1) 162–214.

[9] cf Decock *Theologians and Contract Law* (n 1) 163–92; James Gordley, 'Contract, Property, and the Will—The Civil Law and Common Law Tradition' in Harry N Scheiber (ed), *The State and Freedom of Contract* (Stanford University Press 1998) 66–88; Wim Decock, 'Jesuit Freedom of Contract' (2009) 77 *Tijdschrift voor Rechtsgeschiedenis* 77 423–58.

[10] Knud Haakonssen, 'Protestant Natural Law Theory: A General Interpretation' in Natalie Brender and Larry Krasnoff (eds), *New Essays on the History of Autonomy* (CUP 2004) 92–109. See also Hogg *Promises and Contract Law* (n 5) 127–47.

constraint.[11] It will be suggested that Stair, like many of his contemporaries, adopts different senses of the terms 'freedom' or 'liberty', and the genealogy of his uses is traced through the seventeenth-century literature. It is important to grasp these different meanings of freedom or liberty when considering Stair's contractual and wider legal thought Stair's concept of the will is grounded in a definition of divine law which is voluntarist but draws upon an intellectualist or realist conception of natural law when describing the Moral Law, which applies to man.[12]

The Will in Medieval Theological Philosophy

As a concept, 'the will' was a ubiquitous term within medieval and early modern theological philosophy and ethical teaching. Although there were many complex and nuanced debates, there was a large degree of consistency in terms of language, questions, and the format by which such descriptions were given. Disagreements about the will within medieval or early modern philosophy could be summarized in the most general terms as being between intellectualists or realists on the one hand and voluntarists on the other. Duns Scotus (1266–1308) is taken to be a leading voluntarist, whereas Thomas Aquinas is deemed an intellectualist or realist.[13] These two approaches set the background to disagreements about freedom, will, and human action, but also theological debates about natural law and the nature of God. These debates carried on for centuries. Put very roughly, William of Ockham (1287–1347), Pierre d'Alley (1351–1420), Jean Gerson (1363–1429), and Martin Luther (1483–1546), as well as seventeenth-century Puritan theologians, are said to fall within the voluntarist tradition. On the other hand, the intellectualist or realist tradition includes writers as varied as Gregory of Rimini (1300–58), Francisco de Vitoria (1483–1546), Richard Hooker (1554–1600), and Gottfried Wilhelm Leibniz (1646–1716).

In terms of human action, Hoffmann summarizes the division between the intellectualist and voluntarist approaches as attempts to categorize man's moral psychology according to 'whether primary importance is placed on the intellect or the will in human agency'.[14] Duns Scotus was concerned that the intellectualist understanding of human agency described the human will as wholly reliant on the intellect for all action.[15] In effect, this rendered the decisions of man dependent upon external objects, which the intellect responds to. Such an account, according to Duns Scotus, failed to

---

[11] Thomas Hobbes, *Leviathan* (first published 1651, CUP 1996) Ch 21; Vere Chappell (ed), *Hobbes and Bramhall on Liberty and Necessity* (CUP 1999) 15–42.

[12] Some years ago, Hutton suggested that there was similarity between Stair and Francisco Suárez in this regard: Gordon M Hutton, 'Stair's Philosophical Precursors' in David M Walker (ed), *Stair Tercentenary Studies*, vol 33 (Stair Society 1981) 90–91.

[13] Antonie Vos, *The Philosophy of John Duns Scotus* (Edinburgh University Press 2006) 432–63; Alexander Broadie, *The Shadow of the Scotus: Philosophy and Faith in Pre-Reformation Scotland* (T&T Clark 1995); Brian Davies, *The Thought of Thomas Aquinas* (OUP 1993); Marion Baur, 'Law and Natural Law' in Brian Davies (ed), *The Oxford Handbook of Aquinas* (OUP 2012). For a comprehensive study of the Reformed traditions engagement, see Richard A Muller, *Divine Will and Human Choice* (Baker Academic 2017).

[14] Tobias Hoffmann, 'Intellectualism and Voluntarism' in Robert Pasnau (ed), *The Cambridge History of Medieval Philosophy*, vol 1 (CUP 2009) 414.

[15] This is a drastically simplified version of a very sophisticated account of human action. For a fuller account, see Alexander Broadie, *A History of Scottish Philosophy* (Edinburgh University Press 2008) 7–33.

demonstrate that the free will of man was the seat of human volition. For him, the free will of man was under man's own internal control: that is, it was able to self-determine and was not merely reacting to the dictates of the intellect or the intellect's cognition of external objects.[16] Of the many attempts to find a different way through such debates, the Jesuit Francisco Suárez (1548–1617) is important. Famously, he tried to find a middle ground by proposing that although something is good or right independently of whether or not God willed it to be so, it is not binding or law until God says it is good or right.[17] For Suárez, reason determines the law that the will of man should follow. These debates were not merely medieval. As Haakonssen notes, one way of understanding the Protestant natural law theories of the seventeenth and eighteenth centuries 'is as a prolonged debate about the ontological status of moral values, a debate in which the two sides commonly have been referred to as "realists" and voluntarists'.[18] Scots regents were debating such questions during the early seventeenth century, with or without explicit reference to Duns Scotus or Aquinas, and as a regent Stair would have been very much aware of the voluntarist and intellectualist division, which was central to early modern theories of not just human action but also God's nature.[19] How should Stair's use of the will be understood against this background?

The Will in Stair's Account of Divine Law

Stair speaks of God's will and man's will, which operate differently. Firstly, in the 1681 and 1693 editions of the *Institutions of the Law of Scotland* (*Institutions*), Stair says that the will of man is—ideally—inclined to follow the dictates of reason, which on first glance appears realist.[20] Stair is clear that by 'inclination' he does not mean the ability or power to choose, but rather he means that it is 'determined' or ordered, if working correctly to follow reason. If read without the context of Stair's *Divine Perfections*, an initial impression would be that Stair offers, in broad terms, an intellectualist or realist explanation of the human morality, albeit a Reformed version similar to the *Operum theologicorum* of Girolamo Zanchi (1516–90).[21] Indeed, famously, the opening passages of the first and second printed editions of the *Institutions* say:[22] 'Law is the Dictate of Reason, determining every Rational Being to that which is congruous

---

[16] Allan B Wolter (ed), *Duns Scotus on the Will and Morality* (The Catholic University of America Press 1997) 31, 36.

[17] Knud Haakonssen, *Natural Law and Moral Philosophy* (CUP 1996) 16–24; Thomas Pink, 'Reason and Obligation in Suárez' in Benjamin Hill and Henrik Lagerlund (eds), *The Philosophy of Francisco Suárez* (OUP 2012).

[18] Haakonssen 'Protestant Natural Law Theory' (n 10) 93.

[19] Anfray surmised that 'it is possible to conclude that in the early seventeenth century, the thought of Scotus contributed to a large extent to the shaping of philosophical debates within the Scottish universities'. Jean-Pascal Anfray, 'Scottish Scotism? The Philosophy Theses in the Scottish Universities, 1610–1630' in Mordechai Feingold and Alexander Broadie (eds), *History of Universities: Volume XXIX / 2* (OUP 2017) 120.

[20] Stair *Inst* 1.1.1. See also theses XVI–XXII of his graduation thesis: James Dalrymple, ' "Ethical Theses" in Theses Logicae, Metaphysicae, Physicae, Mathematicae, et Ethicae' (George Anderson 1646). David S Sytsma has provided an English translation recently, which is available here: <https://www.academia.edu/44558898/James_Dalrymple_of_Stair_Ethical_Theses_Glasgow_1646_> accessed 12 December 2022.

[21] *Operum Theologicorum D. Hieronymi Zanchii, 8 vols* (Stephanus Gamonetus & Matthaeus Berjon 1605).

[22] Stair *Inst* 1.1.1. Earlier manuscript versions of the *Institutions* do not include this paragraph.

and convenient for its Nature and Condition; this will extend to the determination of indifferency of all Rational Beings.'

Although Stair appears to be speaking about the law which applies to man, some important theological questions could arise which relate to God's will. These are: is law rational because God willed it to be so? Or because the law was rational, God willed it to be law? Is divine law rational because it had to be rational by necessity or because God made it rational by decision? Is God bound to divine law because he too is a rational being, or is divine law rational and binding because God willed it to be so? In terms of God's will and its relationship to the rational law, Stair offers an important caveat in his two printed editions of the *Institutions*:[23]

> God Almighty, though he be accountable to, and controllable by none, and so hath the absolute freedom of his Choice; yet doth he unchangeably determine himself by his Goodness, Righteousness and Truth; which therefore make the Absolute, Sovereign, Divine law: The same is also the Law of all Rational Creatures, by which they ought to determine and rule their free Actions; but the congruity and conveniency of their Nature affords them other Dictates of their Reason, which quadrat not with the Divine Nature; such as Adoration, Obedience, common to Angels and Men.

According to this, divine law is the will of God: he wills it to be rational. This passage at least suggests that God is not bound by the divine law but he chooses to be bound by it, which is a voluntarist account of divine law. If God chose to be bound by divine law, which is rational, man on the other hand, has been created by God to be rational and created to be bound by God's divine and rational law. This returns things to the will of man. When discussing man's will and reason, Stair evidently draws upon the intellectualist medieval tradition when he says law is the dictate of reason. For his audience in the seventeenth century, this unmistakably invoked Aquinas's conception of law and reason: 'law is nothing else but a dictate of practical reason emanating from the ruler who governs a perfect community'.[24] Although Stair importantly adds the caveat in the 1681 and 1693 editions of the *Institutions* that God chooses to make divine law unchangeable and because of his nature God will not change it, there remains a Thomist tone to how Stair approaches natural law, particularly in his description of how man interacts with the Moral Law.[25] However, Stair's description of man's moral reasoning is complex. Reading Stair's *Institutions* together with his *Divine Perfections* suggests that although the law of nature is rational, how man comes to know the Moral Law is through a process of deduction from axiomatic principles which are anthropological and innate to man. The law may be rational, but the moral epistemology of man and his psychology possessing of moral propositions is through an interaction between reason and the innate principles of law, which are known to him without reasoning.

---

[23] Stair *Inst* 1.1.1.

[24] Thomas Aquinas, *The Summa Theologiæ* (tr Fathers of the English Dominican Province, 2nd edn, 1920, reproduced Kevin Knight) < https://www.newadvent.org/summa/> 1.2.91,1.

[25] Hence, if a voluntarist interpretation can be applied to Stair's God and a realist explanation applied to human psychology, this at least makes it understandable why Hutton went so far as to say 'Stair effects a reconciliation of essentialist and voluntarist views by following a line of reasoning which is substantially Suárezian'. Hutton 'Stair's Philosophic Precursors' (n 12) 90.

Stair's approach in the opening passages appears to characterize right action as the result of the will following the direction of reason, but this should not imply that man's rational capacity alone determines what is good or bad.[26] That is because Stair's description of man's knowledge of the Moral Law includes a process of reasoning from innate principles, which man knows before he uses his rational faculties or his will.

The Will in the *Institutions*

In discussing the will of man, the 'will' appears in three distinct places within the *Institutions*.[27] It initially appears in Stair's opening account of justice;[28] then it reappears in his account of obediential obligations[29] and within his account of conventional obligations.[30] In the opening paragraphs of the first printed edition of the *Institutions*, Stair says that:[31]

> Correspondent to these dictates of reason (wherein law consists) which are in the understanding, there is an inclination in the will to observe and follow those dictates, which is justice; ... where, by the will, is not understood the faculty, but the inclination thereof, determined by the law to give every one that which the law declareth to be due ...

He later says: 'But man being now depraved, and wanting justice, ... or that willingness to give every man his right, and apt to fraud or force',[32] gives up that which is 'profitable for him' and due by equity in order to establish society and positive laws.[33] Accordingly, Stair holds that the will of man is pliable and prone to sin.[34] The implication is that man was designed with an inclination towards justice, but in a postlapsarian world he is no longer capable of directing his action by his will, towards what is good, without God's help.[35] Stair then describes the will in relation to obedience:[36]

> Obedience is that submission and sequacity of the mind and will of man, to the Authority and Will of his Maker, immediately obliging without any tie upon him by himself, intimate to him by the Law of Nature, Light of Reason, and the Conscience, whereby man distinguisheth betwixt Right and Wrong, betwixt what is Duty, and

---

[26] In the *Divine Perfections* (109–10), Stair appears to be somewhat ambivalent about this question of where liberty lies, namely in the will, desire, or intellect, but implies that the soul should ultimately be considered to be the driver of human action.

[27] Stair *Inst* 1.1.2; 1.1.18–19. Also see Stair *Inst* 3.2.4–5 and 3.4.2.

[28] Stair *Inst* 1.1.2.

[29] Stair *Inst* 1.1.18–1.1.19.

[30] Stair *Inst* 1.10 ff.

[31] Stair *Inst* 1.1.2 (emphasis added).

[32] Stair *Inst* 1.1.18.

[33] Stair *Inst* 1.1.18 and *Inst* 1.1.15.

[34] Stair mentions the fall of man in several places: *Inst* 1.1.7; 1.1.18; 1.11.88, 2.4.9.

[35] Stair *Inst* 1.1.7; 1.1.15; 1.1.17 and Stair, *Inst* 1.1.9 (here, Stair claims there was an instability in man even before the fall).

[36] Stair *Inst* 1.1.19.

what is not Duty; hence do arise these Obligations upon man, which are not by his own consent or engagement, nor by the Will of Man, but by the Will of God; and therefore, these are fitly called Obediential Obligations.

Obediential obligations are created by the will of God, and automatically bind man. But the domain of action which obediential obligations regulate should not be viewed as reducing the extent of man's free will. Later in the *Institutions*, Stair explains that 'Though liberty be a most precious right, yet it is not absolute, but limited: First, by the will of God, and our obediential obligations to him, and to men by his ordinance.'[37] He continues: 'men may be restrained or constrained by others, without encroachment upon the law of liberty, in the pursuance of other obediential obligations'.[38] He explains that the liberty of man's will may be diminished in various situations by an obligation, such as man's obligations towards his family, or by delinquence, or where he has contracted with another man.

As will be discussed in the following chapters, Stair used 'liberty' not in the same sense as Grotius or Hobbes but in a more limited pre-natural rights sense, which means he understood the law expressed through obligations as reinforcing or mapping the boundaries of man's liberty rather than as imposed constraints. The next chapter offers an interpretation of Stair's conception of liberty, but for now it is important to note that the contrast is not between a free man who is without obligation and a free man who has his freedom cut away by an obligation, but rather Stair's conception of liberty and obligation is that of a man who is required to do x, y, and z, which are obligations, and in doing so, willingly, is acting with freedom. Stair, however, is clear that there are some obligations which flow from the will of God, which sets the boundaries of man's liberty, and there are some obligations which are created by man's own will, which creates another set of boundaries:[39]

From obediential obligations, flowing from the will of God, order leads us next to conventional obligations, arising from the will of man, whereby our own will tieth us in that, wherein God hath left us free ... yet so as he hath given that liberty in our power, that we may give it up to others, or restrain and engage it, whereby God obliges us to performance, by mediation of our own will; yet such obligations, as to their original, are conventional, and not obediential.

Conventional obligations do arise from our will and consent; for, as in the beginning hath been shown, the will is the only faculty constituting rights, whether real or personal; for it is the will of the owner, that naturally transferreth right from him to the acquirer: so in personal rights, that freedom we have of disposal of ourselves, our actions and things, which naturally is in us, is by our engagement placed in another, and so engagement is a diminution of freedom, constituting that power in another, whereby he may restrain, or constrain us to the doing or performing of that whereof we have given him power of exaction; as in the debtor, it is the debtor's duty

---

[37] Stair *Inst* 1.2.5.
[38] Stair *Inst* 1.2.5.
[39] Stair *Inst* 1.10.

or necessity to perform. But it is not every act of the will that ariseth in an obligation, or power of exaction; and therefore, that it may appear what act of it is obligatory.

Stair goes on to clarify that not every act of the will creates an obligation. That is, after he has established that the will is the source of liability for conventional obligations, he sets out what acts of the will create an obligation. Stair speaks of three acts 'in' the will: desire, resolution, and engagement. Desire is the 'inclination' of the will towards 'its object, and it is the first motion thereof' but not 'sufficient' to create a right. Resolution is the 'determinate purpose to do that, which is without fault altered', and so the resolution of the will, like a desire of the will, is not sufficient to create a right. Stair, however, says that the resolution of the will may create a right if 'by accident the matter is necessary', or that 'resolution he holdeth forth to reassure others'.[40] This careful distinction between an accident and an assurance means that Stair's theory is able to accommodate instances where someone may have internally resolved to do 'something, yet by carelessness or in fact deliberate assurance' they give the external impression that they intended to create an obligation. Stair is prepared to argue that in these two instances, either through negligence or by the will, an obligation is created.[41] Stair explains that a resolution can create an obligation in these instances because it was expressed to another. To alter one's resolution in these circumstances—where one has expressed it to another and expressed the resolution in such a manner that it could be reasonably supposed to be a declaration of the will—would create either 'levity and inconstancy' or 'deceit and unfaithfulness' according to Stair.[42] He is, however, at pains to stress that this is an exception, and, in most circumstances, the expression of one's resolution does not create an obligation.[43] The final movement of the will is engagement, which is the 'only act of the will, which is efficacious' whereby 'the will conferreth or stateth a power of exaction in another, and thereby becomes engaged to that other to perform'.[44]

The Will in Seventeenth-Century Literature

In comparison to the legal sources used by Scots in the early modern period, Stair's *Institutions* demonstrates the most developed use of the terminology of 'the will' within legal literature relating to contracting. Thus, the will of man can create a promise, contract, make an offer to be bound, or create a third-party right of performance. In some instances, the will is conditional[45] upon the acceptance,[46] which is the will of another party, and sometimes the will is pure and unconditional, creating

---

[40] Stair *Inst* 1.10.2. NB: Stair does not appear to use the term 'essential' in a technical Aristotelian sense but rather to mean an unexpected or unintended event.

[41] Stair *Inst* 1.10.2.

[42] Stair *Inst* 1.10.2.

[43] Stair *Inst* 1.10.2.

[44] Stair *Inst* 1.10.2.

[45] Something which Stair says in his *Divine Perfections* is also true of God's will. Stair *Divine Perfections* 78–79.

[46] Stair *Inst* 1.10.3.

an obligation without acceptance.[47] In comparison to canon law,[48] the *Corpus iuris civilis*[49] or the medieval commentaries upon Roman law, which Scots lawyers used in the mid-seventeenth century,[50] Stair's description represents a marked change.

However, it may be said that Stair's use of the term 'will' has much in common with that of Grotius and the late scholastics.[51] In Grotius's *The Rights of War and Peace* of 1625, for example, one can find a very similar description of formation.[52] Grotius uses the term 'will' to describe the trigger for creating an obligation such as a promise or contract (Grotius uses the Latin term *voluntas*).[53] But, as will be described in Chapter 8, Grotius made a significant break from the traditional conception of the will, in contrast to Stair, by stripping it of its metaphysical significance. Grotius does not offer a sophisticated description of human action and relate it to specific doctrines of Dutch law. Nor does Grotius offer an extended discussion of the will in *The Rights of War and Peace*. Indeed, Stair's discussion of the three acts of the will is indicative of the more elaborate descriptions of human action found in Thomist-influenced literature.[54] This raises the question: to what extent can it be said that Stair was influenced by any of the late scholastics? It is very clear that Dominican and Jesuit theologians in the sixteenth and seventeenth centuries wanted to fuse theology and the *ius commune*, and importantly they used the term 'will' to describe the formation of promises and contracts.[55] There may be difficulty in establishing that Stair actually read these texts in the 1640s, but there is good reason to suppose he did. For example, a comparison between Stair's treatment of conventional obligations and Lessius's own treatment of promising and contracting demonstrates a notable degree of affinity.[56] However, for the purposes of this chapter, it is not necessary to establish whether Stair read these texts and took inspiration from them, because it is far more evident that it was a commonplace term

---

[47] Stair *Inst* 1.10.4.

[48] Gordley *Philosophical Origins* (n 1) 41; Hogg *Promises and Contract Law* (n 5) 79–83. In canon law, the term *voluntas* appears in several places, particularly with regard to the regulation of marriage.

[49] It is important to note: Dihle has shown that the term *voluntas* was in the ancient Roman lexicon; indeed, it was used, according to Dihle, within Roman legal literature (Dihle *The Theory of Will* (n 6) 134–36). But the point here is that it did not surface within the legal texts which Scots lawyers were using, such as Justinian's *Institutes* or the *Digest*.

[50] Accursius, Bartolus, and Baldus used the word 'consensus' rather than the word *voluntas* or *voluntatis*; see Gordley *Philosophical Origins* (n 1) 41ff.

[51] It is also used by Pufendorf: Samuel Pufendorf, *The Whole Duty of Man, According to the Law of Nature* (first printed (in English) 1735; Liberty Fund 2003) 1.1–2; 1.10. But, as explained at the outset Stair probably did not read Pufendorf until after the 1670s.

[52] Grotius *The Rights of War and Peace* (n 4) 2.11.11–12.

[53] Grotius *The Rights of War and Peace* (n 4) 2.11.1–4; 2.11.7; 2.11.11–17. Also see, Hugonis Grotii, *De Jure Belli ac Pacis Libri tres, in Quibus Jus Naturæ et Gentium, item Juris Publici Praecipua Explicantur* (Johannem Blaev 1646; reprinted by Carnegie Endowment for International Peace 1946) 2.11.1–4; 2.11.11–17.

[54] Hogg *Promises and Contract Law* (n 5) 11.

[55] For explanations of Aquinas's theory of human action, see Joseph Pilsner, *The Specification of Human Actions in St Thomas Aquinas* (OUP 2006) 10–29; Alan Donagan, 'Thomas Aquinas on Human Action' in Norman Kretzmann, Anthony Kenny, Jan Pinborg, and Eleonore Stump (eds), *The Cambridge History of Later Medieval Philosophy* (CUP 1982) 642–54.

[56] cf Leonardus Lessius, *De Iustitia et Iure Caeterisque Virtutibus Cardinalibus Libri Quatuor/ad Secundam Secundae D. Thomae, à Quaest. 47 Usque Ad Quaest. 171* (Rolin Thierry 1613) (available in Glasgow University 1691 catalogue, GUL Sp Coll Bm6-b.4). Decock 'Jesuit Freedom of Contract' (n 9); Hogg *Promises and Contract Law* (n 5) 136–39.

within the medieval philosophical and theological tradition which shaped university curriculums across Europe, no matter the confessional divide.[57]

Thus what is important from the point of view of language is that Grotius, the late scholastics, and Stair all engaged with the language and ideas of medieval theology.[58] The late scholastics are often described as theologians rather than jurists;[59] and equally Grotius can be seen as a theologian as well as a philosopher and jurist.[60] All of these writers were drawing from the lexicon of theology, which included the works of Aristotle, Augustine, Aquinas, and the countless philosophical-theological commentaries of the sixteenth and seventeenth centuries.[61] Therefore, if Stair had read the late scholastics, he would have recognized the theological pedigree of the term 'will', and when he read Grotius he would have certainly interpreted this word through a theological lens, although Grotius did not use it in that sense in *The Rights of War and Peace*. Moreover, even if Stair did not teach directly from the primary sources of medieval theology whilst a regent at Glasgow University, he most certainly did use and read commentaries and texts which were fundamentally shaped by medieval theology.[62] For now, the task is to give an overview of how theologians, in early modern Scotland, used the term 'will', and to demonstrate that Scots like Stair were drawing from a non-legal lexicon and vocabulary which has a long pedigree dating back to medieval theology.[63]

Classical Conceptions of Human Action

In the centuries before the 1660s, the classic description of human action would involve consideration of desire, intellect, and the will.[64] It would also have involved

---

[57] Lubbe and Reid independently conclude that it is almost certain he did whereas Wilson appears to doubt whether he did. Hogg notes the affinity but does not necessarily claim that Stair read the late scholastics: Gerhard Lubbe, 'Formation of Contract' in Kenneth Reid and Reinhard Zimmermann (eds), *A History of Private Law in Scotland*, vol 2 (OUP 2000) 1–44; Dot Reid, 'Thomas Aquinas and Viscount Stair: The Influence of Scholastic Moral Theology on Stair's Account of Restitution and Recompense' (2008) 29 (2) Journal of Legal History 189–214; Adelyn L M Wilson, 'The Sources and Methods of the Institutions of Scotland, by Sir James Dalrymple 1st Viscount Stair, with Specific Reference to the Law of Obligations' (DPhil thesis, University of Edinburgh 2011) 103–07; Hogg *Promises and Contract Law* (n 5) 136–39. In general terms, the analysis provided in this chapter, however, supports the arguments of Hogg and Reid. In fact, this chapter demonstrates that Aquinas was a common source of Presbyterian theologians when discussing human action.

[58] Gordley *Philosophical Origins* (n 1); Decock 'Jesuit Freedom of Contract' (n 9) 423–58; Decock *Theologians and Contract Law* (n 1).

[59] Decock *Theologians and Contract Law* (n 1).

[60] Jeremy Thomas, 'The Intertwining of Law and Theology in the Writings of Grotius' (1999) 1 (1) Journal of the History of International Law 61–100.

[61] Jill Kraye, 'Moral Philosophy' in Charles B Schmitt, Quentin Skinner, Eckhard Kessler, and Jill Kraye (eds), *The Cambridge History of Renaissance Philosophy* (CUP 1988) 303–86.

[62] Christine M Shepherd, 'Philosophy and Science in the Arts Curriculum of the Scottish Universities in the 17th Century' (DPhil thesis, University of Edinburgh 1975).

[63] The focus here is upon how the will was used within a description of human action. However, as already mentioned, there was a huge literature produced throughout the Middle Ages and into the early modern period about God's will: Mark Murphy, 'Theological Voluntarism' in Edward N Zalta (ed), *The Stanford Encyclopaedia of Philosophy* (2013), Summer 2019 edition <https://plato.stanford.edu/archives/sum2019/entries/voluntarism-theological/> accessed 8 April 2021.

[64] Jeffrey Hause, 'John Duns Scotus (1266–1308)' in *Internet Encyclopedia of Philosophy* <Scotus, John Duns | Internet Encyclopedia of Philosophy (utm.edu)> accessed 2 November 2022. Also, see Thomas Pink

discussion of whether an action was voluntary or involuntary, or whether it was free or unfree, or whether the will was at liberty. First, however, it is important to grasp the dynamics of the apparatus of decision-making before considering how terms such as 'freedom' or 'liberty' were used to describe human action. The tradition of explaining a virtuous action starts with medieval theology's synthesis of Aristotle's discussion of desire and intellect and Christian ideas of the will and sin. St Augustine of Hippo, writing in the fifth century, was the first theologian to introduce the term 'will' to the moral lexicon of philosophical theology.[65] Augustine, however, did not know of Aristotle. It was not until Aquinas in the thirteenth century that one finds the Augustine conception of the will and the Aristotelian conceptions of intellect and desire re-emerging. Aquinas's account, however, diminished the role of sin and promoted the idea of the ability of man to act virtuously. It was the Reformation of the sixteenth century which underscored the destructive nature of sin and brought forth new theories of human action. However, importantly, the Reformation did not break completely from the medieval theological tradition. Jean Calvin in the sixteenth century encapsulates this Protestant re-emphasis upon the Augustinian conception of sin whilst maintaining the language of medieval theology. In the following paragraphs, Aristotle, Augustine, Aquinas, and Calvin will be discussed. The ideas of these philosophers-cum-theologians are important to how one understands Stair's use of the term 'will'. It will be shown that Scots continued to use Aristotle, Augustine, Aquinas, and Calvin during the mid-seventeenth century, and the language and terminology of these writers formed part of the lexicon of mid-seventeenth-century discourse about human action and decision-making.

Aristotle

Aristotle held dominant sway over the syllabus that Stair learned and then taught at the University of Glasgow in the 1630s and 1640s.[66] In year three, students began to study Aristotle's ethics, politics, and economics. In the 1640s, therefore, these classes revolved around Aristotle's *Nicomachean Ethics*. Indeed, the library catalogue of 1691 records numerous copies of Aristotle's ethics[67] and commentaries upon his ethics.[68] A key aspect of Aristotle's ethics is his theory of a virtuous action. In Book VI, he says

---

and M W F Stone (eds), *The Will and Human Action: From Antiquity to the Present Day* (Routledge 2003) 127–54.

[65] For a contrary view, see Michael Frede, *A Free Will: Origins of the Notion in Ancient Thought* (University of California Press 2011).

[66] Shepherd 'Philosophy and Science' (n 62); Broadie *A History of Scottish Philosophy* (n 15) 88–103.

[67] *Aristoteles Ethica Gr: Lat: Antonio Riccobono Interp: Cum Ejusdem Comment: In 8vo* (Padua 1593) (available at the Glasgow University library catalogue of 1690, GUL Sp Coll RB 2858); *Aristotelis Opera Gr: Lat: Cum comment: Gul: Duvallii Tom* (Paris 1629) (available at the Glasgow University library catalogue of 1691, GUL Sp Coll Bi5-a.3–4).

[68] eg *Pet Martyris Commentaria in Ethicam Aristotelis 4to* (Tiguri, 1563) (available at the Glasgow University library catalogue of 1690, GUL Sp Coll Bh9-h.10); *Platonis Cum Aristotile in Universa Philosophia Comparatio autore Jacobo Carpentario in to Edit* (Paris 1573) (available at the Glasgow University library catalogue of 1690, GUL Sp Coll Bh7-g.16); *Idea Œconomicae et Politicae per Fran* (Leyden 1649).

there are 'three things in the soul which control action and truth—sensation, reason and desire'.[69] Sensation cannot cause action, but desire and reason together can. Only when an individual's reasoning is 'true' and their desire is 'right' can a choice be described as good. It is important to emphasize that according to Aristotle a virtuous action was the product of the intellect and desire working together. Desire and the intellect would work together if they were trained; that is, the intellect would need to be taught how to know a virtuous action, which in turn would form a habit to shape the desire towards virtuous actions. 'The origin of action' according to Aristotle—its efficient cause—'is choice, and that choice is desire and reasoning with a view to an end'.[70] Neither reason nor desire can exist without the other; and choice, and therefore action, will not happen without an interaction between desire and reason. Importantly, the Aristotelian texts, which Stair worked with as a student and as a regent, did not have a conception of the will in the same manner as later medieval writers.[71] This notion came from Augustine, and along with it the idea that a man could know what was right but could still, willingly, do that which was wrong.

Augustine

Augustinian theology influenced, inter alia, Aquinas, Luther, and Calvin.[72] Indeed, Scots were still using Augustine during the mid-seventeenth century.[73] The 1691 library of the University of Glasgow contained many Augustinian texts.[74] Therefore, Augustine, like Aristotle, is important, not only for his contribution to medieval theology, but also for his contemporary relevance in the mid-seventeenth century. Augustine invoked the conception of the will as a faculty within human decision-making, which directed human action;[75] therefore it was the prime cause of human

---

[69] Aristotle, *The Nicomachean Ethics* (David Ross tr, revised by J L Ackrill and James O Urmson, OUP 1998) VI.II.

[70] Aristotle *Nicomachean Ethics* (n 69).

[71] Dihle *The Theory of Will* (n 6).

[72] Alastair E McGrath, *The Intellectual Origins of the European Reformation* (2nd edn, Blackwell Publishing 2004) Ch 6.

[73] David G Mullan, 'Theology in the Church of Scotland 1618–c. 1640: A Calvinist Consensus?' (1995) 26 (3) The Sixteenth Century Journal 595–617. Indeed, Henderson reviewed much of the seventeenth century and concluded: 'One notices especially to what an extent the personality of Augustine had impressed those Protestants. Nearly every writer seizes whatever opportunity offers itself of quoting him.' George D Henderson, *Religious Life in Seventeenth-Century Scotland* (CUP 1937) 138.

[74] (1) Augustini Opera in fol (Paris: 1614) (GUL Sp Coll Bi7-b.1–6); (2) Ejusdem dissertio Augustanae confessionis in 8vo (Bremae,1622) (GUL Sp Coll Bi9-l.9); (3) De Quinque propositionibus Jansenii Mens Innocentii Decimi in 4to Edit (London, 1658) (insertion: Theses Germaniae doctrinae Augustini) (GUL Sp Coll Bn3-i.14); (4) Graverus Rediv: seu praelectiones Academicae in Augustanam Confessionem in 8vo edit: Jenae 1654 pars prior (insertion: ab Alberto Grabero) (GUL Sp Coll Bh6-k.6–7); (5) Fran a Sancto Augustino de praedestianatione et Gratia Tract: de adjutorio sine quo non in 4to Edit (London, 1654) (GUL Sp Coll Bm5-g.7); (6) Fran a Sancto Augustino de praedestinatione et Gratia in 4to Edit (Monasterii, 1649) (insertion: It Greg; magni cum D. Augustino de gratia Christi consensio) (GUL Sp Coll Bn3-i.1); (7) Libertatis et Gratiae defensio vindice Toma Augustino in 4to Edit (Paris, 1653) (GUL Sp Coll Bi4-e.10); (8) Confessio Augustiniana in Lib: Quatuor Divisa in 8vo (Paris, 1580) (GUL Sp Coll Bh4-i.1).

[75] Augustine, *Confessions and Enchiridion*, Albert C Outler tr and ed (S C M Press 1955) VII–VIII; St Augustine, 'De Libero Arbitrio' (The Problem Of Free Choice), in Dom Mark Pontifex (tr and ed), *Ancient Christian: The Works of the Fathers* (Longmans, Green & Co 1955) I.II.

action. This was a crucial innovation within the history of moral philosophy,[76] allowing Augustine to explain the failure of man to do that which is right despite knowing what was right. In Greek philosophy, voluntary action was described as a consequence of cognition, whereas Augustine inserted the will between action and cognition.[77] Desire did not follow the intellect automatically, but rather the will directed a desire and could decide whether to respond to the intellect. Hence, the will had to decide first to invoke the intellect before it could have a bearing upon one's actions. However, according to Augustine, the will is constantly misdirected and misguided due to man's sinful nature. It does not have the power to overcome this misdirection. Thus, man may well know what is right by virtue of his intellect, but his will is incapable of directing his action towards what is right. Original sin has impaired permanently the will of man.[78] Despite being permanently impaired, the will of man is still free, according to Augustine: 'There is, to begin with, the fact that God's precepts themselves would be of no use to a man unless he had free choice of will, so that by performing them he might obtain the promised rewards.'[79] Put broadly, a Presbyterian who was engaging with Aristotle would have understood virtue and right action through the lens of Augustinian theology—the very theology that created the concept of a will as an independent cause of human action. Crucially, the will was misguided by sin and needed God's grace if it were to act virtuously. That of Augustine, however, was not the only medieval commentary used by Scots during the seventeenth century; they also used St Thomas Aquinas.

Aquinas

In comparison to all other medieval theologians, Aquinas wrote the most extensive Christian account of Aristotle.[80] Indeed, Aquinas still gave the most extensive account of Aristotle in the seventeenth century, particularly with regard to human action.[81] Protestant and Catholic sixteenth- and seventeenth-century commentaries

---

[76] Dihle *The Theory of Will* (n 6) 123–45; MacIntyre *Whose Rationality? Whose Justice?* (n 6) 103–241; Pink 'Freedom of the Will'(n 6); Porter 'Action and Intention' (n 6) 506–16; Saarinen *Weakness of Will* (n 6); Michael Mendelson, 'Saint Augustine' in Edward N Zalta (ed), *The Stanford Encyclopaedia of Philosophy*, Fall 2019 edition (2012) <https://plato.stanford.edu/archives/fall2019/entries/augustine/> accessed 8 April 2021.

[77] Dihle *The Theory of Will* (n 6) Ch 6.

[78] *De Correptione et Gratia Translated by Peter Holmes and Robert Ernest Wallis, and revised by Benjamin B. Warfield in Philip Schaff (ed) From Nicene and Post-Nicene Fathers, First Series* (Christian Literature Publishing Co 1887; revised and edited for New Advent by Kevin Knight) vol 5, II.

[79] *De Correptione* (n 78) II.II.

[80] Charles H Lohr, 'The Medieval Interpretation of Aristotle' in Norman Kretzmann, Anthony Kenny, Jan Pinborg, and Eleonore Stump (eds), *The Cambridge History of Later Medieval Philosophy* (CUP 1982) 80–98; Gordley *Philosophical Origins* (n 1) Ch 2; MacIntyre *Whose Justice? Which Rationality?* (n 6) Ch 10.

[81] Kraye says:

> The medieval commentator who exerted the widest ranging and longest lasting influence on the interpretation of Aristotle's Ethics was Thomas Aquinas, known by his followers as "the Expositor". His Exposition continued to be printed well into the seventeenth century, and was studied by humanists as well as scholastics, Protestants as well as Catholics' (Kraye 'Moral Philosophy' (n 61) 326–27). Also see Donagan 'Thomas Aquinas on Human Action' (n 55) 642–54.

on Aristotle were still using Aquinas to mediate Aristotle for Christian readers.[82] Thomist-influenced commentaries were used by Scots regents and are listed in the 1691 catalogue of the University of Glasgow, such as the Italian Protestants, Peter Martyr Vermigli (1499–1562) and Girolamo Zanchi (1516–90).[83] These were only the most prominent of a swathe of humanist commentaries influenced by Aquinas.[84] The theses of Stair's students from 1646 offer a good example of how regents used Aquinas to supplement their teaching of Aristotle.[85] In particular, reference was often made to Aquinas when Reformed theologians were discussing the relationship between the will, intellect and desire.[86]

Aquinas was important in fusing Augustine's concept of the will with Aristotle's concept of virtue. He developed this into one of the most elaborate descriptions of human action found in the medieval period.[87] In the *Metaphysics*, Aristotle spoke of 'the apparent good' which 'is the object of appetite', and of 'the real good' which is 'the primary object of [the] rational wish'.[88] In his *Ethics*, Aristotle had said that there are 'three things in the soul which control action and truth—sensation, reason and desire'.[89] Sensation cannot cause action, but desire and reason can. It is, however, only when reasoning is 'true', and the desire 'right', that a choice can be described as good. Virtuous action was the product of right reason and right desire working in harmony. Through teaching, reason would know a virtuous action; and through habit, desire would be moved towards what was right. Within the scholastic tradition, this roughly translated into the movement between the will and the intellect. Aquinas and other medieval philosophical theologians developed this in enormous detail. The purpose here is merely to garner the gist of this description.

Aquinas describes the role of the will within human decision-making in several stages. His particular approach is to set out six steps. In the first step, the will is drawn towards that which is good voluntarily; however, importantly, it is the intellect which informs the will of what is good. The second step is 'the apprehension of the end' and

---

[82] John P Donnelly, *Calvinism and Scholasticism in Vermigli's Doctrine of Man and Grace* (Brill 1976); F Edward Cranz, 'The Publishing History of the Aristotle Commentaries of Thomas Aquinas' (1978) 34 Traditio 157–92; Anthony R D Pagden, 'The Diffusion of Aristotle's Moral Philosophy in Spain, ca. 1400—ca. 1600' (1975) 31 Traditio 287–313; Willem J van Asselt, 'Scholasticism Revisited: Methodological Reflections on the Study of Seventeenth-Century Reformed Thought' in Alister Chapman, John Coffey, and Brad S Gregory (eds), *Seeing Things Their Way: Intellectual History and the Return of Religion* (University of Notre Dame Press 2009) 154–74; Christopher Cleveland, *Thomism in John Owen* (Ashgate Publishing 2013).

[83] *Hieronymi Zanchii de Religione Christiana fides* (Neustadii 1601) (GUL: Sp Coll 1629); *Pet Martyris Commentaria in Ethicam Aristotelis 4to* (Tiguri 1563) (GUL: Sp Coll Bh9-h.10).

[84] Christopher J Burchill, 'Girolamo Zanchi: Portrait of a Reformed Theologian and His Work' (1984) 15 (2) The Sixteenth Century Journal 185–207 at 187ff; Donnelly *Calvinism and Scholasticism* (n 82).

[85] James Dalrimplio, *Theses Logicae, Metaphysicae, Physicae, Mathematicae, et Ethicae. Quas Adolescentes hac Vice Ex Collegio Glasguensi Publice Propugnabunt, ad diem 27 Julii 1646* (Georgius Andersonus 1646) 6–7.

[86] eg George Gillespie, *A Treatise on Miscellany Questions* (Anon. 1647) 145; John Weemes, *The Portraiture of the Image of God in Man* (3rd edn, John Bellamie 1636) 102. See Manfred Svensson, 'Aristotelian Practical Philosophy from Melanchthon to Eisenhart: Protestant Commentaries on the Nicomachean Ethics 1529—1682 '(2019) 21 (3) Reformation & Renaissance Review 218, 277.

[87] cf Joseph Owens, 'Aristotle and Aquinas' in *The Cambridge Companion to Aquinas* (CUP 1996) 38–57; Matthias Perkams, 'Aquinas on Choice, Will and Voluntary Action' in Tobias Hoffmann, Jörn Müller, and Matthias Perkams (eds), *Aquinas and the Nicomachean Ethics* (CUP 2013) 72–90.

[88] Aristotle *Nicomachean Ethics* (n 69) XII.VII.

[89] Aristotle *Nicomachean Ethics* (n 69) VI.II.

'the counsel about the means', whereby the intellect determines what means should be taken towards the end.[90] Although the will and the intellect identify something which is the end or the good, there needs to be a 'desire of the means'.[91] Aquinas says that at this stage the will's desire and the intellect's knowledge of the end 'come under counsel'.[92] If the means is desirable to the will, and, importantly, not contrary to the intellect's knowledge of what is good, then the will 'consents' to the means and the intellect 'assents' to the means.[93] This leads to the third step: the outcome of the process of counsel between the will and the intellect regarding a means to an end is an *intention* to act. Intention, then, is the third step in this process. Aquinas says: 'Intention, as the very word denotes, signifies, "to tend to something" '.[94] Intention means not just an act of the will but also presupposes that there is a means to achieve the end, of which the will is desirous.[95] The fourth step is *choice*: this, according to Aquinas, arises when man compares two alternatives which are approved by the will and intellect.[96] The fifth step is *use*. Aquinas states: 'The use of something means the application of that thing to some operation'.[97] It is explained that 'the operation to which we apply a thing is called its use; thus the use of a horse is to ride, and the use of a stick is to strike'.[98] This leads to the sixth step, which is described by Aquinas as 'fruition', that is: 'Hence fruition seems to have relation to love, or to the delight which one has in realizing the longed-for term, which is the end. Now the end and the good is the object of the appetitive power. Wherefore it is evident that fruition is the act of the appetitive power'.[99] Aquinas's account of human action was to undergo a revival in the early modern period, and his metaphysics was to be developed by Francisco Suárez, who became a towering influence in the early modern period. However, for now, two general points should be made.

First, traditionally, an account of human action which is influenced by Aquinas offers an optimistic description about the possibility, despite the fall, for man to reason alone towards right action, and explains that it is the intellect which guides the will towards right action. In that sense, the intellect and its ability to inform man of what is right and wrong was viewed more favourably by Aquinas in comparison to Protestants, such as Calvin.[100] As Irwin notes:[101]

[90] Aquinas *The Summa Theologiæ* (n 24) I.II 15.3.
[91] Aquinas *The Summa Theologiæ* (n 24) I.II 15.3.
[92] Aquinas *The Summa Theologiæ* (n 24) I.II 15.3.
[93] Aquinas *The Summa Theologiæ* (n 24) 15.1.
[94] Aquinas *The Summa Theologiæ* (n 24) 12.1.
[95] Aquinas says: 'The will does not ordain, but tends to something according to the order of reason. Consequently this word "intention" indicates an act of the will, presupposing the act whereby the reason orders something to the end' (Aquinas *The Summa Theologiæ* (n 24) I.II 12.1).
[96] Aquinas *The Summa Theologiæ* (n 24) I.II 13.3.
[97] Aquinas *The Summa Theologiæ* (n 24) I.II 16.1.
[98] Aquinas *The Summa Theologiæ* (n 24) I.II 16.1.
[99] Aquinas *The Summa Theologiæ* (n 24) I.II 11.1.
[100] Thomas Pink, 'Suarez, Hobbes and the Scholastic Tradition in Action Theory' in Thomas Pink and M W F Stone (eds), *The Will and Human Action: From Antiquity to the Present Day* (Routledge 2003) 127–53; Terence Irwin, *The Development of Ethics: Volume 1: From Socrates to the Reformation* (OUP 2007) 745–75.
[101] Terence Irwin, *The Development of Ethics: Volume 1: From Socrates to the Reformation* (OUP 2007) 753–54.

Aquinas examines our capacity to achieve the virtues and the natural human good, in the light of Christian doctrines of sin, and of the necessity of grace (ST 1–2 q109). He maintains (q109 a2) that we can both will and do good without grace in the state of sin, even though we cannot attain our natural good in the state of sin. According to the Reformers, this concession to human beings in the state of sin underestimates the effects of original sin.

Second, the will of man is said to be free because it works in conjunction with the intellect. The intellect, unlike the will, has access to universals and guides the will, and man is said to be free when he decides to act in accordance with reason. In contrast, to follow the appetite of man, which is animalistic, is not to be free because the appetite responds and moves only in relation to particulars and does not have access to universals. For Aquinas, the will of man is striving towards the good—not a good or singular goods, but the good in general—but it only knows what the good is once counselled by the intellect. Importantly, the universal of a good can be manifest in many different particulars and instances, and so when a decision is presented to the intellect, the intellect of man has several options or choices to make and can direct the will in one direction or another. On that basis, the will of man is free because the intellect is free to choose between alternative particulars; the root of freedom is reason or the intellect of man.[102]

This sort of account of the will and intellect was commonplace amongst scholastic commentaries in the early modern period,[103] but this should not give the idea of uniformity. For example, for Protestants in the sixteenth century, the relationship between the will and intellect was ruptured and Aquinas's account idealistic. Thus, Catholic theologians like Aquinas had failed to give sufficient weight to the destructive effect of sin upon man's decision-making. From the perspective of sixteenth-century theology, Calvin's *Institutes* encapsulates perfectly the Reformation's renewed interest in Augustine and a greater stress on the deficiency of man's decision-making and the irreparable damage done by the fall. Calvin therefore provides an important lens through which to view this break between the intellect and the will, which is evident throughout the sixteenth century. However, before turning to consider Calvin's or indeed Suárez's account of human action, it is important to consider another medieval theologian's account of the will and the intellect, as, although the terminology and the general apparatus of man's decision-making was accepted during the medieval period, there were, nonetheless, vast disagreements about its operation and attributes. Duns Scotus, for instance, influentially departed from Aquinas's account of human action.[104]

---

[102] He says: 'The root of freedom is the will as its subject, but reason as its cause. The will is, in fact, free with regard to alternatives, because reason can have different conceptions of the good. Accordingly, the philosophers defined free decision (liberum arbitrium) as free judgment owing to reason, implying that reason is the cause of freedom' (Aquinas *The Summa Theologiæ* (n 24) I.II 17.1–2).

[103] Donnelly *Calvinism and Scholasticism* (n 82); F Edward Cranz, 'The Publishing History of the Aristotle Commentaries of Thomas Aquinas' (1978) 34 Traditio 157–92; Anthony R D Pagden, 'The Diffusion of Aristotle's Moral Philosophy in Spain, ca. 1400—ca. 1600' (1975) 31 Traditio 3 287–313; Luca Baschera, 'Aristotle and Scholasticism' in Torrance Kirby, William J. Torrance Kirby, Emidio Campi, and Frank A. James, III (eds), *A Companion to Peter Martyr Vermigli* (Brill 2009) 153ff.

[104] Bonnie Kent, *Virtues of the Will: The Transformation of Ethics in the Late Thirteenth Century* (Catholic University of America Press 1995); Vos *The Philosophy of John Duns Scotus* (n 13); Charles B Schmitt,

Aquinas thought that the will strove towards God, the ultimate source of eudaimonia, but while on earth man strove for goodness. It was the intellect which informed man of what was the good and right action in the temporal world. Duns Scotus rather postulated that the free will of man was predetermined to happiness alone, which reduced the freedom of the will of man. The will, according to Duns Scotus, could always choose between alternatives, and it was not always inclined towards happiness; rather, he spoke of the free will of man being inclined towards *affectio commodi*, or an inclination towards benefit or advantage, but also *affectio iustitiae*, or an inclination towards justice. For Duns Scotus, because of 'the will's inclination for justice, one can desire—or fail to desire—an intrinsic good, even when it conflicts with one's personal benefit'.[105] Accordingly, the intellect, for Duns Scotus, and in contrast to Aquinas, is connected to the first inclination of the will, *affectio commodi*, and not the second, *affectio iustitiae*. What was important for Duns Scotus was to demonstrate that the will of man, in any specific instance, could choose between alternatives, whereas Aquinas only demonstrated that the will is free successfully: it can choose between following the intellect or not in successful decisions but was only free when it followed the path directed by the intellect.[106] Duns Scotus argued that the reason the will willed something was ultimately because the will willed it itself. Only on this basis could the will of man be said to be free.

Calvin

The approach of Calvin (1509–64) is somewhat ambiguous in places, but it is clear that he does not reject the traditional language and apparatus of medieval theology. From the point of view of theology more generally, his influence in Scotland during this period cannot be overstated; his books were commonplace in the catalogue of the University of Glasgow library of 1691;[107] his thoughts shaped the orthodoxy of the Church of Scotland;[108] his theology imbued the society within which Stair lived, worked, and worshipped.[109] In his *Institutes*, Calvin follows on from the Aristotelian

---

Quentin Skinner, Eckhard Kessler, and Jill Kraye (eds), *The Cambridge History of Renaissance Philosophy* (CUP 1988); Anfray 'Scottish Scotism?' (n 19) 97–120.

[105] Hoffmann 'Intellectualism and Voluntarism' (n 14) 425.

[106] Thomas Williams, 'John Duns Scotus' in Edward N Zalta (ed), *The Stanford Encyclopedia of Philosophy* (2016) <https://plato.stanford.edu/archives/win2019/entries/duns-scotus/> accessed 8 April 2021; Hoffmann 'Intellectualism and Voluntarism' (n 14) 425.

[107] Twenty-eight titles recorded in the 1691 catalogue of the University of Glasgow are either written by Calvin, or are commentaries upon Calvin concerning his doctrine, including: *Calvini Institutiones* (Geneva 1561) (GUL Sp Coll Bm8-d.11).

[108] Brown says, 'it is important [sic] to highlight the rigorous Calvinism of the Covenanting period, and especially the Westminster Confession that was adopted in the 1640s and still remains the official standard of faith in the Church of Scotland.' Stewart J Brown, 'Religion and Society to c.1900' in Tom M Devine and Jenny Wormald (eds), *The Oxford Handbook of Modern Scottish History* (OUP 2012).

[109] Todd says: 'The received version [of Scottish history] is that Calvinism "provided in the long run to be an abstract, intellectual religion of the elite". Not so. Where the life of the community could be organized around sermons and Bible-reading, and where the most ordinary could be regularly held to a public recitation of their faith, Calvinism became genuinely a religion of the people.' Margo Todd, *The Culture of Protestantism in Early Modern Scotland* (Yale University Press 2000) 83.

exposition of desire and reason, and engages with the medieval explication of the will and intellect. He says, in agreement with Aquinas's Christian formulation of Aristotle, that:[110]

> God has provided the soul of man with intellect, by which he might discern good from evil, just from unjust, and might know what to follow or to shun, reason going before with her lamp; whence philosophers, in reference to her directing power, have called her sovereign [ἡγεμονικόν]. To this he has joined will, to which choice belongs.

He goes on: 'Man excelled in these noble endowments in his primitive condition, when reason, intelligence, prudence, and judgment, not only sufficed for the government of his earthly life, but also enabled him to rise up to God and eternal happiness.' Choice was able to then 'direct the appetites, and temper all the organic motions; the will being thus perfectly submissive to the authority of reason'.[111] However, the key point of departure for Calvin from Aristotle and Aquinas is the degree to which sin has disrupted the harmonious relationship between the intellect and the will:[112]

> Adam, therefore, might have stood if he chose, since it was only by his own will that he fell; but it was because his will was pliable in either direction and he had not received constancy to persevere, that he so easily fell. Still he had a free choice of good and evil; and not only so, but in the mind and will there was the highest rectitude, and all the organic parts were duly framed to obedience, until man corrupted its good properties, and destroyed himself. Hence the great darkness of philosophers who have looked for a complete building in a ruin, and fit arrangement in disorder. The principle they set out with was, that man could not be a rational animal unless he had a free choice of good and evil. They also imagined that the distinction between virtue and vice was destroyed, if man did not of his own counsel arrange his life. So far well, had there been no change in man. This being unknown to them, it is not surprising that they throw every thing into confusion. But those who, while they profess to be the disciples of Christ, still seek for free-will in man, notwithstanding of his being lost and drowned in spiritual destruction, labour under manifold delusion, making a heterogeneous mixture of inspired doctrine and philosophical opinions, and so erring as to both. But it will be better to leave these things to their own place (see Book 2 chap. 2).

Calvin therefore accepts the idealized understanding that the will and intellect of man—they were designed to work harmoniously together and to yield right action. Nevertheless, Calvin stresses that this was only possible in paradise. The will and the intellect cannot therefore work harmoniously in this world without God's help. Calvin maintains that man is still rational, despite the fracture between the will and the intellect. He is not an animal. Moreover, there is still a distinction between vice and virtue. Man still knows right from wrong. Thus, he fundamentally departs from Aquinas

---

[110] Calvin *Inst* 1.15.8.
[111] Calvin *Inst* 1.15.8.
[112] Calvin *Inst* 1.15.8.

and Catholic theologians, who maintain that humanity can build an understanding of right action from reason alone: the intellect and the will are no longer functioning together according to Calvinism. It is only by obedience that man acts virtuously. In book II, chapter II he goes on to say that man is like an animal that follows the inclinations of nature, desires, passions, and appetites, without using reason or deliberation. Even if man is impelled by reason to act virtuously, the impulse of nature weighs heavier on the will of man. He may discern what is good but his will is still inclined towards his appetites and passions, that is sin. It is only through the 'Holy Spirit' that man can break this cycle and do what is virtuous. Thus, the Calvinist theory of action expressly builds upon and consciously modifies the medieval tradition from which it emerges. It borrows from Aristotle, Augustine, and Aquinas and offers an important and influential account of human action. It is a description found in numerous texts written during the mid-seventeenth century by prominent thinkers and theologians, all of whom would have been known to Stair.

Contemporary Scottish literature, 1630–60

It is common to find a discussion of the will, intellect, and desire[113] within Presbyterian theology.[114] For example, Weemes's *The Portraiture of the Image of God* from 1636 contains a lengthy discussion of the will, desire, and the intellect.[115] Samuel Rutherford offers some discussion of the will and the intellect in his *A Sermon Preached to the Honourable House of Commons at their Late Solemne Fast*.[116] Dickson also discusses the will, desire, and intellect in his *Therapeutica Sacra*.[117] However, for present purposes, this chapter examines two theologians whose views are indicative of how Scots Presbyterians analyzed the will, intellect, and desire in mid-seventeenth-century theological literature. Importantly, both were near contemporaries of Stair.

George Gillespie (1613–48) discusses the will within *A Treatise on Miscellany Questions*.[118] He was a Church of Scotland minister and theologian, and brother of Patrick Gillespie (1617–75). Patrick was the minister of the Outer High Kirk

---

[113] Sometimes the Scots theological literature refers to 'affections' instead of desire and 'understanding' or 'wisdom' instead of intellect. It is also noted that these theologians' discussion of the will, intellect and desire is often supplemented with an exposition of the mediating effect man's conscience has upon his decision-making. The role of the conscience, however, is outside the scope of this chapter; but, of course, it is a recurring concept within Stair's discussion of man's decision-making in the *Institutions*: Stair, *Inst* 1.1.3; 1.1.5; 1.1.16; 1.1.18; 1.1.19.

[114] eg (1) Weemes *The Portraiture of the Image of God* (n 86) 96–115; (2) Samuel Rutherford, *A Sermon Preached to the Honourable House of Commons at their Late Solemne Fast, Wednesday, Jan. 31, 1644* (Evan Tyler 1644); (3) Gillespie *A Treatise on Miscellany Questions* (n 86) 141ff; (4) David Dickson, *Therapeutica Sacra Shewing Briefly the Method of Healing the Diseases of the Conscience, concerning Regeneration* (Evan Tyler 1664) 13; (5) Hugh Binning, *The Common Principles of Christian Religion, Clearly Provided, and Singularly Improved* (R S 1666) 160–63.

[115] Weemes *The Portraiture of the Image of God* (n 86).

[116] Weemes *The Portraiture of the Image of God* (n 86) 96–115.

[117] Dickson *Therapeutica Sacra* (n 114) 13.

[118] Gillespie *A Treatise on Miscellany Questions* (n 86).

in Glasgow in 1648 and later became principal of the University of Glasgow.[119] In November 1638, George was invited to preach to the Glasgow General Assembly, and it was here that he rose to prominence within Scottish theological and political polemics. He was a precocious theologian and produced many treatises and pamphlets during his short life. He was moderator of the Church of Scotland and minister of St Giles' Cathedral from 1647 to 1648.

A prolific and influential writer, he published his important *Treatise on Miscellany Questions* in 1649.[120] In a chapter focused upon the errors and false doctrines of the day, Gillespie deploys a theory of human action which resonates with the Calvinist reformulation of Thomist notions of the will and intellect.[121] He identified the concern that some people may be of 'sound heart' but ultimately 'unsound head' in the doctrinal positions they take.[122] '[O]ne of the greatest objections against the suppressing and publishing of Heresies, errors and Schismes', he says, is that 'this is a persecuting of those that are godly, this is a wound to Piety, and the power of godliness'.[123] It is on this basis that he then sets out to explain the root of these false doctrines, which he says come from pride or from error. It is in his discussion of error that one finds his discussion of the will and reason, as well as Aristotle and the 'Schoolmen':[124]

> Secondly, there is a reciprocall influence, as of the will and affections, upon the understanding, so of the understanding upon the will and affections, the will determines the understanding, quo ad exercitium, but the understanding determines the will, quo ad specificationem actus, that is; the will applyes the understanding unto, or hindereth it from the discerning of good, and evill; yet the will it selfe hath not light in its selfe, but is guided by the light of the understanding; wherefore, as the raise makes vapoures, and the vapoures make raise, so a bad understanding, makes a bad will, and a bad will makes a bad understanding, if the eye be single, the body is full of light, Matth. 6. 22. Which makes good what the Schoo[l]men tells us, that bonitas volunta[tis] dependet aréctâ ratione velute regula, the goodnesses of the will depends on right reasons as its rule. See Aquinas qu. 2ae, quest. 19. Art: 3 and the Commentators upon that place. 'Tis to be observed, that sometimes the Scripture speaketh of an error of the judgment concerning the faith, as a fountaine and cause of ungodlinesses, prophanesse, Atheisme, 2 Tim: 2. 16, 17, 18, 19. Gal: 5.4. 2 Epist: of John 9. As contrarie wise, there is a Light and knowledge, which preserveth from sin and ungodlinesse, and leadeth the soul in ways of holynesses and obedience, Psal: 9.10. and 119. 33.34 John 17.17. If the knowledge of God, of his Christ, and of his Word, and Will, and Name, and statutes preserve us from sinne, and lead us in the ways of obedience, then by the rule of contraries, error of judgement in these things, will ensnare us in sinne and

---

[119] K D Holfelder, 'Gillespie, George (1613–1648)' in *Oxford Dictionary of National Biography* (OUP 2004) <Gillespie, George (1613–1648), Church of Scotland minister and theologian | Oxford Dictionary of National Biography (oxforddnb.com)> accessed 2 November 2022.

[120] Gillespie *A Treatise on Miscellany Questions* (n 86).

[121] Calvin *Inst* 1.15.6–7.

[122] Gillespie *A Treatise on Miscellany Questions* (n 86) 141.

[123] Gillespie *A Treatise on Miscellany Questions* (n 86) 144–45.

[124] Gillespie *A Treatise on Miscellany Questions* (n 86) 145.

wickedness, for instance, an error concerning God; whether father, Joh: 15.21. Sonne 1 Cor: 2.8 1 John 2.23.2, Epis: vers 9. Or holy Ghost, Joh: 14.17.

Therefore, as the 'infection of sinne spreadeth it self, throughout the whole soule, and all the faculties and powers therefor', it is important to remember that 'so doth the worke of the Spirit of God'. In a similar manner to Calvin, Gillespie explains right action by saying: 'Wee finde light and holinesses, 1 Pet. 2.9' through the Holy Spirit. Moreover, he says, 'The word of God is so quick and powerfull, as that it pierceth even to the dividing asunder of the Soul and Spirit, if either the intellectuals be not found, or if the vitals and animals bee not right, the word will find it out.' And so, on this basis, he clarifies to his readers that:[125]

> A well meaning pious soul; a good heart and affection, which perhaps, a person may sit down satisfied with, will not excuse a corrupt minde, an erroneous spirit; neither will a sound and orthodox judgement excuse a corrupt heart, and inordinat affections: Aristotle himself could distinguish Art and knowledge from virtue, because the most excellent intellectuals, cannot make a man so much as morally virtuous, without the practice and exercise of virtue. Both soul and spirit, both the inferior and superior part of the soule, must be sanctified. Reason is at the helme, the affections as the sailes, let the helme be stirred never so right, if the winde either blow not at all, or blow crosse in the sailes, the ship makes no speed in her way, let the winde blow never so faire, and fill all the sailes, yet if the helme be off its hinges, or be not rightly stirred, the ship may quickly run upon a rock, or run a shore where its not saife: so he that hath a sound judgement without good affections, cannot move heavenward. He that hath good affections, without a sound judgment, will make more haste than good speed: Reason is as the ride: affections as a nimble horse, a man is but in an ill taking, if either this ride mistake his way, or the horse run away with him out of the way, having no raines to govern him, or if the horse be lame and cannot ride.

Gillespie's discussion shows a familiarity with Aristotle, medieval scholasticism, and a Calvinist reformulation of these ancient understandings of human action. Additionally, as will be discussed below, by saying 'the Schoo[l]men tells us, that bonitas voluntatis is dependent *aréctâ ratione velute regula*, the goodnesse of the will depends on right reasons as its rule', Gillespie demonstrates that Scots theologians would use a particular sense of freedom to describe a free action as that which is a rational or reason-following action. As will be shown, this sense of reason and the will working together in harmony and producing a free action was associated with Thomism in the seventeenth century.

Hugh Binning (1627–53) analyzes the will in his posthumously published work *The Common Principles of Christian Religion* (1666). Binning graduated in 1646 from the University of Glasgow, and was an able student of Stair, succeeding him as regent at the university in 1647. In an extended discussion of Ephesians 1 and Job 23, Binning considers how the will of man resembles the will of God.[126] He says:[127]

---

[125] Gillespie *A Treatise on Miscellany Questions* (n 86) 146.
[126] In Stair's *Divine Perfections*, eg Meditation V, one also finds a similar comparison between God's will and man's will; Stair *Divine Perfections* 67ff.
[127] Binning *The Common Principles of Christian Religion* (n 114) 160–63.

The first [means by which to know God's character] is the constant Doctrine of the Holy Scriptures, of which you should consider four things, 1. 'That his purpose and decree is most wise, therefore Paul cryes out upon such a subject, O the depth of the riches both of the Wisdom and knowledge of God', Rom. 11. 33. His will [is] always one with wisdom, therefore you have the purpose of his will mentioned [the Counsell of his will] for his will (as it were) takes Counsel and advice of Wisdome, & discernes according to the depth & riches of his knowledge and understanding. We see among men those which are separated often, & there is nothing in the world so disorderly, so unruly and uncomely, as when Will is divided from Wisdome, when men follow their own will and lusts as a Law, against their conscience, that is monstruous. The understanding and reason are the eyes of the Will, if these be put out, or if a man leave them behind him, he cannot but fall into a pit. But the purposes of God's will are depths of wisdom nay his very will is a sufficient Rule and Law, so that it may be used of him, stat pro ratione volu[n]tas, Rom. 9. 13, 14. If we consider the glorious Fabrick of the World, the Order established in it, the sweet harmony it keepeth in all its motions & successions: O it must be a wise mind and consell contrived is. Man now having the Idea of this world in his mind, might fancy and imagine many other worlds, being some proportion and resemblance to this: but if he had never so seen nor own this world, he could never have imagined the thousand part of this world, he could in no wise have formed an Image in his mind of all these different kinds of creatures.

Binning's discussion demonstrates a connection with medieval theology and Augustinianism-Calvinism. In this light, one can say that Gillespie and Binning are part of a tradition, along with Weemes, Rutherford, and Dickson, which draws from Augustinianism-Calvinism, but equally reads and takes from Aquinas. This helps to contextualize Stair's use of the term 'will'. The context and use of the will within theological literature in Scotland speak of three things. Firstly, Aristotle offered a philosophical language and conceptual structure, which Scottish Presbyterians used to describe virtuous action without the need for any law, coercion or obedience. Secondly, Augustine and Calvin provided a theory and language by which one could describe man's ability to act morally through the exercises of his will as being completely disabled. Thirdly, Aquinas provided an elaborate language within which Scottish Presbyterians could describe the internal decision-making process of man. For Calvin, God had provided the will with the intellect, which acted as a lamp to guide man towards right action before the fall. Now he needs law and grace to guide him towards right action. The same is true for Gillespie: the will has no light in itself because the understanding (intellect) guides the will. Thus, a bad will makes a bad understanding, and bad understanding makes a bad will. Man, according to Gillespie, has both. Thus, the will and understanding are equally corrupted and incapable of right action. It is only by grace that the light of reason prevents man from sin. Binning too offers a similar Augustinian–Calvinist reworking of the medieval tradition: the will is now separate from wisdom; reason and understanding are the eyes of the will; and it is the lusts and sinful will that dictate the actions of man.

This context is central to how one understands the meaning of 'the will' within the *Institutions*. That is, Stair also draws from this tradition when he uses the term 'will'. He drew this word from this medieval theological tradition, and it would have conveyed an Augustinian-Calvinist theology to his readers. These ideas and notions of the will found in the works of Augustine, Calvin, Gillespie, Binning, and other writers during the sixteenth or early seventeenth centuries were still relevant in the 1650s and 1660s. Calvin was the most influential theologian in Scotland during this period. Gillespie was a prominent member of the Church of Scotland. Binning was Stair's pupil and an influential teacher. Aristotle, Augustine, and Aquinas were authors Stair would have used and could have read in the library in the University of Glasgow. Moreover, when one turns to Stair's own theological writings, remarkably similar accounts of the will, intellect and desire emerge.[128] Indeed, Stair's use of the will in the *Institutions* correlates with Gillespie, Binning, and others. Calvin, Gillespie, and Binning describe a disharmonious relationship between the intellect and the will; they therefore speak of the will as sinful and in need of grace and God's direction. Stair's *Institutions* reflect a legal response to the will's need for direction. In the *Institutions*, Stair says that man's will needs clear instruction and, in some instances, to be compelled.[129] This instruction comes from numerous sources: the Bible,[130] the natural law written on man's heart,[131] man's conscience,[132] the evident utility of positive law, and, importantly, reason. It is also possible to argue that Stair conceived of natural law, via the positive law of Scotland, as the product of reason, and in that regard an encapsulation of the intellect and desire which would in a prelapsarian state guide man independently of positive law.[133] Natural law, and so positive law, rather than the intellect or his desire, tells man what to do. In this light, when Stair then came to say in his 1681 edition of the *Institutions* that 'Law was the dictate of reason', he had in mind the Thomist idea that reason tells man what right and wrong, and so law is a product of reason reflecting the internal workings of man. This statement squares with his statement that, corresponding to:[134]

> these dictates of reason (wherein law consists) which are in the understanding, there is an inclination in the will to observe and follow those dictates, which is justice … where the will, is not understood the faculty, but the inclination therefore, determined by the law to give every one that which the law declareth to be due.

Whether this particular suggestion is convincing should not necessarily detract from the main thrust of the argument: that the will has a philosophical and theological meaning for Stair and many of his readers. Furthermore, this exploration of Stair's contemporaries demonstrates that they were happy to cite Aquinas and express their analysis in a similar language to Aquinas. Indeed, this matches Shepherd's observation that regents during the seventeenth century would often use the

---

[128] Stair *Divine Perfections* 69–70, 80. Stair may here have had in mind Suárez's middle road between intellectualism and voluntarism; Haakonssen *Natural Law and Moral Philosophy* (n 17) 13–24.

[129] Stair *Inst* 1.1.15 and 1.2–16.

[130] Stair *Inst* 1.1.17 ('God doth expostulate and argue with men, even for moral duties, from these common principles of righteousness, which their conscience cannot reject, as is evident everywhere in his Word').

[131] Stair *Inst* 1.1.7.

[132] Stair *Inst* 1.1.5.

[133] cf Stair *Inst* 1.1.9.

[134] Stair *Inst* 1.1.2.

Coimbra Commentaries[135] from the sixteenth century.[136] Given that there is reference to Aquinas in one of his students' theses, it could be argued that Stair possibly looked at these commentaries to aid his understanding of Aquinas if he did not consult the Summa Theologica directly.[137] The Coimbra Commentaries drew heavily upon Thomism.[138] Therefore, it may be that the use of Aquinas found in these mid-seventeenth-century texts was mediated through these commentaries. Nevertheless, the use of Aquinas in mid-seventeenth-century treatises, as well as in the classroom, gives further context and support to the suggestion of Hogg[139] that Stair may have drawn inspiration from Aquinas, and the argument of Reid[140] that Stair, in fact, did draw from Aquinas.

Freedom, Liberty, and Liberation

Pink explains, 'the classical theory of freedom is a theory of the relations between three kinds of freedom', which he describes as concerned with a power, a right, and a desirable condition. From Augustine to Aquinas to Duns Scotus to Suárez, there is an understanding that there are at least two but often three or more different types of freedom which may apply to human action.

Freedom and choice

The first, Pink describes as multi-way freedom of the will, which is the ability of the will to choose between alternatives. He takes a quotation from a key passage in Peter Lombard's twelfth-century *Sentences*: 'a power and capacity of the will and reason that we termed above freedom of choice; which is free to choose between alternatives, since it can be freely moved to this or that'.[141] Sometimes referred to as *liberum arbitrium*, it is a commonplace distinction between different types of freedom found in early modern and seventeenth-century literature. For instance, in the *Divine Perfections*, Stair says: 'Liberty then must be a Power to determine and choose, which cannot be hindered by extrinsick Force, or instrinsick Necessity'.[142] Or, for example, it is something which Calvin was prepared to accept in the *Institutes*, saying: 'In this way, then, man is said to have free will, not because he has a free choice of good and evil, but because he acts voluntarily, and not by compulsion.'[143] It is a distinction found in the

---

[135] This school included, inter alia, the Jesuits theologians-cum-jurists: Luis de Molina (1535–1600) and Francisco Suárez (1548–1617).

[136] Jill Kraye (ed), *Cambridge Translations of Renaissance Philosophical Texts: Moral and Political Philosophy*, vol 2 (CUP 1997) 80.

[137] Dalrimplio *Theses Logicae* (n 85) 6–7.

[138] Dalrimplio *Theses Logicae* (n 85). Such an approach was very common amongst Reformed theologians: David Van Drunen and Manfred Svensson (eds), *Aquinas Among the Protestants* (Wiley Blackwell 2017).

[139] Hogg *Promises and Contract Law* (n 5) 11.

[140] Reid 'Thomas Aquinas and Viscount Stair' (n 57).

[141] Thomas Pink, 'Thomas Hobbes and the Ethics of Freedom' (2011) 54 (5) Inquiry 541, 547.

[142] Stair *Divine Perfections* 106.

[143] Calvin *Inst* 2.2.7.

dispute between Hobbes and John Bramhall (1594–1663), where the archbishop of Armagh said:[144]

> by liberty I do understand neither a liberty from sin, nor a liberty from misery, nor a liberty from servitude, nor a liberty from violence. But I understand a liberty from necessity, or rather from necessitation, that is, a universal immunity from all inevitability and determination to one, whether it be of exercise only, which the Schools call a liberty of contra-diction and is found in God and in the good and bad angels, that is, not a liberty to do both good and evil, but a liberty to do or not to do this or that good, this or that evil, respectively; or whether it be a liberty of specification and exercise also, which the Schools call liberty of contrariety and is found in men endowed with reason and understanding, that is, a liberty to do and not to do good and evil, this or that …

Hobbes too held this to be a definition of liberty; arguably for him it was the only useful definition.[145] Whatever the case, Lombard, Calvin, Stair, and Bramhall appeal to one sense of freedom or liberty. It is a kind of physical but also metaphysical freedom, which is central to questions of responsibility and whether an action is blameworthy. As Suárez explains in his *Treatise on the Laws and God of the Lawgiver*, 'that which does not fall within the realm of freedom does not fall within that of law; but what is absolutely impossible does not come within the realm of freedom, since the latter of its very nature demands power to choose either of two alternatives; and therefore, [what is impossible] cannot be the subject-matter of law'.[146] At a basic level, Suárez, like many other early modern theologians, primarily locates freedom within the human will and, as described above, understands it as the capacity to be motivated, moved or to respond to reason.[147] Pink identifies this as multi-way freedom, the ability to choose between alternatives, which is a characterization of human action often found in medieval and early modern literature.

Freedom and right

Pink speaks of a second sense in which the term 'liberty' or 'freedom' was used in medieval and early modern philosophical theology: the right to liberty. This is a normative sense of liberty; it is to say you have the liberty to use your power to choose between alternatives. As Pink explains, this is not to describe freedom as 'a natural or metaphysical power', but to claim you have legitimacy to act in a certain way.[148] For

---

[144] Chappell *Hobbes and Bramhall on Liberty and Necessity* (n 11) 1. Bramhall's works appear in the 1690 library catalogue of Glasgow University: *The Works of Bishop Bramhall* (Dublin 1677) Sp Coll Bk6-e.4.

[145] Hobbes *Leviathan* (n 11) Ch 21.

[146] Francisco Suárez, *Selections from Three Works: A Treatise on Laws and God the Lawgiver; A Defence of the Catholic and Apostolic Faith; A Work on the Three Theological Virtues: Faith, Hope, and Charity* (Liberty Fund 2015) 1.9.17.

[147] Thomas Pink, 'Suárez, Hobbes and the Scholastic Tradition in Action Theory' in Thomas Pink and M W F Stone (eds), *The Will and Human Action: From Antiquity to the Present Day* (Routledge 2003) 127–53; cf Stair *Divine Perfections* 112–14.

[148] Pink 'Hobbes and the Ethics of Freedom' (n 141) 543.

example, Suárez adopts this second sense of 'liberty' or 'freedom' to capture the notion that there is also a liberty to choose or have control over *how* you choose. Suárez uses this sense of the term 'liberty' in several ways: first, it describes man's condition according to the law of nature, that is, he is born with natural liberty;[149] second, to describe man's ownership of that liberty;[150] third, to refer to a lawful power over another.[151] Each use of the term 'liberty', nonetheless, refers to the claim to have authority over the will and to exercise, choose, or will towards reason's direction. As Pink describes it, man's 'right to liberty is a *dominium libertatis* or right over his own metaphysical freedom'.[152] It is also worth clarifying that Suárez is not suggesting that liberty in this sense is not a space within which man can do anything he wishes. Rather, for him, it is a right, space, or power to do the right thing (*iustum*).[153] This is a key point to note with regard to Suárez's conception of liberty. Such a sense of liberty is absolutely clear to Reformed theologians and philosophers too, but in light of their conception of sin and its effect on the decision-making of man it is something Adam is understood to have before the fall. It therefore appears in descriptions of prelapsarian Adam rather than in a description of man's ability after the fall, which characterizes man as capable, unaided, of controlling his will.[154] Stair did not adopt this sense, but he would have been aware of how Grotius had used the term in *The Rights of War and Peace*.

Freedom and liberation

The third sense of 'freedom' or 'liberty' within early modern theological-philosophical literature is what Pink describes as liberation. He defines this sense of freedom as a 'desirable goal' and as 'the perfection of that power' or the liberty to choose. 'This is a condition', he explains, 'in which the power exists in a form entirely consistent with its function, with a removal of all conditions obstructive to or degrading in relation to that function'.[155] It comes in different forms and expressions but nevertheless relates to moral decision-making and a notion of perfection or happiness or realization of some potential. For example, Calvin would use this sense of freedom in the *Institutes* to describe man's condition in heaven:[156]

> If departure from the world is entrance into life, what is the world but a sepulchre, and what is residence in it but immersion in death? If to be freed from the body is to

---

[149] Suárez *Selections from Three Works* (n 146) 2.14.6.
[150] Suárez *Selections from Three Works* (n 146) 2.14.18.
[151] Suárez *Selections from Three Works* (n 146) 2.14.19.
[152] Pink 'Hobbes and the Ethics of Freedom' (n 141) 547.
[153] That is, he is using the term 'right of liberty' in the objective sense rather than the subjective. For discussion, see Annabel S Brett, *Liberty, Right and Nature: Individual Rights in Later Scholastic Thought* (CUP 2003) 88–122.
[154] Calvin *Inst* 2.3.5 and 14; Chappel *Hobbes and Bramhall on Liberty and Necessity* (n 11) 3; *Westminster Confession of Faith 1647*, Article 4; Samuel Rutherford, *A Treatise of Civil Policy: Being a Resolution of Forty Three Questions Concerning Prerogative, Right and Priviledge, in Reference to the Supream Prince and the People* (Simon Miller 1657) 45–48, 110, 120–21, 147, 411, 418; Samuel Rutherford, *Lex, rex . . .* (Robert Ogle and Oliver & Boyd 1743) 197.
[155] Pink 'Thomas Hobbes and the Ethics of Freedom' (141) 548.
[156] Calvin *Inst* 3.9.4.

gain full possession of freedom, what is the body but a prison? If it is the very summit of happiness to enjoy the presence of God, is it not miserable to want it? But 'whilst we are at home in the body, we are absent from the Lord' (2 Cor. 5:6).

A good example of how different senses of 'liberty' could be used to describe the human will, but where liberation is the final notion, can be found in *The Portraiture of the Image of God in Man* by Weemes (1579?–1636), first published in 1627 and subsequently in 1632 and 1636. There he says:[157]

> The liberty of the will is twofold, the liberty of contrariety and the liberty of contradiction: Man had liberty of contrariety before his fall to chuse good or evil, liberty of contradiction, to doe, or not to doe these two sorts of liberties are not the perfectest estate of the will, for when it hath power to chuse or not to chuse, it imports a weaknesse in it, but when it is determinate to the good, then it is full satisfied, this is reserved for Man in glory. The Apostle, Rom. 6. 18. used this word, liberty, more improperly, when hee saith, free from injustice, and servant to sinne; when hee calleth this freedome, it is most improperly freedome; for, if the sonne make us free, then wee are free, Joh. 8.36. so wee say to serve God, this service is not properly service but, freedome.

Weemes initially uses 'freedom' or 'liberty' to describe the freedom of choice, not just between alternatives, but also to choose right from wrong (liberty of contrariety). He then proceeds to describe the liberty of the will in a perfect state, which for him, as with Calvin, is when man reaches heaven. Rutherford takes a similar approach in *A Survey of the Spiritual Antichrist*, but introduces the rather paradoxical-sounding notion that being unable to choose evil is freedom. Rutherford says: 'True, free-will is a sparkle of God, so much of a loosed and unfettered will to doe good, so much of God, grace is golden wings, for nature to flee to heaven withall. Freedome to doe ill, and to move to hell, is the devil's fetters of vengeance.'[158]

During the mid-seventeenth century, this 'liberation' sense of 'freedom' is frequently associated by Scots theologians with a freedom from law rather than a freedom from the body's passions, sin's yoke, or the burden of choice between right and wrong. Although you find all of these senses of 'liberation' used during the mid-seventeenth century, it is the freedom from law which is the most prominent sense within which a 'liberation' sense of freedom is used.[159] Chapter 20 of the *Westminster Confession of Faith* (1647) reads as follows:

> The liberty which Christ hath purchased for believers under the Gospel consists in their freedom from the guilt of sin, the condemning wrath of God, the curse of the Moral Law; and, in their being delivered from this present evil world, bondage to

---

[157] Weemes *A Portraiture of the Image* (n 86) 128.

[158] Samuel Rutherford, *A Survey of the Spirituall Antichrist* ... (Andrew Crooke 1648) 163.

[159] For example, see Samuel Rutherford, *The Covenant of Life Opened: Or, A Treatise of the Covenant of Grace* (Andrew Anderson 1665) 214; David Dickson, *An Exposition of All St. Pauls Epistles, Together with an Explanation of Those Other Epistles of the Apostles, St. James, Peter, John & Jude* (Francis Eglesfield 1659) 16, 77, 188, 281; Dickson *Therapeutica Sacra* (n 114) 17–18; Hugh Binning, *The Sinner's Sanctuary* ... (George Swintown & James Glen 1670); Stair *Inst* 1.1.9 and 1.2.11.

Satan, and dominion of sin; from the evil of afflictions, the sting of death, the victory of the grave, and everlasting damnation; as also, in their free access to God, and their yielding obedience unto Him, not out of slavish fear, but a child-like love and willing mind. All which were common also to believers under the law. But, under the new testament, the liberty of Christians is further enlarged, in their freedom from the yoke of the ceremonial law, to which the Jewish Church was subjected; and in greater boldness of access to the throne of grace, and in fuller communications of the free Spirit of God, than believers under the law did ordinarily partake of.

Liberation from sin, escaping the wrath of God or being released from the curse of the Moral Law did not mean, importantly, that the Moral Law or indeed human law was no longer applicable to Christians in the temporal pre-glory world. Rutherford, for example, is at pains to stress that 'we are not delivered and freed from the commanding, directing, obliging and binding power of the Law, as a binding rule of life'. To say you were now free from the Moral Law and law entirely, according to Rutherford, would be to claim your liberty as a licence, which is not in fact to be free from sin. Rutherford quotes David, saying: 'I will walk at liberty for I seek thy precepts'.[160] Binning says something similar, when he preaches that 'Man was created for another purpose, and upon other conditions, and a Law of perpetual life and eternal happinesse was passed in his favours, he abiding in the favour, and obeying the will, of Him that gave him life and being'.[161] Once man is free from sin, Binning says, 'A Christian looks to the pattern of the Law, and the word of the Gospel without; but he must be changed into the image of it, by beholding it, and so he becomes a living Law to himself'.[162] The great concern of Presbyterian theologians in the mid-seventeenth century was that they were often cast as rebelliously antinomian or libertine by their interlocutors. The predestinary theology of an elect of God could be caricatured in such debates as if it were a claim of complete licence to do anything, as if liberation from sin and the judgment of the Moral Law granted the elect a sort of immunity within the temporal world. Hence, Rutherford, Dickson, and Binning are keen to stress that liberation does not mean liberation from the Moral Law but liberation from those things which prevent us from obeying the law.

Freedom and reason

Seeking out a middle way or a means by which to describe man's upright state, some mid- to late seventeenth-century writers went further than Rutherford, Dickson, or Binning in describing what liberation was. Offering a description of the relationship of reason, desire, and the will and the law of nature or Moral Law, some writers tried to describe how man's decision-making operated in a regenerated condition, or when he was saved or liberated from sin. Such accounts pose liberty as man's ability to follow

---

[160] Rutherford *A Survey of the Spirituall Antichrist* (n 158) 95.
[161] Binning *The Sinner's Sanctuary* (n 159) 207.
[162] Binning *The Sinner's Sanctuary* (n 159) 76.

reason or law voluntarily or willingly, invoking the realist or intellectualist tradition of Aquinas. For example, Bramhall says in his debate with Hobbes:[163]

> this death in sinne is not a naturall, but a spiritual death, and therefore no utter extinction of the naturall powers and faculties of a man. Such are the understanding and the will, which though they were much weakened by the fall of Adam, yet they were not, they are not utterly extinct, either by originall or actuall sin, but being excited, and, as it were, enlived by preventing grace, they may and do become subservient ... to grace; the understanding being illuminatted by those rays of heavenly light, and the will enabled to consent as freely to the motions of grace, in supernaturall acts, as it did formerly to the dictates of reason in naturall and civill acts.

A similar account is offered in 1673 by the fictional historian, Basil, in a dialogue by Gilbert Burnett (1643–1715):[164]

> I also acknowledge, that great abuse hath followed upon the innovating and prescribing in Divine matters, and that nothing hath occasioned more divisions among Christians, than the overstraining an Uniformity. But if because of abuses you overturn all Legislative Power in matters sacred, nothing that is humane shall scape your fury, since every thing is subject to abuse. And nothing will curb ones Career till he turn Quaker, that follows these Maxims. But one thing is still forgotten, that the dictates of Reason are in their kind the Voice of God; Reason being nothing, save an impress of the Image of God on the Soul of man; which because much obliterated by the fall, was to be supplied by Revelation: but wherein it remains clear, its directions not contradicting any positive or revealed Law, are still to be followed as the Laws of God.

Similarly, Nathaniel Culverwell (1619–51) makes clear that equating reason, law, and decision-making together is to invoke Aquinas and the scholastic tradition which is associated with, inter alia, Suárez. In Culverwell's lectures, he said:[165]

> If you speak of the principles of the Laws of Nature, you shall hear the Schoolmen determining: Infans pro illo statu non obligatur lege naturali, quia non habet usum Rationis & libertatis [an infant, because of its condition, is not obligated by the law of nature, because it does not have the use of reason and free will]. And a more sacred Author saies as much, Lex Naturae est lex intelligentiae quam tamen ignorat pueritia, nescit infantia [the law of nature is the law of reason, of which, however, youth is ignorant and infants unaware]. There's some time to be allowed for the promulgation of Natures Law by the voice of Reason. They must have some time to spell the Νόμοςγραπτὸς [written law] that was of Reasons writing. The minde having

---

[163] John Bramhall, *Castigations of Mr. Hobbes his last Animadversions in the Case Concerning Liberty and Universal Necessity wherein all his Exceptions about that Controversie are Fully Satisfied* (E T 1657) 29–30.

[164] Gilbert Burnett, *A Vindication of the Authority, Constitution, and Laws of the Church and State of Scotland in Four Conferences, wherein the Answer to the Dialogues betwixt the Conformist and Non-Conformist is Examined* (Robert Sanders 1673) 176.

[165] Nathaniel Culverwell, *An Elegant and Learned Discourse of the Light of Nature* (Liberty Fund 2001) 77–78.

such gradual and climbing accomplishments, doth strongly evince that the true rise of knowledge is from the observing and comparing of objects, and from thence extracting the quintessence of some such principles as are worthy of all acceptation; that have so much of certainty in them, that they are neer to a Tautology and Identity, for this first principles are.

Bramhall, Burnet, and Culverwell, as well as Gillespie quoted above, all confirm that in the seventeenth-century theologians could also use 'freedom' in the sense of a reason-bound or rule-bound action. It is something which Stair also clearly invokes in the opening passages of the 1681 and 1693 *Institutions*. These authors also demonstrate that this sense of 'freedom' was associated with Aquinas and scholasticism. Significantly, in the early modern period, one of the most important exponents of this notion of freedom as rule-bound was Suárez, who not only sought a middle way between intellectualism and voluntarism, but also expounded a sophisticated account of law, reason, and obligation. According to him, law as the will of a sovereign embodying reason does not act in opposition to liberty or freedom. For Suárez, law, reason, and obligation work in harmony guiding towards salvation, man's final end and desire.[166] Suárez's approach is important not only due to the influence it had on writings within the Catholic Church and its various religious orders but also because of the similarity between his approach and that of Stair.

In the Preface to *A Treatise on Law and God the Lawgiver*, Suárez says that it should be no surprise that a theologian wishes to speak about the law because God is the ultimate subject of theology, who is 'the last end towards Whom rational creatures tend and in Whom their sole felicity consists'.[167] Suárez observes that God 'directs His creatures', but also 'checks them with admonitions' so that they will remain on 'the path of righteousness', and when they stray he 'counsels' them by 'impelling them by his laws, and above all, succouring them with the aid of His grace'. He finishes, explaining his point, with a quotation from Isaiah: 'the Lord is our lawgiver, the Lord is our king: he will save us'.[168] Therefore 'this salvation lies in free actions and in moral rectitude—which rectitude in turn depends to a great extent upon law as the rule of human actions—it follows thence that the study of law becomes a large division of theology'.[169] Therefore, in a theological sense but also a very practical sense, Suárez frames law as a guide, measure, and counsel for man rather than a restraint or bond placed upon him. Specifically, law regulates man's moral conduct, rendering his actions free, which in turn leads towards man's salvation. Reason, law, freedom, and salvation are combined in Suárez's approach. If an action conforms to the law, then that action is judged to be good, not only because of obedience, but also because the action corresponds to how man should conduct himself. Law may impose an obligation upon man, which he can decide not to follow, but when he does follow it he is acting towards his final end and therefore with freedom. Stair did not believe that man could by his actions gain salvation, but he did, as will be discussed in the following chapters,

---

[166] Suárez *Selections from Three Works* (n 146) 1.1.5.
[167] Suárez *Selections from Three Works* (n 146) Preface.
[168] Suárez *Selections from Three Works* (n 146) Preface.
[169] Suárez *Selections from Three Works* (n 146) Preface.

at times use a conception of freedom which is similar to this generally Thomist approach to freedom.

Hobbes on freedom or liberty

Three senses of 'freedom' or 'liberty' have been discussed so far: freedom as choice, freedom as a right, and freedom as liberation or reason-following. It is necessarily also to gather a sense of how Hobbes's conception of liberty compares to these approaches. Not only is Hobbes a central figure in the emergence of modern notions of liberty, but also it has been commented upon in the past that Stair shares some similarities with Hobbes.[170] Immediately, however, this may seem rather contradictory, as it has also been shown in this chapter that Stair could be said to have a 'freedom is reason' conception of liberty. As subsequent chapters will show, this is not necessarily contradictory, because in fact it was common during this period for theologians and philosophers to use different conceptions of freedom in different contexts. So, Stair could use a rather Hobbesian-sounding conception of freedom when he discusses the positive law but then demonstrate a more Thomist conception when he discusses morality or theology. For now, it is instructive to describe Hobbes's conception of freedom, as it provides an important point of comparison with Stair's conception of freedom, the will and how conventional obligations should be conceived.

Hobbes's description of human action is more familiar to a modern reader—but, as may be clear, Hobbes adopts a variation of the first sense in which freedom may be used, namely a freedom to choose between alternatives. Arguably, Hobbes's definitive account of freedom and liberty is found in the *Leviathan*. 'Liberty, or Freedome,' he says, 'signifieth (properly) the absence of Opposition; (by Opposition, I mean externall Impediments of motion;) and may be applied no lesse to Irrational, and Inanimate creatures, than to Rationall'.[171] He goes on: 'For whatsoever is so tyed, or environed, as it cannot move, but within a certain space, which space is determined by the opposition of some external body, we say it hath not Liberty to go further.' In direct contrast to Stair and the early modern theological tradition, Hobbes made clear that, for him, 'no Liberty can be inferred of the will, desire, or inclination, but the Liberty of the man, which consisteth in this, that he finds no stop in doing what he has the will, desire, or inclination to doe'.[172] Hobbes speaks of 'the right of nature' as the liberty of man to use his power 'for the preservation of his own Nature, that is to say, of his own Life'.[173] He continues that the law of nature and the right of liberty are often 'confounded'; that is, 'Jus, and Lex, Right and Law; yet they ought to be distinguished; because Right, consisteth in liberty to do, or to forbeare; Whereas Law, determineth, and bindeth to one of them; so that Law, and Right, differ as much, as Obligation, and Liberty; which in one and the same matter are inconsistent.'[174] Liberty and right are therefore

---

[170] Archibald H Campbell, *The Structure of Stair's Institutions* (Jackson, Son & Co. 1954).

[171] Hobbes *Leviathan* (n 11) Ch 21.

[172] Hobbes *Leviathan* (n 11) Ch 21.

[173] Hobbes *Leviathan* (n 11) Ch 14.

[174] Hobbes *Leviathan* (n 11) Ch 14.

contrasted by Hobbes with law and obligation. To have a right, according to Hobbes, is to have the power, privilege, or immunity to do what one chooses. In comparison, law and obligation means your right or liberty is bound by a duty, disadvantage, responsibility, or disability.

Hobbes says liberty is 'the absence of externall Impediments: which Impediments, may oft take away part of man's power to do what he would; but cannot hinder him from using the power left him, according as his judgement, and reason shall dictate to him'.[175] But he does demonstrate a sense of normative liberty when he says that the right of nature is a liberty to use judgment and reason as to the best means of self-preservation. Laws, however, are by definition, according to Hobbes, something which stop a man from doing what he wants; they also do not allow him to use his judgment or reason about the best course of action. Laws, obligations, and commands are things which hinder liberty in terms of supplanting your ability to make a choice. Hobbes offers what is sometimes referred to as a negative conception of liberty: the absence of external constraint.[176] It is external in focus, and collapses many of the subtle distinctions found in early modern theological discussion of human action. The different senses of the terms 'liberty' or 'freedom' are central to understanding Stair's contractual thought, his understanding of law and obligation and the relationship between theology and Stair's account of the law of Scotland. As will next be explored, Stair draws on all three of these different senses of 'liberty' in the Institutions.

Conclusion: Scholastic or Humanist?

If Stair used the term 'will' in full knowledge of its origins and theological meaning, should we say this was scholastic? Is Stair's use of the term an example of Reformed Scholasticism?[177] The answer to these questions may be yes, but some caution should be taken when ascribing Stair to a particular genre if that were to be used to preclude him from other genres such as humanism. Indeed, recent scholarship has called into question the usefulness of filing particular substantive topics, such as the relationship between the will, desire, and the intellect, under the headings of 'medieval' or 'early modern scholasticism' as if this were a rival to humanism or Ramist forms of literature.[178] In the history of theology, it is now generally accepted, for instance, that the binary distinction between humanism and scholasticism greatly simplifies the complexity of early modern thinking.[179] Hence, humanists who rejected scholastic methods still spoke of the intellect, desire, and the will.[180] On the other hand, Protestant humanists may have scorned Catholic scholasticism, but in the sixteenth

---

[175] Hobbes Leviathan (n 11) Ch 14.

[176] Isaiah Berlin, 'Two Concepts of Liberty' in Isaiah Berlin (ed), Four Essays on Liberty (OUP 2002) 167–218.

[177] Willem J van Asselt, Introduction to Reformed Scholasticism (Reformation Heritage Books 2011).

[178] Richard A Muller, After Calvin. Studies in the Development of a Theological Tradition (OUP 2003) Ch 2; van Asselt 'Scholasticism Revisited' (n 82) 154–74; Saarinen Weakness of Will (n 6).

[179] For a summary of the literature, see John Coffey, Politics, Religion and the British Revolutions: The Mind of Samuel Rutherford (CUP 1997) Ch 3.

[180] Baschera 'Aristotle and Scholasticism' (n 103) 153ff.

and seventeenth centuries Catholics and Protestants alike continued to draw upon the common pool of medieval theology and philosophy.[181] Scholastic and humanist authors were used in English and Scottish universities to teach logic, ethics, and metaphysics.[182] Thus, scholasticism is better described as a *method* and mode of argumentation rather than a tradition of substantive canonical themes.[183] It may therefore be safer, if a tradition is to be applied to Stair, to describe him as a Protestant natural lawyer on the broad terms which Haakonssen describes.[184]

It is with Hobbes that one begins to see a completely new way of describing human action, which is materialist and without an appeal to theology or Aristotelianism.[185] Hobbes's writing marks a key linguistic and theoretical transformation of terms such as 'the will'.[186] In Hobbes, the will becomes nothing more than a word to describe the last action in man's decision-making. Hobbes, however, saw men as mechanically driven by an aversion to pain and a desire for pleasure; deliberation or reasoning had no meaningful role in man's decision-making, and the will would merely follow the rule of desire.[187] In other words, the will was merely the last stage in a predetermined mechanical process of cause and effect. Stair never expressly refutes Hobbes in the *Institutions*, but he certainly held a different conception of 'the will' from Hobbes. Stair retained the theological, anti-materialist sense of the term which can be found in medieval theological discussions of the will. It is this pre-Hobbesian, trans-confessional philosophical theological language which Stair used as a regent at Glasgow University that connects him with the late scholastics. In drawing from the same lexicon and medieval philosophical traditions, Stair used these ideas, language, and approach into the law of contract. Whether this engraftment is to be classified as scholastic, humanist, or something else is an interesting question. More pertinent or the following discussion is to grasp the detail of Stair's conception of freedom and show how it relates to his account of the law of contract.

[181] Mullan 'Theology in the Church of Scotland 1618–c. 1640' (n 73); Muller *After Calvin* (n 178); McGrath *The Intellectual Origins* (n 72) Ch 2.

[182] John A Trentman, 'Scholasticism in the Seventeenth Century' in Norman Kretzmann, Anthony Kenny, Jan Pinborg, and Eleonore Stump (eds), *The Cambridge History of Later Medieval Philosophy* (CUP 1982) 818–37.

[183] van Asselt 'Scholasticism Revisited' (n 82) 154–74; James H Burns, 'Scholasticism: Survival and Revival' in James H Burns and Mark Goldie (eds), *The Cambridge History of Political Thought 1450–1700* (CUP 1991) 132–56.

[184] Haakonssen 'Protestant Natural Law Theory' (n 10) 92–5.

[185] Jürgen Overhoff, *Hobbes's Theory of the Will: Ideological Reasons and Historical Circumstances* (Rowman & Littlefield Publishers 2000).

[186] Pink 'Suarez, Hobbes and the Scholastic Tradition in Action Theory' (n 100) 127–53.

[187] Hobbes *Leviathan* (n 11) Ch 21.

Stair saw freedom as acting in accordance w/ what God has willed to bring Him glory.

7

Freedom, Liberty, and Conscience

Stair's conception of liberty and freedom emerges from his *Divine Perfections*, read alongside his *Institutions of the Law of Scotland* (*Institutions*). Both sources must be judged against the theological context of mid-seventeenth-century Scotland. Reading these sources together offers an important viewpoint from which to understand Stair's notion of freedom to contract and suggests how his contemporaries would have understood such a notion. What emerges is that Stair held a theologically rich conception of liberty, which meant that when prescribed obligations of divine law were exhausted, man had a discretion to decide how he would bring glory to God. But this was not freedom in a negative Hobbesian or a secular Pufendorfian sense: it was uttered within the context of seventeenth-century Scotland, where the notion of bringing glory to God was central to the social, institutional, and personal organization of an individual's life. Indeed, when Stair is read within the appropriate context, it appears that for him there was a range of permissible actions which man could do with his liberty and which could bring glory to God; but this was not licence or immunity to do whatever you wanted to do. That is, once Stair's approach to liberty is understood within the context of the seventeenth century and his own theological writing, it is clear that for Stair, man is only truly free when he acts in accordance with what God has willed, which was known to man through the Moral Law, which was written on his heart, and through his dialogue with his conscience, reason, and Scripture. Or, to draw upon the explanation of liberty and the will offered in Chapter 7, Stair may have used liberty in its various senses but ultimately held a 'freedom as reason' sense of liberty. It is this that connects to Stair's theological understanding of man's liberty as an expression of following the dictates of reason habitually, and acting as the rational creatures which God created.[1]

However, the analysis in this chapter demonstrates that when Stair spoke of liberty in his *Institutions*, he was cautious in its formulation, acknowledging the practical, jurisdictional, and political limitations of the human law to bring about man's moral rectitude. Stair understood liberty as a gift from God, which allowed him the freedom to bring glory to God in an individual way. As Dunn demonstrated through his interpretation of John Locke, in the seventeenth-century liberty held a political and legal significance for both radical Calvinists and High Church Anglicans because it created the space for men to pursue their calling to God.[2] As will be argued, when Stair is read within this context, there is no tension between either liberty and human law or civil government and man's natural liberty in his account of law, obligations, and contracting. Although Stair uses different senses of 'liberty' or 'freedom' in the *Institutions* and the *Divine Perfections*—liberty to choose, liberty as a right, and liberty

---

[1] Stair *Divine Perfections* 114.
[2] John Dunn, *The Political Thought of John Locke* (CUP 1995) generally, but specifically 245–61.

Contract before the Enlightenment. Stephen Bogle, Oxford University Press. © Stephen Bogle 2023.
DOI: 10.1093/oso/9780192884961.003.0008

as reason—enforcing performance of an obligation is not a deprivation of Stair's theological sense of liberty. As this chapter will argue, according to Stair, in deciding to enter into a contract or to perform one's conventional obligations, you are performing both your moral and your legal obligation; that is, provided man does so willingly and for the glory of God. In such an instance, man's liberty is acting in concert with or in harmony with the human law that implements the Moral Law, and therefore there is no conflict—whereas, when man refuses to perform his obligations, there is a tension between the civil powers' enforcement of that obligation and the liberty of man to choose what he wants to do. On Stair's account, however, the enforcement of an obligation by a civil power withdrew man's choice to act morally, forcing him by restraint, constraint, or force to act in accordance with his legal and moral obligations.

Freedom of and to Contract?

Stair's formulation of legal capacity in terms of liberty is significant both legally and politically.[3] His account of the individual is not about status, as you might expect in the early modern period, but rather about the legal liberty to act without obligation to another individual. Such liberty included the freedom to contract away that liberty. MacCormick has also observed that by stressing a relationship between liberty, conventional obligations, and commerce, Stair was 'in a very real sense the legal prophet for the commercial society which he favoured and which in due course came to pass'.[4] Ford argues that Stair based his account of liberty 'on a political theory that sought to reconcile ascending and descending principles of government, and so began dealing with the legal status of ordinary people'.[5] Stair here views private law as an interpersonal system of personal rights and obligations and not as a directional theory of descending authority akin to theories of divine and absolute monarchism.[6] In terms of Stair's influences, it is also worth noting that Campbell has remarked upon a 'rather unexpected' similarity between Stair and Hobbes: 'namely, the opposition of liberty and obligation'[7] A striking affinity considering their different premises of polity and human personality.[8]

[3] Neil MacCormick, 'Stair as Analytical Jurist' in David M Walker (ed), *Stair Tercentenary Studies*, vol 33 (Stair Society 1981) 196–97.

[4] Neil MacCormick, 'The Rational Discipline of Law' (1981) Juridical Review 146–60, 159.

[5] John D Ford, 'Stair's Title "Of Liberty and Servitude"' in Andrew D E Lewis and David J Ibbetson (eds), *The Roman Law Tradition* (CUP 1994) 156.

[6] eg James Maxwell, *Sacro-Sancta Regum Majestas: or; The Sacred and Royall Prerogative of Christian Kings* (Oxford 1644). See Ford's discussion, John D Ford, 'Lex, Rex Justo Posita: Samuel Rutherford on the Origins of Government' in Roger Mason (ed), *Scots and Britons: Scottish Political Thought and the Union of 1603* (CUP 1994) 262–90.

[7] Archibald H Campbell, *The Structure of Stair's Institutions: Being the Twenty-First Lecture on the David Murray Foundation in the University of Glasgow Delivered on 24th February, 1954* (Jackson, Son & Co 1954) 21.

[8] The only other examination of Stair's theological conception of liberty can be found in Gordon M Hutton, *The Political Thought of Sir James Dalrymple, First Viscount Stair (1619–1695), with Special Reference to his Concepts of Natural Law and Sovereignty, and in Relation to his Political Life* (DPhil thesis, University of Birmingham 1971). Hutton's analysis links Stair's public life to his published work, suggesting contradictions between his practical political and abstract theological conceptions of liberty. This is hardly

Stair's Conception of Freedom, Liberty, and Conscience

Freedom in the *Divine Perfections*

Some of Stair's ideas relating to freedom and liberty are captured in what was to become the *Institutions*, published in 1681 (originating from sometime around 1659–62). And it should be noted that, in painstaking detail, Wilson has demonstrated that Stair did little to alter his title on liberty despite producing various iterations of the *Institutions* between the late 1650s and 1693.[9] Importantly, however, for this chapter, there is a theological account of freedom and liberty offered in his *Divine Perfections*[10] published fourteen years later in 1695 (written, it would appear, sometime between 1681 and 1693).[11] As explained in the Introduction, there is good reason to read both the *Institutions* and the *Divine Perfections* in conjunction with one another—and, that being so, his theological work should inform how we understand his legal and philosophical conceptualization of not just freedom and liberty, but also justice and morality.

In scholastic fashion, he makes four distinctions when giving his account of freedom in the *Divine Perfections*. He starts by observing that freedom 'is a Relative Term, and doth imply something from which, and something to which a Being is free'.[12] Hence he contrasts freedom, as a state of being or conditions, with four other states or conditions, relating to a power to do something or not to do something. He starts by discussing extrinsic forces which can act upon a state of freedom. First, there is the state of constraint, 'making anything act contrary to its free Choice or Inclination'.[13] Second, there is the state of restraint, 'whereby anything is hinder'd to do that which by Choice or natural inclination it might do'.[14] Third, there is the state of resistance or opposition, where 'it can diminish the Effect of the Power of that which is free'.[15] Following this, he describes a fourth category, internal forces, which act upon a state of being; that is, when 'any thing cannot alter its own Power, or the Effect of it, either because it is void of Perception, and so cannot know when and where to alter its Activity'.[16]

In this fourth category, Stair is concerned not with external means which negate freedom, but with the ways by which some things may be constrained by internal

---

surprising; and in any case a close reading of the *Institutions* suggests that Stair did indeed strive to reconcile theory with practical ethics and politics.

[9] Adelyn L M Wilson, 'The Textual Tradition of Stair's *Institutions*, with Reference to the Title "Of Liberty and Servitude" ' in Hector L MacQueen (ed), *Miscellany Seven*, vol 62 (Stair Society 2015) 1–125.

[10] Stair *Divine Perfections*. Indeed, the Divine Perfections appear to be an elaboration of Stair's graduation theses: David S Sytsma, "James Dalrymple of Stair: 'Ethical Theses" in *Theses Logicae, Metaphysicae, Physicae, Mathematicae, et Ethicae* (George Anderson 1646) (2020) <(PDF) James Dalrymple of Stair: Ethical Theses (Glasgow, 1646) | David S. Sytsma - Academia.edu> accessed 15 April 2021.

[11] George Dallas, *System of Stiles as now Practical within the Kingdom of Scotland* (Andrew Anderson 1697) 152–53.

[12] Stair *Divine Perfections* 104.

[13] Stair *Divine Perfections* 104.

[14] Stair *Divine Perfections* 104.

[15] Stair *Divine Perfections* 104.

[16] Stair *Divine Perfections* 104.

forces, which relates to his conception of liberty. This fourth category, however, does not apply universally to objects or animals or brutes. Hence, speaking of 'all creatures', he says that they can experience internal forces in contrast to things such as fire, which can only be constrained or restrained externally but not internally.[17] He goes on to say: 'in a sense Brutes have some kind of freedom, because they act variously, tho they be neither restrained nor constrained'; they can determine their actions according to 'their Sense, Memory, or Imagination'.[18] However, Stair offers a distinction which can be used to differentiate men, who act voluntarily but are nevertheless compelled, from brutes or animals, which act according to absolute necessity. For him, voluntary necessity is 'whereby Rational Beings are free from absolute Necessity, but which they act not as Brutes, but upon comparing the things eligible, they can only choose or act one way'.[19] For example, he says: 'I can choose nothing but under the Appearance of some Goodness: I cannot choose my own Misery; or if it fall in my Consideration, I cannot but desire my own Happiness'; but this, according to Stair, does not equate to the absolute necessity of brutes. Rather, man—in contrast to a brute or animal—is free to follow his 'natural habitual Propension', meaning it is a voluntary necessity.[20] Finally, there is freedom from the 'Prepossession of those Strong Propensions, which are like the Instincts of Brutes', which do not exclude freedom but reduce it. When they prevail, he says, 'the Creature is not free', but you can nevertheless say that someone has the power to act contrary to their prepossessions even if they never do.[21]

There is both a metaphysical or 'liberty as choice' and a theological or 'liberty as reason' implication to Stair's concept of freedom. In terms of metaphysics, 'freedom' is a wide and useful term used to describe behaviour or abilities of things as varied as objects, elements, animals, and persons. Specifically, it is a term that concerns power; in essence, it is the ability to do or not to do something, which is contrasted, by Stair, with resistance to, constraint of or diminution of that power. In contrast to Stair's concept of liberty, which has a narrower ethical or moral meaning, Stair's concept of freedom has an almost scientific or natural philosophical use that enables Stair to describe the freedom of man in a similar manner to that of animals, brutes, elements, and objects while using the concept of liberty to distinguish man from such things. Importantly, the distinction he makes, when speaking about internal freedom, between voluntary necessity and absolute necessity is, arguably, to use more modern philosophical terms, a form of compatibilist understanding of freedom in contrast to determinism, which would discard Stair's distinction between voluntary and absolute—an overly complicated distinction introduced for social or moral purposes. Stair argues that the action of man is free and not technically constrained, even if the desire for happiness and the aversion to misery are a necessary part of man's decision-making. For Stair, man, unlike a brute, chooses or decides or voluntarily opts to respond to these desires or causes.

---

[17] Stair *Divine Perfections* 105.
[18] Stair *Divine Perfections* 105.
[19] Stair *Divine Perfections* 105.
[20] Stair *Divine Perfections* 105.
[21] Stair *Divine Perfections* 106.

Stair's treatment of freedom and his distinction between voluntary necessity and absolute necessity is also important in terms of religious orthodoxy in Scotland in the mid- to late seventeenth century, at least from the perspective of Presbyterians like Stair. In both the *Institutes of Christian Religion* and his subsequent *The Bondage and Liberation of the Will*, John Calvin criticized the ancient philosophers, the Church Fathers, and his contemporaries for using the term 'free will' because it either directly or ambiguously suggests that man retains, without God's help, the ability to act voluntarily and virtuously. Of course, for Calvin, man is corrupted by sin and unable to act morally without God's aid, but this does not mean that man is not free and therefore morally unaccountable for his sinful actions or responsible for his virtuous actions. To say man has free will, therefore, does not allow for his fine distinctions which are central to his theological account of man. Calvin accepts, however, the account of freedom found in Lombard's *Sentences*: freedom from necessity; freedom from sin; and freedom from misery. Picking up on the first sense of 'freedom', Calvin says: 'If freedom is opposed to coercion, I both acknowledge and consistently maintain that choice is free .... If, I say, it were called free in the sense of not being coerced nor forcibly moved by an external impulse, but moving of its own accord, I have no objection.'[22] However, as he explained in the *Institutes*, 'free will does not enable any man to perform good works, unless he is assisted by grace; indeed, the special grace which the elect alone receive through regeneration.'[23] As he further explains in *The Bondage and Liberation of the Will*, the phrase 'free will' unhelpfully implies that man has the power and ability to determine right-action according to his own strength and unaffected will, whereas in fact he can only do so with God's grace, given his sinful nature. Calvin is happy for the term 'freedom' to be used in the sense which Stair adopts: a broader, more descriptive sense, which is contrasted with necessity or constraint.

As Paul Helm summarizes, Calvin believed that in a prelapsarian state man possessed free will, in a moral sense, in order to choose between good and evil, but we 'do not possess such free will now, and so Calvin's advice is that we had better not use the phrase about ourselves lest, by using it to affirm specific human powers that we do not possess, we flatter ourselves that we possess the power to choose either good or evil'.[24] Helm uses the distinction between freedom of action and freedom to elucidate Calvin's theory; it is particularly helpful to understand the distinction between wanting the desire you have and not wanting the desire you have.[25] On this understanding, a person is only free if there is a basic alignment between their desire, their want, and their ability to act. According to Calvin, man has sinful desires, seeks fulfilment of those desires, and so acts upon them; he can only change his sinful desires if he first does not want those desires, which only comes about through his conscience reminding him of what is good and God actively changing man's wants.[26] 'Free will' is

---

[22] Paul Helm, *John Calvin's Ideas* (OUP 2004) 68.

[23] Calvin *Inst* 2.2.6.

[24] Helm *Ideas* (n 22) 161.

[25] Helm *Ideas* (n 22) 174–75. Thomas Pink suggests the distinction should be between voluntariness and self-determination, something he thinks is problematic: Thomas Pink, 'Self-Determination and Moral Responsibility from Calvin to Frankfurt' in M Stone (ed), *Faith and History: Philosophical Essays for Paul Helm* (Ashgate 2008) 145–64.

[26] Calvin *Inst* 2.3.5. Also see contemporary David Dickson's account of how conscience and regeneration operate, which describes this process in intimate detail and retains the notion that man choices to

therefore not a useful term to use when describing human action, according to Calvin; and it is evident that Stair follows this approach, particularly where his account of liberty is concerned.

Stair does not himself use the term 'free will' to describe man's actions, although he does use the terms 'freedom', 'liberty', and 'will' in the *Institutions* and the *Divine Perfections*. Stair does, nevertheless, in the *Divine Perfections* describe and account for what freedom means in relation to both internal and external actions with regard to objects, animals, and man. It is worth noting, therefore, that in comparison to Calvin's account in the *Institutes*, Stair's description of freedom is somewhat more involved and detailed, displaying a scholastic or philosophical approach rather than simply dismissing the need for distinctions or the necessity for precise language. There is a desire in Stair to describe what freedom means and to demonstrate how freedom, namely to be free, is the opposite of to be constrained, hindered, or resisted. It is important, however, to stress that Stair's account of freedom and human action does not suggest that man is constrained, hindered, or resisted by sin in such a way that he cannot do anything else but sin despite willing otherwise. The distinction between freedom of action and freedom of will helpfully captures Stair's approach to human action, first describing the ability to physically control our actions, that is, freedom of action, and then describing our ability to control our decision-making or desires or wants, that is, freedom of will. To account for human action in any other manner would risk contradicting Calvin and the dominant understanding of man's moral responsibility within seventeenth-century Presbyterian thought.[27] Hence, like Calvin, Stair offers an account of the will and liberty of man which is complex and multifaceted, but which ultimately ensures that man's sin is his responsibility and can be described as a choice, wanting to have the desire to sin, rather than something which is determined or necessary, having no control over the want of the desire to sin.

Liberty in the *Divine Perfections*

Stair defines liberty in the *Divine Perfections* as 'the Hability of Self-determination upon a rational Motive'.[28] It is 'a Power to determine and choose, which cannot be hindered by extrinsick Force, or instrinsick Necesity, which may be three ways'.[29] He identifies these three types of liberty: freedom of indifferency; freedom with inclination; and freedom against inclination. Freedom with indifference is when you are inclined by neither your appetite or your desire toward one thing or another. He

---

sin: David Dickson, *Therapeutica Sacra Shewing Briefly the Method of Healing the Diseases of the Conscience, concerning Regeneration* (Evan Tyler 1664) 1.3. Dickson was an influential theologian in the 1630s and 1640, and during the Bishops' Wars he became politically active. As a regent at the University of Glasgow, he would have been known to Stair personally, but whatever the case, Dickson's theology and teaching was orthodoxy for Scottish Presbyterians in the 1640s.

[27] See, for example, Ch IX.I of the *Westminster Confession of Faith* of 1647: 'God hath endued the will of man with that natural liberty, that it is neither forced, nor by any absolute necessity of nature determined to good or evil.'

[28] Stair *Divine Perfections* 113.

[29] Stair *Divine Perfections* 106.

explains: 'consider Adam in his Innocency, choosing the Fruit of the same allowed Tree in Paradise, he could not find a Difference among them all, and so his Choice was freed by indifferency'.[30] Freedom against inclination is when your appetite draws you towards something, but you act contrary 'with the inclination of the rational Appetite'. Thus, he supposes, 'at first view, the natural Affection would incline [Adam] to the forbidden Fruit, tho it might easily have been overcome by minding Gratitude to God who did forbid it, and the Penalty of the Breach of that Command'.[31] In contrast, freedom with inclination is when appetites or affections and the rational appetites act together rather than contrary to each other. Adam, therefore, would have no appetite to eat the forbidden fruit and therefore act in accordance with his rational appetite. To act with liberty, therefore, is to want to act in accordance with a rational motive, and to be free of sinful wants (inclinations, appetites, affections etc.). Hence, Frankfurt's distinction, as with Calvin's, helps to account for how a Protestant theory of human action—which otherwise emphasizes man's inability, due to sin, to act morally and with true freedom—can otherwise be said to act freely.

Four other aspects of liberty are defined by Stair. First, liberty is the power to do what we can do naturally according to our abilities and not simply do whatever we want, such as fly or become invisible.[32] Second, liberty is an *ability* and not merely something we can do at any time; that is, because it is an ability, it 'imports more than a Power, which sometimes is not in a present capacity ... as a sick man hath a Power to walk'.[33] Third, it is the 'last practical Act of the Judgment about that which is in Consideration', and should be taken not to be a single act but over a period of time. However, it is not 'what is judged to be just, but what is judged to be fit in the present Circumstances, or to be either good, as just, profitable, or pleasant'.[34] This last point may need further clarification, as it is not entirely clear what Stair means here. One possible explanation is that Stair does not want to confuse an act of man's reason with liberty. Thus, reason or the intellect, informed by man's conscience, may determine what one ought to do morally, and thus what is just. Ultimately, however, the last stage in human action involves a process of determining how to bring about that which is not determined by reason or the intellect. And, for Stair, it is that last stage where you can say whether a man has liberty or not. He does not want to suggest that the process of deliberation or reflection can be free or not free. It is following deliberation, when man moves towards implementing what he has decided to do or not to do, that the steps taken by a man can be called free or not free.[35] Fourth, it is the ability to decide to act or not to act (*liberty ad contradictoria*) or to prefer one thing over another (*liberty ad contraria*).

---

[30] Stair *Divine Perfections* 107.
[31] Stair *Divine Perfections* 107.
[32] Stair *Divine Perfections* 114.
[33] Stair *Divine Perfections* 114.
[34] Stair *Divine Perfections* 114.
[35] This suggestion is based on a reading of pages 110–11 of the *Divine Perfections*. It is argued that Stair would prefer this interpretation of human action as the alternative errs towards a more intellectualist rather that voluntarist account of action. It is plausible that Stair was influenced by Scotus' critique of Aquinas on this point: See Terence Irwin, *The Development of Ethics: Volume 1: From Socrates to the Reformation* (OUP 2007) Ch 25 for a summary of Scotus's views on the will, freedom, and reason and Aquinas.

Therefore, in the *Divine Perfections*, Stair adopts an intricate understanding of freedom and liberty. In his specific definition of liberty, Stair connects a rational motive and self-determination with liberty, and stresses that 'no Rational Creature could be ... infallible by its own intrinsick Perfections' and emphasizes, again, that it is God who ultimately ensures man does good over evil, and that man is not free whilst subject to sin.[36] On this basis, it would be fair to say that Stair holds a somewhat commonplace position: man is not truly at liberty until he acts in accordance with natural law and is unable to sin.[37] It is unsurprising that Stair holds such an opinion, but making this point underlines the significance of Stair's description of the role of human law and civil government in the *Institutions*, and especially the notion that man is left free by natural law and human law and is permitted to enter into a contract of his choice. It is suggested, therefore, that Stair's description of freedom and liberty in the *Institutions* and his description of man's freedom to contract should be informed by how he described these terms in the *Divine Perfections*. According to Stair, legally you could enter into whatever contract you wanted provided it was permissible according to human law and your conscience. You did not have unfettered licence to do as you wished but should rather do within your contracting affairs what you determined would bring glory to God.

This leaves the difficult question of how Stair's theological concept of liberty relates to his understanding of the role of human law in society and with regard to individual freedom. It also raises the question of how far Stair was prepared to go to ensure, through human law, the fulfilment of natural law, and man's liberty. Stair does not wish to use human law or civil government to enforce ethical action other than those basic obligations necessary for peace and society. Indeed, Stair had witnessed both the radical 1649 parliament in Scotland,[38] which sought to bring about Godly rule in Scotland, as well as the Westminster parliament of saints in 1653,[39] which also sought to create through temporal powers and law a Godly society in Britain. More widely, Stair would have been conscious of the control and power exerted by the Roman Catholic Church through ecclesiastical courts and their supervision of contracts in Scotland during the early modern period.[40] For those who could afford the services of the court, they were often used for the registration or enforcement of contracts and promises. In practical terms, then, how should a legal system be understood and implemented when it is informed by a Calvinist conception of liberty? Or, to what extent does the human law of Scotland articulated by Stair embody natural law imperatives;

---

[36] Stair *Divine Perfections* 16.

[37] Pink characterizes this sort of conception of freedom, as 'a desirable goal or condition' sense of freedom, which, importantly, during the medieval period existed alongside the notion that freedom was a power. Thomas Pink, 'Freedom of the Will' in John Marenbon (ed), *The Oxford Handbook of Medieval Philosophy* (OUP 2012) 570–87. Such an opinion is commonplace within medieval literature, for example Lombard's *Sentences* II.25.156.

[38] Michael Lynch, 'The Wars of Covenant' in Michael Lynch (ed), *The Oxford Companion to Scottish History* (OUP 2001) 112. For reference to the Court of Session during this period, see David Stevenson, 'The Covenanters and the Court of Session, 1637–1650' in David Stevenson (ed), *Union, Revolution and Religion in 17th-century Scotland* (Variorum 1997) 227–47.

[39] For discussion of law-reform projects during this period, see Blair Worden, *The Rump Parliament, 1648–53* (first published 1977, CUP 2010) 105–18.

[40] James J Robertson, 'Canon Law as a Source' in David M Walker (ed), *Stair Tercentenary Studies*, vol 33 (Stair Society 1981) 122–27.

or in what circumstances should it tell men and women what to do with their freedom; how far should the law and its enforcement ensure man's moral rectitude; how does a legal system ensure that people act in accordance with a rational motive; and how does law relate to liberty? Before dealing with the political and legal meaning of 'liberty', it is important first to establish how Stair addresses the requirement that man use his freedom to bring glory to God.

Freedom to Bring Glory to God

It is possible to offer an answer to these questions if the *Institutions*, the *Divine Perfections*, and other texts from the seventeenth century are read in conjunction. Answering the larger questions posed above also offers an interpretation of what Stair envisaged when he spoke of man's freedom to create a conventional obligation, which is very different from nineteenth-century notions of freedom of contract. In the *Institutions*, Stair makes the general point that 'man by nature is free in all things, where this obedience has not tied him, until he oblige himself'. Stair then adds the crucial caveat that God has left man with this freedom so that he may choose between alternatives 'providing that whatsoever he do (even where he is free) be ordered and directed to the glory of God'.[41] He explains:

> God seemeth to do with men, as Princes do with their Ambassadors, to whom they give some express instructions, wherein they have no latitude in their Negotiations, and for the rest to do as they shall judge most fit upon the place, wherein, if acting bona fide, they mistake, and do not that which is most fit, they are not culpable.[42]

This example could easily be overlooked as ornamental or somewhat insignificant if modern conceptions of religious freedom are read into this passage. When placed within mid- to late seventeenth-century Scotland, however, and alongside other texts from this period, this passage invokes a very different and regulated sense of freedom and what it means for man to act with liberty.

Stair wrote within the context of a Calvinist sense of personal calling, where individuals were made free but also responsible. Although the context of Scotland is important to how this is understood, the experience of the British Isles more generally in the seventeenth century was similar. As Walzer noted, in the seventeenth century, Puritan theologians-cum-politicians—or 'saints' as they were sometimes referred to—'attempted to fasten upon the necks of all mankind the yoke of a new political discipline—impersonal and ideological, not founded upon loyalty or affection, no more open to spontaneity than to chaos and crime'.[43] Calvinist-inspired ideas, which emerged in both England and Scotland, no longer made discipline reliant upon 'the authority of paternal kings and lords or upon the obedience of childlike and trustful subjects'. Rather, 'Puritans sought to make it voluntary, like the contract itself, the

---

[41] Stair *Inst* 1.1.20.
[42] Stair *Inst* 1.1.20.
[43] Micheal Walzer, *The Revolution of the Saints* (Harvard University Press 1965) 302.

object of individual and collective wilfulness.'[44] Dunn has also noted, in describing the context of Locke's conception of liberty and political obligation: 'It was a central fact of Calvinist theology, both in its radical development among the Saints and a fortiori in its more conservative articulation in the Anglican church ... that the intensely religious individualism of the doctrine of the calling was intimately bound to the social discipline of the religious community.'[45] Stair may not have been a Puritan, but in Scotland in the 1660s, and again in the 1680s and 1690s, he was writing and publishing within a community that was deeply shaped by these ideas and debates about the proper jurisdiction, institutional and social boundaries of what it meant to have the freedom to bring glory to God.

The *Larger Catechism*

In mid-seventeenth-century Scotland, there were very clear and exacting expectations as to how individuals should live their lives, including what they should say, think, and do; that is, how they should use whatever freedom they might have.[46] These expectations were not just legal, in the sense of being articulated in the statutes of human law, nor were they just unwritten social norms or informal conventions or religious customs: these expectations were expressed in sermons,[47] treatises on heresies or erroneous religious practices and beliefs,[48] handbooks on what individuals should do in their daily lives,[49] and other literature promulgated by the Church of Scotland[50] or Scottish universities.[51] Hence, when Stair wrote that man should use his freedom to

---

[44] Walzer *The Revolution of the Saints* (n 43) 302.

[45] Dunn *The Political Thought of John Locke* (n 2) 248.

[46] See, generally, Michael F Graham, *The Uses of Reform: Godly Discipline and Popular Behaviour in Scotland and Beyond, 1560–1610* (Brill 1996); Margo Todd, *The Culture of Protestantism in Early Modern Scotland* (Yale University Press 2002); Jenny Wormald, 'Reformed and Godly?' in Tom M Devine and Jenny Wormald (eds), *The Oxford Handbook of Modern Scottish History* (OUP 2012) 204–19.

[47] For some examples, see *A Collection of Lectures and Sermons, Preached upon Several Subjects, Most in the Time of Persecution* (H & S Crawford 1809). For surveys of seventeenth-century preaching, see William G Blaikie, *The Preachers of Scotland: From the Sixth to the Nineteenth Century* (T&T Clark 1888) 123–84; Crawford Gribben, 'Preaching the Scottish Reformation, 1560–1707' in Hugh Adlington, Peter McCullough, and Emma Rhatigan (eds), *The Oxford Handbook of the Early Modern Sermon* (OUP 2011) 272–86.

[48] Robert Baillie, *A Dissvasive from the Errours of the Time* (Samuel Gillibrand 1645). Indeed, Robert Baillie, a high-profile Presbyterian minister from the mid-1640s until his death in 1662, was practically prolific in this genre producing many tracts on related topics.

[49] For example, see Richard Baxter's voluminous (over 1,200 pages), *A Christian Directory: or a Summ of Practical Theologie, and Cases of Conscience, Directing Christians, how to USE their Knowledge and Faith; How to improve all Helps and Means, and to Perform all Duties; How to Overcome Tempations, and to Escape or Mortifie every Sin* (Robert White 1673), a copy of which was held in Glasgow University Library in 1691. See also the popular and detailed statement of Presbyterian ethics found in James Durham, *A Practical Exposition of the X commandments with a Resolution of Several Momentous Questions and Cases of Conscience* (Andrew Anderson 1676). Durham's treatise was published in London in 1675 and Edinburgh in 1676 and 1677. It was published numerous times in the eighteenth century in Edinburgh in 1715, 1735, 1777, and 1798.

[50] Alexander Henderson, *The Government and Order of the Church of Scotland* (James Bryson 1641; reprint by George Mosman 1690).

[51] Christian Maurer, '"A Lapsu Corruptus": Calvinist Doctrines and Seventeenth-Century Scottish Theses Ethicæ' in Mordechai Feingold and Alexander Broadie (eds), *History of Universities: Volume XXIX/2* (OUP 2017) 189–209.

bring glory to God, it should not be overlooked that he did so within the context of a deeply religious environment, and where what it meant to bring glory to God was expressed in a variety of literatures.[52] Notably, Stair wrote this passage in the *Institutions* within living memory of the *Westminster Confession of Faith* (*Confession*) which was passed by the Church of Scotland in 1647 and adopted by the radical Scottish Parliament of 1649.[53] It was within the context of strict corporate religion, the Church of Scotland's dominance, and a society shaped by Calvin's vision of a Godly community that Stair said man should use his liberty to bring glory to God. It is not only the context, however, which directs the reader of Stair's *Institutions* towards the orthodoxy of the Church of Scotland: Stair's directive that man should bring glory to God with his freedom invokes the first passage of the *Larger Catechism of the Westminster Confession of Faith* (*Larger Catechism*).[54]

The 1647 *Larger Catechism* which accompanied the 1647 *Confession* specified what men and woman should believe and what their duties were. The opening passage of the *Larger Catechism* says: 'What is the chief and highest end of man?' To this, the answer is: 'Man's chief and highest end is to glorify God, and fully to enjoy him forever.' Answer 21 states that 'Our first parents [Adam and Eve] being left to the freedom of their own will, through the temptation of Satan, transgressed the commandment of God in eating the forbidden fruit; and thereby fell from the estate of innocency wherein they were created.' After describing the role of Christ within salvation, answers 91 and 92 state that man's first duty is to be obedient to God's will, which was first revealed to Adam, but which is now known as the Moral Law. Answer 94 says: 'Although no man, since the fall, can attain to righteousness and life by the moral law; yet there is great use thereof, as well common to all men, as peculiar either to the unregenerate, or the regenerate.' Following from this, answer 95 confirms that the Moral Law nevertheless informs men of their duty to God and reminds them of their inability to follow the expectations of morality. The Moral Law, it is stated, serves to awaken the conscience of the 'unregenerate' and to remind the 'regenerate' of how far they are from God and thus what they have received by grace. Thereafter, over ninety of the answers deal with the specific duties of men and women which are based on the Moral Law; mostly this is done by extrapolating from the Ten Commandments in the Books of Exodus and Deuteronomy of the Bible.

---

[52] Indeed, in terms of what type of worship would bring glory to God was one of the key points of controversy during the seventeenth century, particularly in Scotland.

[53] Stewart J Brown, 'Religion and Society to c.1900' in Tom M Devine and Jenny Wormald (eds), *The Oxford Handbook of Modern Scottish History* (OUP 2012) 79, 84.

[54] See also, David Dickson's discussion of this very question—what should man do with his freedom? In keeping with the *Larger Catechism*, Dickson said:

> All that Christian liberty granteth unto us, is, that whether we eat or drink, or what lawful thing else we do, we do all for the glory of God, 1 Cor.10.31, that is, so as we may be strengthened and set forward, to glorifie God in Christ in necessar duties. As for the manner and measure to be keeped in the use of things lawfull, prudence must be asked of God, who will direct us in this as in other Christian duties (Dickson *Therapeutica Sacra* (n 26) 469).

Dickson was influential during this period, and his writings popular during both the Interregnum and the Restoration. This specific treatise was published numerous times during the mid- to late seventeenth century, originally in Latin in 1656, published in both London and Edinburgh; subsequently, it was published in 1664 (Evan Tyler), 1694 (James Watson), and 1695 (James Watson).

The extrapolations found in the *Larger Catechism* are extensive and practical in focus, with something to say about almost all aspects of social life. Importantly, from the perspective of contracting, in answer to the question of what duties were required by the eighth commandment—thou shall not steal—the *Larger Catechism* said:[55]

> The duties required in the eighth commandment are, truth, faithfulness, and justice in contracts and commerce between man and man; rendering to everyone his due; restitution of goods unlawfully detained from the right owners thereof; giving and lending freely, according to our abilities, and the necessities of others; moderation of our judgments, wills, and affections concerning worldly goods; a provident care and study to get, keep, use, and dispose these things which are necessary and convenient for the sustentation of our nature, and suitable to our condition; a lawful calling, and diligence in it; frugality; avoiding unnecessary lawsuits, and suretyship, or other like engagements; and an endeavor, by all just and lawful means, to procure, preserve, and further the wealth and outward estate of others, as well as our own.

It is noteworthy to read in this passage both the religious regulation of commercial activity by primarily one's conscience, which the Catechism introduces, but also the duty to pursue the lawful and just accumulation of wealth for oneself. That said, how one maintains and procures wealth is a dangerous moral activity. For example, in answer to the question of what sins are forbidden by the eighth commandment, the *Larger Catechism* said:[56]

> The sins forbidden in the eighth commandment, besides the neglect of the duties required, are, theft, robbery, man-stealing, and receiving anything that is stolen; fraudulent dealing, false weights and measures, removing landmarks, injustice and unfaithfulness in contracts between man and man, or in matters of trust; oppression, extortion, usury, bribery, vexatious lawsuits, unjust enclosures and depredation; engrossing commodities to enhance the price; unlawful callings, and all other unjust or sinful ways of taking or withholding from our neighbor what belongs to him, or of enriching ourselves; covetousness; inordinate prizing and affecting worldly goods; distrustful and distracting cares and studies in getting, keeping, and using them; envying at the prosperity of others; as likewise idleness, prodigality, wasteful gaming; and all other ways whereby we do unduly prejudice our own outward estate, and defrauding ourselves of the due use and comfort of that estate which God hath given us.

Although the Westminster Standards were abandoned during the Restoration period and restored by the Church of Scotland after 1690, they remained culturally and theologically important throughout this period. In 1660 and 1661,[57] the *Confession*,

---

[55] Answer 142. Of course, this is a summary of Calvin *Inst* 2.8.45. Compare Beveridge's translation (1845) of the 1536 edition with that of Battles (Ford L Battles (tr), *Institutes of the Christian Religion* (William B Eerdmans Publishing Company 1975)), where the latter speaks of contracts, rather than the former, who speaks of hidden 'craft which takes possession of them with a semblance of justice'.

[56] Answer 143. Again, a summary of Calvin's exposition of the Moral Law: Calvin *Inst* 2.8.46.

[57] It was also printed in 1652 in Edinburgh: *Westminster Assembly, The Confession of Faith, and the Larger and Shorter Catechisms First Agreed upon by the Assembly of Divines at Westminster, and Now Appointed by*

the *Shorter Catechism*, and the *Larger Catechism* were republished in Edinburgh and Glasgow in an edition which contained Scriptural references to accompany each stipulation of a duty or sin, including eighty Scriptural references, from both the Old and New Testaments, to support these two answers given above.[58] The *Confession* demonstrates the direct and clear instructions given to Scottish parishioners in the mid-seventeenth century, which was contained in a very public and influential document of the Church of Scotland. Indeed, Wallace has argued that popular unrest in early eighteenth-century Scotland about food prices was often motivated by a sense of moral economy and notions of fairness which were religiously inspired.[59] Equally, Waterman stresses that the duty to accrue and maintain wealth is remarkable given that 'no other catechism, Protestant or Catholic of the period from the Reformation to the eighteenth century interprets the commandment against the thief in anything like this way'.[60] Therefore, when Stair speaks of a freedom which should be directed towards the glory of God, he was invoking a spiritual dimension to how the *Institutions* was importing a system of duties which direct implications to how the freedom to create a conventional obligation should be used and understood.

Durham's *Practical Exposition of the Ten Commandments*

James Durham (1622–58) was a near-contemporary of Stair and a student at Glasgow University during the same period as Stair was a regent (1645–47). Stair and Durham participated in the Bishops' Wars of 1639 and 1640, and later that decade they both adopted moderate views (during both the later stages of the Civil War and Commonwealth). As with Stair, Durham came to public prominence in 1649; but, unlike Stair, he was not called upon in diplomatic or civil affairs, but rather appointed to the General Assembly's standing committee, which engaged, on behalf of the Church, in public affairs when the Assembly was not in session. He spent a period in the 1650s as chaplain to Charles II, but in 1651 he took a high-profile appointment as the minister for Glasgow High Church, which was close to the university and is now part of Glasgow Cathedral. He led a large congregation, over 1,000, and is said to have preached, lectured, and written with a precociousness and industry.[61] During his lifetime, Durham contributed to a popular title, *The Sum of Saving Knowledge*, which

---

the *Generall Assembly of the Kirk of Scotland, to be a Part of Uniformity in Religion Between the Kirks of Christ in the Three Kingdomes* (Lithgow 1652).

[58] *Westminster Assembly, The Confession of Faith, and the Larger and Shorter Catechisms First Agreed upon by the Assembly of Divines at Westminster, and Now Appointed by the Generall Assembly of the Kirk of Scotland, to be a Part of Uniformity in Religion Between the Kirks of Christ in the Three Kingdomes* (Society of Stationers 1661); and by Evan Tyler, in Edinburgh in 1660, printer to Charles II.

[59] Valerie Wallace, 'Presbyterian Moral Economy: The Covenanting Tradition and Popular Protest in Lowland Scotland, 1707–c. 1746' (2010) 89 (277) Scottish Historical Review 54–72.

[60] Anthony M C Waterman, 'Moral Philosophy or Economic Analysis? *The Oxford Handbook of Adam Smith*' (2015) 27 (2) Review of Political Economy 218, 223.

[61] K D Holfelder, 'Durham, James (1622–1658)' in *Oxford Dictionary of National Biography* (OUP 2004) <Durham, James (1622–1658), Church of Scotland minister | Oxford Dictionary of National Biography (oxforddnb.com)> accessed 2 November 2022.

was published just after the *Confession*, and often accompanied later editions of the *Confession*. Although he died aged thirty-six, he had already prepared several titles, including his large *Practical Exposition of the X Commandements*, which provide an insight into what Godly discipline meant during the mid-seventeenth century.[62] It also provides an important perspective against which to understand what Stair envisaged when he spoke of using one's liberty to bring glory to God.

Although it might be surprising, as a minister Durham has a great deal to say about contracting ethics or the transfer of goods and services between persons. In his extrapolation of the eighth commandment (thou shall not steal), Durham explains that through this commandment God, 'regulateth them [man] in the use of their riches and estates, and setteth bounds to the lust of the eye, and the covetousness of the heart'.[63] Further, he says, it applies to 'the outwards estate of our selves and others, that we fail not either in wronging, or in inordinate and excessive profiting them or ourselves', which would otherwise amount to stealing.[64] On reading this commandment's 'general scope', Durham claims that 'men have not liberty to manage these things of the world according to their meer pleasure and arbitrement, but these are rules set to them, by which they are to be governed in reference to them'.[65] He tells his reader that there is a 'religion in buying and selling, and such like, as well as there is in praying and hearing the word, though the thing be of a different nature'.[66] After discussing different kinds of theft and how it is committed, Durham examines the 'duties commanded, and Questions that may be moved concerning them, as about Charity or giving Alms, Usury, making of bargains or contracts, pursuing of riches, &c'.[67] He addresses three topics with copious references to Scripture: how, through trading, a man can wrong others, wrong his own estate, and acquire and gain for his estate without doing wrong to himself or another. Each topic is dealt with by Durham by offering an account of what duties are incumbent upon a man in pithy statements, which are sometimes explained in more detail.

After speaking about theft by robbery, he addresses ways 'whereby, without pretext of violence, another is wrong'. Dividing this into four separate headings, he comes to the last, which is 'the wronging of a man in his private and personal estate' where a 'filthy lucre' is gained 'either by simply unlawful, or by dishonest, unworthy, and base ways and means'.[68] He speaks of nine ways by which a gain can be ill-gotten: (1) miserliness; (2) taking too much when a gift is offered; (3) offering one's self for employment, which is below one's station; (4) by 'vice or villainy'; (5) 'By squeezing, under colour of Law, as by biting Usury, forging of Writs, by moyen and buds prevailing in law to dwang a man from his right'; (6) 'excessive and hurtful travel and pains to win a very little and inconsiderable things'; (7) by robbery and murder; (8) tomb-raiding; and (9) by gambling.[69] After speaking about the different types of ill-gotten gain, he then

---

[62] Durham *A Practical Exposition of the X Commandments* (n 49).
[63] Durham *A Practical Exposition of the X Commandments* (n 49) 395.
[64] Durham *A Practical Exposition of the X Commandments* (n 49) 395.
[65] Durham *A Practical Exposition of the X Commandments* (n 49) 395.
[66] Durham *A Practical Exposition of the X Commandments* (n 49) 396.
[67] Durham *A Practical Exposition of the X Commandments* (n 49) 396.
[68] Durham *A Practical Exposition of the X Commandments* (n 49) 402.
[69] Durham *A Practical Exposition of the X Commandments* (n 49) 402–03.

proceeds to speak of how a man can wrong another's estate by focusing almost solely on the motive of the one who had gained. Under this heading, he lists over twenty-four types of motive which are not always related strictly speaking to contracting but which do nonetheless relate to the transfer of a thing or service from one person to another.[70]

On Durham's account, you can wrong the estate of another in these ways: (1) by the slightest of margins; it is not the quantity that matters but the wrong itself; (2) you should consider not only what was done by the hand of a man, but also the heart; (3) wrong can be committed, even if you do not know you have done so but did know of a means to determine whether or not you have done wrong but you choose not to use those means; (4) when you convince another, when they have a right against you, that you have not wronged them; (5) when you know it is the thing of another, but you nevertheless take it; (6) you take, in a time of necessity, more than you need; (7) 'In contracts or bargains to our neighbours prejudice; as by too close sticking to clauses or Writs beyond it maybe, the intention of the makes, and when there is some pretext of Law, this is against the end of the Writs and Law'; (8) in buying and selling, when we exchange with only a care for what we get, when we sell a thing which we know should not be sold, when we sell a thing for a higher price than it is worth, when our measure and scale is 'fearce [fierce]', or when we commend a good to be better than it is;[71] (9) in just debts, when we do not pay on time, avoid paying, allow the case to come to court, or constrain and force the creditor to forego a due debt; (10) when we take advantage of another's need; (11) by vexatious cases relating to our bargains; (12) mishandling goods entrusted to us; (13) by bribery; (14) when there is inequality between parties; (15) when we damage a neighbour's estate by negligence or laziness; (16) by asking someone to guarantee a debt we know we cannot pay, or guaranteeing a debt we know we cannot pay; (17) retaining what we know or discover to belong to another; (18) failing to restore to another what is theirs; (19) using another's goods or wasting their time; (20) taking from another, albeit lawful, that which we know is of great sentimental value to another; (21) when we take wages for a job we are not qualified to do; (22) when we do not offer to help someone who we know is in need; (23) buying or selling things we know should not be sold; (24) acting as an accessory of some sort in the buying and selling of things which should not be sold; and (25) ceasing upon things 'under the pretext of escheats'.[72] Durham also stresses during this long list of personal motives, which contribute to the diminishing of a neighbour's estate, that it is important always to distinguish between the 'Lords Court' or the 'Court of Conscience' and the 'Civil Courts', whereby some things may be allowable by the latter but not the former.[73] Durham, however, does not explore this distinction in any more detail, rather leaving it as a general statement of competence, upon which a great deal rests.

He them proceeds to discuss first how a man may wrong his own estate and then how a man may better his estate. Starting with the means by which you might wrong your own estate, Durham speaks of five general ways this can be done: (1) 'by not

---

[70] Durham *A Practical Exposition of the X Commandments* (n 49) 404.
[71] Durham *A Practical Exposition of the X Commandments* (n 49) 405.
[72] Durham *A Practical Exposition of the X Commandments* (n 49) 410.
[73] Durham *A Practical Exposition of the X Commandments* (n 49) 402–10.

providently caring for its preservations and increase, or improvement, when he is not frugal, or not so frugal as he ought to be'; (2) 'By unnecessary waste in prodigality and lavishness'; (3) by negligence, laziness, and carelessness; (4) by spending on yourself, rather than giving generously; and (5) by failing to appreciate what you have, and so you are never satisfied.[74] This leads to a discussion of the ways by which a man can appropriately improve his estate or make gains which do not contravene the duty prescribed by the eighth commandment. He says that man should be guided by the end, the measure, and the means. In familiar terms to that of Stair and the structuring of the opening titles of the *Institutions*, Durham says that the end of a man should first be the glory of God, then others' needs, and then lastly ourselves.[75] When it comes to keeping a measure of our own estate's increase, he acknowledges it 'is hard to determine', yet 'sure folks are not left to gather as much as they may even by lawful means attain to ... adding one thing to another'. It is only through prayer and diligence that a man can determine what is necessary, convenient, and honest for him to have. Durham spends a fair amount of time considering the right means by which you can improve your estate, speaking in passing about occupation and conquering but moving on to address the question of 'trading and merchandize', which 'is lawful in its self, as a mean[s] to the end proposed'.[76] Although there is tendency amongst men to buy, cheat, and sell dearly, a just price should be paid. Durham offers a fairly developed account of what should determine a just price, recognizing, however, that it can be difficult to fix at times.

Some of these duties or wrongs that Durham outlines could be said to be covered by the existing doctrines or rules of the human law, which Stair describes in the *Institutions*. Nonetheless, it is also clear that others are not so easily articulated or recognizable as a doctrine or rule of the law of Scotland in the mid-seventeenth century. Some certainty could not be said to be part of the law at this time. This is unsurprising, however, given that the *Larger Catechism* and Durham's treatise sought to be more wide-ranging, covering areas of social life not always accounted for in a legal treatise, and in a language which does not have legal precision. But, for Stair, the performance of those duties is hard to measure and should be judged by man's conscience and not by the human law of Scotland. In making this point, he mirrors Durham's distinction between the Lord's Court and the Civil Court. For instance, in the opening passages of the *Institutions*, Stair gives an example of how the human law may require much less in comparison to what our consciences tells us:[77]

Conscience relates more to the principles of religion, than of morality .... For instance, the law excludes discharges of debts, if a term be assigned to prove payment, and the term be circumduced; yet a conscientious creditor ought not to take twice payment: so a great estate may be carried away by apprising for a small sum, but just ones will not for conscience sake so extend it.

[74] Durham *A Practical Exposition of the X Commandments* (n 49) 411–12.
[75] Durham *A Practical Exposition of the X Commandments* (n 49) 413.
[76] Durham *A Practical Exposition of the X Commandments* (n 49) 416.
[77] Stair *Inst* 1.1.4–5.

In terms of understanding the spiritual dimension of such duties and whether they should be implemented or enforced by institutions in Scotland, more needs to be said about how the performance of these duties should be measured; it is this which, in part, shapes Stair's views on the jurisdictional, practical, and necessary limits of human law.

Inward performance of duties

Of central importance to the question of enforcement and judgement of performance of these duties prescribed in the *Westminster Confession of Faith* and in practical ethical treatises, such as Durham's, is that outward performance was not enough—or, as the seventeenth-century preacher Donald Cargill said, you also need 'inward purity of conscience, and righteousness of mind'.[78] Indeed, it was a central tenet of Protestant theology overall that external works do not gain salvation.[79] Cargill was a popular preacher in the mid- to late seventeenth century and a former (devoted) student of Samuel Rutherford. He preached hundreds of sermons across Scotland, some of which are still accessible. Although he was later to be more far more radical in his politics and ecclesiology in comparison to Stair, his field preaching gives a good sense of orthodox preaching in the seventeenth century with regard to inner and outer obedience and the importance of motive.

Of relevance to this chapter is a sermon delivered on or around 3 November 1678 in Partick-loan, near Glasgow; there Cargill offered an exposition of John 8:34–35 expressing a very intricate but common theme amongst Scots preachers, relating to freedom and performance of duties to God. Imagining Christ challenging his followers, Cargill says:

> You say, ye are free; but ye are servants; and the servant abideth not in the house for ever. Ye are in bondage. But say ye, we are so past feeling that we cannot tell whether we are bond or free men. There are some when they boast most of freedom, that are most in slavery to sin.[80]

He continues: 'What is freedom?' and answers: 'In a word, a man is free, when he has got, by the Spirit of God, such a power over himself, as to govern himself by divine laws, religion, and right reason.'[81] He asks his congregation if they are free or if they are in slavery; he asks if they are serving God or serving themselves; he asks them to search their conscience. After this, he challenges the notion of outward service when the will of man is otherwise. He uses the example of a heritor and their charter—someone legally bound, by a feudal obligation, to make a payment to the parish towards things such as minister's stipends:[82]

---

[78] *A Collection of Lectures and Sermons* (n 47) 392.
[79] Alastair E McGrath, *Reformation Thought: An Introduction* (2nd edn, Wiley-Blackwell 1993) 87–131.
[80] *A Collection of Lectures and Sermons* (n 47) 389.
[81] *A Collection of Lectures and Sermons* (n 47) 389.
[82] *A Collection of Lectures and Sermons* (n 47) 389, 391–92.

If ye are doing [your duties] out of obedience to God; then are ye servants to him; but otherwise, to speak with reverence, ye are putting a cheat on God, if ye could. Ye meet under his banner, and then just turn back to the enemy again. There are some heritors bound to little more by their charters, than to answer fore the court thrice a year: And we are such gentlemen's tenants as these. We think it enough to appear at court. But will God regard you as servant on that account?

Stair agrees that it is our inward choices and attitude to our duties which are of import- ance, not our external acts. Or rather, the effect of our external acts is meaningless if the choice to take such an action was not motivated to bring glory to God. Hence, he takes issue with those who say 'that everything is a duty or a sin: and because all things must be done to the glory of God … and so we are not free'.[83] Complaining that this position focuses upon the actions of men rather than their choices, he makes several Biblical references which stress it is the inward choice which God sees. Continuing to argue for the importance of inward performance of duties rather than outward per- formance, he turns matters around, saying: 'there is a great difference betwixt duty which is necessary, and wherein we are obliged, though we mistake and be wilfully ignorant' in our performance of it, and the situation where we act contrary to 'what is forbidden to God's glory' but nevertheless those actions bring about some good.[84] It should also be noted that Stair devotes serious discussion to this question and places it towards the end of his open passage of the *Institutions*, following his statement that where 'obedience ends, there freedom begins'.[85] He is therefore signalling clearly how we should approach our judgment and assessment of man's actions which are beyond the scope of human law and within his God-given freedom. Moreover, it needs to be clarified that when Stair is speaking about inward performance, choices, and bringing glory to God, it is with reference to what God's divine law and Christian morality re- quires of man and not, crucially, human law, because he has already made it clear that he is no longer speaking of what the law of Scotland requires of a man. Therefore, in practice, what this means is that Stair would have distinguished the duties prescribed in the *Larger Catechism*, which prescribes Christian morality and articulates divine law according to Scripture, by whether they were contained also in the law of Scotland or not.[86] Only if it were the former would these duties be judiciable and therefore en- forceable by a Scottish secular court.

Stair further clarifies this last point later in the *Institutions*; under title 3 of Book I, he continues the discussion of where human law ends but the Moral Law continues. Speaking of the distinction between legal and natural obligations, he says: 'Natural Obligations are these, which have a ty by the Law of Nature, and raise a right in the person to whom they relate; but the Civil Law … do not second them with legal Remedies or executions'.[87] He explains that some natural obligations have no legal remedy because 'they oblige to inward duties of the mind', others because 'the manner

---

[83] Stair *Inst* 1.1.20.
[84] Stair *Inst* 1.1.20.
[85] Stair *Inst* 1.1.20.
[86] See his explanation at Stair *Inst* 1.3.4.
[87] Stair *Inst* 1.3.5.

and measure is left to the discretion and Arbitriment of the obliged', and lastly because some 'relate to duties performable to God, whereof he hath given no power nor command to man; ... to vindicate for him'. Some of these duties or obligations which fall into this last category may indeed be owed to other parties, such as beneficence, charity, assistance to those in danger, and relief to those who are oppressed. Stair says that 'so the Creditor is God', but 'there is no correspondent Right or power of Compulsion in man'. He also argues at this point that there are some natural obligations which relate to 'matters of small moment, *nam prætor non curat minima*', which should not benefit from the use of human law and civil enforcement, and there are in contrast 'things of greater importance' where a legal process is prescribed, and there is a penalty rightly imposed for 'non-observance' and the withdrawal of civil enforcement. In regard to the latter, he gives the example of *nudum pactum* and the strict requirements of stipulation to illustrate that although an agreement should be performed by virtue of a natural obligation, the failure to clothe your pact in the formal legality of a stipulation was, according to Stair, penalized in Roman law by non-enforcement. On this basis, Stair draws an analogy between the strict formality of stipulations and the formal requirements of Scots law in the mid-seventeenth century which otherwise required a morally binding agreement or promise to be executed in writing.[88]

Civil government and ecclesiastical government

In the *Divine Perfections*, Stair's view is more explicit about the general political theory which informs his understanding about the difference between those natural laws which are enforceable by a civil authority and those which are not, or at least he offers more of an indication of who should enforce what. Stair's account is almost wholly consistent, too,[89] with Calvin's account in the *Institutes of the Christian Religion*.[90] In contrast to Calvin, Stair's account is brief and vague in terms of the extent to which civil powers can enforce religious conformity. Calvin is, of course, far more specific about civil and religious power.[91] Offering a history, Stair says that before the flood 'God exerciseth his Dominion not only by the Laws of Nature, but by human laws and Institutions, which are not known by the Light of Nature, but by Revelation'.[92] Nonetheless, after the flood, civil government was introduced by God, whereby he transmitted the 'power and burden' of government to fathers of families but mostly to 'the Governors of those Societies' or civil government.[93] Significantly, Stair says that

---

[88] Stair *Inst* 1.3.5.

[89] Although as discussed above, see Stair *Inst* 1.3.5, regarding the enforcement of natural obligations where he says, inter alia, there are some natural obligations which man owes to God, where God 'hath given no power nor commanded to man ... to vindicate for him'. In the prior paragraph, 1.3.4, Stair says that man is 'warranted to vindicat ... the Crimes of Witchcraft, Blasphemy, Bestiality and the like' and is also entitled to vindicate obedential obligations, which give rise to not just reparation but also punishment from God, and man is authorized, by God to carry out such punishments.

[90] Calvin *Inst* 3.19.15.

[91] eg cf Stair *Divine Perfections* 265 and Calvin *Inst* 4.10.1.

[92] It is interesting to see Stair's version of a sacred or theo-political history and to compare it with his history of science offered in his *Physiologica Nova Experimentalis*.

[93] Stair *Divine Perfections* 265.

at this time God also created a 'distinct Government for his own Worship, and separated it from the Paternal and Civil Authority'. He goes on to explain that for Christians 'a Church became a distinct Society from a State, and hath its proper Ecclesiastick Government, tho services may concur in the same Persons'.[94] Civil government, therefore, on Stair's account, was separated by God from ecclesiastical government. Alluding to the familiar idea of a temporal and spiritual sword, Stair then clarified in the *Divine Perfections*:[95]

> The Ecclesiastick Government is about the inward State of those of their Society, in so far as Man's Knowledge can reach, to promote Holiness, and internal and eternal Happiness, and about their outward Acts only, as they signify their inward Condition; and their Rewards and Punishments are only by application of ther Divine Ordinances, in exciting Joy or Grief, Fear or Hope, as conducible for the inward State, but without temporal Rewards, and forcible Punishments.

In contrast, civil government is for 'the outward State of Society' and the mode of its rule is outward and conducted by 'extrinsick Rewards and forcible Punishments'.[96] Stair, however, stresses another form of government: conscience. He describes this as 'yet a more inward and Secret Dominion of God' which acts as 'his Deputy, by which he distributes the most powerful and important Rewards and Punishments, not only in this Life, but chiefly after Death'.[97] Stair does not say, however, where or when or if the ecclesiastical government can ask the civil government to act on its behalf. Nor does he speak of places whether civil and ecclesiastical government may overlap in their concerns, such as marriage. However, Stair does indicate in the *Institutions* that human law and by consequence civil government has its practical limitations, which may give some indication as to whether Stair draws a line between ecclesiastical jurisdiction and civil.[98]

For example, as already mentioned above, he speaks of a creditor's conscience preventing him from taking payment of a debt twice, even though the human law would allow for him to do so. He suggests there that 'conscience relates more to the principles of religion, than morality', with the implication that such things are best left to one's conscience to decide according to what God requires of one.[99] Moreover, he says later in the opening passages of the *Institutions* that human laws may in some instances fail to fully enforce the equity of natural law, 'as it may be more profitable for people to forbear the pursuance of them, than to be at the trouble and the expenses of the pursuit'. He explains, preferring to 'take themselves to the honesty of the party, than to compulsion by remeid of law'.[100] Stair writes about the 'obligations of gratitude,

[94] Stair *Divine Perfections* 266.
[95] Stair *Divine Perfections* 266.
[96] Stair *Divine Perfections* 266.
[97] Stair *Divine Perfections* 266.
[98] Although beyond the scope of this study, it could be suggested that as well as comparing Stair to Rutherford, as Ford has done, it would be profitable to compare Stair with the lesser-known Irvine minister, Alexander Nisbet (1623–69): *A Brief Exposition of the First and Second Epistles General of Peter* (Christopher Higgins 1658) and *An Exposition with Practical Observations upon the Book of Ecclesiastes* (George Mosman 1693) (compiled in 1658 and published posthumously).
[99] Stair *Inst* 1.1.15.
[100] Stair *Inst* 1.1.15.

and the inward obligations of the mind, as of affection, love, kindness ..', telling the reader that there are many more inward obligations placed upon man in contrast to the handful of fundamental 'outward obligations'. On his account, outward obligations are far more easily enforced, in contrast to inward obligations. His concern, however, is the 'vexation it might breed' if all such obligations were pursued and enforced by the human law. He speaks there, too, of men concentrating their efforts, through the human law and civil government, on compelling men not to do evil rather than to do good.[101]

Freedom to Contract Prior to Civil Government and Human Law

As has been shown, Stair divides the duties of natural law into those which can be enforced by a civil government and human law and those spiritual duties which cannot, leaving them to spiritual authorities and man's own conscience. This, however, places the focus upon the temporal sphere and civil government. For example, how does Stair describe the relationship between human law and an individual's liberty? In Stair's system of human law, how is liberty understood and accommodated for? Is liberty prior to human law and constitutive of law, or does liberty come after human law is established? How does liberty relate to the enforcement of human law by a civil authority? These questions were of central importance in the mid- to late seventeenth century, as new political ideologies and philosophies emerged to support resistance to royal or papal authority and the reimagining of political communities within Europe more generally.[102]

Definitions of liberty in the *Institutions* and the *Divine Perfections*

Before addressing these wider questions, the first point to address is whether Stair is consistent when speaking about liberty in the *Institutions* with his account in the *Divine Perfections*. In the *Institutions*, Stair speaks of liberty in numerous places;[103] initially, however, he speaks of it in relation to slavery, saying that although it is 'against the natural law of liberty, yet it is received for conveniency by the nations, being more willing to lose liberty than life'.[104] He subsequently discusses liberty when speaking of the freedom which God has given men: 'God hath obliged him only in a few necessary Moral Duties, and has left him free in much more, without any ty upon him, as to the matter, but with a Liberty, *ad contradictiora*, that he may do or not do; and *ad contraria*, that he may do this or that contrair.'[105] He continues to discuss the freedom which God has given man, saying: 'From this freedom doth arise, not only our personal

---

[101] Stair *Inst* 1.1.15.
[102] See Quentin Skinner, *The Foundations of Modern Political Thought, Vol 2: The Age of Reformation* (CUP 1978).
[103] Including: Stair *Inst* 1.1.11; 1.1.20–22; 1.2.1–16; 2.7.4–5; 4.52.18–29.
[104] Stair *Inst* 1.1.11.
[105] Stair *Inst* 1.1.20.

freedom and liberty, whereby men are *sui juris*, but also their power of the disposal of other things within their reach, or that dominion which God hath given them over the creatures.'[106] He then discusses in the following passage conventional obligations, saying: 'every such Obligation, is a diminution of that Freedom, for thereby we are either restrained from that power of disposal of the Creatures, or may be constrained to some performance contrair to our natural Liberty'.[107] There is a subsequent mention of liberty when discussing the 'Rights of men', saying there are three within the law of Scotland, 'Personal Liberty, Dominion, and Obligation; Personal Liberty, is the power to dispose of our Persons, and to live where, and as we please, except in so far, as by Obedience or Ingagement we are bound'.[108] Lastly, in the second title of Book I, he discusses liberty and servitude over sixteen paragraphs, where in the opening paragraph he says:

> Liberty is that natural power which man hath of his own person, whence a free man is said to be *suæ potestatis*, in his own power; and it is defined in the law to be a natural faculty to do that which every man pleaseth, unless he be hindered by law or force.[109]

On the basis of these passages alone, it is fair to conclude that there is not only a conceptual consistency—describing it as a power, ability, faculty, and something which is unique to men—but also a consistency in language—using phrases such as *ad contradictiora, ad contraria*, restraint, constraint. If this is acceptable, then his specific title, in the *Institutions*, on liberty and servitude can be informed by what he says in the *Divine Perfections*, and can on that basis be used to answer the above questions relating to human law's authority in relation to liberty, and whether liberty and man's freedom to contract is prior to civil government.

Limited, restrained, constrained, diminished, and taken away

Stair's overall discussion of the relationship between liberty and servitude can be taken to set out the boundaries of liberty and to explain the apparent restraint, constraint, or diminishing of man's liberty that human law imposes. Stair says liberty is not absolute in title 2 of Book I of the *Institutions*. The fact that Stair makes this clear is, of course, to be expected, given that Stair believes God gave man liberty, and therefore its bounds are predetermined by what God decided to give to man. As already discussed, from a theological perspective the bounds of man's liberty are predefined in natural law, and not shaped by the extent of other men's liberty. God has given liberty, and he decides the extent of that liberty. Hence, Stair lists the limits of our liberty, which ends where God wills us to do something, with ownership of my body, with my status as a spouse, with my status as a child, or when I suffer from a mental disorder. To put things another way, for Stair: I can still be said to have liberty despite God telling me what to do;

---

[106] Stair *Inst* 1.1.20
[107] Stair *Inst* 1.1.20.
[108] Stair *Inst* 1.1.22.
[109] Stair *Inst* 1.2.1.

despite having no ownership of my body; despite my husband telling me what to do; when my father tells me what to do; or when others, who care for me, when I suffer from a mental disorder, tell me what to do, I still have liberty. In all of these instances, God has decided that we have no choice or power in the matter, and thus liberty just is not something that we can have or not have. When, therefore, the human law ensures man adheres to God's moral expectations or performs his duties under natural law, it has not infringed upon man's liberty. In other words, from this perspective, titles III to IX of Book I of the *Institutions* discuss areas of the human law, obligations, which implement God's natural law and have nothing to do with man's liberty.

But when we do have liberty, Stair's treatment demonstrates that liberty is something which is internal and related to decision-making, choices, and power rather than something which is external. This is important when it comes to the question of whether Stair considers liberty to be a right but also liberty's relationship to human law. Further, in his title 'Of Liberty and Servitude', he speaks of restraint and constraint as being opposed to liberty—but this does not mean that an obligation placed upon man is in opposition to his liberty.[110] As will be shown, for Stair the loss of liberty is the loss of a choice or power to do something, and in that regard liberty remains something which has an internal dimension to Stair, albeit effected or lost by or through external things. Therefore, he says that restraint stops a man from going where he wills and doing what he wills, whereas constraint forces a man to do something he does not want to do. Note that in both instances Stair is emphasizing the absence of the ability to choose one action over another, or at least you are left with very little option but to do what you would not want to do. Therefore, despite the restraint or constraint being very much external and inflicted on the body, whether by imprisonment or being physically forced, what is lost or absent is something internal, the ability to choose to do something. Being constrained or restrained, therefore, are examples of when liberty is lost; but, importantly in such situations, liberty may resume or be restored. Stair goes on to say that we lose liberty due to our delinquency, using the example of being punished for non-payment of a debt through the loss of our property. Again, what is lost, when liberty is lost, is the choice to do something, namely transfer property voluntarily in lieu of payment; rather, we are punished and the decision is taken from us.

The examples of constraint or restraint show that liberty is only diminished temporarily by a punishment and not permanently: that is, our goods are forfeit for the debt, but we nonetheless retain the liberty to dispose of the rest of our property in the future. Next, he says that our engagements, by which he includes contracts, diminish our liberty when we refuse to perform what we owe to our creditor and are, for example, imprisoned until we do so. Stair also speaks of liberty being diminished by 'subjection unto authority', where we give that power over us to 'a society', 'a few persons' or 'one sovereign'. He describes this in terms of power being given to others, saying: 'tho man by nature be a free creature and in his own power, he doth then become in the power of others'.[111] Presumably, our choice and power is only diminished and not completely negated, because the transfer of power to authority is not absolute, leaving areas in

---

[110] In the 1681 edition, the title is merely called 'Liberty'.
[111] Stair *Inst* 1.1.8.

which man can still determine some things himself. Stair poses authority to be a rather minor reduction of liberty in comparison to servitude. He says: 'liberty is wholly taken away by bondage, slavery or servitude, which is diametrically opposite to liberty', because in effect servitude creates a thing of a man and therefore man no longer has any choice or liberty remaining.

As Dickson says:

For, the nature of the conscience and will, is to determine freely what the man shall do; and the Lords people must be a willing people, Ps. 110. 3 He must know, that albeit the will and conscience cannot be compelled, yet the carnal lusts which have seduced the conscience, may be crossed and curbed by ecclesiastick censures and civil punishments, that the conscience and will, being better informed, after the discovery of the deceitfulnesse of their lusts, which did mislead them, they may freely disclaim the error, & their unhappy venting thereof.

He continues:

In which case albeit the acts commanded by the will and conscience, are curbed and restrained, yet the will and conscience, is not compelled, but is brought to a better determination of its own elicit acts, that having obtained a clearer light about its duty, it may command the outward man to say & do what is right.[112]

If this reading of Stair's discussion of liberty is plausible, then the human law is not in tension with liberty and should not, theologically speaking, require man to forego that liberty completely in order to enjoy civil government and the benefits of human law, although he may give up some liberty. If we do not give away our liberty to choose, Stair explains that we lose our liberty, when we deserve to lose it, because we are, in fact, misusing it or not using it correctly or are acting beyond the bounds of liberty which God has given us.[113] From both a theological and a legal perspective, the only time liberty and human law could be in tension or opposed to each other is if the human law in some way compelled man to act in a manner contrary to natural law. Stair, as has been explained, nevertheless sought to leave aside those potential areas of conflict to man's own conscience or ecclesiastical government, and did not extend the human law, on his account, into such areas. Such conflicts or tensions between man's liberty and human law arise when it comes to the duty to bring glory to God, or those duties (described by Stair as natural obligations) that we owe to others, such as gratitude, kindness, or forgiveness, and the duty we might otherwise have to ensure that men do good rather than evil. Stair, as has been shown, stresses that these are not for the human law to adjudicate upon. Even then, however, when there are things, in the human law, which are contrary to natural law and liberty, such as slavery, private ownership, or formalities in the conclusion of contracts, Stair is pragmatic and suggests man has in the past introduced such things because of circumstances or should be in the present reasonable in giving up on those areas of natural law, where human law

---

[112] Dickson *Therapeutica Sacra* (n 26) 435–36.
[113] Calvin *Inst* 3.19.3.

and natural law diverge. From a legal perspective, Stair does see human law, in some instances, constraining, restraining, or diminishing liberty, but from a broader theological perspective it was ensuring that man uses his liberty as God intended.

Importantly, Stair does not suggest that man formally transfers his right of remedy, or natural power to enforce natural law, or his liberty and choice, to a civil government. Rather, he suggests that the utility and expediency of human law means that such things are justified, and that we rely on long-established custom, judges, and, to a lesser extent, the king's statutes to embody natural law in human law.[114] Indeed, he is keen to show, in the *Institutions*, that for the most part, and where possible, the human law of Scotland does implement natural law. Therefore, if there is a tension between man and the human law, it is between his sinfulness and God's will. But the question of whether man is sinful or not is not the focus of human law, as sinfulness is generally considered by Stair to be a matter of conscience and between God and man, whereas the focus of human law is upon the external temporal world, on ensuring utility and the common good. Human law, therefore, only requires external compliance—unlike God, who requires internal compliance or willing obedience. Human law, therefore, contrasts more easily with freedom because Stair's concept of freedom, as explained above, is a broader descriptive term which can cover both internal and external things. Therefore, it can be said that the human law can be in conflict with man's freedom, in some sense because it forces external compliance, but not his liberty, because man either chooses to obey the law or does not, which, in that case, on Stair's account, would most probably be an instance where man was not acting with liberty—although he might act freely.

Performing a contract with liberty; performing a contract against your will

This interpretation of Stair's conception of liberty and human law provides a theological viewpoint on Stair's treatment of conventional obligations and why they are enforced. Liberty, for Stair, comes prior to the human law and can run in conjunction with it or operate simultaneously with it. It is God-given, natural, and 'the most native and delightful right of man'.[115] If it is used correctly, then in theory man would never lose any of it. However, 'through sin and evil custom the natural law in man's heart' is much 'defaced, disordered, and erroneously deduced', and so in addition to Scripture God has 'also given men voluntary and human laws, which though not at the pleasure of men' have the end of 'exigences and utility'.[116] Moreover, he says, given the difficulties of individual men determining for themselves what is right according to natural law, human law should take its place. Human law is needed therefore for coordination and peace and quiet in the temporal world, and may lead to man giving up some of his God-given liberty.[117] Or, to put it another way, if man is Godly, acting in accordance

---

[114] Stair *Inst* 1.1.10.
[115] Stair *Inst* 1.2.2.
[116] Stair *Inst* 1.1.6–7.
[117] Stair *Inst* 1.1.18–20; cf Calvin *Inst* 4.20.2.

with his conscience and by God's grace with obedience, then he is acting with liberty and will never come into conflict with the law; he will always willingly obey it.[118] In that sense, human law is not needed for someone of this make-up—a willingly obedient man—although it can of course help guide them and inform them of what they should do in the temporal world. But not all society is made up of such men.

On this description, liberty, in terms of the ability to create a conventional obligation, is the ability to engage not only the law but also the moral natural law of God. Creating a conventional obligation is the creation of an obligation which is both moral and legal. Of course, you can have a moral obligation to perform an inchoate, informal, or insufficiently executed contract, but you cannot have a legally enforceable contract, which does not carry with it a moral dimension for Stair. Hence, we can use our liberty to create a moral obligation to another person and an obligation which the human law recognizes. This demonstrates then a dual obligation, to the Moral Law and to the human law, and also demonstrates how liberty cannot in general terms come into conflict with the human law. That is, if man did not perform his obligation, as he was unwilling, then the enforcement of that obligation would not, from a theological perspective, be a constraint on man's liberty; indeed, it would be ensuring that he acts in accordance with it. But, because man is choosing not to perform the obligation, he does lose his choice or liberty. Of course, he may still not freely perform the obligation because of the threat of human law's sanction, but in that instance human law is not, from a theological point of view, acting as a constraint, restraint, or diminution on his liberty by forcing him to perform. That is, if liberty is taken to be a choice alone, the enforcement in the event of unwillingness would be a diminution of your liberty. Indeed, this reframes a central passage in title 10 of Book I, where Stair discusses liberty and contract. Stair says there that by creating a conventional obligation one gives the 'liberty in our power, that we may give it up to others, or restrain and ingage it, whereby God obliges us to performance, by mediation of our own will; yet such Obligations, as to their Original, are conventional, not obediential'.[119] It follows then, that when man performs a conventional obligation, it is not only out of an obligation to God but also because God tells man to perform this obligation, and he can do so willingly and so act with liberty when performing his obligation. When it is created, he has created a duty to God to perform it because it is a moral duty under the natural law and an obligation under the human law.

Choosing to obey the law; freely performing obligations

Nor should any praise, credit, or virtue be given to man for doing so. Man performed his conventional obligations because of God's natural law, his Biblical teaching, and his direct instructions to man: it was his duty. This offers an explanation of not only how Stair understood the creation of conventional obligations, their normativity, and the justification of their performance, but also his overall understanding of what it means to adhere to the human law and moral duties. If Stair is read as a Presbyterian natural

---

[118] cf Calvin *Inst* 3.19.4.
[119] Stair *Inst* 1.10.

law jurist, then his understanding of the duty to perform the law (including conventional obligations) should be framed against a broadly Calvinist perspective. It should therefore be recalled that Calvin said that it is 'beyond dispute, that free will does not enable any man to perform good works, unless he is assisted by grace',[120] and he goes on to say: 'no will is free which has not been made so by divine grace ... that the righteousness of God is not fulfilled when the law order and man acts, as it were, by his own strength, but when the Spirit assists, and the will (not the free will of man, but the will freed by God) obeys'.[121] Aristotelian ethics places value upon choosing rightly, something Presbyterians in the mid-seventeenth century studied and knew well. According to Aristotle, what is virtuous was the decision to act virtuously without hesitation or compulsion. For Aristotle, when someone does a virtuous action, they should receive praise; the man who chooses rightly should be praised. However, against the context of Calvinism, a virtuous action is not something which man is capable of. Man is 'devoid of all uprightness', and he 'cannot arrogate anything, however minute, to himself without robbing God of his honour'.[122] Calvin corrects the:[123]

> Philosophers [who] set it down as beyond dispute, that virtue and vice are in our own power. For (say they), If it is in our choice to do this thing or that, it must also be in our choice not to do it ... if we do good when we please, we can also refrain from doing it; if we commit evil, we can also shun the commission of it (Aristot. lib. iii. c.5).

Performing a promise or a contract could therefore not be deemed a virtuous act if Stair were to offer a theory in line with Calvinist orthodoxy. Man could only act virtuously through God's grace.

Incoherent, inconsistent, and contradictory?

It might seem that Stair is being inconsistent, or that the analysis provided here is strained by trying to demonstrate coherence between the *Institutions* and the *Divine Perfections*. On the one hand, the interpretation given above suggests that Stair does not think man is acting freely and with liberty, unless he is acting morally and how God intended (which he does not do without God's aid). Therefore, there should be no mention or notion that human law, when it compels man to do what the Moral Law requires, is taking away man's liberty. Rather, on the analysis so far provided, it has been argued that human law would only be encountered by a man when he acts without Christian liberty, that is, sinfully and unfreely. On the other hand, however, on first appearances, this is not what Stair says in the *Institutions*. Rather, there he says that when man has acted contrary to human law (and thereby natural law) he is made to obey the human laws, and his liberty is lost: his liberty is restrained, constrained, or diminished. Prima facie, in the *Institutions*, therefore, liberty is present and is lost to

---

[120] Calvin *Inst* 2.2.6.
[121] Calvin *Inst* 2.2.8.
[122] Calvin *Inst* 2.2.1.
[123] Calvin *Inst* 2.2.3.

human law when it ensures man does the right thing or what natural law requires of him. Liberty, therefore, can be contrasted with human law and the obligations it places upon man, and you cannot have liberty and be under the human law. Hence, in order to justify human law and its infringement of man's natural God-given liberty, Stair, it would appear, needs to offer some justification or legitimization of civil authority's infringement of man's liberty and potentially to acknowledge that man's law, temporal society, and civic government can aid, and do help, man towards acting with Christian liberty.[124] That may be unproblematic for him, and it was an option open to him. However, taking such a route, intellectually, would risk suggesting that liberty could be achieved by the force of human law upon man's external actions; potentially, such a theory or explanation of the role of human law in the temporal world raises the profile and standing of human law on man's road to salvation, that is, gives it a spiritual dimension.

This, however, if it is a contradiction or tension, is something that is lies at the very heart of the Calvinist tradition. It emerges through the need to hold man accountable, morally for his actions, on the basis of a common-sense theory of responsibility but not to ascribe credit to man when a good deed is done. Calvinism needs to maintain that moral responsibility is based on the power or liberty of an agent to make a decision between right and wrong and direct their actions accordingly. But, at the same time, there is the need to give no moral accountability to man when he does do something good, as to do so would encroach upon the idea that since the fall man has been unable to do nothing but sin, unless prompted by God. As Pink notes, this is not something necessarily confined to the Calvinist tradition, as it is a tension found in medieval theories of freedom;[125] but it is something particularly problematic for the Calvinist tradition, which strongly emphasized man's complete moral corruption—in comparison to other theories, such as Arminianism or Catholicism, which were prepared to find some indwelling grace or righteousness within man despite his fall from grace.[126] For Calvin, and for Stair, to have liberty is to have the choice to do something or not to do something, which man retains despite sin, and when he acts morally he is acting with liberty, and therefore is not enslaved to sin. However, due to sin, unless aided by God to do otherwise, man will always choose to sin rather than do what is good. In other words, human law, in forcing a man to do what he should do according to the Moral Law, is restraining, constraining, or hindering man's ability to choose sin. Whether this is always coherent from a philosophical perspective is a different question from its theological significance to the Reformed tradition. It may, therefore, be something that is to be expected in Stair, that this tension or contradiction arises here in his suggestion that liberty is lost when man does something contrary to the Moral Law, which is enforced by the human law. Stair wants to hold man accountable, therefore give to him liberty, but at the same time does not want to say that it is the human law of man which helps him to do the right thing, as such praise should be given to

---

[124] Arguably, in the eyes of Calvinists and Counter-Remonstrants, this is what the Arminian theology enabled, and Grotius demonstrated, see Marco van Gelderen, 'Arminian Trouble: Calvinists Debates on Freedom' in Quentin Skinner and Marco van Gelderen M (eds), *Freedom and the Construction of Europe*, vol 1 (CUP 2013) 21–37.

[125] Pink 'Freedom of the Will' (n 37) 570–87.

[126] Pink, 'Self-Determination and Moral Responsibility from Calvin to Frankfurt' (n 25) 145–64.

God. For Stair, liberty is lost because the human law by restraint or constraint negates man's ability to choose to sin, but when man does the right thing then his liberty is being exercised in harmony with the human law and not because of it.

Conclusion

Stair's *Divine Perfections* provide a deeper understanding of his conception of freedom and liberty. As has been suggested in this chapter, Stair gave wide meaning to 'freedom', using it to describe actions in general and the ability to choose between possibilities or to move freely, whereas he gave 'liberty' a narrower meaning, understanding it as the power of self-determination in accordance with a rational motive. Nevertheless, it was argued that Stair's understanding of that freedom was shaped overall by a Calvinist understanding of man's moral psychology. Additionally, it was explained that, despite having a somewhat dim view of man's moral capacities, Stair spoke of man using his freedom to create conventional obligations, which, it could be suggested, demonstrates a reasonable degree of faith in men and resists a paternalism that you might otherwise expect, given the Calvinist moral psychology which he adopted. However, this apparent laissez-faire approach to man's liberty was framed against the context of Presbyterian views about the role of the church in Scottish society and the power of civil authorities to create and administer civil laws. Hence, it was shown that where this power to contract was given juridically, it was, nevertheless, politically and theologically taken away in terms of social and ethical expectations as to how this juridical liberty could be used. Other political and theological contexts, however, shaped different conceptions of liberty, authority and contracting, and this is what the next chapter explains.

8

Freedom to Contract in the Seventeenth Century

main argument of book?

Grotius' conception of freedom to contract provides a crucial point of comparison to Stair's theory. Stair can be seen as providing a Calvinist reworking of Grotius's account of contracting. Stair ultimately understood liberty or freedom as how man brought glory to God. Importantly, for Stair this did not translate into a civil power of the church or ecclesiastical authority to regulate individual contracts with the aid of the temporal sword, because that would be potentially harmful. Stair saw man's liberty to contract as coexisting with Calvinist social organization; individual liberty at the contracting level did not challenge the need for overall social and religious discipline at the collective level. Stair shares Grotius' concern with the promotion of commerce and trade through free contract, but this is not the core of Stair's theorizations. It is important to register how far Stair's theologically based contractual ideas depart from Grotian natural law; and this takes on added significance as we trace the influence of Stair's contract jurisprudence into the Enlightenment theories of commercial society in the eighteenth century.[1]

Freedom to Trade, Commerce, and Contract

In both *The Free Sea*[2] and *The Rights of War and Peace*,[3] Grotius draws upon antiquity to support his free-trade arguments, which unsurprisingly points to a literary catalogue of ideas available to seventeenth-century writers. It is not difficult to find descriptive statements in Classical literature that explain contracting, transacting, or exchanging goods as inherently human or as an instinctive part of any community.[4] Observing that mankind needs to enter into commerce, through either barter or buying and selling of property, is a familiar idea found in the opening book of Aristotle's *Politics*.[5] It is also common to find an explanation that men need to share their individual goods due to the otherwise vulnerable position they are in without community cooperation. For Philo, God intended men to be interdependent upon each other for survival, precipitating that men enter into reciprocal and mutual agreements. In his *On*

---

[1] See, Joost Hengstmengel, *Divine Providence in Early Economc Thought* (Routledge 2019) for a key discussion of how early modern Christian economic thought relates to eighteenth century ideas and, particularly, Adam Smith.

[2] (First published 1609, Liberty Fund 2004) 1.9.

[3] Hugo Grotius, *The Rights of War and Peace* (first published 1625, Liberty Fund 2005) 2.2.15.

[4] Some but not all of the quotations cited here were highlighted by Douglas Irwin in his Douglas Irwin, *Against the Tide: An Intellectual History of Free Trade* (Princeton University Press 1995) 11–25.

[5] Aristotle, *Politics* (Ernest Barker tr, revised by Richard Stalley, OUP 2009) 1.9.

Contract before the Enlightenment. Stephen Bogle, Oxford University Press. © Stephen Bogle 2023.
DOI: 10.1093/oso/9780192884961.003.0009

the Cherubim, The Flaming Sword, and Cain, Philo explained that 'as a lyre is formed of unlike notes, God meant that they [men] should come to fellowship and concord and form a single harmony; and that a universal give and take should govern them, and lead up to the consummation of the whole world.'[6] Plutarch argues in one of his *Moralia* that water creates a fifth element, the sea, which is 'no less beneficial' to man than any of the other elements because 'when our life was savage and unsociable, [sea] linked it together and made it complete, redressing defects by mutual assistance and exchange and so bringing about co-operation and friendship.'[7] Suggesting that by honouring an agreement or promise, man was doing more than serving self-interest, but acting in a morally and politically commendable way, is almost a platitude within Classical literature from Aristotle to Cicero.[8] One of the famous examples of this is in Plato's *Crito*, where Socrates draws the answer from Crito that 'One should keep agreements.'[9] Xenophon calls agreements 'the greatest blessing of cities: their senates and their best men constantly exhort the citizens to agree, and everywhere in Greece there is a law that the citizens must promise under oath to agree, and everywhere they take this oath.' He explains: 'without agreement no city can be made a good city; no house can be made a prosperous house.'[10] Discerning a basic commonality amongst different systems of human law which emerge out of man's common nature, and specifically similar laws about contracting, is famously found in Justinian's *Institutes*.[11] However, as this chapter will show, Grotius and Stair approached this in a different manner from these Classical writers whose focus was upon communities or cities rather than individuals.

Conscience, Ethics, and Restraints on Trade

Whether trade was viewed as divinely instituted or a natural outcome of man's basic temporal needs, writers and jurists in antiquity were generally suspicious of commerce, trade, and money,[12] and this continued into the early modern period. Even if there could be said to be a natural right to contract, it was something which should be

---

[6] Philo, *On the Cherubim. The Sacrifices of Abel and Cain. The Worse Attacks the Better. On the Posterity and Exile of Cain. On the Giants* (Francis H Colson and George H Whitaker trs, Harvard University Press 1929) 73–75. This is very similar to Libanius, who Grotius quotes in Grotius *The Rights of War and Peace* (n 3) 2.2.15, 5.

[7] Plutarch, *Moralia, Volume XII: Concerning the Face Which Appears in the Orb of the Moon. On the Principle of Cold. Whether Fire or Water Is More Useful. Whether Land or Sea Animals Are Cleverer. Beasts Are Rational. On the Eating of Flesh* (Harold Cherniss and William C Helmbold trs, Harvard University Press 1957) 288–99.

[8] Although self-interest is, of course, the most common judgement and frequent criticism of trade in Classical literature, at least trade leads to profit rather than subsistence or need.

[9] Plato, *Euthyphro. Apology. Crito. Phaedo* (Christopher Emlyn-Jones and William Preddy trs, Harvard University Press 2017) 243.

[10] Xenophon, *Memorabilia. Oeconomicus. Symposium. Apology* (Edgar C Marchant and O J Todd trs, revised by Jeffrey Henderson, Harvard University Press 2013) 333.

[11] *Justinian Inst* 1.1.3.

[12] Jacob Viner, *Religious Thought and Economic Society: Four Chapters of an Unfinished Work* (Duke University Press 1978); Irwin *Against the Tide* (n 4) 17–25; Christopher Berry, *The Idea of Luxury* (CUP 1994); Neville Morley, *Trade in Classical Antiquity* (CUP 2007) 79–89; James Davis, *Medieval Market Morality: Life, Law and Ethics in the English Marketplace, 1200–1500* (CUP 2011).

done judiciously. For example, medieval and early modern writers approached commerce as a branch of ethics, while legal systems, through canon law, customary laws, or via legislation of civil- powers, regulated prices, usury, and who could trade and with whom.[13] Irwin observed, however, that by the sixteenth century the shame and suspicion associated with trade receded somewhat, with some writers approaching trade and commerce as 'ethically neutral', but nevertheless with the looming potential for unethical, sinful behaviour.[14] John Calvin, for example, said in his *Institutes* that God desired that whilst man is under civil government, 'the public quiet be not disturbed, that every man's property be kept secure, that men may carry on innocent commerce with each other, that honesty and modesty be cultivated; in short, that a public form of religion may exist among Christians, and humanity among men.'[15] Although the important reassessment of such things had begun,[16] which would lead to eventual liberalization in these areas,[17] canon law, local laws, and customs continued to enforce rules with regard to usury, credit, prices, and foreign trade throughout Europe.

Attitudes about commerce may have been relaxing during the early modern period, but there was, nevertheless, a voluminous casuistic literature and a strong pastoral focus on Christian ethics, which drew upon not just Biblical but also Classical sources.[18] Produced, preached, and circulated by Protestant and Catholic theologians, ministers, and those charged with guiding the laity to salvation, this teaching and literature was related to commerce and trade as well as other aspects of a Christian's life.[19] As has been shown, for example, Calvinist theologians and ministers in Scotland, such as James Durham, had extremely high expectations of what 'innocent commerce' meant for an individual.[20] Indeed, in different ways, and for different purposes, this ethical literature and pastoral guidance is something which both English and Scots clergy produced during the seventeenth century, including discussion of contracting

---

[13] Richard H Helmholz, *The Oxford History of the Laws of England, Vol I: The Canon Law and Ecclesiastical Jurisdiction from 597 to the 1640s* (OUP 2004); Avner Greif, *Institutions and the Path to the Modern Economy: Lessons from Medieval Trade* (CUP 2006); Stephan R Epstein, *Freedom and Growth: The Rise of States and Markets in Europe, 1300–1750* (Routledge 2000); Shellagh Ogilvie, *Institutions and European Trade: Merchant Guilds, 1000–1800* (CUP 2011).

[14] Irwin *Against the Tide* (n 4) 20.

[15] Calvin *Inst* 4.20.3.

[16] For example, see Wolfgang Musculus, *Commentary on Psalm 15 (1551)*, T Rester tr (2008) 11 (2) Journal of Markets & Morality 349–460; Michael Wykes, 'Devaluing the Scholastics: Calvin's Ethics of Usury' 38 Calvin Theological Journal (2003) 27–51; Wim Decock, 'The Catholic Spirit of Capitalism' in Wim Decock, Jordan J Ballor, Michael Germann, and Laurent Waelkens (eds), *Law and Religion: The Legal Teachings of the Protestant and Catholic Reformations* (2014) 22–44; Paolo Astorri, *Lutheran Theology and Contract Law in Early Modern Germany (ca. 1520–1720)* (Brill 2019) 47–109.

[17] Richard H Tawney, *Religion and the Rise of Capitalism: A Historical Study* (first published 1926, Verso 2015); Margaret Sampson, 'Laxity and Liberty in Seventeenth-Century English Political Thought' in Edmund Leites (ed), *Conscience and Casuistry in Early Modern Europe* (CUP 1988) 72–119; Charles R Geisst, *Beggar Thy Neighbor: A History of Usury and Debt* (University of Pennsylvania Press 2013) 97–137; Davis *Medieval Market Morality* (n 12).

[18] Margo Todd, *Christian Humanism and Puritan Social Order* (CUP 1987); Jill Kraye, 'Moral Philosophy' in Charles B Schmitt, Quentin Skinner, Eckhard Kessler, and Jill Kraye (eds), *The Cambridge History of Renaissance Philosophy* (CUP 1988) 319–25.

[19] Leites *Conscience and Casuistry* (n 17).

[20] James Durham, *A Practical Exposition of the X Commandments with A Resolution of Several Momentous Questions and Cases of Conscience* (Dorman Newman 1675).

and trading.[21] Although this literature would never claim to help man towards salvation, the mid-seventeenth-century literature did instruct the laity on Scripture's relevance to everyday life and remind parishioners of their inadequacy when faced with God's law and hence their need for God's grace. It was not about virtue or civic duty, for these writers, but rather extrapolating, explaining and applying Scripture to everyday life and understanding what the law of God was.[22]

Jesuits too, from the late sixteenth century into the seventeenth century, were engaged in developing an ethically orientated guidance for the laity,[23] but for a different purpose. Decock explains: 'as theologians and confessors, the Jesuits wanted to give advice to Christians of all walks of life, particularly businessmen and princes, so that they would be able to save their souls on the day of Last Judgment.'[24] The jurisdiction of the conscience, for the Catholic Church, was of central importance in the post-Trent era as 'moral theologians constructed the *forum internum* as a parallel jurisdiction that competed for normative power with the secular State.'[25] It is no surprise, therefore, that it was voluminous and juridical in nature. Importantly, as Decock has shown, Jesuit theologians were very much interested in commerce and the laws which applied to trading and contracting.[26] Indeed, Jesuits gave confessors advice on law, ethics and contracting with an intensity and familiarity with legal sources that make it sometimes difficult to differentiate their work from that of jurists.[27] In contrast, seventeenth-century Protestants in Scotland and England never attempted anything like this; but they, like their Jesuit counterparts, were intensely concerned with the

---

[21] For example, see William Perkins, *Epieikeia, or a Treatise of Christian Equity and Moderation* (Legatt 1604); Christopher Love, *Scriptural Rules to be Observed in Buying and Selling* (unknown 1652); Joseph Hall, *Cases of Conscience Practical Resolved: Containing a Decision of the Principall Cases of Conscience, of daily Concernment, and Continuous Use amongst Men* (R H & J G 1654) 1–66; Thomas Nicols, *An Abridgement of the Whole Body of Divinity, Extracted from the Learned Works of the Ever-Famous and Reverend Divine* (W B 1654) 107–17; Francis Taylor, *An Exposition with Practical Observations upon the three first Chapter of the Proverbs* (E C 1655); George Fox, *A Warning to All the Merchants in London, and such as Buy and Sell* (London: Thomas Simmons, 1658); Richard Allestree, *The Practice of Christian Graces, or The Whole Duty of Man* (Maxwell 1658) 238–74, 459.

[22] This continued into the eighteenth century: see Valerie Wallace, 'Presbyterian Moral Economy: The Covenanting Tradition and Popular Protest in Lowland Scotland, 1707–c. 1746' (2008) 89 (277) Scottish Historical Review 54–72. NB there existed too, a healthy and burgeoning literature within the Lutheran strand of reformed theology: Astorri *Lutheran Theology* (n 16) 47–109.

[23] Stefania Tutino, 'Ecclesiology/Church–State Relationship in Early Modern Catholicism' in Ulrich L Lehner, Richard A. Muller, and A. G. Roeber (eds), *The Oxford Handbook of Early Modern Theology, 1600–1800* (OUP 2016) 151–64; Jean-Louis Quantin, 'Catholic Moral Theology, 1550–1800' in Ulrich L Lehner, Richard A. Muller, and A. G. Roeber (eds), *The Oxford Handbook of Early Modern Theology, 1600–1800* (OUP 2016) 75–88.

[24] Wim Decock, 'From Law to Paradise: Confessional Catholicism and Legal Scholarship' (2011) 18 Rechtsgeschichte 12, 17.

[25] Decock 'From Law to Paradise' (n 24) 13.

[26] See Wim Decock, *Theologians and Contract Law: The Moral Transformation of the Ius Commune (ca. 1500–1650)* (Brill 2013) 22–49.

[27] For example, Flemish Jesuit, Leonardus Lessius (1554–1623) produced a treatise in 1605, entitled *De Justitia et Jure Caeterisque Virtutibus Cardinalibus Libri Quatuor*, a copy of which was held in Glasgow University, printed in Paris in 1613. Glasgow's copy is over 800 pages long, divided into four books, weaving together a commentary on the *Prima Secundæ Partis* of Aquinas' *Summa Theologica*, local rules relating to trade and finance and discussion of various *Ius Commune* rules. See Wim Decock, 'Leonardus Lessie's on Buying and Selling (1605). Translation and Introduction' (2007) 10 (2) Journal of Markets and Morality 433–516.

jurisdiction of conscience and how it related to the use of one's liberty.[28] Viner noted, inter alia, the one central difference between Protestant and Catholic casuistry: the former emphasized 'what should be done' rather than what was 'permissible to do'.[29] As will be explained, a reconsideration of jurisdiction and conscience is central to how Grotius and Stair approached the notion of freedom of contract. By limiting or re-defining the jurisdictional and legal reach of commercial ethics' expectations of men, Grotius's idea that man was free to contract found a clear demarcation and a wide scope for individual decision-making in terms of trade and a broader area of dis-cretion when it came to contracts. In responding to Grotius and incorporating this into the *Institutions of the Law of Scotland* (*Institutions*) , Stair too creates this space for trade and commerce, but he only creates this space within his description of the positive law and his definition of civil power's jurisdiction. Stair adapted Grotius's ap-proach to Calvinist expectations and concepts of conscience, while Grotius sought to diminish the influence and control of clerics and Protestant casuistry over individuals.

Grotius

Grotius's conception of liberty and rights

From an analytical perspective, Grotius's account of liberty includes three elements, namely ownership, status, and freedom of action. In *The Rights of War and Peace*, pub-lished in 1625, Grotius wrote:

> Civilians call a Faculty that Right which a Man has to his own; but we shall hereafter call it a Right properly, and strictly take. Under which are contained: A Power either over ourselves, which is term'd Liberty; or over others, such as that of a Father over his Children, or a Lord over his Slave.[30]

Grotius had previously articulated these ideas in 1603 in his unpublished *Commentary on the Law and Prize of Booty*,[31] where he said:

---

[28] Bruce Lenman, 'The Limits of Godly Discipline in the Early Modern Period with Particular Reference to England and Scotland' in Kasper von Greyerz (ed), *Religion and Society in Early Modern Europe, 1500–1800* (Allen & Unwin1984) 142; Sampson 'Laxity and Liberty in Seventeenth-Century English Political Thought' (n 17); James Tully, 'Governing Conduct' in Edmund Leites (ed), *Conscience and Casuistry in Early Modern Europe* (CUP 1988) 12–71; ; Richard J Ross, 'Puritan Godly Discipline in Comparative Perspective: Legal Pluralism and the Sources of "Intensity"' (2008) 113 American Historical Review 975–1002; Richard J Ross, 'Binding in Conscience: Early Modern English Protestants and Spanish Thomists on Law and the Fate of the Soul' (2015) 33 Law and History Review 803–37; Dennis R Klinck, *Conscience, Equity and the Court of Chancery in Early Modern England* (Ashgate 2010) 107–218; Astorri *Lutheran Theology and Contract Law* (n 16) 8–9.

[29] Viner *Religious Thought and Economic Society* (n 12) 155.

[30] Grotius *The Rights of War* (n 3) 1.1.5.

[31] Hugo Grotius, *Commentary on the Law of Prize and Booty* (tr *Martine Julia van Ittersum*, Liberty Fund 2006). Only discovered in 1864, it was not published until 1868, van Ittersum's 2006 translation is the first extensive, critical edition in English. Sometimes it is referred to as *De Jure Praedae Commentarius*.

For what is that well-known concept, 'natural liberty', other than the power of the individual to act in accordance with his own will? a Liberty and ownership. And liberty in regard to actions is equivalent to ownership in regard to property. Hence the saying: 'Every man is the governor and arbiter of affairs relative to his own property'.[32]

Furthermore, in his *Introduction to Dutch Jurisprudence*, written in 1619–20[33] and published in 1631,[34] he speaks of contracting away freedom; he says that contracts, more than a promise, give away freedom because:[35]

> this [contracting] consists in a man's free disposal of his acts: for just as the power which a man has over his own property, whether in complete or incomplete ownership, enables him by delivery or sufferance to make another person owner, ... so too a man may make over to another who accepts the same, a portion, or rather a consequence of his own freedom, so that the other acquires a right over it, which right is termed a personal right.

On the basis of these three works, it is clear that for Grotius liberty is a power to act (*potestas*) or, as described in Chapter 7, a metaphysical freedom to choose. However, liberty is also a thing which is owned by the self (*potestas in se*), which relates to the second sense of 'liberty' or 'freedom', the normative sense of 'liberty'.[36] Moreover, Grotius makes a political point based on the notion of a social contract rather than a theological or anthropological point, which might be associated with Calvinists like Stair. That is: for Grotius, man is by nature his own master or within his rights to act freely (*sui iuris*). Importantly, this was not just a legal claim as to juridical capacity, but rather an assertion of capacity or competence in a pre-legal state of nature; that is, he was without a master, or enjoyed self-mastery, prior to the creation of civil government and human laws. In so giving liberty a multi-dimensional meaning, Grotius drew upon the Roman law conceptions of *libertas* rather than the medieval philosophy previously discussed. For Grotius, *libertas* is the ability to do as one pleases, and *sui iuris*, as in the status of a free man rather than an *alienus iuris*, is to be under the power of another.[37] Rather than using the term 'liberty' in different senses, Grotius synthesizes into the concept of a normative right the conception of liberty as ownership, liberty as status and liberty as freedom of action.

---

[32] Grotius *The Law of Prize* (n 31) 34–35. Prior to this, he says at p 34: 'God created man αὐτεξούσιον, "free and sui iuris" ', so that the actions of each individual and the use of his possessions were made subject not to another's will but to his own. Moreover, this view is sanctioned by the common consent of all nations.'

[33] For discussion of whether Stair would have read or had access to the *Introduction to Dutch Jurisprudence* (or *Inleydinge*) see Adelyn L M Wilson, 'Stair and the Inleydinge of Grotius' (2010) 14 (2) Edinburgh Law Review 239–68.

[34] Hugo Grotius, *The Introduction to Dutch Jurisprudence* (first published 1631, tr Charles Herbert, John van Voorst 1903).

[35] Grotius *Introduction* (n 34) 294–95.

[36] As discussed in chapter 7.

[37] For a convincing account of how and why Grotius drew concepts from the *Corpus Iuris Civilis* to develop his notion of liberty, see Daniel Lee, *Popular Sovereignty in Early Modern Constitutional Thought* (OUP 2016) 258–64.

In comparison, Stair uses these terms for different contexts; that is, liberty in terms of the metaphysical ability to choose, which can be relevant when forced to perform an action; liberty when it is used within its lawful boundaries; and liberty when it acts as an evaluation of whether or not someone is acting according to a rational motive or not, which is liberty in the sense of reason or liberation. Stair does not understand man as owning his liberty; nor does he see liberty as a normative right which man can claim, other than when it is recognized within the positive law. Grotius, on the other hand, does not use 'liberty' in this way. It is simpler and relatively consistent no matter the context; it is the free capacity of a man to act, whether expressed in the arena of theology, history, law, or politics. On this basis, Grotius offers a political theory in which a commonwealth or *polis* is created which involves the transfer of that essential natural liberty to a civil power. In fact, because liberty is stripped of a theological or liberation sense, Grotius is comfortable with a civil power overseeing a large amount of what Stair would have understood to be ecclesiastical or spiritual affairs.[38] Therefore, for both Stair and Grotius, their description of liberty had implications in terms of describing who could tell an individual what to do with their respective freedoms and what powers they might have. If the church is subject to the civil power's control, then its ability to regulate, determine, or influence individuals' use of their power to contract is limited to moral teaching. To fully consider Grotius's notion of freedom we must also address his ideas about freedom to trade.

The content of rights: Freedom to trade

Grotius does not merely offer an analytical account of rights: he wants to demonstrate that the law of nature is constituted by individual rights, and that this applies universally, and that this can provide a basic account of the content of natural law.[39] This means that Grotius deduces some basic principles which contribute to the establishment of civil society, which he then proceeds to explain on the basis of man's sociability but also their necessity for man's individual preservation. First, for Grotius, it appears indisputable that man is an animal of 'higher order' who has a desire to live in society with other men.[40] From this desire and instinct, one can deduce some basic principles which provide the content of the rights men can legitimately exercise against others:[41]

[38] See Grotius, *The Rights of War* (n 3) 1.3.8; Hugo Grotius and Edwin Rabbie (ed), *Hugo Grotius Ordinum Hollandiae ac Westfrisiae pietas (1613)* (Brill 1995) generally. For discussion, see Martin van Gelderen, 'Arminian trouble: Calvinist debates on freedom' in Quentin Skinner and Martine van Gelderen (eds), *Freedom and the Construction of Europe* (2013) vol 1, 21–37.

[39] Hugo Grotius 'Preliminary Discourse' in Hugo Grotius, *The Rights of War and Peace* (first published 1625, Liberty Fund 2005), I–VII.

[40] In making this statement, Grotius is significantly changing his emphasis from his earlier writings on why man establishes society and laws. That is, his account of the basis of natural law, rights and human law changes between 1603, when he wrote his *Commentary on the Law of Prize and Booty*, and 1625 when he published *The Rights of War and Peace*: Annabel Brett, 'Natural Right and Civil Community: The Civil Philosophy of Hugo Grotius' (2002) 45 (1) The Historical Journal 31, 37–45.

[41] Grotius 'Preliminary Discourse' (n 39) VIII.

This Sociability, which we have now described in general, or this Care of maintaining Society in a Manner conformable to the Light of human Understanding, is the Fountain of Right, properly so called; to which belongs the Abstaining from that which is another's, and the Restitution of what we have of another's, or of the Profit we have made by it, the Obligation of fulfilling Promises, the Reparation of a Damage done through our own Default, and the Merit of Punishment among Men.

There is, however, an indirect relationship between these basic rights of men and civil society, including its laws. Grotius continues to explain that civil law, namely human law, is originally founded upon a contract, saying:[42]

since the fulfilling of Covenants belongs to the Law of Nature (for it was necessary there should be some Means of obliging Men among themselves, and we cannot conceive any other more conformable to Nature) from this very Foundation Civil Laws were derived. For those who had incorporated themselves into any Society, or subjected themselves to any one Man, or Number of Men, had either expressly, or from the Nature of the Thing must be understood to have tacitly promised, that they would submit to whatever either the greater part of the Society, or those on whom the Sovereign Power had been conferred, had ordained.

One of the rights which Grotius speaks of in *The Rights of War and Peace* is the right to trade.[43] In numerous places in his 1609 treatise, *The Free Sea*, Grotius sought to defend the right of nations and individuals to trade and travel. The law of nations, he argued, makes clear that 'all men should have free liberty of negotiation among themselves which no man could take away.'[44] He refers to Book I of Aristotle's *Politics*, saying that there it was suggested that 'what was wanting to nature was supplied by negotiation that everyone conveniently might have enough.'[45] He goes on:

the liberty of trading is agreeable to the primary law of nations which hath a natural and perpetual cause and therefore cannot be taken away and, if it might, yet could it not but by the consent of all nations, so far off is it that any nation, by any means, may justly hinder two nations that are willing to trade between themselves.[46]

Grotius's *Introduction to Dutch Jurisprudence*, written a few years before *The Rights of War and Peace*, offers further insight into the content of civil rights and their relationship to the law of nature and how this right of trade is manifest in human law. For example, in discussing obligations, such as contracts, Grotius says that our rights arise out of obligations, which relate to the corresponding duties of benevolence, good faith, and gratitude.[47] According to Grotius, these are virtues which stem from either the natural law principles of fellowship of nature or the necessity of mutual intercourse.

---

[42] Grotius 'Preliminary Discourse' (n 39) XVI.
[43] Richard Tuck, *Natural Rights Theories* (CUP 1979) 69–71.
[44] Grotius *Free Sea* (n 2) 1.9.
[45] Grotius *Free Sea* (n 2) 1.9.
[46] Grotius *Free Sea* (n 2) 1.9.
[47] Grotius *Introduction* (n 34) 3.1.3.

However, human law, in addition to natural law, places a new obligation upon man 'to check the want of caution on the part of men in binding themselves'.[48] We have civil rights because they emerge from natural law, but we also have them because they are necessary to ensure that men adhere to the natural law. In taking this approach in *The Rights of War and Peace* and in the *Introduction to Dutch Jurisprudence*, Grotius offers a positive, optimistic theory of commerce and its sociable origins in man's nature, which is reflected in the law of nature and by consequence of the human law of nations and the Dutch Provinces. Rather than being a dangerous activity fraught with the risks of greed, acquisitiveness, and corruption, commerce was part of the foundation to nature and to the law of nature. It is in our nature, and it is good for civil society, and it is right that we do it.

Utility, rights, and justice

The dual nature of Grotius's explanation of natural law is repeated in *The Preliminary Discourse* to *The Rights of War and Peace*, where he says 'Civil Laws' are derived from the law of nature whose 'mother' is human nature, which would have desired society, out of man's sociable nature, even if it was not necessary due to the vulnerable circumstances of man, who needs to establish civil society.[49] For Grotius, the 'Mother of Civil Law' is the consent which man gives to create society and human laws, whether that be due to his sociable nature or out of necessity. Or, as Grotius puts it, to 'the Law of Nature Profit is annexed', meaning that although man would have created civil society, without any consideration of its profit to him individually or its necessity, there are, nevertheless, clear benefits to man to establish civil society and introduce human laws. Prima facie, Stair would agree. That is, Grotius's stress on the necessity and utility of rights is repeated in Stair.[50] Furthermore, there is the notion in Stair that human law involves the consent of man and his acquiescence.[51] For both, the utility and necessity of rights is a means to determine the scope, content, and use of rights in civil society, but the differences in coming to this conclusion, between Grotius and Stair, are fairly evident. But there are important differences too.

Firstly, the two passages quoted above demonstrate that Grotius's account of natural law, rights, and civil law is only indirectly theistic and, importantly, does not have a necessary connection to divine law, conscience, or Scripture,[52] something which Grotius acknowledges himself.[53] Stair does not, like Grotius, establish a pre-civil natural state where there is a system of natural rights from which man is able to determine the nature and content of natural law. In the *Divine Perfections*, Stair offers an account of civil society's creation which is, in essence, 'a divine creation'.[54] In contrast to Grotius,

---

[48] Grotius *Introduction* (n 34) 3.1.21.
[49] Grotius 'Preliminary Discourse' (n 39) XVII.
[50] Stair *Inst* 1.1.6; 1.1.17–18.
[51] Stair *Inst* 1.1.10; 1.1.15.
[52] In his *Introduction to Dutch Jurisprudence* (viz. Stair *Inst* 1.2.1), Grotius does, however, make some mention of conscience, but he does not invoke it, in contrast to Stair, as a structural or fundamental concept in terms of man's cognition of or obedience of the law of nature or human law.
[53] Grotius 'Preliminary Discourse' (n 39) XI.
[54] Stair *Divine Perfections* 265.

Stair draws upon a Scriptural history and divine law—which gives man power over his wife and family, and the notion that 'fathers of families' gave power over most aspects of their families to civil government—in order to account for the authority of a sovereign.[55] As the *Institutions* demonstrate, the sovereign does not have absolute sovereignty to do as they wish, but is rather subject to the system of divine law, the agreement made with fathers of fathers, and human law created by man in accordance with equity. Stair places theology at the root of his explanation of commerce and why it is beneficial to society. Grotius's approach reaches similar conclusions, but the detailed arguments are made without recourse to theology. Albeit he ultimately accepted the divine origins of natural reason, Grotius demonstrates that it can be argued for independently.

Secondly, Stair is far more sceptical about the abilities of man to undertake a project as ambitious as Grotius's,[56] holding instead that man only knows a few essentials of natural law and that his ability to reason from those essentials is liable to error.[57] In comparison, therefore, rather than determine an overarching system of natural law, man must proceed carefully from case to case when trying to establish what is right and in accordance with natural law.[58] Additionally, for Stair, if man had not fallen, there would be no distinction between what is good and what is equitable in civil society; but, as man is now fallen, he needs to determine the civil law according to what is profitable to him and within the confines of his God-given freedom, that is, not encroaching upon the divine law of God. He needs to trade and enter into commerce, and he realizes the benefits of it, but much of this comes from working out the basic principles of the law of nature in practice rather than knowing that it is necessary for man on the basis of first principles.

Thirdly, as Tuck notes, in *The Rights of War and Peace* Grotius's focus upon subjective rights allowed him 'to treat the law of nature as totally to do with the maintenance of other people's rights, whether of property or merit'.[59] In other words, rights, under Grotius's theory, 'have come to usurp the whole of the natural law theory, for the law of nature is simply, respect one another's rights'.[60] Additionally, as Brett argues, Grotius's account of what is a right is notable:[61] he says that that which is right is that which is 'not not-right or unjust'.[62] In that sense, by reducing natural law to the maintenance of others' rights, Grotius did not just diminish the extent of duties which it can be said natural law imposes on a man, but also he created a space for man to claim it is right for him to act without interference—at least, provided he has not transferred that liberty away or it is not 'repugnant to the Nature of a Society of reasonable Creatures'.[63] This is connected to how Grotius sought to construct a theory which was acceptable to different Christian faiths, but one which importantly reduced the need for casuistry,

---

[55] Stair *Divine Perfections* 264–65.
[56] Stair *Inst* 1.1.17.
[57] Stair *Inst* 1.1.4–5.
[58] Stair *Inst* 1.1.4–7.
[59] Tuck *Natural Rights Theories* (n 43) 67.
[60] Tuck *Natural Rights Theories* (n 43) 67.
[61] Grotius *The Rights of War* (n 3) 1.1.3–8.
[62] Brett 'Natural Right and Civil Community' (n 40) 44.
[63] Grotius *The Rights of War* (n 3) 1.1.3.

clerical instruction, or theological interpretation of what the natural law requires of individual men, namely appeals to the jurisdiction of conscience.[64]

The approach taken by Grotius was to claim that questions of justice were 'the exclusive territory of the lay casuist (or natural rights theorists)' and 'that the function of the divine was to promote piety by preaching up the counsels of perfection to be found in the Gospel of Charity'.[65] Unlike Grotius, Stair did not wish to reduce natural law to these basic rights, but he was nevertheless willing to accept that the rights men have according to human law are the result of utility and what can be determined for the good of the community. Stair made a distinction between natural and legal obligations in the *Institutions*,[66] where he spoke of the practical and jurisdictional limits of the law: charity, assistance, alms, kindness, and so on were all obligations placed upon man by natural law, but they were not something which human law could or should enforce. Stair explained this in theistic and practical terms. Grotius explains his distinction in practical and theoretical terms. Stair had a much wider conception of what natural law included; Grotius's reduction of the duties of men to the respect of basic rights does not fit with Stair's conception of natural law. Moreover, the related notion that divines are restricted in what is their proper domain would run counter to Stair's understanding of Presbyterian government as per the 1647 *Westminster Confession of Faith*. Stair may have said they had no temporal power, but his account of liberty allowed for the clergy to give strong and direct instruction as to what an individual should do. This, however, raises the question of what role Grotius saw for the church within his political philosophy.

God, theology, and the maintenance of society

It is clear that the role and place of God, theology and religious duty is limited in what might be called Grotius's civil philosophy—namely his explanation of civil powers and human law's foundations, purpose, limits, and relationship to the law of nature—when compared to Stair.[67] Unlike Stair, Grotius does not approach the question of freedom and liberty from a metaphysical or scholastic point of view, which was otherwise common in seventeenth-century theological literature.[68] Instead, Grotius adopts a humanistic and historical approach to explain liberty, using sources from antiquity, such as the *Corpus Iuris Civilis*, poets, orators, historians, and, also importantly, rational

---

[64] Richard Tuck, 'Grotius and Selden' in James H Burns and Mark Goldie (eds), *The Cambridge History of Political Thought* (CUP 1991) 499–529.

[65] Sampson 'Laxity and Liberty in Seventeenth-Century English Political Thought' (n 17) 117.

[66] Stair *Inst* 1.3.5–6, discussed also in Chapters 5 and 7.

[67] Even in his theological or theological-politico writing, his emphasis is upon reducing the influence of the church and prioritizing the affairs of the civil powers, see, for example, *De Imperio Summarum Potestatum circa Sacra* discussed later in this chapter.

[68] See further Chapter 7. For a detailed and revealing interpretation of Grotius's working methods and use of sources, including Roman law, with reference to his writings on natural law and rights, see Martine J van Ittersum, 'The Working Methods of Hugo Grotius: Which Sources Did He Use and How Did He Use Them in His Early Writings on Natural Law Theory?' in Paul J du Plessis and John W Cairns, *Reassessing Legal Humanism and its Claims: Petere Fontes?* (Edinburgh University Press 2016) 155–93.

self-interest to elucidate his argument.[69] Indeed, in his legal and political writing you find copious citation of classical writers like Cicero and very little reference to the Old or the New Testament—something for which William Welwood (1578–1622) criticized Grotius in title 27 of *An Abridgement of all Sea-Lawes*.[70] Nor is his account shaped by a postlapsarian narrative[71] or an underlying proposition that man needs God's help in determining what natural law is[72]—something for which the Calvinist jurist, Johannes Voet (1647–1713), notably criticized Grotius in his *Commentarius ad Pandectas*.[73] In comparison to Calvinists like Stair, Grotius starts from a far more positive perspective about man's ability to synchronize with God's design by creating a civil society based on individual rights. Grotius, however, does maintain in *The Rights of War and Peace* that the law of nature, 'whether it be that which consists in the Maintenance of Society, or that which in a looser Sense is so called, though it flows from the internal Principles of Man, may notwithstanding be justly ascribed to God, because it was his Pleasure that these Principles should be in us'.[74] God's place is therefore accounted for within Grotius's civil philosophy, but it does not, importantly, require God for any knowledge of natural law or man's rights. As Haakonssen explains, the medieval concept of *ius* meant:[75]

in both Aristotelian and the Thomistic tradition the right action and the right state of affairs ... which fits into a law-governed whole. And for the Thomists this whole includes God, so that by living socially in accordance with natural law, we are in the end living in society with God. But for Grotius this right action is the one which each person has an individual natural right to do, subject to the essential requirements of social life—which, as we know, for him amount to no more than the noninfringement of the similar rights of others.

For now it is the 'secularizing effect' of Grotius upon natural rights theories, and specifically the conception of liberty, which is of interest in comparison to Calvinists like Stair.[76] By reducing natural law to basic notions of rights, including liberty, property, and contract, and reducing the scope and jurisdiction of spiritual powers within the

---

[69] Richard Tuck, 'Introduction' in Hugo Grotius, *The Rights of War and Peace* (first published 1625, Liberty Fund 2005) xiv; also see Benjamin Straumann, *Roman Law in the State of Nature: The Classical Foundations of Hugo Grotius' Natural Law* (CUP 2015).

[70] (Humfrey Lownes 1613) 62–63. For discussion of Grotius's understanding of the Bible, see Mark Somos, *Secularisation and the Leiden Circle* (Brill 2011) 383–97. Despite the exiguity of Scripture in Grotius's civil philosophy, it still nonetheless appears often in *The Rights of War and Peace*, but is often cited alongside a classical source like the *Corpus Iuris Civilis*.

[71] See H J Erasmus, 'Natural Law: Voet's criticism of De Groot' (2016) 22 (1) *Fundamina* 40–52.

[72] See Hugo Grotius, 'Preliminary Discourse' (n 39), but also Hugo Grotius, *The Truth of Christian Religion in Six Books by Hugh Grotius Corrected and Illustrated with Notes, By Mr. Le Clerc*. (J Clarke tr, 2nd edn, J Knapton 1719) I.XIX (p 75). Originally published in Hugo Grotius, *De Veritate Religionis Christianae* (Thomas B. Wait et sociis 1627).

[73] Johannes Voet, *His Commentary on the Pandects ... translated by James Buchanan* (J C Juta 1880) 17–18. Originally published Johannes Voet, *Commentarius ad Pandectas*, vol 2 (Abrahamum de Hondt 1698); Johannes Voet, *Commentarius ad Pandectas*, vol 1 (Johannem Verbessel 1704) 1.1.15.

[74] Grotius 'Preliminary Discourse' (n 39) XII.

[75] Knud Haakonssen, 'Hugo Grotius and the History of Political Thought' (1985) 13 (2) *Political Theory* 239–65 at 249.

[76] Haakonssen, 'Hugo Grotius' (n 75) 249.

political community, Grotius redefined the boundaries of natural law and left far more discretion to individuals when it came to the use of their liberty. Of course, no matter the differences, it should be noted that Grotius did not wish to exclude God—but he did, nevertheless, offer a theory which did not rely on theistic premises in order to articulate his natural rights theory and thereby explain the relationship between liberty, civil government, and human laws. Stair differs in this regard but is, nevertheless, in the *Institutions* demonstrating that although the roots of social order in Scotland are theistic, it is nonetheless possible to see the benefits and utility of those roots within society.[77] This explains why Stair says that rights are the 'formal and proper object of law'. He draws upon the Aristotelian notion of causation to give an analytical framework to describe the relationship between rights and the law of nature. Yet, because this analytical system does not necessarily undermine a divine role in law, Stair can both say that rights constitute law, that is, they are the formal cause, and hold that God is the ultimate source of law.[78]

Civil and ecclesiastical powers

Grotius, however, still had to navigate and articulate a theory of civil government and individual liberty that explained the place and role of God and religious belief within the maintenance and formation of Dutch society.[79] That is, the right of liberty, which Grotius spoke of, had to be used in a deeply religious and theologically fractious society. Unlike Stair, however, Grotius formulated a far clearer conception of how the civil powers and the ecclesiastical powers should relate to man's liberty, notwithstanding, as has been shown, that it is possible to map Stair's approach in broad outline.[80] For Grotius, there should be liberty to hold unorthodox views, albeit ones which did not contradict the basic tenets of the Reformed Church in the States of Holland. Early in the 1610s, at a time when religious liberty was significantly limited, Grotius's position was well defined and came to be known latterly as Erastianism:[81] in response to strict Calvinists who thought otherwise, Grotius held that religious tolerance should be enforced by the temporal powers in order to maintain peace. That is, civil powers held supremacy over the church in the States of Holland and West Friesland.

In 1613, Grotius contributed to a famous debate concerning the academic appointment of Conrad Vorstius (1569–1622) to the chair of theology in Leiden. In his *Ordinal Hollandiae ac Westfrisiae Pietas*,[82] which circulated widely, and in England

---

[77] Stair *Inst* 1.1.17–22.

[78] Stair *Inst* 1.1.22.

[79] Hans W Blom and Harm-Jan van Dam, 'Dossier: Ordinum Pietas (1613): Its Context and Seventeenth-Century Reception' (2013) 34 Grotiana 7–10.

[80] Grotius wrote extensively on this topic. Only ten months after publishing the *Ordinum Pietas*, Grotius wrote a more theoretical work on the relationship between the church and state, *Tractatus de Jure Magistratuum* discovered in 1997, and in 1647 published his '*magnum opus*' on the supremacy of civil government, *De Imperio Summarum Potestatum circa Sacra*. For discussion, see Harm-Jan van Dam, 'Second Thoughts: Ordinum Pietas and the Tractatus de Jure Majistratuum' (2013) 34 Grotiana 120–37. Also see Hugo Grotius and Harm-Jan van Dam (eds), *Hugo Grotius, De Imperio Summarum Potestatum circa Sacra: Critical Edition with Introduction, English Translation and Commentary*, 2 vols (Brill 2001).

[81] Grotius and van Dam *Hugo Grotius, De Imperio Summarum Potestatum* (n 80) 29.

[82] Grotius and Rabbie *Ordinum Hollandiae* (n 38).

and Wales,[83] and most probably having made it to Scotland too,[84] Grotius launched into religious debates with a fierce polemic and defence of the States. Grotius attacked hard-line Calvinists in the *Ordium Hollandiae*, particularly Sibrandus Lubbertus (c.1555–1625), who objected to Vorstius's appointment on theological grounds (his views on, inter alia, predestination). Grotius, however, Judge Advocate at the time, defended the right of the States of Holland and West Friesland to appoint who they wished despite theological differences within the Reformed church concerning matters of doctrine, such as predestination. He argued that the 'administrators, who until now have used their authority and their means to support the Reformed religion ... who have refused to tolerate the public exercise of any other religion' were now being unjustly accused of heresy by some Calvinists.[85] Grotius quotes James VI and I with approval, saying: 'His Majesty holds that there will be no shorter way to reach concord than carefully to separate the necessary from non-necessary; as to the non-necessary points, room should be given to Christian liberty.'[86] Very little, for Grotius, was necessary, and the Church should not therefore insist on those things that are unnecessary.

In arguing for 'Christian liberty', Grotius said he was engaging with an English form of Calvinism, namely puritanism—a charge Sibrandus was keen to avoid. 'Everybody knows', Grotius said, 'that that name comes from England, where it is unusually assigned to some stubborn people who approve of nothing except of what they do themselves.'[87] According to his definition, puritans 'deny that the King is the head of the external Anglican Church', disapprove of the government of the Anglican Church where 'presbyters' are subordinate to bishops and archbishops, and 'in every controversy they assign almost no authority to Antiquity, but every authority to recent teachers'.[88] But this, for Grotius, was what Sibrandus and other strict Calvinists were calling for and was something which, if taken further, would threaten peace and order in the states in Holland, for the king in England, and for the senate in Venice.[89] In granting a large degree of authority and latitude to the theologians, the synods and strict Calvinists had encroached upon the jurisdiction of the civil powers. But they had also, according to Grotius, created uncertainty as to whether 'some young minister or village presbyter', or the nobility or archbishops were qualified to determine such matters.[90] To insist on observance of the unnecessary was to risk revolt, for the

---

[83] Hugo Dunthrone, 'History, Theology and Tolerance: Grotius and his English Contemporaries' (2013) 34 Grotiana 107–19.

[84] A copy was held in Glasgow in, and probably before, 1691; see Stephen Rawles, *The 1691 Catalogue of Glasgow University Library* (unpublished 2005) based on GUL Sp Coll Bm6-b.4. It is, however, thought to have been circulated around reformed churches in Europe, including Scotland; see Freya Sierhuis, *The Literature of the Arminian Controversy: Religion, Politics and the Stage in the Dutch Republic* (CUP 2015) 66. In relation to the use and circulation in Scotland of Grotius's larger treatise, *De Imperio Summarum Potestatum circa Sacra*, see George D Henderson, *Religious Life in Seventeenth-Century Scotland* (CUP 1937) 75, 78, 131, 260. A copy of the *De Imperio* was also held in Glasgow on and probably before 1691.

[85] Grotius and Rabbie *Ordinum Hollandiae* (n 38) 111.

[86] Grotius and Rabbie *Ordinum Hollandiae* (n 38) 171.

[87] Grotius and Rabbie *Ordinum Hollandiae* (n 38) 173.

[88] Grotius and Rabbie *Ordinum Hollandiae* (n 38) 173–75.

[89] Grotius and Rabbie *Ordinum Hollandiae* (n 38) 175.

[90] Grotius and Rabbie *Ordinum Hollandiae* (n 38) 165.

argument of Sibrandus was seeking to undermine the authority of the magistrates and state and to claim for the Church influence in the temporal world of the state.

For Grotius, quoting Erasmus, the 'essence of our religion is peace and unanimity', which can 'hardly last unless we define only the absolutely minimum and leave to each individual his own free judgment on many questions, because many things are very obscure'.[91] For Grotius, there were very few things the civil power could not rightfully claim authority over: it was only those who 'command things forbidden by God or forbid things commanded by Him' that temporal authorities had no jurisdiction over.[92] In effect, as he explained in detail in a later treatise, this was a very small area of human action where civil powers did not have authority.[93] Although Stair may have been somewhat sympathetic to the call for peace and unanimity, and does not appear to insist on civil enforcement of the finer points of doctrine, unlike Grotius, he was writing for or, at the least, with such a puritan audience in mind.[94] Certainly, this would have been his context in the mid-seventeenth century, and possibly to a lesser extent in the 1680s. Indeed, if the debate about Vorstius's appointment and Grotius's views about the powers of the civil authorities is placed against the context of an earlier and comparable period in Scottish history, namely James VI and I's introduction of the Perth Articles in 1618, the Dutch debate about Christian liberty would have been well understood and its implications recognized by a Scottish audience. At the risk of oversimplifying, it could be said Grotius was addressing a very similar audience to that which Stair also addressed; but, where Stair was seeking to appease and accommodate, Grotius was trying to oppose and resist. It is not hard to see that the puritans Grotius spoke of in the 1610s and considered again in the 1640s were, in effect, the same puritans Stair worked with in 1649,[95] who formed part of his context in the 1650s[96] and remained part of the discourse in the 1680s.[97]

A right and liberty to do what nature prescribes

In 1617, Grotius finished a draft of a far more extensive work on the relationship between the church and civil power. Although not published until 1647, two years after his death, his *De Imperio Summarum Potestatum circa Sacra* can be read alongside the *Ordinum Hollandiae* as he expands greatly upon the arguments he made in 1613. Importantly, in this treatise, you can find Grotius offering an answer to how man's liberty relates to the power of the church, civil authority, and human laws. After explaining that 'human authority removes the objects for actions which are forbidden by

[91] Grotius and Rabbie *Ordinum Hollandiae* (n 38) 169.

[92] Grotius and van Dam *Hugo Grotius, De Imperio Summarum Potestatum* (n 80) 211–19.

[93] Grotius and van Dam *Hugo Grotius, De Imperio Summarum Potestatum* (n 80) 221.

[94] For discussion of whether puritanism is a useful modern label to use in Scottish history, see David Mullen, *Scottish Puritanism, 1590–1638* (OUP 2000). Using Grotius's somewhat disparaging definition, it can be used to apply to political groups in Scotland during the seventeenth century.

[95] Aeneas J G Mackay, *Memoir of Sir James Dalrymple* (Edmonston and Douglas 1873) 35–45.

[96] R Scott Spurlock, *Cromwell and Scotland: Conquest and Religion, 1650–1660* (John Donald 2007).

[97] See Gillian H MacIntosh, *The Scottish Parliament under Charles II, 1660–1685* (Edinburgh University Press 2007), and also Alasdair Raffe, 'Presbyterianism, Secularization, and Scottish Politics after the Revolution of 1688–1690' (2010) 53 (2) The Historical Journal 317–37.

God [viz. divine law]', he explains that 'civil law' removes obstacles to man and 'creates the right and the external liberty to do what nature prescribes'.[98] He then continues to speak of things not determined by divine law (which, according to Grotius, is found in man's heart or Scripture), making the point that whether these areas of conduct are considered sacred or not, civil powers have authority to make laws and commands within such areas, and not the church. For example, he says: 'Roman emperors made constitutions concerning formalities and the effects of contracts and testament and innumerable other things.'[99] He goes on: 'there is no need to read the Holy Bible', for it is clear that there are many examples in history of Godly rulers who have legislated in sacred areas.

For Grotius, the church's authority was limited and ultimately subject to overview by the civil powers; and, importantly for present purposes, civil authority would rarely encroach upon God's divine law or indeed what God requires of men morally, because human law, in fact, enforces and works in harmony with the divine law. According to Grotius, human laws create the space within which men can exercise their liberty and live in a peaceful society.[100] To use a modern phrase, Grotius appears content to give man autonomy where there are no laws otherwise prescribing what he should do, and therefore offers an account of law where man's decision to contract and determine the terms of that contract are dealt with adequately already. Thus, in terms of Christian ethics and the disposal of that freedom so long as the human law did not prevent it, you were at liberty to pursue it. Indeed, to an extent, this also reflects his opinion when it comes to the form of civil government that individuals choose to adopt, saying in *The Rights of War and Peace*: 'But as there are several Ways of Living, some better than others, and every one may chuse which he pleases of all those Sorts; so a People may chuse what Form of Government they please.'[101] Therefore, when compared to Stair there are similarities: Stair too gives man freedom where the human law ends; but, as has been shown previously, matters do not stop there. Rather, Stair offers an account of human law which complements ecclesiastical claims of jurisdiction over Christian ethics. On this point, however, Grotius is far more resistant to, and bullish about protesting against, the power of spiritual authorities over individual decision-making. That is, Grotius is not framing his conception of liberty to fit with ecclesiastical authorities' strict catechisms, prescriptive instructions as to what to do with liberty emanating from theologians, ministers, or church authorities, or offering an account which accommodates the shaping of Christian ethics through ecclesiastical powers using civil authority.

Trade, Contracts, and Social Order

If this explains how Grotius reduced and limited the surveillance and role of the church within temporal affairs, including in areas of commerce, it does not

---

[98] Grotius and van Dam *Hugo Grotius, De Imperio Summarum Potestatum* (n 80) 225.
[99] Grotius and van Dam *Hugo Grotius, De Imperio Summarum Potestatum* (n 80) 225.
[100] Grotius 'Preliminary Discourse' (n 39).
[101] Grotius *The Rights of War* (n 3) 1.3.8.

explain how Grotius differs from Classical writers. However, upon examination, the first thing that becomes clear is that, in Classical literature, statements about free trade or commerce often related to foreign trade and communities or cities rather than the individual and their trading with other individuals. This is where Grotius and Stair, in different ways, depart from these otherwise commonplace statements regarding free trade: they drew upon the notion of free trade in their accounts of the law of nature and the origins of civil society, and they often did so in a new way. First, both Stair and Grotius had a positive attitude towards trade, commerce, and contracting. Second, they spoke of property and contracting as *distinctive* *features* forming part of a foundational structure of justice for society. This was to speak of individual interpersonal relationships, including contracting as forming part of the basis for civil order and political legitimacy. Third, neither had an individual-versus-state model of conceptualizing liberty, law, and contracting, which you find in later centuries: Grotius saw freedom as preceding the establishment of civil powers, whereas Stair had a notion of it coexisting with civil powers within a Godly society.

The language too changed in comparison to Classical literature. Grotius and Stair conceptualized in their respective works what was natural, necessary, and morally commendable into a language of individual politics, and structured natural law around interpersonal relations. Therefore, in different ways, each laid on top of a natural description of man and his needs or habits a framework of juridical concepts, such as liberty and right, which was a development within the natural law tradition. To say that man has a liberty to contract was the demarcation of the individual and his rights in contrast to something external to him, such as other men, the *polis*, or a king. In this process, human law found foundations beyond and prior to the sovereign's claims of authority, or a way to avoid the king's direct appeal to a divine right. To shape things in this manner is to situate what could be called the natural habits or needs of men into a language where the use of that liberty or the restriction of that liberty had to be justified and explained in terms of man's consent or otherwise. It fitted with and sustained the notion that man had a right against the ruling authority, and that infringements had to be explained.

In the seventeenth century, writers such Stair and Grotius sought to find a new discourse and language through which to describe civil society and its establishment, and, importantly, the place of the individual within the temporal political order. They did so through their different descriptions of what natural law was and its content. However, they each characterized man as, by nature, free, but that he was also in need of trade and commerce in order to survive and thrive. In different ways, this helped each writer to describe and justify a political order based on not only defence and peace, but also trade and commerce. As part of this process, legal concepts like a contract were used in connection with liberty to describe the fundamental rights of men. These natural law theories attached to private law doctrines, like contract or property, in such a manner that private law gained sophisticated political, philosophical, and theological explanations. Albeit these explanations were not seen as immediately judiciable or necessarily generative of a particular remedy in local courts, the understanding that man has an inherent right to contract is nonetheless part of the legal history of contractual thought, as much as it is part of the history of political or economic thought. Each writer characterized the place of natural law and its relationship to civil authority and human law within a society where theology, religion, and faith were central to the characterization of man, civil government, and his ethical decisions.

Origins of Civil Society, Natural Law, and Jurisdiction

Importantly, Grotius and Stair are positive about the role of commerce and contracting, and they frame it as foundational to justice and social order; however, Grotius, unlike Stair, offered an account of political communities which was not wholly dependent upon contentious theological premises. Indeed, Grotius was a Protestant, sympathetic to the Arminian doctrine, critical of puritanism and claims of religious supremacy, and he wished to give the utmost power to the civil authorities. Stair too was a Protestant, but of the Calvinist variety; he wished to limit the authority of the civil powers when it came to spiritual matters but also to find a balance between the spiritual and temporal authorities in establishing a Godly society. In that regard, Stair could be said to share a similar theological position to that of Jesuits, such as Francisco Suárez who sought to establish the place and role of religious authority within the life of an individual, which included giving guidance as to how your liberty to contract should be used. Grotius based his natural law account on the sociability of man and the ability of reason. He had a positive attitude about man's ability to act in accordance with God's design and create a civil society and human laws. Stair did not share the same confidence as Grotius in his ability to determine and articulate what natural law was beyond the basics, which he saw as imprinted upon man's heart, informed by man's conscience, confirmed in Scripture and cautiously guided by reason in particular instances. Far less agency was given to man, by Stair, in determining what natural law was when compared to Grotius. However, what Grotius did and what Stair emulated was to offer an account of political communities and social order founded on basic ideas of justice, including the notion of freedom to contract. This was an attempt to find another way through the religious turmoil which otherwise divided writers like Stair and Grotius.

Perfect and Imperfect Duties

Another important aspect of this new theory offered by Grotius was that it included the notion that there were natural rights which the civil authority should concern itself with and those which it did not. This was an important move in minimizing and restricting suspicions about the moral dubiety of trade found in medieval law, Christian teaching, and contemporary casuistry literature. That is, Grotius's conception of natural law could be termed as including a political and ethical division, which excluded a great deal of moralizing about the ethics and duties of trading. The political notion offered a limited sense of natural law: it gave men basic rights, which included a bare idea of freedom to trade and contract, but said very little about how this freedom should be directed or guided. It was to strip natural law down to very simple things, which were arguably unrelated to theological or personal ethics, but only civil order and the basic organization of a community, including the freedom to contract as you like. This was what civil powers should concern themselves with; to go further was to wander beyond the basic foundations of civil society. In doing so, Grotius created what could be called a second sense of natural law, which was related to personal ethics: who should one contract with, what should the terms of that contract be, should I allow a debt to go unpaid, should I be generous, and so on. Unlike the political sense of man's freedom to contract, this division created an ethical sense of what it meant to have contractual freedom, which could be tutored by man's sense of right and wrong. But, importantly, such things were beyond the remit of civil powers. In the moral philosophy which dominated Scotland and parts of Europe during the eighteenth century, this distinction was formulated in terms of perfect and imperfect duties—or, as Grotius termed it, negative and positive justice, the former being the domain of civil government, the latter being personal and relating to an individual's private sphere. Here is a modernistic notion that individuals ought to have a presumptive freedom when exercising their powers to contract: that is, contractual freedoms are predominantly private and personal, not a matter for the state. Stair subscribed to such a private-public division, but there is an important caveat which separates him from Grotius: the role of conscience, or the notion that man should use his liberty to bring glory to God.

Conscience, Contract, and Control

We have seen how Stair's view of human laws and civil authority in the *Institutions* promoted a conception of liberty relatively unhindered by ecclesiastical oversight. But he also offered an account of liberty which allowed for man to be instructed and for his conscience to be shaped by clergy, the church, and casuistry literature. Grotius, in contrast, was far less willing to offer the clergy a power over man's ethical decisions. It can therefore easily be overlooked how conscience plays a key role in Stair's account of freedom to contract. For Stair, the freedom to contract should be tutored, instructed, and shaped by pastors, clergy, and the church because it related to questions of salvation and Godly order. For Grotius, the role of the church in relation to man's conscience was to be greatly limited, as part of his project of minimizing theological and confessional accounts of civil society and human law. Stair was more tentative, looking for an account of society and human law in response to, on the one hand, claims of absolute sovereignty made by Stuart monarchs, and, on the other hand, the clergy's claim of Godly rule. In offering a new account, Stair nonetheless saw an important role for man's individual conscience together with a role for the church in cultivating that conscience. Liberty here joins the theological through the telos of seeking to bring glory to God (whether or not you were ultimately saved). Civil powers may have been sidelined, and trade and freedom championed, but this was done on the major premise that conscience played a governing role in how man used his freedom to contract.

Commerce before the Commercial Society

Grotius was far from the only writer in the seventeenth century to make these connections or to express a more positive attitude towards trade and commerce.[102] However, he is important because he attempted to give his ideas of contract and of commerce a prominent place within his description of natural law, yet with a minimal theological content. This stance is unsurprisingly mirrored in Stair's *Institutions* but with modifications.[103] Stair's conception of liberty also derives from natural law, but the norms governing contractual behaviour may be governed dualistically by the jurisdiction of both temporal and spiritual powers where the art of the jurist-theologian was to show how these powers would not encroach upon each other's rightful domain. That is, Stair may have limited the power and reach of human law to regulate individual trading, but he nonetheless did not expressly restrict the spiritual reach of the Church to guide and shape the conscience of an individual towards the glory of God. This was a Calvinist adaptation of Grotius's approach.

Conclusion

This chapter has not explored the wider politics of Stair or Grotius[104] with regard to commerce in an age of nationalism and empire, nor has it examined the historical or sociological significance of Grotius's or Stair's treatments of liberty within their respective, often troubled societies.[105] Rather, it has considered their theory-making on their own terms: as an analytical framework which connects liberty, trade, and contract with a natural law theory within the context of strong theological notions of how man should live his life. Grotius and Stair drew on classical and medieval traditions in their natural law theories but with a fresh focus on interpersonal relationships as the core site of human action and identity.[106] They used a language of rights supporting liberty to evoke a division between the spiritual and temporal authority. It is clear that Grotius and Stair's theories of contracting and liberty had political implications for the

---

[102] For summaries, see various entries in Nicholas Canny (ed), *The Oxford History of the British Empire: Volume 1* (OUP 1998); David Ormrod, *The Rise of Commercial Empires: England and the Netherlands in the Age of Mercantilism, 1650–1770* (CUP 2003); Tom Leng, 'Commercial Conflict and Regulation in the Discourse of Trade in Seventeenth-Century England' (2005) 48 (4) The Historical Journal 933–54; István Hont, *Jealousy of Trade: International Competition and the Nation-State in Historical Perspective* (CUP 2010).

[103] See Stair *Inst* 1.14. Here Stair describes barter and exchange as a 'mutual obligation of mankind' which should be encouraged by civil authorities, commonwealths, and nations around the world.

[104] For Grotius, see, for example: Martine van Ittersum, *Profit and Principle: Hugo Grotius, Natural Rights Theories and the Rise of Dutch Power in the East Indies, 1595–1615* (Brill 2006).

[105] For example: Henry S Maine, *Ancient Law: Its Connection with the Early History of Society, and its Relation to Modern Ideas* (1861) 109–66; Max Weber, *Wirtschaft und Gesellschaft. Grundriß der verstehenden Soziologie* (1922) in Gunter Roth and Claus Wittich (trs), *Max Weber, Economy and Society* (University California Press 1978), specifically 666–729; Roscoe Pound, 'Liberty of Contract' (1909) 18 Yale Law Journal 454–87; Léon Duguit, 'Collective Acts as Distinguished from Contracts' (1918) 27 Yale Law Journal 753–68.

[106] Benedict Kingsbury and Benjamin Straumann, 'The State of Nature and Commercial Sociability in Early Modern International Legal Thought' (2010) 31 Grotiana 22–43.

understanding of civil and spiritual powers in relation to not just contract law but private law more generally. They each sought to limit the scope, reach, and areas within which a civil or spiritual power could introduce laws without consideration of the basic rights to trade. It is this restraint of state and ecclesiastical coercion which could be said to connect these authors to eighteenth-century conceptions of contract, which define the right of an individual to contract as being central to political and legal order as well as the best path to prosperity. Stair and Grotius may have come to this conclusion in different ways to writers such as David Hume or Adam Smith, but the result of Grotius's theory (and Stair's Calvinist version) was to introduce a discourse conceptualizing the individual as someone with the right to own property and the right to trade as essential expressions of the right to liberty. Moreover, Grotius and Stair introduce a means by which to distinguish between different duties, natural and legal or the perfect and imperfect duties—distinctions we will explore next within eighteenth-century moral philosophy. Stair's translation of Grotian ideas into the law of Scotland turns out be both subtle, and momentous.[107] Inspired by Grotius and possibly derivative of him, Stair ensured that Grotius's naturalist freedom of contract could be fitted within basic Calvinist premises and so take root within Scottish legal thinking.

---

[107] Neil MacCormick, 'Stair as Analytical Jurist' in David M Walker (ed), *Stair Tercentenary Studies*, vol 33 (Stair Society 1981) 194–95.

9

The Reception of Stair's Contractual Thought

This chapter examines how Stair's contractual thought relates to other accounts of contracting given in the late seventeenth and early eighteenth century. There may be several ways to investigate the reception of an author's ideas,[1] but the approach taken in this chapter is to examine the contractual thought of Stair in comparison to George Mackenzie (1636/8–1691) and Gershom Carmichael (1672–1729). Both of these writers were influential in Scotland during their lifetimes and in the years that followed.[2] Although the contractual thought of Mackenzie has never been systematically compared to Stair,[3] the general contrast between these two jurists' legal thought is well known and the differences relatively well documented.[4] However, Stair is not often compared to Carmichael. One reason why is that this involves adopting a wider conception of what might usually be considered to be legal thought. Carmichael for some is a moral philosopher, while Stair is a jurist. However, Scots lawyers and moral philosophers of the age did not make a sharp distinction between what we might call

---

[1] For example, Blackie's analysis generally considers *dictum*: John W G Blackie, 'Stair's Later Reputation as a Jurist' in David M Walker (ed), *Stair Tercentenary Studies*, vol 33 (Stair Society 1981) 207–37. Alternatively, Hogg compares Stair juristic work, including Lord Kames (1696–1782), John Erskine (1695–1768), and George Bell (1770–1843): Martin Hogg, 'Perspectives on Contract Theory from a Mixed Jurisdiction' (2009) 29 (4) Oxford Journal of Legal Studies 643–67. Another approach is to track various developments in legal education and associated institutions: John W Cairns, 'Introduction' in John W Cairns (ed), *Enlightenment, Legal Education and Critique*, vol 2 (Edinburgh University Press 2017). Generally, the approach taken here is mindful of what Dunn has described as a mixture between the examination of ideas and their context: John M Dunn, 'The Identity of the History of Ideas' in John M Dunn, *Political Obligation in its Historical Context* (CUP 1980).

[2] On Carmichael, see James Moore and Michael Silverthorne, 'Gershom Carmichael and the Natural Jurisprudence Tradition in Eighteenth-Century Scotland' in István Hont and Michael Ignatieff (eds), *Wealth and Virtue* (CUP 1983) 73–87; James Moore, 'Natural Rights in the Scottish Enlightenment' in Mark Goldie and Robert Wokler (eds), *The Cambridge History of Eighteenth-Century Political Thought* (CUP 2006) 291–316. On Mackenzie, see John W Cairns 'The Formation of the Scottish Legal Mind in the Eighteenth Century: Themes of Humanism and Enlightenment in the Admission of Advocates' in Neil MacCormick and Peter Birks (eds), *The Legal Mind: Essays for Tony Honore* (OUP 1986) 253–77; John W Cairns 'The Moveable Text of Mackenzie: Bibliographical Problems for the Scottish Concept of Institutional Writing' in John W Cairns and Olivia F Robinson (eds), *Critical Studies in Ancient Law, Comparative Law and Legal History* (Hart 2001) 235–48.

[3] Although see Holligan's analysis of Stair's conception of restitution, Bonnie Holligan, 'Ownership and Obligation: Restitution, Vindication and the Recovery of Moveables in Stair's *Institutions*' (2017) 21 (2) Edinburgh Law Review 169–91.

[4] Hector L MacQueen, 'Mackenzie's *Institutions* in Scottish Legal History' (1984) 29 Journal of the Law Society of Scotland 498–501; John D Ford, 'Stair's Title "Of Liberty and Servitude"' in Andrew D E Lewis and David J Ibbetson (eds), *The Roman Law Tradition* (CUP 1994) 135–58; John W Cairns, 'The Civil Law Tradition in Scottish Legal Thought' in David L Carey Miller and Reinhard Zimmermann (eds), *The Civilian Tradition and Scots Law* (Duncker & Humblot 1997) 207–12; Clare Jackson, 'Natural Law and the Construction of Political Sovereignty in Early Modern Scotland' in Ian Hunter and David Saunders (eds), *Natural Law and Civil Sovereignty* (Palgrave 2002) 155–69; John D Ford, *Law and Opinion in Scotland during the Seventeenth Century* (Hart 2007) 473–573; Olivia F Robinson, 'Law, Morality and Sir George Mackenzie' in Hector L MacQueen (ed), *Miscellany Six*, vol 54 (Stair Society 2009) 11–28.

Contract before the Enlightenment. Stephen Bogle, Oxford University Press. © Stephen Bogle 2023.
DOI: 10.1093/oso/9780192884961.003.0010

today the positive law of Scotland and its moral or normative justification.[5] For most, consideration of the rules and doctrines of the law in Scotland, or indeed any legal system, was only one part of understanding the nature of the law applied in Scotland or within any given national jurisdiction. Grasping this is also vital to understanding the type of natural law theory which emerged in northern Europe during the seventeenth and eighteenth centuries and the natural law jurisprudence of writers such as Carmichael.[6] Many lawyers and philosophers in the eighteenth century understood the law of Scotland to be a specific expression of universal principles of the law of nature, including idealized conceptions of the law relating to contracts and promises.[7] In the immediate years following the publication of Stair's *Institutions of the Laws of Scotland* (*Institutions*), mainstream consideration of natural law was often legalistic in nature, whether it was discussed by a lawyer or a moral philosopher.[8] To these lawyers and philosophers, studying contracts or promises included an examination of the underlying principles or historical causes of the law of contract. As Haakonssen explains, this examination of juristic concepts, such as contracting, was a normative exercise and connected to some form of natural law theory, whether it be realist, voluntarist, rationalist, or utilitarian.[9] Stair advocated seeking out the causes, principles, and origins of laws, which is well captured in his contractual thought; and it is an approach that Carmichael and others continued into the eighteenth century. To explore the reception of Stair is therefore to explore the reception of this methodology and approach to natural law.

Mackenzie

On the basis of printing alone, Mackenzie's approach to the law of Scotland appears to have been the most popular and influential student text. He was by far the most published legal author in the period between 1681 and 1762.[10] In his life, he saw five treatises on the subject of law published,[11] and numerous of his essays on legal topics were published after his death in 1691.[12] Mackenzie's *Institutions* in the end went through

---

[5] Neil MacCormick, 'Law and Enlightenment' in R H Campbell and Andrew Skinner (eds), *The Origins and Nature of the Scottish Enlightenment* (John Donald 1982) 150–66.

[6] Knud Haakonssen, 'Protestant Natural Law Theory: A General Interpretation' in Natalie Brender and Larry Krasnoff (eds), *New Essays on the History of Autonomy* (CUP 2004) 92–109.

[7] Peter Stein, 'The General Notions of Contract and Property in Eighteenth-Century Scottish Thought' [1963] Juridical Review 1–13.

[8] See Haakonssen 'Protestant Natural Law Theory' (n 6) 92–109.

[9] Knud Haakonssen, *Natural Law and Moral Philosophy: from Grotius to the Scottish Enlightenment* (CUP 1996) 15–61.

[10] For discussion, Cairns 'The Moveable Text Of Mackenzie' (n 2) 235–48.

[11] (1) George Mackenzie, *Pleadings in Some Remarkable Cases before the Supreme Courts of Scotland since the Year 1661* (George Swintoun, James Glen and Thomas Brown 1673); (2) George Mackenzie, *Observations upon the 28. (i.e. 18.) Act, 23. Parl. K. James VI. against dispositions made in defraud of creditors, &c.* (His Majesties Printers 1675); (3) George Mackenzie, *The Laws and Customes of Scotland, in Matters Criminal* (James Glen 1678); (4) George Mackenzie, *The Institutions of the Law of Scotland* (John Reid 1684); (5) George Mackenzie, *Observations on the Acts of Parliament, made by King James the First, King James the Second, King James the Third, King James the Fourth, King James the Fifth, Queen Mary, King James the Sixth, King Charles the First, King Charles the Second* (Andrew Anderson 1686).

[12] George Mackenzie, *The Works of that Eminent and Learned Lawyer, Sir George Mackenzie*, vols 1 and 2 (James Watson 1716–22). Volume 1 of the 1716 collection contains within the open pages a collection of

eight editions,[13] with the last being published in 1758.[14] Of course, Lord Bankton sought to emulate Stair in the 1750s, with his *An Institute of the Laws of Scotland*,[15] which is significant; but, when placed within the context of legal publishing and education of the eighteenth century, it was Mackenzie's approach that appears to have been the most influential. Therefore, Mackenzie is central to any consideration of the reception of Stair's approach to the law of contract.

Natural law and the known way of law

Mackenzie represents an affirmation of what he calls the known way of Justinian's *Institutes* in his own *Institutions*, published in 1684.[16] Although Mackenzie's *Institutions* should be understood as an elementary student textbook,[17] it is still profitable to examine it for an indication of Mackenzie's contractual thought. For, when compared with Carmichael's equivalent textbook also produced for students, Mackenzie's style, approach, and language suggest that his elementary approach is not merely because he envisaged his *Institutions* being used by relative novices, but also because it represents a more general point about how the law of Scotland should be understood. Reading Mackenzie's account of the law of contract in the *Institutions* alongside his other works, such as the *Observations on the Acts of Parliament*[18] from 1687 and his unpublished *Discourse on the 4 First Chapters of the Digest*[19] (*Discourse*) composed at the end of his life, suggests that he had an overview of the law which he wished to express to students through his *Institutions*.

Mackenzie did not offer a sophisticated account of natural law and did not attempt to explain individual rules of Scots law in terms of their natural law origins. In many respects, his natural law theory is medieval; that is, divine law, the law of nature, the law of nations, and the civil law of Scotland are coexistent and apply to different aspects of society and jurisdictions of human life. On his account, there is no hierarchy where a higher level corrects a lower level, but rather there are different jurisdictions of competence whereby different aspects of the law of nature apply.[20] Mackenzie did

---

letters, poems, and testimonials written about Mackenzie. These letters display a huge degree of admiration towards Mackenzie as a jurist.

[13] George Mackenzie, *The Institutions of the Law of Scotland* (1st edn, John Reid 1684) (403 pages); 2nd edn (John Reid 1688) (209 pages); 3rd edn (Thomas Broun 1699) (141 pages); 4th edn (John Vallange 1706) (263 pages); 5th edn (William Brown & Co 1719) (561 pages); 6th edn (William Brown & Co 1723) (347 pages); 7th edn (William Brown 1730) (339 pages); 8th edn (E & J Robertsons 1758) (325 pages).

[14] George Mackenzie, *The Institutions of the Law of Scotland* (9th edn, E & J Robertsons 1758).

[15] Andrew MacDowall, Lord Bankton, *An Institute of the Laws of Scotland in Civil Rights: With Observations upon the Agreement or Diversity between Them and the Laws of England. In four books* (A Kincaid & A Donaldson 1751–53).

[16] George Mackenzie, *The Institutions of the Law of Scotland* (John Reid 1684) dedication.

[17] John W Cairns, 'Institutional Writings in Scotland Reconsidered' (1983) 4 Journal of Legal History 76–117.

[18] Mackenzie *Observations on the Acts of Parliament* (n 11).

[19] George Mackenzie, *A Discourse on the 4 First Chapters of the Digest to Show the Excellence and Usefulness of the Civil Law*, BL Add Ms 18236.

[20] Merio Scattola, 'Before and After Natural Law' in Tim J Hochstrasser and Peter Schröder (eds), *Early Modern Natural Law Theories: Context and Strategies in Early Enlightenment* (Kluwer 2003) 30, 10–11.

not seek to offer a theory of the common principles of human law: the civil or positive law of Scotland was the will of the sovereign.[21] Mackenzie generally follows the traditional formula of Justinian's *Institutes*,[22] but innovates in how he describes the law of nations or *ius gentium*, saying that the law of nations should be divided into those laws which are 'dictated by right Reason' and those laws which countries agree upon, such as 'promises, or contracts, the liberty of Commerce, the ransoming of Prisoners, securities of Ambassadors'.[23] He develops this further in his *Discourse*, saying that:[24]

> From these same Principles also I conclude that though the Consent of Nations be a general Measure by which men determine what is the Law of Nature—*omnia autem in re consensus omnium Gentius Lex Naturæ putanda est* which made the Civil Law distinguish—*Ius Gentium in primævam quod Naturalis Ratio inter omnes-homines constituit Et serudiarium*, which is made of Principles derived from these first Principles, yet we must certainly go higher in seeking the pure foundation of the Laws of Nature.

Nevertheless, there is very little in Mackenzie's *Institutions* or *Discourse* to suggest that he was concerned to offer a justification or exploration of how positive law relates to the nature of people or society. For Mackenzie, it was created by parliament and by the will of the sovereign. It was coexistent with the law of nature. There was no need to explore further. Unlike Stair, he does not endorse the approach of François Douaren, or Hugo Grotius who cast aside the traditional Justinianic formula and sought to place law upon a rational basis. There is no extended discussion of concepts such as liberty, or obligation, and how such ideas relate to the law of nature.

Opening his *Institutions*, Mackenzie emulates the first sentences of Justinian's *Institutes*: 'Justice, is a constant and perpetual Will, and Inclination to give every Man what is due to him.' He continues: 'The Law is a Science, which teacheth us to do Justice.'[25] In comparison to Stair, it is evident that Mackenzie does not feel his reader needs any further explanation or examination of what justice means or how the perpetual will towards justice relates to positive law or indeed divine law. Rather, Mackenzie continues by introducing the divisions between the law of nature, the law of nations, and the civil law or municipal law. Explaining these concepts of Roman law briskly, he proceeds to explain to his readers that there is a reliance in Scotland upon the traditions and texts of Roman law, saying the 'Romans having studied with great Exactness the Principles of Equity and Justice their Emperor Justinian did cause digest all their Laws into one Body, which is now called by most polite Nations (for its Excellency) the Civil Law.' Accordingly, 'it has great Influence in Scotland, except

---

[21] Mackenzie *Discourse* (n 19) ff 18–20. For discussion, see MacQueen, 'Mackenzie's *Institutions* in Scottish Legal History' (n 4); Cairns 'The Civil Law Tradition in Scottish Legal Thought' (n 4) 207–12.

[22] For discussion, see Alan Watson, *Roman Law and Comparative Law* (University of Georgia Press 1991) 217–20.

[23] Mackenzie *Institutions* 1.1.1. For comment on this section, see Alan Watson, 'Transformations of Law: Justinian's Institutes 1.2 pr., 1; Stair; Mackenzie' in Hector L MacQueen (ed), *Miscellany Four*, vol 49 (Stair Society 2002), 243–54.

[24] Mackenzie *Discourse* (n 19) ff 6–7.

[25] Mackenzie *Institutions* 1.1.1–2.

where our own express Laws or Customs have receded from it'.[26] In his style, arrangement, language, and description of the law, Mackenzie reasserted a more traditional and familiar approach to the arrangement and description of private law in Scotland.[27]

Structure and language

In comparison to Stair, one of the most noticeable things is the structure Mackenzie adopts in his *Institutions*. Watson has suggested that one of Mackenzie's aims was to correct Stair's structure. Stair had put forward this structure in his original manuscripts from the 1660s, and it was repeated in his 1681 edition of his *Institutions*—that is, three books.[28] Stair added a fourth book in the second edition of 1693, but it was not his original intention. Watson suggests that Stair did this in response to Mackenzie's implied criticism.[29] MacQueen has also suggested that there is 'some internal evidence that in part at least Mackenzie's work was a reaction against rather than a derivation from or an "epitome" of Stair'.[30] He draws attention to the dedication Mackenzie gave in the *Institutions*, saying: 'the natural and easie way of writing [institutions] is by going from the first principle to a second and from that to a third, the admired method of Euclid in his elements, though much neglected by all who have written Institutions of Law'.[31] As alluded to earlier, Mackenzie says in his dedication: 'I have often observed, that more Lawyers are ignorant for not understanding the first Principles, than for not having read many Books, as it is not the having travelled long, but having *known the way*, which brings a man to his Lodging soon, and securely'.[32] Stair's *Institutions*, in comparison to Mackenzie's, make many references to different jurists and texts. It is a long book too, whereas Mackenzie's is short. Mackenzie explains the private law of Scotland, including the law of contract, briefly, whereas Stair explains the private law of Scotland with reference to the law of nature, other nations, other jurists, and decisions of the Court of Session; that is, he explains things at length. In that way, it could also be said that Mackenzie was keen to return to the known way of Justinian's *Institutes* and demonstrate that this was the correct model and structure by which to introduce the law of Scotland, including the law applying to contracting. Stair's approach was novel and sought to introduce a new system.[33]

---

[26] Mackenzie *Institutions* 1.1.7.

[27] As described in Chapter 1. However, as Cairns explains when Mackenzie's *Institutions* are placed against the context of legal education in Dutch universities of the late seventeenth century, he is adopting a new method of teaching of Roman law through a customary compendium. In that sense, Mackenzie's *Institutions* is an example of a *methodus compendiaria* of Justinian's *Institutions*, which was an innovation in itself: John W Cairns, 'Teaching Criminal Law in Early Eighteenth-Century Scotland: Collegia and Compendia' (2012) 20 (1) Fundamina 90–99.

[28] See further Chapter 5; also Alan Watson, 'Some Notes of Mackenzie's *Institutions* and the European Legal Tradition' (1989) 16 Ius Commune 303–13.

[29] Alan Watson, *The Making of the Civil Law* (Harvard University Press 1981) 30–31.

[30] MacQueen, 'Mackenzie's *Institutions* in Scottish Legal History' (n 4) 499.

[31] Mackenzie *Institutions* Dedication.

[32] Mackenzie *Institutions* (emphasis added).

[33] Indeed, as discussed, Stair's contemporaries possibly viewed his approach as distinctive: Ford *Law and Opinion* (n 4) 87 ff. John Lauder, Lord Fountainhall, refers to 'Stair's System' in 1677: David Laing (ed), *Historical Notices of Scottish Affairs, selected from the Manuscripts of Sir John Lauder of Fountainhall, Bart*, vol 1 (Bannatyne Club 1848) 134.

Unsurprisingly, Mackenzie's *Institutions* is arranged over four books: (1) Persons (including Law and Government), (2) Real Rights, (3) Personal Rights (including Wills and Succession), and (4) Actions, including Crimes. In Book 3, he gives the classic definition of an obligation found in Justinian's *Institutes*, namely a legal tie whereby we are bound to pay or perform a thing. Echoing the *Institutes*, he speaks of a division between natural and civil obligations, which is suggestive that he does not take the same approach as Stair.[34] He says some obligations are natural 'because they arise from the Principles of right Reason, or Laws of Nature', whereas civil obligations 'arise from positive Laws, or Municipal Customs'.[35] He does say 'a contract is an agreement entered into by several persons, inducing an Obligation', but this serves more as a commonplace gloss rather than an analysis of the general features and single cause of a contract, which can be found in Stair's *Institutions*. On Mackenzie's account, contracts arise by thing, word, writ, or consent, which is the structure around which he discusses individual contracts. When describing each of these contracts, Mackenzie is concise and at points terse rather than discursive and explanatory. Where Stair uses terms or concepts which were unfamiliar to legal writing in Scotland, such as 'the will', 'conventional obligations', and 'obediential obligations', Mackenzie's language, terminology, and definition are familiar and recognizable. Stair used terms such as 'offer', 'acceptance', and 'conditional obligation'. Again, in his dedication, he says: 'in all which I have proceeded, building always one Principle upon another; and expressing everything in the Terms of the Civil Law, or in Stile or Ours respectively; so that if any Man understand full this Little Book . . '. Although Stair too used the language of civil law, he did not do so exclusively, but rather intermingled it with scholastic, theological, and political terminology.

Promising and *nuda pacta*

Promises and *nuda pacta* are enforceable, according to Mackenzie's account. But, unlike Stair, as explained in Chapter 4, Mackenzie presents this as an exception rather than as a plain example of natural law's expression within the law of Scotland. However, this should not suggest that Mackenzie did not think that pactions or promises were not enforceable according to the law of nature. In his *Discourse*, he says: 'by the Law of Nature, Pactions should be observed', but he goes on to say: 'yet by the Civil Law and the Law of England there arises no action upon them, exception the Paction or Promise to be founded on a reasonable cause'. Again, however, it is notable that he actually considers the enforcement of a pact or promise, namely a *nuda pacta*, as an exception to civil law or Roman law, which for him was the embodiment of 'the principles of Reason into a Body of positive law' which was inspired by 'God Almighty' so that 'Nations might have common principles wherein they agree'. Mackenzie therefore accepts the enforcement of pacts as being according to the law of nature, but presents the traditional approach of Roman law and its departure from the law of nature as the preferred approach, something which embodied a legal wisdom found in the *Digest*.

---

[34] See J A C Thomas, *Textbook on Roman Law* (North-Holland Publishing Co 1976) 236 ff.
[35] Mackenzie *Institutions* 3.1.2.

In direct contradiction to Stair, Mackenzie suggests that the approach of the law of Scotland departs from the common approach of nations who follow the traditional Roman approach. Mackenzie, in both the *Discourse* and the *Institutions*, tells his reader that promises and pacts are now enforceable 'with us', suggesting some frustration with regard to this innovation within the tradition of Roman law and the common-sense approach of the *Digest*. However, when discussing this in the *Discourse* or the *Institutions*, he adds the important caveat that they are only enforceable if proved by a writ or oath.[36] In taking this approach, he tries to incorporate his account of pacts and promises in the *Institutions* by including this within his discussion of obligations created by writs. No attempt is made to explain this other than as an example of a customary amendment to the approach of Roman law, which Scotland had thus far followed. However, the enforcement of promises does not sit well within Mackenzie's account. In his *Observations*, Mackenzie explains further:[37]

> That in our practice; all Writs exceeding an hundred pounds, are Interpreted to be Writs of importance, and so to need Witnesses, January ult, 1623. But if any sum be to need annualy pay'd, that Writ whereby it is to be pay'd, requires Witnesses, though never so small, because yearly Prestations may arise to a considerable sum. July 4 1632. And though sums above 100 pounds, require Writs; Yet intromission with victual or any thing else, probable by witnesses, as all other things consisting in *facto are*; as also intromission with uncoyne'd Money or Silver in mass, is provable by Witnesses, though exceeding 100 pounds, *But promises & nuda emissio verborum though for less sums than 100 pounds, are only probable by Writ*, because Bystanders may mistake the position and force of Words, January 19. 1672 Douchar con. Brown.

Mackenzie starts by advising that all writs exceeding £100 must be witnessed, and clarifies that this includes annual contracts which otherwise fall under £100. If there has been a transfer of a thing, money, or anything else corporeal and the value is over £100, then technically, according to Mackenzie, there is no obligation unless the transaction was executed in a writ. In some instances, however, witnesses can be used to prove that there was a transfer of a thing or payment in money, even if the transaction's value exceeds £100. He says 'promises & nuda emission verborum ... are only probable by Writ' if they are under the value of £100. This is effectively the same rules of law which Stair described in his *Institutions* and which are examined in Chapter 1. But there are several notable things about how Mackenzie approaches this which are different from Stair. Significantly, Mackenzie acknowledges that *nuda pacta* or promises are legally significant when they are provable by writ, but does not suggest that they create an obligation. Mackenzie presents this as a customary change to the law, which is implicitly endorsed by the 1579 Act. Stair presented this change as an example of Scots law edging closer to the divinely ordained natural law. Mackenzie presents this new practice of enforcing a promise and *nudum pactum* as an additional means by which a party may be compelled to perform, not as an obligation. Returning to the *Institutions*, this explains why for Mackenzie the enforcement of promises was

---

[36] Mackenzie *Institutions* 3.2.3.
[37] Mackenzie *Observations* (n 11) 192–93 (emphasis added).

untidy. First, he does not make explicit the status of *nuda pacta* or a promise. Second, Mackenzie needs to clarify the distinction between probative and constitutive writs, which introduces a discussion of process and evidence to a discussion about the formation of obligations. This uneasiness represents a broader difference between Stair and Mackenzie regarding the authority of Roman law.

Roman law and legal science

Mackenzie went further than Stair in appraising the authority of Roman law,[38] and this in turn shaped his understanding of the law applying to contracting. Roman law had authority, according to Mackenzie, because it was received into the law of Scotland by custom, which was then endorsed by the sovereign in the form of statute.[39] For Stair, it only held authority when it replicated equity and was thereafter received into the customary law of Scotland through decisions of the Court of Session.[40] In his *Discourse*, Mackenzie says:

> it seems that God Almighty did inspire the Romans to digest the principles of Reason into a Body of positive Law to the End Nations might have common principles wherein they might agree, and it is therefore called by the French and us and by most of all other Nations, the Common Law.[41]

Cairns has also drawn attention to Mackenzie's inaugural oration of the Advocates' Library, where he said: 'Of books on Roman Law, pride of place must be given to the text itself and its various editions, since on it both our calling and our library are based.'[42] He goes on to declare: 'It is a divine achievement, which we owe more to Heaven than to Rome, vouchsafed to us on earth to be a pattern to legislators and an arbiter among the races of men.'[43]

Stair does not share Mackenzie's admiration for the science of Justinian's *Institutes*. He said the 'distinction [between obligations within Roman law] insinuates no reason of the cause or rise of these distinct obligations, as is requisite in a good distinct division.'[44] He goes on to say: 'therefore, they may be more appositely divided, according

---

[38] Cairns 'The Civil Law Tradition in Scottish Legal Thought' (n 4) 191–220. Also see Holligan, who demonstrates how this affects their respective approaches to restitution of moveable property: Holligan 'Ownership and Obligation' (n 3) 171–92.

[39] In his *Discourse*, Mackenzie explains that the 'Old Customs of Scotland are originally derived from the Roman Law in what Concerns moveable; From the Feudal [*sic*] in what Concerns heritage, and the Cannon, in what Concern Ecclesiastical [*sic*] Matters.' He goes on: these 'Customs have been [*sic*] much augmented by the Books of Regiam Majestatem ... [*sic*] a writ by the Command of King Malcolm 2nd ... which was afterwards much augmented by our own Lawyers'. Mackenzie *Discourse* (n 19) f16.

[40] Stair *Inst* 1.1.12.

[41] Mackenzie *Discourse* (n 19) f18. For discussion, see MacQueen, 'Mackenzie's *Institutions*' (n 4) 498–501; Cairns 'The Civil Law Tradition in Scottish Legal Thought' (n 4) 204; Ford *Law and Opinion* (n 4) 498–507, 524–39.

[42] George Mackenzie, *Oratio Inauguralis* (J H Loudun tr, first published in 1689, Edinburgh Bibliographical Society 1946) 278. Cairns, however, suggests that Mackenzie's 'approach to the authority of civil law [Roman law] in Scotland was mixed.' See Cairns 'The Civil Law Tradition in Scottish Legal Thought' (n 4) 211.

[43] Mackenzie *Oratio Inauguralis* (n 42) 278.

[44] Stair *Inst* 1.1.23.

to the principle or original from whence they flow, as in obligations obediential, and by engagement, or natural and conventional'. Therein follows his definition of conventional obligations, which are 'put upon men by their own will ... such as we are bound to perform solely by our obedience to God'.[45] Stair does, of course, feel it is necessary to explain how the Roman categories relate to his 'more appositely divided' description. Therefore, despite saying lawyers in Scotland no longer follow the Roman division, he reluctantly acknowledges the Roman approach before entering into a lengthy discussion, saying: 'This so much ... for clearing this Matter, their Contracts were four kinds, either perfect by Things, Words, Writ or sole consent'.[46] From this point on, Stair discusses the law in Scotland applying to contracts using the Justinianic division of contracts—but the order is important.

Mackenzie has no hesitation in adopting the Justinianic structure, nor does he give a detailed analysis of contracts and their origins in the law of nature; rather, he starts with a division and definition: 'Obligations arising from Contracts are divided and distinguished according as they are perfected, either by the Sole Consent of the Contractors, or by the Intervention, or Tradition of Things, Or lastly By Word or Writ'.[47] Stair says, 'Pactions, contracts, covenants, and agreements, are synonymous terms ... according to the recent customs of this and other nations; so that it will be unnecessary to trace the many subtilties and differences amongst pactions and contracts in Roman law'.[48] Conventional obligations are created by the will of man; the tradition of things, the use of words, and completion of writs are a mere mode of expression of the will.[49] Nevertheless, Stair retains the nomenclature of different types of contract but the reader is in no doubt: there is a general notion of contract of which these are examples.[50] In essence, Stair's basic account of these contracts does not vary from Mackenzie in that he discusses the same contracts, yet as has been shown in previous chapters, his approach is very different in style. For example, whereas Mackenzie describes this as 'that remarkable Division of Contracts', Stair describes the division of contracts with a degree of frustration: 'the many subtleties and differences amongst pactions and Contract in the Civil law'.[51] As Stair turns to look at loan, commodatum, and bills of exchange,[52] and then to address mandate,[53] deposit,[54] sale,[55] location,[56] and society,[57] he says: 'Having thus treated of contracts in general in the preceding title, we come now to particular contracts'.[58] On Stair's analysis, the Roman law is merely divided up into competent parts which express a general overarching principle of natural law. Yet it is evident for Mackenzie not only that he wanted to return to the

---

[45] Stair *Inst* 1.3.3.
[46] Stair *Inst* 1.10.11.
[47] Mackenzie *Institutions* 3.1.5.
[48] Stair *Inst* 1.10.10.
[49] Stair *Inst* 1.10.10.
[50] Stair *Inst* 1.10.13.
[51] Stair *Inst* 1.10.10.
[52] Stair *Inst* 1.11.1.
[53] Stair *Inst* 1.12.1.
[54] Stair *Inst* 1.13.1.
[55] Stair *Inst* 1.14.1.
[56] Stair *Inst* 1.15.1.
[57] Stair *Inst* 1.16.1.
[58] Stair *Inst* 1.11.1.

'known way' of Roman law, starting from the competent parts and going no further, but also that he considered there was much to admire in the Roman classification of contracts.[59]

Law and theology

Mackenzie wished for the study of law to be separated from a study of philosophy, theology, or natural law. He believed that these subjects should be studied but should not be woven together with the study of law. In 1663, and again in 1684, Mackenzie made a strong argument against theological and religious ideas and teaching which wandered beyond that which for him was its appropriate domain.[60] For Mackenzie, in the years prior to the Restoration, religion and theology had gone far beyond their rightful place, not just in urging men to take up arms against the king, but also in how they were used in discourse to justify otherwise bloody acts.[61] In the opening, 'Address to the Fanatics of all Sects and Sorts', of his *Religious Stoic*, he says: 'I am none of those who acknowledge no Temples beside those of their Heads. And I am of Opinion, that such as think that they have a Church within their own Breast, should likewise believe their Heads are Steeples, and so [we] should provide them with Bells.'[62] He goes on to argue that 'The God (who loves us all infinitely better than any one of us doth another) leaves us, upon our own hazard, a freedom in our choice' but, despite this, 'poor miscreants compel one another, denying to our Fellow-creatures that Freedom which he allows all the Creation.'[63] Mackenzie said that 'this makes me apt to believe, that if Laws and Law-givers did not make Heretics vain, by taking too much notice of their Extravagancies, the World should be no more troubled with these, than they are with the Chimera's of Alchemists and Philosophers.'[64] He later bemoans the argumentation of Presbyterian polemics as proceeding 'by the curiosity of School-men and the bigotry of Tub-preachers' and 'is now formed into the Body of Divinity'.[65]

Mackenzie's critique continues. Presbyterian pulpits, he says, have become 'either a Bar, whereat secular quarrels, are with passion pleaded, or a stage whereon revenge is, by Satryes satisfied; or a School-chair, from which unintelligible questions are mysteriously debated'.[66] Mackenzie was gravely concerned that the boundaries between law

---

[59] Mackenzie *Discourse* (n 19) f54.

[60] For a discussion of Mackenzie's religious views, see Clare Jackson, 'Religious Latitude, Secular Theology and Sir Thomas Browne's Influence in George Mackenzie's *Religio Stoici* (1663)' (2014) 29 The Seventeenth Century 73–94. Also see David Allan, ' "In the Bosome of a Shaddowie Grove": Sir George Mackenzie and the Consolations of Retirement' (1999) 25 History of European Ideas 251–73; Giovanni Gellera, 'Pride Aside: James Dundas as a Stoic Christian' (2019) 17 (2) Journal of Scottish Philosophy 157.

[61] George Mackenzie, *Religio Stoici: Or, A Short Discourse on These Several Subjects . . .* (R Broun 1663).

[62] Mackenzie, *Religio Stoici* (n 61) ii. Jackson suggests that Mackenzie contributed to a new-found culture of religious tolerance during the Restoration period, which transformed 'former divisions between Episcopalians and Presbyterians were, to some extent, redefined along lines whereby the preservation of civil order was ultimately accorded a higher priority than religious orthodoxy': Clare Jackson, *Restoration Scotland: Politics, Religion and Ideas* (Boydell 2003) 169; see Chs 6 and 7 passim.

[63] Mackenzie *Religio Stoici* (n 61) v.

[64] Mackenzie *Religio Stoici* (n 61) iv.

[65] Mackenzie *Religio Stoici* (n 61) 22.

[66] Mackenzie *Religio Stoici* (n 61) 168–69.

and theology had been blurred by radical Presbyterians. He argued that, in the years prior to the Restoration, passions had ruled men's reason and that lawmakers had been too eager to listen to religious fanatics.[67] Mackenzie warned that it was dangerous for the Church to 'encroach' upon the 'Laws of the State', as one would thereby trample on people's liberties. Mackenzie surely has in mind here, inter alia, the Covenanting ministers who urged the hanging of Sir Robert Spottiswood, Lord Dunipace (1596–1646), on 20 January 1646—or even the radicals of the 1649 Parliament who 'zealously' sought 'godly rule'—and, of course, those implicated in the execution of Charles I. None of this is to say that Mackenzie was in any way advocating a secular vision of legal education. In his *Discourse*, he says for example: 'I may conclude that no Man can be a true and profound Lawyer except he acknowledge the being of a God, and an immortality of the Soul.'[68] However, he was very clear that the study of law and a knowledge of the law of Scotland did not require an exploration of theology or elaborate natural law systems.[69]

Stair was far from being a religious fanatic,[70] but Mackenzie may well have understood Stair to be a 'philosopher' or even a 'School-man' rather than a learned lawyer who could be a reliable guide to the law of Scotland or its foundations. Mackenzie would have known that Stair had served on the Radical Parliament's Law Commission of 1649, which was 'zealously desirous for the glory of God, the good of his people and for the furtherance of the administration of justice within this kingdom to have as far as possible may be by the blessing of God'.[71] He may have read Stair's *Institutions* and considered the opening passages as being too sectarian and theological. It is possible that he felt Stair had listened too much to the religious and theological debates of fanatics and risked too much by offering a Calvinist natural law justification for the law of Scotland, including the law of contract. In Mackenzie's *Discourse*, he too offers an account of natural law which could be said to be broadly Calvinist, but he does not seek to mix it together with his account of the positive law of Scotland. Nor does he wish to give an overly theistic account. Rather, he appears to have understood that knowledge of law and following learned jurists was a far better guide to law and its equity. He explains in his dedication to the *Institutions* that he has offered a simple account of the law of Scotland, going on to say: 'Natural Reason, and Thinking, will easily supply much of what is diffused, through our many Volumes of Treatise, and Decisions'. But he also makes clear in his *Discourse* that he would much prefer the development of law to be directed by jurists advising the lawmakers, rather than judges or statesmen making law without such advice:[72]

---

[67] Mackenzie *Religio Stoici* (n 61) 168–90.

[68] Mackenzie *Discourse* (n 19) f8.

[69] For further elaboration of why Mackenzie may have thought the study of Roman law in of itself was sufficient, see Cairns 'The Formation of the Scottish Legal Mind in the Eighteenth Century' (n 2). Cairns also makes reference to Kelley's argument that within a particular strand of legal humanism: 'the study of law, more than any other field, represented an encyclopaedia, a total *Weltanschauung*, expressed concretely in various philosophical systems modelled on classical jurisprudence.' Donald R Kelley, *The Beginning of Ideology: Consciousness and Society in the French Reformation* (CUP 1981) 186.

[70] Gordon M Hutton, 'Stair's Public Career' in David M Walker (ed), *Stair Tercentenary Studies*, vol 33 (Stair Society 1981) 1–65.

[71] RPS 1649/1/306.

[72] Mackenzie *Discourse* (n 19) f54.

I should like much better to have our Law directed by the Writing of Learned Lawyers who give their Judgment in abstract Cases wherein none are concerned but their own Souls, Reputation and Posterity, which generally lye men to be Just, and who have great Leisure to mediate upon what they transmit to Posterity as Law. It is from the opinions of such as these that the admired Digest did arise, and though the codex be only be Constitutions of Emperors, and as such is not in the same Reputation, yet all the Emperors had the Council of the most Learned Lawyers of their age to assist them in forming their acts and constitutions and Alexander Severus never past any without the assistance of 20: of the best Lawyers of the age But yet I think that the Concilia or Constitutions of Lawyers where of these are very many extent should have but small authority, because they have been interested for those who employed them.

It could be suggested that Mackenzie would have been apprehensive of Stair's approach to the law of Scotland in the *Institutions*, which relied heavily on a Calvinist reworking of Grotius's natural law theory along with an account of the individual rules, customs, and practices of the law in Scotland.[73] Stair attempted to show a direct link between equity and the law of Scotland, somewhat shortcutting the known ways of reasoning and explaining the law of Scotland and the traditional Justinian description of the natural law. Mackenzie said in his *Discourse* that 'Equity doth the blood circle through the whole Body of our Law and animates it as the Blood doth the body for *ratio est anima Legis* but it is very dangerous when it goes out of its due course, as blood doth when it extravasates.'[74]

Throughout the *Institutions*, Stair sought to demonstrate the equity of the law of Scotland and prove its closeness to equity. Mackenzie would not disagree that the law in Scotland should be founded on equity, but he did not wish for there to be a direct appeal to equity. If there was to be use of equity, it should be determined via the existing law, which already embodied equity—and, if that failed, then through the use of learned legal writing.[75] It is possibly not too much of a conjecture to say that such concerns would have equally translated into Mackenzie's perception of Stair's contractual thought, which was overtly underpinned by a direct appeal to equity or natural law. Indeed, in his *Discourse*, Mackenzie often speaks of Roman law and equity, and uses pactions, promises, or the conclusion and proof of writs as an example of where Roman law has for good reason departed from the requirements of the law of nature.[76] For Mackenzie, the wisdom of Roman law often points towards a safer way to engage with equity or the law of nature, which shapes how he approaches contracting.

It could be suggested, however, that in writing the *Institutions* Stair was concerned with offering an account of the law which restored a sense of order and authority while

---

[73] Indeed, the use of natural law arguments in the style formulated by Stair could quickly become political, eg James Steuart, *Naphtali, or, The Wrestlings of the Church of Scotland for the Kingdom of Christ* ... (S N 1667); Andrew Honeyman, *A Survey of the Insolent and Infamous Libel, Entituled, Naphtali* (Anon. 1668) James Steuart, *Jus Populi Vindicatum* (Anon. 1669). For analysis, see Neil McIntyre, 'Saints and Subverters: The Later Covenanters in Scotland, c. 1648–1682' (DPhil thesis, University of Strathclyde 2016) 81–144.

[74] Mackenzie *Discourse* (n 19) f45. For discussion of this passage, see Ford *Law and Opinion* (n 4) 488 ff.

[75] Mackenzie *Discourse* (n 19) f54–55.

[76] Mackenzie *Discourse* (n 19) f15, f16, f45, f71–72.

possibly also neutralizing radical Presbyterianism, which disturbed traditional conceptions of authority and order. That is, Stair wished to present the law of Scotland as ordered and rational, and to demonstrate that it was also Godly, but he did not use his natural law theory to underpin the law as practised in Scotland. Nor did he try to challenge existing legal institutions in Scotland. Indeed, as Ford has demonstrated, Stair wished to offer a theory of sovereignty and judicial decision-making which greatly restricted those who could claim legitimacy in making direct claims to natural law. In contrast to Mackenzie, in writing the *Institutions* Stair was to an extent actively placating the radicals but with the aim of maintaining the status quo. However, by doing so he placed a theological gloss upon the law of Scotland, including the law applying to contractual behaviour. This is particularly evident if one considers Stair's moralization of the law but also his use of theology and Biblical references in how he described the law. This approach fell out of favour in Scotland soon after the Glorious Revolution.

Overall, it could be said that Mackenzie's attitude is something which the first Professor of Scots Law at Edinburgh University, Alexander Bayne, captured well in 1726:[77]

All the Sciences are, in the General, useful, as they convey to our Minds the Knowledge of Truths of different Natures, by which we not only improve and cultivate the natural Lights of Reason, but in the Exercise of our Faculties, in our Enquires of that Kind, we attain to a Habit of discerning accurately, the different Natures of Things, of distinguishing them with Exactness, and of judging better of them by those acquired Helps; than it is possible for us to do, by the bare Lights of our natural Reason, without the Aid of the Sciences For, by their Means, we are enabled to range our Thoughts into better Order, and to communicate and explain them, with great Perspicuity in all Matters wherein we happen to be conversant.... Of all the Sciences, that which tends directly to the Service of Religion, claims the first Place; the other being of a lower Rank, are properly distinguished from that of Theology, by the Name of Humane Sciences.... Among the humane Sciences, that which has the nearest, and most immediate Relation to the Order of Society, and to the public Good, is without Question, the Science of the highest Character; and as being the most useful to Mankind, is best entitled to the first Place, and such is the Science of Law.... It is the Law which regulates the Justice that Men owe to one another, in all the various Affairs and Intercourse of Life; and it comprehends not only the Rules by which these Affairs and Intercourses are governed, but the Rules or the Functions, and Duties of those to whom the Administration thereof, is committed.

One interpretation of the reception of Stair is to say that Mackenzie and other lawyers in Scotland, during the Restoration and thereafter, would have found his manuscripts and eventually his *Institutions*, including his account of contract, theological in places and using unpopular scholastic ideas and language. In directly relating the performance of one's civil obligation to one's duty to God, Stair was cutting across

---

[77] Alexander Bayne, 'Discourse on the Rise and Progress of the Law of Scotland and the Method of Studying It' in Thomas Hope, *Minor Practicks or A Treatise of the Scottish Law ...* (Thomas Ruddiman 1726) 151–52.

numerous modes of thinking which were established and familiar to seventeenth- and eighteenth-century lawyers. Stair's approach would have been understood to emanate from his new description of the law of Scotland, which was shaped by a Calvinist reading of Grotius. Mackenzie rejects this approach. It might be suggested that Mackenzie not only produced his *Institutions* in 1684 to right the wrongs of Stair's legal treatment of the law of Scotland, but he also published his *Religious Stoic* in the same year to remind his readers that, contrary to the approach of Stair, lawyers and judges should not take 'too much notice' of the 'extravagances' of philosophers, theologians, ministers, and radicals. None of this is to say that Mackenzie did not see a relationship between theology and law. He was religious and, in his *Discourse*, presents an account of the law of nature which is in keeping with the main tenets of Reformed theology. Indeed, his stress on the will of the sovereign fits well with Lutheran theology as much as it does with Restoration politics. To take this approach is, however, to limit the necessity of developing a sophisticated natural law account of society, authority, and basic legal concepts such as property, contract, or rights. To understand the law, according to Mackenzie, you had to first grasp the primacy of sovereign authority and accept a Royalist account of legitimacy.[78] It could be said that, for Mackenzie, exploring the natural law foundations of society or fundamental laws should not undermine the will of the sovereign or parliaments but reinforce their authority. Hence, on that basis, to explore, develop, or articulate an alternative natural law authority for the positive law of Scotland was unnecessary for him; but this was arguably central to the jurisprudential moral philosophy of the eighteenth century.[79]

Natural Law Education and Writing

In contrast to Mackenzie's approach, the form of natural law teaching which Scottish students encountered from the 1660s to 1760 increasingly displaced notions that positive law merely emanated from the will of a sovereign and reformulated ideas of authority and the basis for sovereign power. Arguably, for Scots, this begins in the Dutch Provinces but continues with later developments in Scotland from the 1690s onwards.[80] Between the 1660s and the 1750s, a relatively large number of Scots students studied in Leiden, Franeker, Groningen, and Utrecht, and around two-fifths of these students proceeded to become advocates in Scotland.[81] Scots students were studying

---

[78] Mackenzie *Discourse* (n 19) f7–8.

[79] For discussion, see Jackson 'Natural Law and the Construction of Political Sovereignty in early modern Scotland' (n 4) 155–69; John W Cairns, 'Attitudes to Codification and the Scottish Science of Legislation 1600–1830' (2007) 22 Tulane European and Civil Law Forum 1, 32ff.

[80] Moore 'Natural Rights in the Scottish Enlightenment' (n 2) 291–316.

[81] Robert Feenstra, 'Scottish-Dutch Legal Relations in the Seventeenth and Eighteenth Centuries' in Thomas C Smout (ed), *Scotland and Europe, 1200–1850* (John Donald 1986) 128–42 at 132–33; Paul Nève, 'Disputations of Scots Students Attending Universities in the Northern Netherlands' in William M Gordon and T D Fergus (eds), *Legal History in the Making* (Hambledon Press 1991) 93–108; John W Cairns, 'Importing Our Lawyers from Holland: Netherlands Influences on Scots Law and Lawyers in the Eighteenth Century' in John W Cairns (ed), *Law, Lawyers, and Humanism*, vol 1 (Edinburgh University Press 2015) 223–41. Kees Van Strien and Margreet Ahsmann, 'Scottish Law Students in Leiden at the End of the Seventeenth Century: The Correspondence of John Clerk 1694–1697' (1992) 19 Lias: Sources and Documents Relating to the Early Modern History of Ideas 271 and (1993) 20, 1.

not only Roman law or the practicks of the Court of Session prior to admission to the Faculty, but also, importantly, if in the Dutch Provinces, they would often take private classes on the law of nature and nations.[82] As a form of jurisprudence or legal theory, students would learn during these classes the theories of Grotius, Pufendorf, Huber, and the less innovative, but nonetheless influential Voet.[83] Although aspiring advocates were often advised to concertate upon the *Institutes*, *Digest*, and *Code* during their studies, as this was the best preparation for entry to the Scots bar, private lessons on Grotius were very popular.[84] Along with the cost, convenience, and variety it offered students to study Grotius in this manner, it appears to have been a very common practice in Leiden and Utrecht and something students did not want to miss out on.[85]

Students who studied in Scotland rather than elsewhere would also have encountered modern ideas of natural law as part of their degree. Originating out of the traditional master-of-arts curriculum of Scottish universities, this form of jurisprudential teaching and writing was produced to supplement the traditional lectures on ethics delivered at Scottish universities.[86] Whether at home or in the Netherlands, Cairns has suggested that interest in the '*ius naturale* and *ius gentium* had been developed and sustained in the later seventeenth century by the education of advocates'.[87] This interest developed throughout the early eighteenth century, and arguably reached an important point in 1760.[88] In that year, Cairns has highlighted that the Faculty of Advocates resolved that candidates proposing to become members of the Faculty should attend classes on the law of nature. 'They do therefore recommend', said the resolution, 'to all young Gentlemen who intend to offer themselves for Candidates for the office of Advocate, to apply to the study of the law of Nature & Nations.'[89] As part of this study of the law of nature and nations, Scots learned that justice, rights, property, and, importantly, contract were at the foundation of civil society. Against this background, consideration of Carmichael's approach to contracting is an important starting point in understanding how close his approach to contracting is to Stair's approach.

---

[82] K V Strien and M Ahsmann 'Scottish Law Students' (n 81).

[83] Robert Feenstra and Clarissa J D Wall, *Seventeenth-Century Leyden Law Professors and their Influence on the Development of the Civil Law* (North-Holland Publishing 1975); Cairns 'Attitudes to Codification' (n 79) 34.

[84] Strien and Ahsmann 'Scottish Law Students' (1993) (n 82) 279 ff.

[85] Govaert C J J Van den Bergh, *The Life and Work of Gerard Noodt (1647–1725)* (Clarendon Press 1988), 269. Strien and Ahsmann, 'Scottish Law Students' (1992) (n 82) 1–7 and Strien and Ahsmann 'Scottish Law Students' (1993) (n 82) 290 ff.

[86] Haakonssen *Natural Law and Moral Philosophy* (n 9); John W Cairns, 'The First Edinburgh Chair in Law: Grotius and the Scottish Enlightenment' (2005) 11 (32) Fundamina 31–57; John W Cairns, 'The Legacy of Smith's Jurisprudence in Late Eighteenth-Century Edinburgh' in Ian Hunter and Richard Whatmore (eds), *Philosophy, Rights and Natural Law* (Edinburgh University Press 2019) 278–305.

[87] Cairns 'Attitudes' (n 79) 34.

[88] Cairns 'The First Edinburgh Chair in Law' (n 86) 42–43.

[89] Angus Stewart and David Parratt (eds), *The Minute Book of the Faculty of Advocates*, vol 46 (Stair Society 1999) 94.

Carmichael

Pufendorf, Grotius, and moral science

If it was moral professors in Scotland who first introduced the ideas of Grotius and of Samuel Pufendorf (1632–94) to the Scottish university curriculum, then it could be said that a jurisprudential exploration of law, morality, and the foundations of civil society originated in moral philosophy.[90] William Scott, a regent at Edinburgh University, demonstrated one of the earliest and most sustained engagements with this type of jurisprudence, possibly offering private classes on Grotius from the 1690s, but also producing an abridgment and commentary upon *De jure belli ac pacis* for his students in 1707 and an updated version in 1718.[91] In Glasgow, however, Carmichael is a notable turning point, not only because he taught Pufendorf and Grotius, but also because he also introduced a commentary upon Pufendorf's *De Officio Hominis*, which was subsequently published.[92] A comparison between Carmichael's and Stair's contractual thought demonstrates clearly the lines of similarity and indicates how the type of approach Stair took was continued in Scotland. Like Grotius, Pufendorf, and Stair, Carmichael sought to establish the foundations of civil society, human law, and notions of contract and property with a direct appeal to the law of nature mediated through a form of scientific examination of general principles which govern interpersonal relationships rather than through an appeal to Roman law, sovereign or monarchical authority, or a notion of direct divine creation. Indeed, Carmichael's discussion of human action, Roman law, the structure of man's duties, and the distinction between perfect and imperfect rights can be profitably compared to Stair's approach, demonstrating a significant degree of continuity.

Human action, liberty, and morality

Happiness is the ultimate goal of man, according to Carmichael. Such a notion is unsurprising, given that his lectures develop out from the traditional university curriculum, where Aristotle's ethics would be taught along with a scholastic gloss upon

---

[90] Christine M Shepherd, *Philosophy and Science in the Arts Curriculum of the Scottish Universities in the 17th Century* (DPhil thesis, University of Edinburgh 1975) 170ff. See Andrew Massie's lectures (1682): EUL DK.5.29 (critical of Cumberland); Andrew Massie's lectures (1682): EUL DK.5.29. John Wishart's lectures (1675 and 1679) (References Stair, Mackenzie, Grotius, More): EUL DK.5.96 and EUL Gen 690 D Herbert Kennedy (1692): EUL DK.8.118; John Law's lectures (References Pufendorf) (1699–1700): GUL Ms Mu 49.

[91] Hugo Grotius, *Hugonis Grotii De jure Belli ac Pacis Librorum III. Compendium, Annotationibus & Commentariis Selectis Illustratum. In usum Studiosae Juventutis Academiae Edinensis* (Andrew Anderson 1707; T Ward (reprint) 1718).

[92] Samuel Puffendorfii, *De Officio Hominis et Civis, Juxta Legem Naturalem, Libri Duo. Supplementis et Observationibus in Academicae Juventutis Auxit et Illustravit Gerschomus Carmichael, Philosophiae in Academia Glasguensi Professor. Editio Secunda Priore Auctior et Emendatior* (John Mosman 1724). References to Carmichael's notes in this chapter refer to the English translation of his notes which was produced in 2002: Gershom Carmichael, *Natural Rights on the Threshold of the Scottish Enlightenment: The Writings of Gershom Carmichael*, James Moore and Michael Silverthorne (eds) (Liberty Fund 2002). Quotations from Carmichael's *Supplementis et Observationibus* are taken from the 2002 Liberty Fund edition.

the concept of *eudaimonia*. Adding the familiar caveat found within Christian interpretations of *eudaimonia*, Carmichael tells his students that man only finds his true happiness if he first gives glory to God, but nevertheless man's first inclination is towards his own happiness (contrary to God). However, if man does not direct his actions towards giving glory to God and following his divine will, then—in this life or in the afterlife—man will experience misery. According to Carmichael, it is reason, however, which tells us to obey God: the 'human mind is fitted to feel the greatest pleasure and delight in actions which are most conformable to reason.'[93] He says that God demands certain actions from man as a sign of love and veneration from man towards God, and that God interprets anything to the contrary as contempt and hatred. For him, this is known as divine law and leads him to conclude: 'law must be recognised as the highest norm for human action.'[94] However, he makes clear that law only applies to free actions, and he disagrees with Pufendorf in saying that the law of nature, which is part of divine law, applies to both internal and external actions.[95] On this basis, Carmichael offers an account of human action. Much of this resonates with Stair's approach found in the *Divine Perfections*.

Carmichael says that obedience of God's law is determined by examining whether the will of man freely obeys or not. Saying that ignorance and incapacity render actions beyond the domain of law, he stresses that some of the distinctions found in earlier theological writing are unhelpful, such as the distinction between liberty of contradiction or contrariety and spontaneity or liberty.[96] Carmichael is also keen to stress that, unlike for scholastics, in his system of natural jurisprudence some actions can be indifferent, which Pufendorf describes as 'those actions which law makes no provision in either way.'[97] Nor does he care for the scholastic debate about where freedom resides; whether it is in the intellect or in the will, he says freedom or free action applies to the actions of man. Preferring a Lockean definition of liberty or freedom, he expressly refers his students to the discussion of liberty in *An Essay Concerning Human Understanding*. There his students would have found Locke's definition:[98]

> So that the Idea of Liberty, is the Idea of a Power in any Agent to do or forbear any particular Action, according to the determination or thought of the mind, whereby either of them is preferr'd to the other; where either of them is not in the Power of the Agent to be produced by him according to his Volition, there he is not at Liberty, that Agent is under Necessity, So that Liberty cannot be, where there is no Thought, no Volition, no Will; but there may be Thought, there may be Will, there may be Volition, where there is no Liberty.

Carmichael paraphrases for his students that liberty is either to act as one chooses or not to act as one chooses, which is to invoke what Pink would term the 'ability to

---

[93] Carmichael *Natural Rights* (n 92) 24.
[94] Carmichael *Natural Rights* (n 92) 25.
[95] Carmichael *Natural Rights* (n 92) 30–31.
[96] Carmichael *Natural Rights* (n 92) 34.
[97] Carmichael *Natural Rights* (n 92) 41.
[98] John Locke, *An Essay Concerning Human Understanding* (first published 1689, OUP 1979) Ch 21, para 7.

choose' sense of liberty. However, Carmichael also alludes to the second sense of liberty Pink speaks of, which is the normative or right-based conception. He tells his students that if the law is the ultimate judge of our actions and following the law of nature, as a part of God's divine law, is what leads us to happiness, then we must have a right to exercise our liberty. If justice requires us to have regard for others, then 'it assumes in the person for whom justice is to be done, some right of facility afforded by the law, of doing, having, obtaining something from someone else'.[99] For Carmichael, a good man obeys the law and is just when he uses his free will to choose to obey the law, and this therefore implies that there is a right in the law of nature for man to perform those duties.

There is a great deal of Carmichael's description of human action which is similar to Stair. Additionally, the theological tone of Carmichael's characterization of divine law, his description of the law of nature and his description of justice resembles Stair's own description of these subjects. There are important differences too. Carmichael does not speak of sin or man's fallen nature as necessarily preventing him from acting morally, albeit he does stress the role of grace in certain places. However, Carmichael's approach is first to describe how the just and right actions of man operate, and then to add caveats. Stair does not take this approach. Moreover, Stair is more explicit about the relationship between reason and law, whether that be in his description of what the law is, namely the dictate of reason, or in describing liberty in the *Divine Perfections*, that is, as the habit of following reason. Stair more explicitly uses different senses of 'liberty' in both the *Institutions* and the *Divine Perfections*, whereas Carmichael prefers to use Locke's sense. Carmichael does not offer a detailed account of human law and its relationship to the law of nature. However, what he does say on these topics is consistent with Stair's account, particularly in relation to how natural law obligations are embodied in positive law and how law relates to liberty.

Roman law, scholasticism, and natural law

Carmichael does not share Mackenzie's level of admiration for Roman law, nor does he appear as critical of scholastic ideas or methods. In that regard, Carmichael is similar to Stair.[100] For example, Carmichael says that someone 'who cares sincerely about duty, and recognizes that a common rule of duty is given to all men', will gain knowledge of their duty from scholastics.[101] He goes on, however, to criticize those who do not think that 'the discipline of philosophy is necessary for this pursuit' because they think that natural theology or casuistry is sufficient, or 'others [who] think this knowledge may be found in the study of the civil law'.[102] By civil law he means the positive law of a nation, and he explains that 'the place of moral philosophy' cannot 'be taken by

---

[99] Carmichael *Natural Rights* (n 92) 43.

[100] Holligan persuasively demonstrates that Stair's ambivalence towards Roman law in comparison to his direct use of natural law, contributed to Mackenzie and Stair taking a different approach to restitution: Holligan, 'Ownership and Obligation' (n 3) 177–88.

[101] Carmichael *Natural Rights* (n 92) 12.

[102] Carmichael *Natural Rights* (n 92) 12–13.

the Roman or any other particular system of jurisprudence'.[103] For Pufendorf, as with Carmichael, the civil law of a country and the Roman law presuppose the existence of a moral law, which is part of the law of nature. They do not embody it.[104] Carmichael explains that in the books of Roman law there may be 'innumerable declarations of the law of nature, in light of which Ulpian says that he and his friends aspire to true philosophy'. But it is important 'not to credit any man or nation with authorship of the laws of nature'.[105] He diminishes the authority of Roman law by historicizing it, saying:

> just as the authority of the Roman government adds nothing to the sanctity of the law
> of nature; so the mixture of natural laws with merely civil laws and things of that
> order prevents one from deducing the natural and genuine precepts contained in the
> books of Roman law from their own principles and from seeing that those precepts
> are connected with each other by the native genius of the Roman jurists.[106]

He accepts that there may well be a grounding in the law of nature, which forms the basis of some Roman laws, but complains that jurists of Roman law 'did not normally trouble themselves to deduce that law from some higher source nor was it pertinent to their task to do so'.[107] If Stair was never explicit himself as to why he did not grant Roman law the same authority as many of his peers, Carmichael's approach may best capture why Stair was ambivalent towards Roman law in his *Institutions* and approached the law of contract in a different manner from Mackenzie's *Institutions*.

Carmichael prefers to appeal directly to the law of nature when considering the foundation of men's duties. In doing so, he speaks of a scientific approach, but he also shares Stair's general openness to using scholastic concepts or ideas in how he describes the law of nature. He says it should not be 'objected that subjects which form a great part of the scholastics ethics are not to be found in the recent writings on the doctrine of natural law'. He explains that 'if one cuts out some of ... the empty quibblings and arguments about words' and those things which should be left to natural theology (the logic of divinity) or pneumatology (the study of the Holy Spirit), 'what remains can easily find its place in the style of natural law'. When speaking about the science to be used when determining the law of nature, he says: 'there is no other genuine philosophy of morals than the philosophy that elicits and demonstrates from evident principles found in the nature of things and those duties of men and citizens which are required in the individual circumstances of human life'.[108] Speaking of Pufendorf's adaptation of Grotius's approach, he says: 'the science of the law of nature [found in *Of the Law of Nature and Nations*] ... however different in appearance it might seem from the ethics which had long prevailed in the schools, was no different in aim and subject matter; it was the same subject, more correctly taught, and therefore better able to reach the goal which the other had sought with uncertain direction'.[109] He

---

[103] Carmichael *Natural Rights* (n 92) 14.
[104] cf Mackenzie *Oratio Inauguralis* (n 42) 278; Mackenzie *Discourse* (n 19) f16.
[105] Carmichael *Natural Rights* (n 92) 14.
[106] Carmichael *Natural Rights* (n 92) 14.
[107] Carmichael *Natural Rights* (n 92) 14.
[108] Carmichael *Natural Rights* (n 92) 11.
[109] Carmichael *Natural Rights* (n 92) 10–11.

continues: 'all writers on ethics had always professed that it was the science which would direct human actions to goodness, that is, to conformity with the law of nature or, as they commonly say in the schools, with the right dictates of reason'.[110] He therefore stresses that whatever 'distinctions one may make between scholastic ethics and natural jurisprudence, one must not attribute them to the nature of moral science itself but to the spurious or genuine manner of teaching it'.[111] Stair used scholastic language, referred to scholastic writers, and in his *Divine Perfections* and the *Institutions* demonstrates a theory of human action which could be classified as scholastic; but ultimately his theory of human action and ethic is congruent with Carmichael's naturalism; the debates of theological and philosophical scholars, like those of lawyers, provide paths to natural truths embedded in human striving. Moreover, Stair shared with Carmichael, and demonstrates in the *Institutions*, an admiration for presenting natural law entwined with positive law, in a Grotian format, that is, demonstrating a simple pattern of reasoning from self-evident principles to yield specific rules which should govern human interactions.

Structure

Carmichael was just as concerned as were his predecessors in finding an appropriate structure for the law of nature. Unlike Grotius and Pufendorf, however, Carmichael saw the primary duty of man as his duty towards God. Only with this basic norm in place could he lay out a system of personal ethics and moral duties. Of course, this theism represents a major departure from Pufendorf, but it very much echoes the approach taken by Stair in the opening passages of the *Institutions*. Pufendorf and Grotius would never dispute that man has a primary obligation to God first and foremost, but their accounts minimize or exclude this from consideration of what men owe to each other. Carmichael draws a clear line against this almost Epicurean stance, avowing his intentions to 'elevate the moral science from the human forum to which it has been too much reduced by Pufendorf to the loftier forum of God'.[112] Although Carmichael never published a treatise which followed the order he described, he gave a very clear indication as to how he would arrange a discussion of the law of nature, human law, and civil government in the commentary he published on Pufendorf. Therefore, in 1724, he republished his edition of Pufendorf's *The Whole Duty of Man* and included a revised appendix where he set out how the rights and duties of man should be arranged.[113] By way of preface in the introduction, he says that in 'almost every discipline, the evidence of the propositions taught depends on their connections with one another, with the principles on which they are based'.[114] He continues: 'I made an attempt to set out the order which nature seems to have directed us to follow in the moral science'. Matters are arranged over thirty-eight headings, starting with the

---

[110] Carmichael *Natural Rights* (n 92) 11.
[111] Carmichael *Natural Rights* (n 92) 11.
[112] Carmichael *Natural Rights* (n 92) 17.
[113] Puffendorfii, '*De Officio Hominis et Civis*' (n 92).
[114] Carmichael *Natural Rights* (n 92) 221.

fundamental law that man 'exhibits love and veneration for the supreme being' and finishing with a heading on the duties of sovereigns. Carmichael's opening few titles are concerned with the type of action which divine law applies to, the different ways by which divine law is applied, namely the court of conscience or the human court, and a discussion about the concept of law in general. After several titles on divine law, natural law and the concept of law, he discusses rights. He discusses under these titles the division between rights, the different types of rights and the various subject matter of rights, including contracts, promises and property. Titles 25 to 38 cover the origins of society, forms of civil government, and the creation and authority of human law and the duties of sovereigns.

Carmichael's innovation within Pufendorf's layout and subject matter is twofold. First, by reintroducing God to the centre of his description of the substance of natural law, Carmichael discusses in more detail the relationship of divine law to individual decisions and civil institutions, including the sovereign. Of course, this affects the structure, whereby he needs first to distinguish what divine law is and then to distinguish how divine law applies to individual actions but without undermining the notion that there is a temporal civil society and sovereign created by men and working in tandem with a spiritual world. Much of this recalls Stair, who began his *Institutions* with a wide-ranging discussion of the different sources of law, and which importantly enables him to distinguish between divine law and the human law. Second, Carmichael reintroduces a Grotian consideration of rights to the description of the law of nature. He criticizes Pufendorf for this neglect of rights and demonstrates an account of natural law should incorporate rights. Similarly, Stair too introduces the concept of rights as a means by which to view the other side of duties.

From duties to rights

Pufendorf said in *The Whole Duty of Man* that 'this is a fundamental Law of nature, That every man ought, as much as in him lies, to preserve and promote society: That is the Welfare of Mankind.'[115] Carmichael makes two additions or corrections. First, he says: 'but there are three fundamental precepts: that God is to be worshipped; that each man should pursue his own interests without harming others; and that sociability should be cultivated.'[116] Unlike Pufendorf, Carmichael did not confine his account of man's natural law duties to the temporal world but also considers spiritual things. But he is also dissatisfied with the underlying causes which Pufendorf attributes to man's sociability, which comes from a recognition of man's frailty and weakness in the state of nature. Second, Carmichael wants to stress that sociability is not just a consequence but is part of the cause of society. Hence, he says, 'there are certain advantages and pleasures which men can get either from their own actions or from external objects or from the actions of other men', and it is in the interests of society to promote and protect these. These things should not be 'obstructed, withdrawn, or intercepted, since

---

[115] Samuel Pufendorf, *The Whole Duty of Man, According to the Law of Nature* (first printed (in English) 1735; Liberty Fund 2003) 1.3.9.

[116] Carmichael *Natural Rights* (n 92) 51.

they contribute to the preserving and strengthening of social inclination and social life among men.[117] Developing this insight, Carmichael is theologically motivated to turn the focus from the duty to preserve and promote the welfare of mankind to a consideration of mankind's right to the promotion and preservation of welfare.

Perfect and imperfect rights

Carmichael says that Pufendorf's title on the duties men incur when making contracts 'relies heavily on the distinction between "absolute" and "hypothetical" duties … but he does not explain it with sufficient clarity'.[118] For Carmichael, the starting point is to make clear that 'perfect rights' belong to individuals and that these rights are either 'natural or adventitious'.[119] Adventitious rights, he explains, 'arise from some human action or event'. They include the right to life, physical integrity, the right to chastity, and also reputation. He adds to this the right to liberty, which is a power 'of ordering one's actions as one pleases within the broad limits of the common divine laws. As well as the closely related ability to use in common things which are by nature positively common.' These rights are authorized by the general principle of natural law, that 'every man is forbidden from violating any of these rights in another'. Carmichael proceeds to develop with precision the duties that men incur when concluding contracts, by making clear that some adventitious rights are personal, relating to individuals and what they owe by way of things or services to another, whereas others are real, relating to the possession and use of a thing. He explains that a personal right is 'simply a certain particle of a man's natural liberty which is transferred to another man by some act or event'. Personal rights are created by 'mutual consent' and produce three effects: the transfer of liberty to another party; the transfer of a right against a third party to another; or the transfer of liberty back to the person who originally transferred it, restoring them to natural liberty. On his account, these acts can be either unilateral or reciprocal.[120]

Pactions, promises, and bare agreements

After giving what he believes is a more precise analytical framework upon which to analyze the duties men owe to each other when creating contracts, Carmichael returns to Roman law, saying that the term *pactum*, which is used in the *Digest*, 'stands for a variety of ideas which do not all have the same extension'.[121] He notes that Pufendorf restricted the word *pactum* to 'one species within that genus, namely, that which is obligatory on both sides'. However, for Carmichael, there should be a distinction made here between 'an act obligatory by mutual consent between one which created

---

[117] Carmichael *Natural Rights* (n 92) 51.
[118] Carmichael *Natural Rights* (n 92) 77.
[119] Carmichael *Natural Rights* (n 92) 77.
[120] Carmichael *Natural Rights* (n 92) 78.
[121] Carmichael *Natural Rights* (n 92) 80.

the obligation on one side only and one which created an obligation on both sides'.[122] The former, he says, is 'not so well named a gratuitous promise' because, according to him, there is nevertheless in such situations a corresponding right, either to return something or the waiver of a right. Nonetheless, whether Pufendorf should have been clearer or not about whether a promise can bind the recipient, he does make the distinction between a contract and a promise, saying there was a general duty 'of the Law of Nature, that every Man keep his Word, or fulfil his Promises and make good his Contracts'. Pufendorf does say, in the text Carmichael gave to his students, 'Our Word may be given, either by a single Act, where one Party only is obliged; or by an Act reciprocal, where more than one are Parties.'[123] However, Carmichael does point out to his students that when it comes to promises, Pufendorf only makes a distinction between imperfect promises, which are only due according to courtesy, and perfect promises, where performance is due as a matter of necessity and can be compelled. For Carmichael, there should equally be a distinction between perfect and imperfect contracts on similar grounds.

Later on, in his commentary, Carmichael criticizes Pufendorf's use of the distinction between a bare agreement and a contract, stating that Pufendorf is unable to explain the distinction other than by saying that a contract relates to commerce whereas a bare agreement is connected to other matters. Unconvinced, Carmichael says:[124]

> The author could safely have omitted this distinction since, as it is understood by jurists, it arises from a superfluous subtlety of Roman law … it obviously seems of the notary's art. The author evidently felt this and does not explain the difference between these two things according to the maxims of Roman jurisprudence but rather by natural reason, though he seem to think that they come to more or less the same thing.… But the distinction is not much use in itself, and does not square properly with the accepted application among the Roman jurists (for there may be innumerable agreements about things or actions occurring in commerce, which would not be called contracts by the nomenclature of the Romans, for example exchange of things by consent alone).

For Carmichael, equity and natural law suggest that the distinction should be dropped from 'natural jurisprudence altogether'; however, he does agree that the distinction introduced by Pufendorf between gratuitous and chargeable agreements is helpful. Nevertheless, Carmichael adds the caveat that the same can apply to promises as well as contracts. That being so, Pufendorf explains that a gratuitous transaction is where there is an advantage given to one of the parties, whereas a chargeable or onerous contract puts an obligation which is 'equally burdensome' upon both parties.[125] He uses this then to divide the nominate Roman law contracts into those which are chargeable and those which are gratuitous, and, as Carmichael notes, 'rightly drops the [Roman]

---

[122] Carmichael *Natural Rights* (n 92) 81.
[123] Pufendorf *The Whole Duty of Man* (n 115) 1.10.6.
[124] Carmichael *Natural Rights* (n 92) 107.
[125] Pufendorf *The Whole Duty of Man* (n 115) 1.15.2.

distinctions of nominate and innominate … [and] once one removes the contrast be-tween bare agreements and contracts, all these finicky distinctions converge of their own accord'.[126] Much of this, again, is similar to how Stair described promises and contracts in the *Institutions*.

Fraud, fear, and error

In *The Whole Duty of Man*, Pufendorf follows on from his discussion of promises and contracts and their obligatory effect with a discussion of situations where a contract or promise may fail to become effective due to capacity, fraud, fear, or error. Carmichael is less willing than Pufendorf to grant as many exceptions, which is reminiscent of Stair. First, Pufendorf says that if an error becomes apparent to one party after the contract has been formed but before it has been performed, then:

> it is but Equity that I should be at liberty to retract; especially if upon the Contract making, I plainly signify'd for what Reason I agreed to it; more particularly, if the other Party suffers no Damage by my going off from my Bargain, or, if he does, that I am ready to make Reparation.[127]

Carmichael's students are told that 'this privilege cannot be claimed by perfect right, unless the error concerns something which the person who was in error at least thought was assumed as a condition on both sides'.[128] Second, Pufendorf says that where there is an error with regard to the subject of the agreement, the contract is 'invalid, not for the sake of the Mistake, but because the Laws and Terms of the Agreement are not really fulfilled'.[129] Carmichael disagrees that this should be the ground upon which the contract is invalid, saying that such an agreement should be set aside only if the error was about the nature of the subject of the contract. In such a situation, it can be set aside and parties restored to their prior position, but if the contract is partly or fully performed and the reason for the error can be attributed to fault of the party in error, then compensation may be due if a loss is incurred by virtue of the fact that the contract has been set aside.[130] When it comes to agreements or promises made due to 'unjustified force',[131] Pufendorf says they are 'invalid',[132] whereas Carmichael says that although they are not enforceable by the extorter they are binding upon the conscience of the promisee, so long as what has been promised is lawful.[133]

---

[126] Carmichael *Natural Rights* (n 92) 108.
[127] Pufendorf *The Whole Duty of Man* (n 115) 1.10.12; Carmichael *Natural Rights* (n 92) 114–15.
[128] Carmichael *Natural Rights* (n 92) 83.
[129] Pufendorf *The Whole Duty of Man* (n 115) 1.10.12.
[130] Carmichael *Natural Rights* (n 92) 84.
[131] Carmichael *Natural Rights* (n 92) 85.
[132] Pufendorf, *The Whole Duty of Man* (n 115) 1.10.15.
[133] Carmichael *Natural Rights* (n 92) 85.

Carmichael Compared to Stair

Although there is a great deal to suggest that Stair and Carmichael offered a broadly similar natural law account of contracting, there is one significant and obvious difference. Carmichael was not interested in demonstrating in any detail about how these natural law propositions related to the specifics of Scots contract law. As discussed previously, Stair had two overriding objectives: one was to provide a description of the customary law of Scotland, demonstrating its equity and closest to natural law, and the second was to establish that law was a rational discipline, not the mere will of a law maker. It was argued that Stair's experiences of the seventeenth century would have certainly influenced both objectives, but particularly the second whereby he tried to place discussions of law's authority on to a new philosophical basis. Although Carmichael did not share Stair's first objective, he shared his second. Indeed, as has been shown, if one takes each of Stair's individual propositions of natural law and compares them to Carmichael, they share a great deal in common. Moreover, they each express the interpersonal nature of natural law by laying emphasis on the interaction between rights and duties. So once Stair's application of the principles of natural law to the specific rules of Scots law is extracted—if you look beyond Stair's first objective—and focus on his standalone account of natural law, there is a great deal of similarity between the *Institutions*' account of the natural law of contracting and Carmichael's own account in his *Supplementis et Observationibus*. Importantly, both writers, inspired by Grotius, converted the traditional Christian focus on obligations imposed by natural law into a more specific juristic language of interpersonal and corresponding rights and duties.

Natural Law and Contracting

If Carmichael's natural law teaching based on Grotius and Pufendorf is taken as an example of what Haakonssen terms Protestant natural law, then it could be said that Scots students were encountering from the late 1660s into the late eighteenth century a type of natural law examination of contracting which Stair demonstrates in the *Institutions*. Indeed, this engagement with Grotius and Pufendorf often involved the adaptation of their theories to accommodate theistic premises in a similar manner to Stair. On that basis, the question of how Stair's contractual thought was received could be framed to demonstrate that Stair was just one of several writers in Scotland who developed a natural law consideration of basic concepts of private law in light of Grotius or Pufendorf's theories and to a greater or lesser extent, theistic premises. If framed in this manner, such a tradition could include the teaching and writings of Gershom Carmichael,[134] George Turnbull,[135] Thomas

---

[134] Puffendorfii '*De Officio Hominis et Civis*' (n 92).

[135] George Turnbull, *A Methodical System of Universal Law: Or, The Law of Nature and Nations ... written in Latin by the Celebrated Jo. Got. Heineccius with Supplements and a Discourse by George Turnbull* (J Noon 1741, Liberty Fund (republished) 2008).

Reid,[136] and James Beattie.[137] In terms of these individual writers' treatment of contracting, each offered to a greater or lesser extent a theistic account; each considered human action and man's access to moral knowledge; each drew from the tradition of Grotius and Pufendorf, speaking of natural law in terms of rights and duties; and each used Roman law as a point of comparison when discussing the specifics of natural law. Stair may be the first Scot writing exemplary texts about natural law and private law concepts; but he was certainly not the last when the teaching of moral philosophy in the eighteenth century is considered. Contract, along with other conceptions such as rights, duties and obligations, and property, became commonplace topics of exploration and consideration of natural law within eighteenth-century moral philosophy. This arguably starts with Scots' engagement with Grotius through legal education but develops in numerous different directions within Scottish civil society, the *belle lettres* movement, and in the shaping of institutions in Scotland.[138] Although an analysis of each of these writers is beyond the scope of this book, it is important nevertheless to signal a longer period of legalistic natural law theories in Scotland of which Stair's project is just one, possibly overlooked, part.[139] That is, framing Stair as offering a moral philosophy of contracting in similar terms to Carmichael, Turnbull, Reid, and Beattie demonstrates that a natural law consideration of legal practices and concepts in Scotland potentially started with Stair, but continued well into the eighteenth century.[140]

Conclusion

Stair offered a distinctive account of the law in Scotland and the law applying to contracting. His description aimed to be comprehensive and to give an integrated account of the various sources of law used in Scotland during the seventeenth century. He wished to start from the beginning or first causes—common principles—and demonstrate their manifestation in the positive law of Scotland, namely the principles of society, property, and commerce. In doing this, he offered a unique taxonomy and attempted to justify the law of Scotland based on a form of Calvinist natural law theory. He connected liberty, commerce, and contract to a theory of private law based on rights governing interpersonal rather than status-based relationships, and he provided a relatively sophisticated theory of human action, making a discriminating

---

[136] For an analysis of Reid's unpublished lectures on ethics, see Haakonssen, *Natural Law and Moral Philosophy* (n 9) 201–16. See Stein 'General Notions of Contract' (n 7) 2–3.

[137] James Beattie, *Elements of Moral Science*, vol 2 (William Creech 1790).

[138] Richard B Sher, *Church and University in the Scottish Enlightenment* (first published 1985, Edinburgh University Press 2015) 93–119.

[139] Stein notes: 'Curiously, although the intellectual life of eighteenth-century Scotland centred around a small group of personal acquaintances, there seems to have been little, if any, contact between the institutional writers and the moral philosophers'. Stein 'General Notions of Contract' (n 7) 2.

[140] Duncan Forbes, 'Natural Law and the Scottish Enlightenment' in R H Campbell and Andrew Skinner (eds), *The Origins and Nature of the Scottish Enlightenment* (John Donald 1982) 186–204; Haakonssen *Natural Law and Moral Philosophy* (n 9); Cairns 'Attitudes' (n 79) 32–51. It could also be that in addition to Stair jurists such as John Erskine (1695–1768), William Forbes (1668–1745), and Lord Bankton (1685–1760) fall within this classification of natural law. Both MacCormick and Stein appear to suggest this type of classification: Stein 'General Notions' (n 7) 1–13 and MacCormick 'Law and Enlightenment' (n 5) 150–66.

investigation of freedom. Stair innovated within the Roman law taxonomy rather than following the received wisdom of the past; he crucially asserted that *nuda pacta* were enforceable; whilst using much of Roman law in the construction of modern doctrine, he was also confident enough to depart from the hallowed traditions of Romanist classical and medieval legal writing. Most startlingly, he could displace or adapt authoritative Roman law principles with a new type of equity based on natural law and conscience. This equitable technique is particularly apparent in his handling of the law applying to contracting behaviour.

Stair was evidently inspired by Grotius when he drafted the *Institutions*. Grotius's natural law theory provides a template for Stair in his ambitions to describe the law of Scotland from first principles. The Grotian approach gave Stair a style, a method, and a collection of natural law propositions helping him to identify the foundations of the private law of Scotland. At the same time, Stair made important modifications and alterations to the Grotian approach in order to fit with his Calvinist world view. He melded Calvinist theology creatively with scholastic learning, particularly in his formulation of the human will and its role in the creation of an obligation. Stair's *Divine Perfections* and *Institutions*, in all their dense and detailed arguments, allow us to reconstruct the bases of Stair's contractual thought. Indeed, reading these texts together demonstrates that Stair had an overarching theory which was able to integrate theology, justice, and law into the social and political conditions of Scotland during the seventeenth century. This was bold, innovative, and ambitious. Our concluding discussion of later writers shows that his project was just the start of a Protestant natural law tradition in Scotland, and possibly Europe more generally, which sought to explore basic juristic concepts such as the power and freedom to contract.

Nevertheless, if the approaches of the later jurists Mackenzie and Carmichael are to be used to measure the reception of Stair's innovations, then the story is mixed. On the one hand, Stair had little impact upon legal education—or, as MacCormick put it, 'as a model for the study of Scots law [the *Institutions*] was a failure'. It was Mackenzie's structure which moulded the organization of Scots private law around Justinian's *Institutes* and his terse consideration of the origins of law, which prevailed in Scottish legal education and legal writing well into the late eighteenth century. On the other hand, Stair's natural law conception to the praxis of contract echoed well into the eighteenth century, even if Stair's name was not so often invoked in the later debates. Moreover, as MacCormick has suggested, Stair's *Institutions* were of lasting influence at a higher level by providing a 'still-persuasive method of exposition of the law, always trying to connect positive legal doctrine to underlying equitable principle'.[141]

One can also claim that Stair's style of contractual thought, stripped of its overt Calvinist and Aristotelian expression, fitted well with the emergence of a modern society based upon commerce in the eighteenth century. As social organization became increasingly regarded as the product of a market equilibrium, the centrality of contracting as the key political institution in national life formed a new common sense. Here, Stair's temporal account of the liberty to contract appeared to be apt, even if his theology was not of the modern enlightenment world. It was possible to keep

---

[141] Neil MacCormick, 'Stair and the Natural Law Tradition: Still Relevant?' in Hector L MacQueen (ed), *Miscellany Six*, vol 54 (Stair Society 2009) 1–10, 6.

Stair's methods and accept his celebration of the binding force of contract as the expression of man's will, without also accepting his stress on the role of conscience, his recognition of the persistent claims of religion, and his understanding of the priority of natural obligations. These parts of Stair's contractual thought lost their grip upon mainstream accounts of man's right to contract. Indeed, in the modern world such ideas might even seem incomprehensible, though as historians we may recover them and realize what we have lost.

Bibliography

Primary Sources

Manuscripts
Adv Ms 6.1.3
Adv Ms 24.1.3 (Thomas Wallace?)
Adv Ms 24.1.3 (Peter Wedderburn?)
Adv Ms 24.2.2
Adv Ms 24.2.3 (John Thomson)
Adv Ms 24.2.10 (1659–62)
Adv Ms 24.3.2 (Thomas Wallace?)
Adv Ms 24.3.9 (George Lockhart?)
Adv Ms 24.3.10
Adv Ms 24.4.8–13
Adv Ms 24.4.14 (George Lockhart?)
Adv Ms 24.5.7
Adv Ms 25.1.13
Adv Ms 25.1.14 (1671?)
Adv Ms 25.3.2 (1666?)
Adv Ms 25.3.3
Adv Ms 25.4.2 (John Nisbet?)
Adv Ms 25.5.14
Adv MS 25.7.12
NLS Ms 943 (Thomas Wallace?)
NLS Ms 3171 (Thomas Wallace?)
NLS Ms 5435 (Robert Ker?)
NLS Ms 5437 (Nisbet)
NLS Ms 8490 (John Nisbett?)

Published Sources

——*Calvini Institutiones* (Geneva 1561) GUL Sp Coll Bm8-d.11.
——*A Collection of Lectures and Sermons, Preached upon Several Subjects, Most in the Time of Persecution* (H & S Crawford 1809).
——*The Confession of Faith, and the Larger and Short Catechism, Agreed upon by the Assembly of Divines at Westminster* (1655).
——'Decretals of Gregorii IX 1.35.1' in *Corpus Iuris Canonici* (In aedibus Populi Romani 1582) <http://digital.library.ucla.edu/canonlaw> accessed 5 April 2021.
——*Hugonis Grotii De Jure Belli ac Pacis Librorum III. Compendium, Annotationibus & Commentariis Selectis Illustratum. In Usum Studiosae Juventutis Academiae Edinensis* (Andrew Anderson 1707; reprinted by T Ward 1718).
——*Munimenta Alme Universitatis Glasguensi: Records of the University of Glasgow from its Foundation until 1727*, vol 3 (Maitland Club 1854).

——*Nisbet's Practicks: 'A Treatise anent Scotts Law in Civills 1666'* (1681), NLS MS 8490 ff144–54.

——*Summary of Catalogue of the Advocates' Manuscripts* (National Library of Scotland 1971).

——*Westminster Confession of Faith* (1647).

——*Westminster Assembly, The Confession of Faith, and the Larger and Shorter Catechisms First Agreed upon by the Assembly of Divines at Westminster, and Now Appointed by the Generall Assembly of the Kirk of Scotland, to be a Part of Uniformity in Religion Between the Kirks of Christ in the Three Kingdomes* (Lithgow 1652).

——*Westminster Assembly, The Confession of Faith, and the Larger and Shorter Catechisms First Agreed upon by the Assembly of Divines at Westminster, and Now Appointed by the Generall Assembly of the Kirk of Scotland, to be a Part of Uniformity in Religion Between the Kirks of Christ in the Three Kingdomes* (Evan Tyler 1660, Society of Stationers 1661).

Allestree R, *The Practice of Christian Graces, or The Whole Duty of Man* (Maxwell 1658).

Anon, *A Vindication of the Proceedings of the Convention of the Estates in Scotland* (Ric Chinwell 1689).

——*Catalogus Librorum Bibliothecae Juris Utriusque, tam Civilis Quam Canonici, Publici Quam Privati, Feudalis Quam Municipalis Variorum Regnorum, cum Historicis Graecis & Latinis, Literatis & Philosophis Plerisque Celebrioribus* (George Mosman 1692).

——*A Vindication of Divine Perfections* (Leiden c. 1695).

——*The Decisions of the English Judges, during the Usurpation, from the Year 1655, to His Majesty's Restoration, and the Sitting Down of the Session in June 1661* (Hamilton & Balfour 1762).

Aquinas T, 'The Summa Theologiæ' (Fathers of the English Dominican Province trs, 2nd edn, reproduced by Kevin Knight 1920), *New Advent* <https://www.newadvent.org/summa/> accessed 6 November 2022.

Aristotle, *Metaphysics* (W Ross and J A Smith trs, Clarendon Press 1908).

——*Posterior Analytics* (G R G Mure tr, Clarendon Press 1928).

——*Physics* (R P Hardie and R K Gaye trs, Clarendon Press 1930).

——*The Nicomachean Ethics* (D Ross tr, revised by John L Ackrill and James O Urmson, OUP 1998).

——*Politics* (E Barker tr, revised by R Stalley, OUP 2009).

Augustine, 'De Correptione et Gratia' in P Schaff (ed), *From Nicene and Post-Nicene Fathers. First Series, Vol. 5.* (P Holmes and R E Wallis trs, revised by B Warfield, Christian Literature Publishing Co 1887).

Baillie R, *A Dissuasive from the Errours of the Time* (Samuel Gillibrand 1645).

Balfour J, *Practicks: Or, a system of the more ancient law of Scotland.* Compiled by Sir James Balfour of Pettindreich, carefully published from several manuscripts (Thomas & Walter Ruddimans 1754).

Baxter R, A *Christian Directory: Or a Summ of Practical Theologie, and Cases of Conscience, Directing Christians, how to USE their Knowledge and Faith; How to improve all Helps and Means, and to Perform all Duties; How to Overcome Temptations, and to Escape or Mortifie every Sin* (Robert White 1673).

Bayne A (ed), *Minor Practicks, or, a Treatise of the Scottish Law* (Thomas Ruddiman 1726).

Beattie J, *Elements of Moral Science*, vol 2 (William Creech 1790).

Binning H, *The Common Principles of Christian Religion, Clearly Provided, and Singularly Improved* (R S 1666).

——*The Sinner's Sanctuary* ... (George Swintown & James Glen 1670).

Bramhall J, *Castigations of Mr. Hobbes his Last Animadversions in the Case Concerning Liberty and Universal Necessity wherein all his Exceptions about that Controversie are Fully Satisfied* (E T 1657).

——*The Works of the Most Reverend Father in God John Bramhall* (Dublin 1677).

Burnett G, *A Vindication of the Authority, Constitution, and Laws of the Church and State of Scotland in Four Conferences, wherein the Answer to the Dialogues betwixt the Conformist and Non-Conformist is Examined* (Robert Sanders 1673).

Burnett R, 'Ad Lectorem' in Thomas Craig, *Jus Feudale*, vol 1 (L Dodd tr, Stair Society, volume 64, 2017).

Calvin J, *Institutes of the Christian Religion* (F L Battles tr, W B Eerdmans 1975).

——*Institutes of the Christian Religion* (H Beveridge 1845 tr, W B Eerdmans 1994).

Cicero *De Officiis* (W Miller tr, Harvard University Press 1913).

Clyde J A, *Sir Thomas Craig of Riccarton the Jus Feudal with an Appendix containing the Books of the Feus*, 2 vols (Stair Society 1934).

——(ed), *Hope's Major Practicks, 1608–1633*, vol 3 (Stair Society 1937).

Corvinus J A, *Digesta per Aphprosmos Strictim Explicate* (Elzvir 1636).

Craig T, *Jus Feudale Tribus Libris Comprehensum Quibus Non Solùm Consuetudines Feudales & Prædiorum Lura* (Impensis Societatis Stationariorum 1655).

——*Jus Feudale*, vol 1 (L Dodd tr, Stair Society, volume 64, 2017).

Crawford D, *Journals of Sir John Lauder Lord Fountainhall with His Observations on Public Affairs and Other Memoranda 1665–1676* (Scottish History Society 1900).

Culverwell N, *An Elegant and Learned Discourse of the Light of Nature* (Liberty Fund 2001).

Dallas G, *System of Stiles* (Andrew Anderson 1697).

Dalrymple J, *Theses Logicæ, Metaphysicæ, Physicæ, Mathematicæ. Quas Adolescentes hac vice ex Collegio Glasguensi Publice Propugnabunt, ad diem 27 Julii 1646* (Georgius Andersonus 1646).

——*Modus Litigandi or Form of Process observed Before the Lords of Council and Session in Scotland* (Andrew Anderson 1681).

——*The Decisions of the Lords of Council and Session. In the Most Important Cases Debate before Them, with Acts of Sederunt*, 2 vols (Andrew Anderson 1681 and 1683).

——*Physiologia Nova Experimentalis in qua, Generales Notions Aristotelis, Epicuri, & Cartesii Supplentur: Errores Deterguntur & Emendantur* (Cornelium Boutesteyn 1686).

——*The Decisions of the Lords of Council and Session. In the Most Important Cases Debate before Them, From July 1671 to July 1681* (Andrew Anderson 1687).

——Viscount Stair, *Institutions of the Law of Scotland* (Andrew Anderson 1693).

——*An Apology for James Dalrymple, Viscount Stair* (first published 1690, J Ballantyne & Co 1825).

—— 'Scotstarvet's "Trew Relation"' (1916) 13 (52) *Scottish Historical Review* 380–92.

Dickson D, *An Exposition of All St. Pauls Epistles, Together with an Explanation of Those Other Epistles of the Apostles, St. James, Peter, John & Jude* (Francis Eglesfield 1659).

——*Therapeutica Sacra Shewing Briefly the Method of Healing the Diseases of the Conscience, concerning Regeneration* (Evan Tyler 1664).

Doneau H, *Commentarii de Iure Civilii*, vol 2 (1589–90).

Du Moulin C, 'Nova et Analytica Explicatio Rvbr. et Leg …' in Charles du Moulin, *Opera Quae Extant Omnia, ex Variis Librorum Apothecis* (Paris 1658) IV, cols 127–287.

Duareni F, 'Epistula de Ratione Docendi Discendi Iuris (1544)' in *Francisci Duareni Jurisconsulti Celeberrimi: Opera Omnia. Diligenter Emendate & Aucta Opportunis Notis. Volumen Quartum* (Typis Josephi Rocchii 1768) 364–65.

Durham J, *A Commentarie upon the Book of Revelation* (Christopher Higgins 1658).

——*A Practical Exposition of the X Commandments* (Kings Armes 1675).

——*A Practical Exposition of the X Commandments with a Resolution of Several Momentous Questions and Cases of Conscience* (Andrew Anderson 1676).

Durham J and Dickson D, *The Sum of Saving Knowledge* (Anon 1605).

Erskine J, *An Institute of the Law of Scotland* (first published 1773, Edinburgh Legal Education Trust 2014).

Fergusson J, *A Brief Exposition of the Epistles of Paul to the Philippians and Colossians* (Christopher Higgins 1656).

Filmer R, *Patriarcha: or the Natural Power of Kings* (Walter Davis 1680).

Forbes W, *A Journal of the Session* (Edinburgh 1714).

——*Institutes of the Law of Scotland* (first published 1722, Edinburgh Legal Education Trust 2012).

Fox G, *A Warning to all the Merchants in London, and such as Buy and Sell* (Thomas Simmons 1658).

Garcia F, *Tractus de Ultimo Fin Iuris Civilis et Canonici* (Apud Joannem Gymincum 1585).

Gibson A (ed), *The Decision of the Lords of Council and Session in Most Cases of Importance, Debated, and Brought before Them; from July 1621 to July 1642* (Andrew Anderson 1690).

Gillespie G, *A Treatise of Miscellany Questions wherein many useful Questions and Cases of Conscience are Discussed and Resolved* (Thomas Whitaker 1649).

Gillespie P, *The Ark of the Testament Opened, or ... a Treatise of the Covenant of Grace* (Edinburgh 1655).

——*The Ark of the Covenant Opened, or; A Treatise of the Covenant of Redemption between God and Christ, as the Foundation of the Covenant of Grace* (London 1677).

Grotii H, *De Jure Belli ac Pacis Libri tres, in Quibus Jus Naturæ et Gentium, item Juris Publici praceipua explicantur* (Johannem Blaev 1646; reprinted by Carnegie Endowment for International Peace 1946).

Grotius H, *The Truth of Christian Religion in Six Books by Hugh Grotius Corrected and Illustrated with Notes, By Mr Le Clerc* (J Clarke tr, 2nd edn, J Knapton 1719). Originally published as Hugo Grotius, *De Veritate Religionis Christianae* (Paris 1627).

——*The Introduction to Dutch Jurisprudence* (first published 1631, C Herbert tr, J van Voorst 1903).

——*Hugo Grotius Ordinum Hollandiae ac Westfrisiae Pietas (1613)* (E Rabbie ed, Brill 1995).

——*De Imperio Summarum Potestatum circa Sacra: Critical Edition with Introduction, English Translation and Commentary*, 2 vols (H-J van Dam ed, Brill 2001).

——*The Free Sea* (first published 1609, Liberty Fund 2004).

——*The Rights of War and Peace* (first published 1645, Liberty Fund 2005).

——*Commentary on the Law of Prize and Booty* (first published 1868, M J van Ittersum tr, Liberty Fund 2006).

Gudelinus P, *Commentariorum de Jure Novissimo Libri Sex: Optimia Methodo, Accurateac Erudite Conscripti, Additis Harum Vicinarumque Region Moribus* (Ex Officina Hieronymi Verdus 1620).

Hall J, *Cases of Conscience Practically Resolved: Containing a Decision of the Principall Cases of Conscience, of Daily Concernment, and Continuous Use amongst Men* (R H & J G 1654).

Henderson A, *The Government and Order of the Church of Scotland* (Anon 1641).

Hilliger O, *Donellus Enucleatus siue Commentarii* (Peter Bellerum 1642).

Hobbes T, *Leviathan* (first published 1651, CUP 1996).

Honeyman A, *A Survey of the Insolent and Infamous Libel, Entituled, Naphtali* (Anon Edinburgh 1668).

Innes C (ed), *Munimenta Alme Universitatis Glasguensis. Records of the University of Glasgow, from its Foundation till 1727* (Maitland Club 1854).

Laing D (ed), *The Letters and Journals of Robert Baillie 1632–1642, vol 2* (Bannatyne Club 1842).

——*Historical Notices of Scottish Affairs, selected from the Manuscripts of Sir John Lauder of Fountainhall, Bart.*, vol 1 (Bannatyne Club 1848).

Lauder J, Lord Fountainhall, *The Decisions of the Lords of Council and Session, from June 6th, 1678, to July 30th, 1712*, vols 1 and 2 (Hamilton & Balfour 1759–61).

Lessius L, *De Iustitia et Iure Caeterisque Virtutibus Cardinalibus Libri Quatuor / ad Secundam Secundae D. Thomae, à Quaest. 47 Usque ad quaest. 171* (Rolin Thierry 1613) (available in Glasgow University 1691 catalogue, GUL Sp Coll Bm6-b.4).

Locke J, *An Essay Concerning Human Understanding* (first published 1689, OUP 1979).

Love C, *Scriptural Rules to be Observed in Buying and Selling* (London 1652).

MacDowall A, Lord Bankton, *An Institute of the Laws of Scotland in Civil Rights: With Observations upon the Agreement or Diversity between Them and the Laws of England. In four books* (A Kincaid & A Donaldson 1751–53).

Mackenzie G, *A Discourse on the 4 First Chapters of the Digest to Show the Excellence and Usefulness of the Civil Law* BL Add Ms 18236 (unpublished).

——*Religio Stoici: Or, A Short Discourse on These Several Subjects . . .* (R Broun 1663).

——*Pleadings in Some Remarkable Cases before the Supreme Courts of Scotland since the year 1661* (George Swintoun, James Glen and Thomas Brown 1673).

——*Observations upon the 28. (i.e. 18.) Act, 23. Parl. K. James VI. Against Dispositions made in Defraud of Creditors, &c.* (His Majesties printers 1675).

——*The Laws and Customes of Scotland, in Matters Criminal* (James Glen 1678).

——*Observations on the Acts of Parliament, made by King James the First, King James the Second, King James the Third, King James the Fourth, King James the Fifth, Queen Mary, King James the Sixth, King Charles the First, King Charles the Second* (Andrew Anderson 1686).

——*Observations on the Acts of Parliament* (1687).

——*Oratio Inauguralis* (first published, J H Loudun tr, Edinburgh Bibliographical Society 1689).

——*The Works of that Eminent and Learned Lawyer, Sir George Mackenzie*, vols 1 and 2 (James Watson 1716–22).

——*The Institutions of the Law of Scotland*, 1st edn (John Reid 1684) (403 pages); 2nd edn (John Reid 1688) (209 pages); 3rd edn (Thomas Broun 1699) (141 pages); 4th edn (John Vallange 1706) (263 pages); 5th edn (William Brown & Co 1719) (561 pages); 6th edn (William Brown & Co 1723) (347 pages); 7th edn (William Brown 1730) (339 pages); 8th edn (E & J Robertsons 1758) (325 pages); 9th edn (E & J Robertsons 1758).

Maxwell J, *Sacro-Sancta Regum Majestas: Or; The Sacred and Royall Prerogative of Christian Kings* (first published 1644, Tho Dring 1680).

Morison W M (ed), *Decisions of the Court of Session, from its First Institutions to the Present Time* (2nd edn, Archibald Constable 1811).

Nicols T, *An Abridgement of the Whole Body of Divinity, Extracted from the Learned Works of the Ever-Famous and Reverend Divine* (W B 1654).

Nisbet A, *A Brief Exposition of the First and Second Epistles General of Peter* (Christopher Higgins 1658).

——*An Exposition with Practical Observations upon the Book of Ecclesiastes* (George Mosman 1693).

Owen J (ed), *Commentaries on the Epistle of Paul the Apostle to the Romans* (Calvin Translation Society 1849).

Pareus D and Zacharias U, *Corpus Doctrinae Christinae, Eccelesiarum a Papatu Reformation, Contenens Explicationes Catcheticas D Zachariae Ursini* (Iona Rosa 1621).

Perkins W, *Epieikeia, or a Treatise of Christian Equity and Moderation* (Legatt 1604).

Philo, *On the Cherubim. The Sacrifices of Abel and Cain. The Worse Attacks the Better. On the Posterity and Exile of Cain. On the Giants* (Francis H Colson and George H Whitakerb trs, Harvard University Press 1929).

Plato, *Euthyphro. Apology. Crito. Phaedo* (Christopher Emlyn-Jones and William Preddy trs, Harvard University Press 2017).

Plutarch, *Moralia, Volume XII: Concerning the Face Which Appears in the Orb of the Moon. On the Principle of Cold. Whether Fire or Water Is More Useful. Whether Land or Sea Animals*

Are Cleverer. Beasts Are Rational. On the Eating of Flesh (Harold Cherniss and William C Helmbold trs, Harvard University Press 1957).

Pufendorf S, *The Whole Duty of Man, According to the Law of Nature* (first printed (in English) 1735, Liberty Fund 2003).

Puffendorfii S, *De Officio Hominis et Civis, Juxta Legem Naturalem, Libri Duo. Supplementis et Observationibus in Academicae Juventutis Auxit et Illustravit Gerschomus Carmichael, Philosophiae in Academia Glasguensi Professor. Editio Secunda Priore Auctior et Emendatior* (John Mosman 1724).

Ross W, *Lectures on the History and Practice of the Law of Scotland Relative to Conveyancing and Legal Diligence* (Bell & Bradfute 1822).

Rutherford S, *A Sermon Preached to the Honourable House of Commons at their Late Solemne Fast, Wednesday, Jan. 31, 1644* (Evan Tyler 1644).

——*A Survey of the Spirituall Antichrist . . .* (Andrew Crooke 1648).

——*The Covenant of Life: or A Treatise of the Covenant of Grace* (Andrew Anderson 1654).

——*A Treatise of Civil Policy: Being a Resolution of Forth three Questions Concerning Prerogative, Right and Privilege* (London 1656).

——*A Treatise of Civil Policy: Being a Resolution of Forty Three Questions Concerning Prerogative, Right and Priviledge, in Reference to the Supream Prince and the People* (Simon Miller 1657).

——*The Covenant of Life Opened: Or, A Treatise of the Covenant of Grace* (Andrew Anderson 1665).

——*Lex, Rex: The Law and the Prince, a Dispute for the Just Prerogative of King and People* (Robert Ogle and Oliver & Boyd 1843).

Skene J (ed), *Regiam Majestatem Scotiae, Veteres Leges et Constitutiones . . .* (London 1613).

Skenc J, *The Lawes and Actes of Parliament, Maid be King Iames the First, and his Successours Kinges of Scotland Visied, Collected and Extracted Furth of the Register. The Contentes of this Buik, are Expremed in the Leafe Following* (Robert Walde 1597, republished in 1681).

Spotiswoode J (ed), *Practicks of the Laws of Scotland observed and collected by Sir Robert Spotiswoode* (James Watson 1706).

Steuart J, *Naphtali, or, The Wrestlings of the Church of Scotland for the Kingdom of Christ . . .* (Edinburgh 1667).

——*Jus Populi Vindicatum* (London 1669).

Strang J, *De Voluntate et Actionibus Dei circa Peccatum* (Apud Ludovicum & Danielem Elzevirios 1657).

——*De Interpretatione et Perfectione Scripturae, una cum Opusculis de Sabbato* (Ex Officina Arnoldi Leers 1663).

Suárez F, *Selections from Three Works: A Treatise on Laws and God the Lawgiver; A Defence of the Catholic and Apostolic Faith; A Work on the Three Theological Virtues: Faith, Hope, and Charity* (Liberty Fund 2015).

Taylor F, *An Exposition with Practical Observations upon the Three First Chapter of the Proverbs* (E C 1655).

Tillotson J, *Sermons concerning the Divinity and Incarnation of our Blessed Saviour* (Aylmer 1695).

Turnbull G, *A Methodical System of Universal Law: Or, The Law of Nature and Nations . . . Written in Latin by the Celebrated Jo. Got. Heineccius with Supplements and a Discourse by George Turnbull* (J Noon 1741, republished Liberty Fund 2008).

Van Christinaeus P, *Practicarum Quaestionom Rerumque in Supremis Belgarum Curiis Iudicatarum Observatarumque volume II et III* (Antwerp 1626).

Vermigli P M, *Pet Martyris Commentaria in Ethicam Aristotelis 4to* (Tiguri 1563) GUL: Sp Coll Bh9-h.10.

Vinnius A, *Commentarius Locupletissimus, Academicus & Forensis, in Quatuor Libros Institutionum Imperialium* (ex officina Joannes Maire 1642).

——*Institutionum Imperialium Commentaries Academicus & Forensis* (1659).

Voet J, *His Commentary on the Pandects* . . . (J Buchanan tr, J C Juta 1880). Originally published as Voet J, *Commentarius ad Pandectas*, vol 2 (Abrahamum de Hondt 1698, reprinted Johannem Verbessel 1704).

Weemes J, *The Portraiture of the Image of God in Man* (John Bellamie 1636).

Welwood W, *An Abridgement of all Sea-Lawes* (Humfrey Lownes 1613).

Wesenbecius M, *Paratitla in Pandectarum iuris Civilis Libros Quinquaginta* (Basile 1568).

Xenophon, *Memorabilia. Oeconomicus. Symposium. Apology* (E C Marchant and O J Todd tr, revised by Jeffrey Henderson, Harvard University Press 2013).

Zanchi G, *Operum Theologicorum D Hieronymi Zanchii, 8 vols* (Stephanus Gamonetus & Matthaeus Berjon 1605).

——*Hieronymi Zanchii de Religione Christiana fides* (Neustadii 1601) GUL: Sp Coll 1629.

Secondary Sources

Allan D, ' "In the Bosome of a Shaddowie Grove": Sir George Mackenzie and the Consolations of Retirement' (1999) 25 History of European Ideas 251–73.

Allen D and Springsted E O, *Philosophy for Understanding Theology* (2nd edn, Westminster John Knox Press 2007).

Anfray J-P, 'Scottish Scotism? The Philosophy Theses in the Scottish Universities, 1610–1630' in Feingold M and Broadie A (eds), *History of Universities: Volume XXIX/2* (pp 133–59) (OUP 2017).

Anstey P R, *The Idea of Principles in Early Modern Thought* (Routledge 2017).

Astorri P, *Lutheran Theology and Contract Law in Early Modern Germany (ca. 1520–1720)* (Ferdinand Schöningh 2019).

——'Grotius's Contract Theory in the Works of His German Commentators: First Explorations' (2020) 41 (1) Grotiana 88–107.

Atiyah P, *The Rise and Fall of the Freedom of Contract* (OUP 1979).

——*Promises, Morals and Law* (OUP 1983).

Backus I, 'Bucer's view of the Roman and Canon Law in his Exegetical Writings and in his Patristic Florilegium' in Strohm C and Jürgens H P (eds), *Martin Bucer und das Recht* (pp 83–100) (Droz 2002).

Baird Smith D, 'Canon Law' in *An Introductory Survey of the Sources and Literature of Scots Law*, vol 1 (pp 183–92) (Stair Society 1936).

Barry J C (ed), *William Hay's Lectures on Marriage*, vol 24 (Stair Society 1967).

Barton J L, 'Causa Promissionis Again' (1966) 34 Tijdschrift voor Rechtsgeschiedenis 41–73.

Baschera L, 'Aristotle and Scholasticism' in Torrance Kirby W J, Campi E, and James F A III (eds), *A Companion to Peter Martyr Vermigli* (pp 133–59) (Brill 2009).

Baur M, 'Law and Natural Law' in Brian Davies (ed), *The Oxford Handbook of Aquinas* (pp 238–54) (OUP 2012).

Berlin I, 'Two Concepts of Liberty' in Isaiah Berlin, *Four Essays on Liberty* (pp 167–218) (OUP 2002).

Berman H, *Law and Revolution II: The Impact of the Protestant Reformation in the Western Legal Tradition* (Harvard University Press 2006).

Berry C, *The Idea of Luxury* (CUP 1994).

Berry C J, *The Idea of a Commercial Society in the Scottish Enlightenment* (EUP 2013).

Birks P, 'Definition and Divisions: A Meditation on Institutes 3.13' in Peter Birks (ed), *The Classification of Obligations* (pp 1–36) (OUP 1997).

Birocchi I, *Causa e Categoria General del Contratto* (G Giappichelli 1997).

Black A C, 'Institutional Writers' in *An Introductory Survey of the Sources and Literature of Scots Law*, vol 1 (Stair Society 1936).

Black G, *Woolman on Contract* (4th edn, W Green 2010).

Blackie J W G, 'Stair's Later Reputation as a Jurist' in David M Walker (ed), *Stair Tercentenary Studies*, vol 33 (pp 207–37) (Stair Society 1981).

Blaikie W G, 'Ferguson, James (1621–1667)' in *Oxford Dictionary of National Biography*, vol 18 (Smith, Elder & Co 1885–1900) 342–43.

——*The Preachers of Scotland: From the Sixth to the Nineteenth Century* (T&T Clark 1888).

Blom H W and van Dam H-J, 'Dossier: Ordinum Pietas (1613): Its Context and Seventeenth-Century Reception' (2013) 34 Grotiana 7–10.

Bogle S, 'Law and Religion' (2015) 19 (2) Edinburgh Law Review 285–87.

Brett A, 'Natural Right and Civil Community: The Civil Philosophy of Hugo Grotius' (2002) 45 (1) The Historical Journal 31–51.

Brett A S, *Liberty, Right and Nature: Individual Rights in Later Scholastic Thought* (CUP 2003).

Broadie A, *The Shadow of the Scotus: Philosophy and Faith in Pre-Reformation Scotland* (T&T Clark 1995).

——*A History of Scottish Philosophy* (EUP 2008).

——'James Dundas on the Hobbesian State of Nature' (2013) 11 (1) The Journal of Scottish Philosophy 1–13.

——'James Dundas, the First Lord Arniston, on the Idea of Moral Philosophy and the Concept of Will' in A Broadie (ed), *Scottish Philosophy in the Seventeenth Century* (p 158–73) (OUP 2020).

Brown J J, 'The Social, Political and Economic Influences of the Edinburgh Merchant Elite, 1600–1638' (DPhil thesis, University of Edinburgh 1985).

Brown K M, 'Aristocratic Finances and the Origins of the Scottish Revolution' (1989) 104 (410) English Historical Review 46–87.

Brown, Stewart J, 'Religion and Society to c.1900' in T M Devine and J Wormald (eds), *The Oxford Handbook of Modern Scottish History* (pp 79–99) (OUP 2012).

De Bruijn N, '"No One Is A Better Jurist than Accursius": Medieval Legal Scholarship as the Fountainhead of Inspiration for Jacques Cujas and Huges Doneau?' (2014) 82 Legal History Review 72–99.

Buckland W W, *A Textbook of Roman Law* (CUP 1921) 410–11.

Buckroyd J M, 'Bridging the Gap: Scotland 1659–1660' (1987) 66 (181) The Scottish Historical Review 1–25.

Burchill C J, 'Girolamo Zanchi: Portrait of a Reformed Theologian and His Work' (1984) 15 (2) The Sixteenth Century Journal 185–207.

Burns J H, 'Scholasticism: Survival and Revival' in J H Burns and M Goldie (eds), *The Cambridge History of Political Thought 1450–1700* (pp 132–56) (CUP 1991).

Cairns J W, 'Institutional Writings in Scotland Reconsidered' (1983) 4 Journal of Legal History 76–117.

——'The Formation of the Scottish Legal Mind in the Eighteenth Century: Themes of Humanism and Enlightenment in the Admission of Advocates' in N MacCormick and P Birks (eds), *The Legal Mind: Essays for Tony Honore* (pp 253–77) (OUP 1986).

——'The Law, the Advocates and the Universities in Late Sixteenth-Century Scotland' (1994) 73 (196) Scottish Historical Review 171.

——'The Civil Law Tradition in Scottish Legal Thought' in D I C Miller and R Zimmermann (eds), *The Civilian Tradition and Scots Law: Aberdeen Quincentenary Essays* (pp 191–223) (Duncker & Humblot 1995).

——'Historical Introduction' in K Reid and R Zimmermann (eds), *A History of Private Law in Scotland*, vol 2 (pp 14–184) (OUP 2000).

——'The Moveable Text of Mackenzie: Bibliographical Problems for the Scottish Concept of Institutional Writing' in J W Cairns and O F Robinson (eds), *Critical Studies in Ancient Law, Comparative Law and Legal History* (pp 235–48) (Hart 2001).

——'Jus Civile in Scotland, ca. 1600' (2004) 2 Roman Legal Tradition 136.

——'The First Edinburgh Chair in Law: Grotius and the Scottish Enlightenment' (2005) 11 (32) Fundamina 31–57.

——'Attitudes to Codification and the Scottish Science of Legislation 1600–1830' (2007) 22 Tulane European and Civil Law Forum 1.

——'National, Transnational and European Legal Histories: Problems and Paradigms. A Scottish Perspective' (2012) 5 Clio@Themis: Revue Électronique d'Histoire du Droit 1.

——'Teaching Criminal Law in Early Eighteenth-Century Scotland: Collegia and Compendia' (2012) 20 (1) Fundamina 90–99.

——'Importing Our Lawyers from Holland: Netherlands Influences on Scots Law and Lawyers in the Eighteenth Century' in J W Cairns (ed), *Law, Lawyers, and Humanism: Selected Essays on the History of Scots Law*, vol 1 (pp 223–41) (EUP 2015).

——'Natural Law, National Laws, Parliaments, and Multiple Monarchies: 1707 and Beyond' in J W Cairns (ed), *Law, Lawyers, and Humanism: Selected Essays on the History of Scots Law*, vol 1 (pp 115–43) (EUP 2015).

——'Introduction' in J W Cairns (ed), *Enlightenment, Legal Education and Critique*, vol 2 (pp x–xxviii) (EUP 2017).

——'The Legacy of Smith's Jurisprudence in Late Eighteenth-Century Edinburgh' in I Hunter and R Whatmore (eds), *Philosophy, Rights and Natural Law* (pp 278–305) (EUP 2019).

Fergus T D and MacQueen H L, 'Legal Humanism in Renaissance Scotland' (1990) 11 *Journal of Legal History* 40–69.

Campbell A H, *The Structure of Stair's Institutions* (Jackson, Son & Co 1954).

Canny N (ed), *The Oxford History of the British Empire: Volume 1* (OUP 1998).

Carey Miller D L and Zimmermann R (eds), *The Civilian Tradition and Scots Law: Aberdeen Quincentenary Essays* (Duncker & Humblot 1995).

Carmichael C (ed), *The Deed and the Doer in the Bible: David Daube's Gifford Lectures*, vol 1 (Templeton Press 2008).

Chappell V (ed), *Hobbes and Bramhall on Liberty and Necessity* (CUP 1999).

Clarke D M, 'Descartes' Philosophy of Science and the Scientific Revolution' in J Cottingham (ed), *The Cambridge Companion to Descartes* (pp 258–85) (CUP 1992).

Cleveland C, *Thomism in John Owen* (Ashgate Publishing 2013).

Coffey J, *Politics, Religion and the British Revolutions: The Mind of Samuel Rutherford* (CUP 1997).

Coing H, 'English Equity and The Denunciatio Evangelica of the Canon Law' (1955) 71 Law Quarterly Review 223.

Collinet P, 'The evolution of contract as illustrating the general evolution of Roman law' (1932) 48 Law Quarterly Review 488.

Coutts J, *A History of the University of Glasgow, from its Foundation in 1451 to 1909* (James Maclehose and Sons 1909).

Cranz F E, 'The Publishing History of the Aristotle Commentaries of Thomas Aquinas' (1978) 34 Traditio 157–92.

Davies B, *The Thought of Thomas Aquinas* (OUP 1993).

Davis J, *Medieval Market Morality: Life, Law and Ethics in the English Marketplace, 1200–1500* (CUP 2011).

Dawson J E A, 'Bonding, religious allegiance and covenanting' in J Goodare and S I Boardman (eds), *Lords and Men in Scotland, 1300–1625* (pp 155–72) (EUP 2014).

Decock W, 'Leonardus Lessius on Buying and Selling (1605). Translation and Introduction' (2007) 10 (2) Journal of Markets and Morality 433–516.

——'Jesuit Freedom of Contract' (2009) 77 Tijdschrift voor Rechtsgeschiedenis 423–58.

——'From Law to Paradise: Confessional Catholicism and Legal Scholarship' (2011) 18 Rechtsgeschichte 12–34.

——*Theologians and Contract Law: The Moral Transformation of the Ius Commune (ca 1500–1650)* (Brill 2013).

——'The Catholic Spirit of Capitalism' in W Decock, J J Ballor, M Germann, and L Waelkens (eds), *Law and Religion: The Legal Teachings of the Protestant and Catholic Reformations* (pp 22–44) (Vandenhoeck & Ruprecht 2014).

—— 'Hugo Grotius's Views on Consent, Contract and the Christian Commonwealth' (2020) 41 (1) Grotiana 1–176.

Decock W, Ballor J J, Germann M, and Waelkens L (eds), *Law and Religion: The Legal Teachings of the Protestant and Catholic Reformations* (Vandenhoeck & Ruprecht 2014).

Dihle A, *The Theory of Will in Classical Antiquity* (California University Press 1982).

Dolezalek G, 'The Court of Session as a Ius Commune Court—Witnessed by "Sinclair's Practicks", 1540–1549' in H L MacQueen (ed), *Miscellany Four*, vol 49 (pp 51–84) (Stair Society 2002).

——'Introduction: The Purpose of this Book' in *Scotland under the Ius Commune*, vol 55 (pp 1–12) (Stair Society 2010).

——*Scotland under Jus Commune*, vol 55 (Stair Society 2010).

Donagan A, 'Thomas Aquinas on Human Action' in N Kretzmann, A Kenny, K Pinborg, and E Stump (eds), *The Cambridge History of Later Medieval Philosophy* (pp 642–54) (CUP 1982).

Donnelly J P, *Calvinism and Scholasticism in Vermigli's Doctrine of Man and Grace* (Brill 1976).

Du Plessis P J, 'Legal History and Legal Method(s)' (2010) 16 (1) Fundamina 47.

Duguit L, 'Collective Acts as Distinguished from Contracts' (1918) 27 Yale Law Journal 753–68.

Dunn J M, 'The Identity of the History of Ideas' in *Political Obligation in its Historical Context* (pp 13–28) (OUP 1980). Originally published as Dunn J, 'The Identity of the History of Ideas' (1968) 43 (164) Philosophy 85–104.

Dunn J, *The Political Thought of John Locke* (CUP 1995).

Dunthrone H, 'History, Theology and Tolerance: Grotius and his English Contemporaries' (2013) 34 Grotiana 107–19.

Epstein S R, *Freedom and Growth: The Rise of States and Markets in Europe, 1300–1750* (Routledge 2000).

Erasmus H J, 'Natural Law: Voet's Criticism of De Groot' (2016) 22 (1) Fundamina 40–52.

Ewan L A, 'Debt and Credit in Early Modern Scotland: The Grandtully Estates 1650–1765' (DPhil thesis, University of Edinburgh 1988).

Feenstr R, 'Scottish–Dutch Legal Relations in the Seventeenth and Eighteenth Centuries' in T C Smout (ed), *Scotland and Europe, 1200–1850* (pp 128–42) (John Donald 1986).

——'Pact and Contract in the Low Countries from the 16th to the 18th century' in J Barton (ed), *Towards a General Law of Contract* (pp 197–213) (Duncker & Humblot 1990).

——'La Systématique du Droit dans l'œuvre de Grotius' in L M Friedman, Istituto della Enciclopedia Italiana, Accademia Nazionale dei Lincei, and Convegno Internazionale su la Sistematica Giuridica (eds), *La Sistematica Giuridica: Storia, Teoria e Problem Attuali* (pp 333–45) (Istituto della Enciclopedia Italiana 1991).

——'The Development of European Private Law: A Watershed?' in D L C Miller and R Zimmermann, *The Civilian Tradition and Scots Law* (pp 103–66) (Duncker & Humblot 1995).

——and Ahsmann M, *Contract: Aspecten van de Begrippen Contract en Contractsvrijheid in Historisch Perspectief* (Kluwer 1988).

——and Wall C J D, *Seventeenth-Century Leyden Law Professors and their Influence on the Development of the Civil Law* (North-Holland Publishing 1975).

Fiori R, 'The Roman Concept of Contract' in T A J McGinn (ed), *Obligations in Roman Law* (pp 40–75) (University of Michigan Press 2013).

Flint T P and Rea M C (eds), *The Oxford Handbook of Philosophical Theology* (OUP 2011).

Forbes D, 'Natural Law and the Scottish Enlightenment' in R H Campbell and A Skinner (eds), *The Origins and Nature of the Scottish Enlightenment* (pp 186–204) (John Donald 1982).

Ford J D, 'The Rational Discipline of Law' (DPhil thesis, University of Cambridge 1988).

——'Lex, Rex Iusto Posita: Samuel Rutherford on the Origins of Government' in R A Mason (ed), *Scots and Britons: Scottish Political Thought and the Union of 1603* (pp 262–90) (CUP 1994).

——'Stair's Title "Of Liberty and Servitude"' in A D E Lewis and D J Ibbetson (eds), *The Roman Law Tradition* (pp 135–58) (CUP 1994).

——'The Civilian Tradition and Scots Law: Aberdeen Quincentenary Essays. Edited by David L Carey Miller and Reinhard Zimmermann' (1998) 57 (2) Cambridge Law Journal 415–18.

——'A History of Private Law in Scotland, 2 vols' (2001) 60 (3) Cambridge Law Journal 630.

——'Dalrymple, James, first Viscount Stair (1619–1695)' in H. C. G. Matthew and B Harrison (eds), *Oxford Dictionary of National Biography* (OUP 2004) < Dalrymple, James, first Viscount Stair (1619-1695) | Oxford Dictionary of National Biography (oxforddnb.com)>, accessed 9 November 2022.

——*Law and Opinion in Scotland during the Seventeenth Century* (Hart 2007).

——'Protestations to Parliament for Remeid of Law' (2009) 85 (225) The Scottish Historical Review 57–107.

——(ed), *Alexander King's Treatise on Maritime Law*, vol 65 (Stair Society 2018).

Frede M, *A Free Will: Origins of the Notion in Ancient Thought* (University of California Press 2011).

Freedman J S, 'Aristotle and the Content of Philosophy Instruction at Central European Schools and Universities during the Reformation Era' (1993) 137(2) Proceedings of the American Philosophical Society 213–53.

——*Philosophy and the Arts in Central Europe, 1500-1700: Teaching and Texts at Schools and Universities* (Taylor Francis 1999).

Fried C, *Contract as Promise: A Theory of Contractual Obligations* (first published 1981, OUP 2015).

Gardiner S R, *History of the Great Civil War, 1642–1649* (vol 4) (Longmans, Green & Co 1901).

Geisst C R, *Beggar Thy Neighbor: A History of Usury and Debt* (University of Pennsylvania Press 2013).

Gellera G, 'Natural Philosophy in the Graduation Theses of the Scottish Universities in the First Half of the Seventeenth Century' (DPhil thesis, University of Glasgow 2012).

——'Pride Aside: James Dundas as a Stoic Christian' (2019) 17 (2) Journal of Scottish Philosophy 157–74.

——*The Philosophy of James Dundas* (Edinburgh University Press forthcoming).

Gilbert N W, *Renaissance Concepts of Method* (Columbia University Press 1960).

Gordley J, *The Philosophical Origins of Modern Contract Doctrine* (OUP 1991).

——'Contract, Property, and the Will—The Civil Law and Common Law Tradition' in H N Scheiber (ed), *The State and Freedom of Contract* (pp 66–88) (Stanford University Press 1998).

——'Why Look Backward' (2002) 50 (4) The American Journal of Comparative Law 657–70.

——'Ius Quaerens Intellectum: The Method of the Medieval Civilians' in J W Cairns and P J du Plessis (eds), *The Creation of the Ius Commune: From Casus to Regula* (pp 77–102) (Edinburgh University Press 2010).

——'The Method of the Roman Jurists' (2013) 87 (4) Tulane Law Review 933–54.

Gordon W M, 'A Comparison of the Influence of Roman Law in England and Scotland' in W M Gordon (ed), *Roman Law, Scots Law and Legal History: Selected Essays* (pp 309–23) (Edinburgh University Press 2007).

——'Stair, Grotius and the Sources of Stair's *Institutions*' in W Gordon and E Reid (eds), *Roman Law, Scots Law and Legal History* (pp 225–66) (EUP 2007).

Gordon W M, 'Risk in Sale—From Roman to Scots Law' in W M Gordon (ed), *Roman Law, Scots Law and Legal History* (pp 164–76) (Edinburgh University Press 2007).

Gouldesbrough P (ed), *Formulary of Old Scots Legal Documents*, vol 36 (Stair Society 1985).

Gow J J, 'The Constitution and Proof of Voluntary Obligations' (1961) 6 Juridical Review 1–124.

Graham J M (ed), *Annals and Correspondence of the Viscount and the First and Second Earls of Stair*, vol 1 (William Blackwood & Sons 1875).

Graham M F, *The Uses of Reform: Godly Discipline and Popular Behaviour in Scotland and Beyond, 1560–1610* (Brill 1996).

Green T M (ed), *The Consistorial Decisions of the Commissaries of Edinburgh, 1564–1576/7*, vol 61 (Stair Society 2014).

Green T, *The Spiritual Jurisdiction in Reformation Scotland: A Legal History* (EUP 2019).

Greif A, *Institutions and the Path to the Modern Economy: Lessons from Medieval Trade* (CUP 2006).

Gribben C, 'Preaching the Scottish Reformation, 1560–1707' in H Adlington, P McCullough, and E Rhatigan (eds), *The Oxford Handbook of the Early Modern Sermon* (pp 272–86) (OUP 2011).

Haakonssen, K, 'What Might be Called Natural Jurisprudence?' in R H Campbell and A Skinner (eds), *The Origins and Nature of the Scottish Enlightenment* (pp 205–25) (John Donald 1982).

Haakonssen K, 'Hugo Grotius and the History of Political Thought' (1985) 13 (2) Political Theory 239–65.

——*Natural Law and Moral Philosophy: From Grotius to the Scottish Enlightenment* (CUP 1996).

——'Protestant Natural Law Theory: A General Interpretation' in N Brender and I Krasnoff (eds), *New Essays on the History of Autonomy* (pp 92–109) (CUP 2004).

——and Seidler M J, 'Natural Law: Law, Rights and Duties' in R Whatmore and B Young (eds), *A Companion to Intellectual History* (pp 383–94) (Wiley-Blackwell 2015).

Hallebeek J, 'Medieval Legal Scholarship' in J Hallebeek and H Dondorp (eds), *Contract for a Third-Party Beneficiary* (1–28) (Brill 2008).

Halpérin J-L, *Five Legal Revolutions Since the 17th Century: An Analysis of Global Legal History* (Springer 2014).

Hause J, 'John Duns Scotus (1266–1308)' in *Internet Encyclopedia of Philosophy* <Scotus, John Duns | Internet Encyclopedia of Philosophy (utm.edu)> accessed 10 November 2022.

Helm P, *John Calvin's Ideas* (OUP 2004).

Helmholz R H, *The Spirit of Classical Canon Law* (University of Georgia Press 1996).

Helmholz R (ed), *The Oxford History of Laws of England, Vol I: The Canon Law and Ecclesiastical Jurisdiction from 597 to the 1640s* (OUP 2004).

Henderson G D, *Religious Life in Seventeenth-Century Scotland* (CUP 1937).

Hirschman A O, *The Passions and the Interests: Political Arguments for Capitalism Before Its Triumph* (first published 1977, Princeton University Press 2013).

Hochstrasser T J, *Natural Law Theories in the Early Enlightenment* (CUP 2000).

Hoeflich M H, 'A Seventeenth-Century Roman Law Bibliography: Jacques Godefroy and his "Bibliotheca Juris Civilis Romani"' (1982) 75 Law Library Journal 514–52.

Hoffmann T, 'Intellectualism and Voluntarism' in R Pasnau (ed), *The Cambridge History of Medieval Philosophy*, vol 1 (pp 414–27) (CUP 2009).

Hogg M, 'Perspectives on Contract Theory from a Mixed Jurisdiction' (2009) 29 (3) Oxford Journal of Legal Studies 643–67.

——'Promises: The Neglected Obligation in European Private Law' (2010) 59 International Comparative Law Quarterly 461,

——*Promises and Contract Law: Comparative Perspectives* (CUP 2011).

Holfelder K D, 'Durham, James (1622–1658)' in *Oxford Dictionary of National Biography* (OUP 2004) <Durham, James (1622–1658), Church of Scotland minister | Oxford Dictionary of National Biography (oxforddnb.com)>, accessed 10 November 2022.

——'Gillespie, George (1613–1648)' in *Oxford Dictionary of National Biography* (OUP 2004) <Gillespie, George (1613–1648), Church of Scotland minister and theologian | Oxford Dictionary of National Biography (oxforddnb.com)> accessed 10 November 2022.

Holligan B, 'Ownership and Obligation: Restitution, Vindication and the Recovery of Moveables in Stair's *Institutions*' (2017) 21 (2) Edinburgh Law Review 169–91.

Hont I, 'The Language of Sociability and Commerce' in A Pagden (ed), *The Languages of Political Theory in Early-Modern Europe* (pp 253–76) (CUP 1987).

——*Jealousy of Trade: International Competition and the Nation-State in Historical Perspective* (CUP 2010).

——and Ignatieff M, 'Needs and Justice in the *Wealth of Nations*: An Introductory Essay' in *Wealth and Virtue: The Shaping of Political Economy in the Scottish Enlightenment* (pp 1–44) (CUP 1983).

Hutton G M, *The Political Thought of Sir James Dalrymple, First Viscount Stair (1619–1695), with special reference to his concepts of Natural Law and Sovereignty, and in Relation to his Political Life* (DPhil thesis, University of Birmingham 1971).

——'Stair's Philosophical Precursors' in D M Walker (ed), *Stair Tercentenary Studies*, vol 33 (pp 90–91) (Stair Society 1981).

——'Stair's Public Career' in D M Walker (ed), *Stair Tercentenary Studies*, vol 33 (pp 1–65) (Stair Society 1981).

Hutton S, *British Philosophy in the Seventeenth Century* (OUP 2015).

Hyland R, 'Pacta Sunt Servanda: A Meditation' (1993–94) 34 Virginia Journal of International Law 405.

Ibbetson D, *A Historical Introduction to the Law of Obligations* (OUP 2001).

——'Natural Law and Common Law' (2001) 5 (1) Edinburgh Law Review 4–20.

——'What is Legal History a History of?' in A Lewis and M Lobban (eds), *Law and History: Current Legal Issues 2003*, vol 6 (pp 33–40) (Oxford 2004).

Irvine Smith J, 'The Transition to the Modern Law 1532–1660' in *An Introduction to Scottish Legal History*, vol 20 (pp 25–43) (Stair Society 1958).

Irwin D, *Against the Tide: An Intellectual History of Free Trade* (Princeton University Press 1995).

Irwin T, *The Development of Ethics: Volume 1: From Socrates to the Reformation* (OUP 2007).

Jackson C, 'Natural Law and the Construction of Political Sovereignty in Early Modern Scotland' in I Hunter and D Saunders (eds), *Natural Law and Civil Sovereignty* (pp 155–69) (Palgrave 2002).

——*Restoration Scotland, 1660–1690: Royalist Politics, Religion and Ideas* (Boydell Press 2003).

——'Religious Latitude, Secular Theology and Sir Thomas Browne's Influence in George Mackenzie's *Religio Stoici* (1663)' (2014) 29 *The Seventeenth Century* 73–94.

Kelley D R, *The Beginning of Ideology: Consciousness and Society in the French Reformation* (CUP 1981).

Kent B, *Virtues of the Will: The Transformation of Ethics in the Late Thirteenth Century* (Catholic University of America Press 1995).

Kim M, 'Custom, Community, and the Crown: Lawyers and the Reordering of French Customary Law' in C H Parker and J H Bentley (eds), *Between the Middle Ages and Modernity: Individual and Community in the Early Modern World* (pp 169–86) (Rowman & Littlefield 2007).

Kingsbury B and Straumann B, 'The State of Nature and Commercial Sociability in Early Modern International Legal Thought' (2010) 31 Grotiana 22–43.

Klinck D R, *Conscience, Equity and the Court of Chancery in Early Modern England* (Ashgate 2010).

Koch S, 'Grotius's Impact on the Scandinavian Theory of Contract Law' (2020) 41 (1) Grotiana 59–87.

Kotlyar I A, 'The Influence of European Ius Commune on the Scots Law of Succession to Moveables, 1560–1700' (DPhil thesis, University of Edinburgh 2017).

Kraye J, 'Moral Philosophy' in C B Schmitt Q Skinner, E Kessler, and J Kraye (eds), *The Cambridge History of Renaissance Philosophy* (pp 303–86) (CUP 1988).

——(ed), *Cambridge Translations of Renaissance Philosophical Texts: Moral and Political Philosophy*, vol 2 (CUP 1997).

Kuhn H, 'Aristotelianism in the Renaissance' in E N Zalta (ed), *The Stanford Encyclopedia of Philosophy Archive*, Spring 2018 Edition (first published 2005, Stanford University 2018) <https://plato.stanford.edu/archives/spr2018/entries/aristotelianism-renaissance/> accessed 8 April 2021.

Lane A N S, *John Calvin Student of Church Fathers* (T&T Clark 1999).

Lee D, *Popular Sovereignty in Early Modern Constitutional Thought* (pp 258–64) (OUP 2016).

Lee R W, *An Introduction to Roman-Dutch Law* (5th edn, Clarendon Press 1953).

Leites E (ed), *Conscience and Casuistry in Early Modern Europe* (CUP 1988).

Leng T, 'Commercial Conflict and Regulation in the Discourse of Trade in Seventeenth-Century England' (2005) 48 (4) The Historical Journal 933–54.

Lenman B, 'The Limits of Godly Discipline in the Early Modern Period with Particular Reference to England and Scotland' in K von Greyerz (ed), *Religion and Society in Early Modern Europe, 1500–1800* (pp 124–45) (Allen & Unwin 1984).

Lesaffer R, *European Legal History: A Cultural and Political Perspective* (CUP 2009).

Lohr C H, 'The Medieval Interpretation of Aristotle' in N Kretzmann, A Kenny, K Pinborg, and E Stump (eds), *The Cambridge History of Later Medieval Philosophy* (pp 80–98) (CUP 1982).

Lorenzen E G, 'Causa and Consideration in the Law of Contracts' (1919) 28 (7) Yale Law Journal 621–46.

Lubbe G, 'Formation of Contract' in K Reid and R Zimmermann (eds), *A History of Private Law in Scotland*, vol 2 (pp 1–46) (OUP 2000).

Luig K, 'The Institutes of National Law in the Seventeenth and Eighteenth Centuries' (1972) 17 Juridical Review 193.

——'Stair from a Foreign Standpoint' in D M Walker (ed), *Stair Tercentenary Studies*, vol 33 (pp 239–52) (Stair Society 1981).

Lynch M, 'The Wars of Covenant' in M Lynch (ed), *The Oxford Companion to Scottish History* (OUP 2001).

Lythe S G E, *The Economy of Scotland 1550–1625* (Oliver & Boyd 1960).

McBryde W W, 'Promises in Scots Law' (1993) 41 International Comparative Law Quarterly 48.

——*The Law of Contract in Scotland* (3rd edn, W Green 2007).

McClelland P, 'The Seller's Liability for Sale of Fault Goods in Scots Law' (pp 14–28) (LLM thesis, University of Glasgow 2015).

McLeod G, 'The Romanization of Property Law' in K Reid and R Zimmermann (eds), *A History of Private Law in Scotland*, vol 1 (pp 220–42) (OUP 2000).

MacCormick N, 'Stair as Analytical Jurist' in D M Walker (ed), *Stair Tercentenary Studies*, vol 33 (pp 187–99) (Stair Society 1981).

——'Law and Enlightenment' in R H Campbell and A Skinner (eds), *The Origins and Nature of the Scottish Enlightenment* (pp 150–66) (John Donald 1982).

——'The Rational Discipline of Law' (1982) 26 Juridical Review 146–60.

MacCormick, Neil, *Legal Right and Social Democracy: Essays in Legal and Political Philosophy* (OUP 1984).

——'Stair and the Natural Law Tradition: Still Relevant?' in H L MacQueen (ed), *Miscellany Six*, vol 54 (pp 1–10) (Stair Society 2009).

McGrath A E, *Reformation Thought: An Introduction* (2nd edn, Wiley-Blackwell 1993).

——*The Intellectual Origins of the European Reformation* (2nd edn, Blackwell 2004).

Macinnes A I, *The British Revolution, 1629–1660* (Macmillan 2005).

MacIntosh G H, *The Scottish Parliament under Charles II, 1660–1685* (Edinburgh University Press 2007).

MacIntyre A, *Whose Justice? Which Rationality?* (Duckworth 1988).

McIntyre N, 'Saints and Subverters: The Later Covenanters in Scotland c. 1648–1682' (DPhil thesis, University of Strathclyde 2016).

Mackay A J G, *Memoir of Sir James Dalrymple, First Viscount Stair* (Edmonston & Douglas 1873).

McKechnie H, 'Practicks, 1469–1700 Part 1. Native Sources' in *An Introductory Survey of the Sources and Literature of Scots Law*, vol 1 (pp 28–41) (Stair Society 1936).

Mackenzie Stuart A J, 'Contract and Quasi Contract' in *An Introduction to Scottish Legal History*, vol 20 (pp 241–64) (Stair Society 1958).

Macleod J, 'Error Before Bell: The Roots of Error in the Scots Law of Contract' (2010) 14 (3) Edinburgh Law Review 385–417.

MacMillan C, *Mistakes in Contract Law* (Hart 2010).

McNeill P G B, 'Introduction' in P G B McNeill (ed), *The Practicks of Sir James Balfour of Pittendreich*, vol 1 (pp xi–lxvii) (Stair Society, vol 22, 1963).

——(ed), *The Practicks of Sir James Balfour of Pittendreich*, vol 2 (Stair Society, vol 22, 1963).

MacQueen H L, 'Mackenzie's *Institutions* in Scottish Legal History' (1984) 29 Journal of the Law Society of Scotland 498–501.

——'"Regiam Majestatem", Scots Law, and National Identity' (1995) 74 (197) Scottish Historical Review 1–25.

MacQueen H and Thomson J, *Contract Law in Scotland* (3rd edn, Bloomsbury Professional 2012).

Maine H S, *Ancient Law: Its Connection with the Early History of Society, and its Relation to Modern Ideas* (John Murray 1861).

Mann A, *The Scottish Book Trade, 1500 to 1720* (Tuckwell 2000).

Mathieson W L, *Politics and Religion; a Study in Scottish History from the Reformation to the Revolution*, vol 2 (James MacLehose and Sons 1902) 175.

Maurer C, '"A Lapsu Corruptus": Calvinist Doctrines and Seventeenth-Century Scottish Theses Ethicæ' in M Feingold and A Broadie (eds), *History of Universities: Volume XXIX/2* (pp 189–209) (OUP 2017).

Mendelson M, 'Saint Augustine' in E N Zalta (ed), *The Stanford Encyclopedia of Philosophy*, Fall 2019 Edition (Stanford University Press 2012) <https://plato.stanford.edu/archives/fall2019/entries/augustine> accessed 8 April 2021.

Miller J, 'Innate Ideas in Stoicism and Grotius' in H W Blom and L C Winkel (eds), *Grotius and the Stoa* (pp 157–76) (Royal van Gorcum 2004).

Mitchison R, *Lordship to Patronage Scotland 1603–1745* (Edinburgh University Press 1983) 68.

Moore J, 'Natural Rights in the Scottish Enlightenment' in M Goldie and R Wokler (eds), *The Cambridge History of Eighteenth-Century Political Thought* (pp 291–316) (CUP 2006).

——and Silverthorne M, 'Gershom Carmichael and the Natural Jurisprudence Tradition in Eighteenth-Century Scotland' in I Hont and M Ignatieff (eds), *Wealth and Virtue* (pp 73–87) (CUP 1983).

——(eds), *Natural Rights on the Threshold of the Scottish Enlightenment: The Writings of Gershom Carmichael* (Liberty Fund 2002).

Morley N, *Trade in Classical Antiquity* (CUP 2007).

Mullan D G, 'Theology in the Church of Scotland 1618–c. 1640: A Calvinist Consensus?' (1995) 26 (3) *The Sixteenth Century Journal* 595–617.

——*Scottish Puritanism, 1590–1638* (OUP 2000).

Muller R A, 'Calvin and the "Calvinists": Assessing Continuities and Discontinuities between the Reformation and Orthodoxy' (1995) 30 *Calvin Theological Journal* 345–75.

——'Reformation, Orthodoxy, "Christian Aristotelianism", and the Eclecticism of Early Modern Philosophy' (2001) 81 (3) Dutch Review of Church History 306–25.

——*After Calvin. Studies in the Development of a Theological Tradition* (OUP 2003).

——*Divine Will and Human Choice* (Baker Academic 2017).

Murphy M, 'Theological Voluntarism' in E N Zalta (ed), *The Stanford Encyclopedia of Philosophy*, Summer 2019 Edition (Stanford University Press 2013) <https://plato.stanford.edu/archives/sum2019/entries/voluntarism-theological/> accessed 8 April 2021.

Murray M J and Rea M, 'Philosophy and Christian Theology' in E N Zalta (ed), *The Stanford Encyclopedia of Philosophy*, Spring 2020 Edition (Stanford University Press 2014) <https://plato.stanford.edu/archives/spr2020/entries/christiantheology-philosophy/> accessed 8 April 2021.

Musculus W, 'Commentary on Psalm 15 (1551)', tr T M Rester (2008) 11 (2) Journal of Markets and Morality 349–460.

Nanz K P, *Die Entstehung des Allgemeinen Verstagsbegriffs im 16. bis 18. Jahrhundert* (Schweitzer 1985).

Nève P, 'Disputations of Scots Students Attending Universities in the Northern Netherlands' in W M Gordon and T D Fergus (eds), *Legal History in the Making* (pp 93–108) (Hambledon Press 1991).

Nicholas B, *An Introduction to Roman Law* (OUP 1962).

Normand W G, 'Consideration in the Law of Scotland' (1939) 55 Law Quarterly Review 359.

Nussbaum M C, *Philosophical Interventions: Reviews 1986–2011* (OUP 2012).

Ogilvie S, *Institutions and European Trade: Merchant Guilds, 1000–1800* (CUP 2011).

Ollivant S, *The Court of the Official in Pre-Reformation Scotland, based on the Surviving Records of the Officials of St Andrews and Edinburgh*, vol 34 (Stair Society 1982).

Ong W J, *Ramus, Method, and the Decay of Dialogue: From the Art of Discourse to the Art of Reason* (first published 1958, Chicago University Press 2004).

Ormrod D, *The Rise of Commercial Empires: England and the Netherlands in the Age of Mercantilism, 1650–1770* (CUP 2003).

Osler D, 'Legal Humanism' Max Planck Institute <http://www.rg.mpg.de/research-project/legal-humanism> accessed 7 April 2021.

Overhoff J, *Hobbes's Theory of the Will: Ideological Reasons and Historical Circumstances* (Rowman & Littlefield 2000).

Owens J, 'Aristotle and Aquinas' in *The Cambridge Companion to Aquinas* (pp 38–57) (CUP 1996).

Ozment S and Witte J, 'Luther' in J Witte Jr and G S Hauk (eds), *Christianity and Family Law* (pp 179–94) (CUP 2017).

Pagden A R D, 'The Diffusion of Aristotle's Moral Philosophy in Spain, ca. 1400–ca. 1600' (1975) 31 Traditio 287–313.

Parkinson G H R (ed), *The Renaissance and Seventeenth-Century Rationalism: Routledge History of Philosophy*, vol IV (Routledge 1993).

Perkams M, 'Aquinas on Choice, Will and Voluntary Action' in T Hoffmann J Müller, and M Perkams (eds), *Aquinas and the Nicomachean Ethics* (pp 72–90) (CUP 2013).

Pilsner J, *The Specification of Human Actions in St Thomas Aquinas* (pp 10–29) (OUP 2006).

Pink T, 'Suárez, Hobbes and the Scholastic Tradition in Action Theory' in T Pink and M W F Stone (eds), *The Will and Human Action: From Antiquity to the Present Day* (pp 127–53) (Routledge 2003).

——'Self-Determination and Moral Responsibility from Calvin to Frankfurt' in M Stone (ed), *Faith and History: Philosophical Essays for Paul Helm* (pp 145–64) (Ashgate 2008).

——'Thomas Hobbes and the Ethics of Freedom' (2011) 54 (5) Inquiry 541–63.

——'Freedom of the Will' in J Marenbon (ed), *The Oxford Handbook of Medieval Philosophy* (pp 570–87) (OUP 2012).

——'Reason and Obligation in Suárez' in B Hill and H Lagerlund (eds), *The Philosophy of Francisco Suárez* (pp 175–208) (OUP 2012).

——and M W F Stone (eds), *The Will and Human Action: From Antiquity to the Present Day* (Routledge 2003).

Pitkin B, 'John Calvin' in J Witte Jr and G S Hauk (eds), *Christianity and Family Law* (pp 195–210) (CUP 2017).

Pocock J G A, *Virtue, Commerce, and History: Essays on Political Thought and History* (CUP 1985).

Poggi G, *The Development of the Modern State: The Sociological State* (Stanford University Press 1978).

Poldnikov D, 'Origins of General Concept of Contract in Western European Legal Science' (2016) 2 Journal on European History of Law 53–59.

Porter J, 'Action and Intention' in R Pasnau and C van Dyke (eds), *The Cambridge History of Medieval Philosophy*, vol 2 (pp 506–16) (CUP 2010).

Pothier R J, *A Treatise on the Law of Obligations, Or Contracts*, vol 1 (Robert H Small 1853).

Pound R, 'Liberty of Contract' (1909) 18 Yale Law Journal 454–87.

Quantin J-L, 'Catholic Moral Theology, 1550–1800' in U L Lehner, R A Muller, and A G Roeber (eds), *The Oxford Handbook of Early Modern Theology, 1600–1800* (pp 119–34) (OUP 2016).

Raffe A, 'Presbyterianism, Secularization, and Scottish Politics after the Revolution of 1688–1690' (2010) 53 (2) The Historical Journal 317–37.

Rawles S, *The 1691 Catalogue of Glasgow University Library* (unpublished 2005).

Reid D, 'Thomas Aquinas and Viscount Stair: The Influence of Scholastic Moral Theology on Stair's Account of Restitution and Recompense' (2008) 29 Journal of Legal History 189–214.

——'The Doctrine of Presumptive Fraud in Scots Law' (2013) 34 (3) Journal of Legal *History* 307–26.

--'Fraud in Scots Law' (DPhil thesis, University of Edinburgh 2013).

Reid K and Zimmermann R (eds), *A History of Private Law in Scotland* (OUP 2000).

——'The Development of Legal Doctrine in a Mixed System' in *A History of Private Law in Scotland*, vol 1 (pp 1–13) (OUP 2000).

Richter T, 'Molina, Grotius, Stair and the Jus Quaesitum Tertio' (2001) 14 Juridical Review 219.

Robertson J J, 'Canon Law as a Source' in D M Walker (ed), *Stair Tercentenary Studies*, vol 33 (pp 122–27) (Stair Society 1981).

Robinson O, *The Sources of Roman Law: Problems and Methods for Ancient Historians* (Routledge 1996).

Robinson O F, 'Law, Morality and Sir George Mackenzie' in H L MacQueen (ed), *Miscellany Six*, vol 54 (pp 11–28) (Stair Society 2009).

Rodger A F, 'Molina, Stair and the Jus Quaesitum Tertio' (1969) 14 Juridical Review 34–44, 128–51.

Ross R J, 'Puritan Godly Discipline in Comparative Perspective: Legal Pluralism and the Sources of "Intensity"' (2008) 113 American Historical Review 975–1002.

——'Binding in Conscience: Early Modern English Protestants and Spanish Thomists on Law and the Fate of the Soul' (2015) 33 Law and History Review 803–37.

Saarinen R, *Weakness of Will in Renaissance and Reformation Thought* (OUP 2011).

Sampson M, 'Laxity and Liberty in Seventeenth-Century English Political Thought' in E Leites (ed), *Conscience and Casuistry in Early Modern Europe* (pp 72–119) (CUP 1988).

Scattola M, 'Before and After Natural Law: Models of Natural Law in Ancient and Modern Times' in T J Hochstrasser and P Schröder (eds), *Early Modern Natural Law Theories: Context and Strategies in Early Enlightenment* (pp 1–30) (Kluwer 2003).

Schmitt C B, Skinner Q, Kessler E, and Kraye J (eds), *The Cambridge History of Renaissance Philosophy* (CUP 1988).

Scotland, Courts of Session, *The Acts of Sederunt of the Lords of Council and Session, from the 15th of January 1553, to the 11th of July 1790* (Elphingston Balfour 1790).

Scottish Records Office, *Guide to the National Archives of Scotland* (The Stationery Office 1996).

Schüssler R, 'On the Anatomy of Probabilism' in J Kraye and R Saarinen (eds), *Moral Philosophy on the Threshold of Modernity* (pp 91–113) (Springer 2005).

Sellar W D H, 'Promise' in K Reid and R Zimmermann (eds), *A History of Private Law in Scotland*, vol 2 (pp 252–81) (OUP 2000).

Sellberg E, 'Petrus Ramus' in E N Zalta (ed), *The Stanford Encyclopedia of Philosophy* (Stanford University Press 2014) <https://plato.stanford.edu/archives/win2020/entries/ramus> accessed 8 April 2021.

Shepherd C, 'Philosophy and Science in the Arts Curriculum of the Scottish Universities in the 17th Century' (DPhil thesis, University of Edinburgh 1975).

Shulz, F, *Principles of Roman Law* (M Wolff tr, OUP 1936).

Sierhuis F, *The Literature of the Arminian Controversy: Religion, Politics and the Stage in the Dutch Republic* (CUP 2015).

Simpson A W B, *A History of the Common Law of Contract: The Rise of the Action of Assumpsit* (OUP 1975).

Simpson A R C and Wilson A L M, *Scottish Legal History Volume 1: 1000–1707* (Edinburgh University Press 2017).

Skinner Q, 'Meaning and Understanding in the History of Ideas' (1969) 8 (1) *History and Theory* 3–53.

——*The Foundations of Modern Political Thought, vol 1: The Renaissance* (CUP 1978).

——*The Foundations of Modern Political Thought, vol 2: The Age of Reformation* (CUP 1978).

Smith D B, 'The Spiritual Jurisdiction 1560–64' (1993) 25 *Records of the Scottish Church History Society* 1–18.

Somos M, *Secularisation and the Leiden Circle* (Brill 2011).

Spence C, *Women, Credit, and Debt in Early Modern Scotland* (Manchester University Press 2016).

Spurlock R S, *Cromwell and Scotland: Conquest and Religion, 1650–1660* (John Donald 2007).

Stair, James Dalyrymple Viscount of, *A Vindication of Divine Perfections* (Brabazon Aylmer at the Three Pigeons in Cornhill c. 1695).

Stein P, *Fault in the Formation of Contract in Roman Law and Scots Law* (University of Aberdeen Press 1958).

——'The General Notions of Contract and Property in Eighteenth-Century Scottish Thought' (1963) 6 Juridical Review 1–13.

——'The Influence of Roman Law' (1963) 8 Juridical Review 205.

——'The Source of the Romano-Canonical Part of Regiam Majestatem' (1969) 48 (14) Scottish Historical Review 107–23.

——'The Fate of the Institutional System' in P van Warmelo and J van de Westhuizen (eds), *Huldigingsbundle Paul van Warmelo* (pp 218–27) (Universiteit van Suid-Afrika 1984).

——'Legal Humanism and Legal Science' (1986) 54 (2) The Legal History Review 297–306.

——'Roman Law, Common Law, and Civil Law' (1991–92) 66 Tulane Law Review 1591–604.

——'Donellus and the Origins of the Modern Civil Law' in J A Ankum et al (eds), *Mélanges Felix Wubbe* (pp 439–52) (Editions Universitaires 1993).

——'The Quest for a Systematic Civil Law' (1995) 90 Proceedings of the British Academy

——*Roman Law in European History* (CUP 1999).

Stevenson D, 'The National Covenant: A List of Known Copies' (1988) 23 Records of the Scottish Church History Society 255–99.

——'The Covenanters and the Court of Session, 1637–1650' in D Stevenson (ed), *Union, Revolution and Religion in 17th-century Scotland* (pp 227–47) (Variorum 1997).

——*Revolution and Counter-Revolution in Scotland, 1644–1651* (John Donald 2003).

Stewart A and Parratt D (eds), *The Minute Book of the Faculty of Advocates*, vol 46 (Stair Society 1999).

Stewart L A M, *Urban Politics and the British Civil Wars: Edinburgh, 1617–53* (Brill 2006).

——'Authority, Agency and the Reception of the Scottish National Covenant of 1638' in R Armstrong and T Ó Hannracháin (eds), *Insular Christianity: Alternative Models of the Church in Britain and Ireland, c.1570–1700* (p 88–106) (OUP 2013).

——*Rethinking the Scottish Revolution* (OUP 2016).

Straumann B, *Roman Law in the State of Nature: The Classical Foundations of Hugo Grotius' Natural Law* (CUP 2015).

Strien K V and Ahsmann M, 'Scottish Law Students in Leiden at the End of the Seventeenth Century: The Correspondence of John Clerk 1694–1697' (1992) 19 Lias: Sources and Documents Relating to the Early Modern History of Ideas 271–330.

Strien K V and Ahsmann M, 'Scottish Law Students in Leiden at the End of the Seventeenth Century: The Correspondence of John Clerk 1694–1697' (1993) 20 Lias: Sources and Documents Relating to the Early Modern History of Ideas 167–92.

Svensson M, 'Aristotelian Practical Philosophy from Melanchthon to Eisenhart: Protestant Commentaries on the Nicomachean Ethics 1529–1682' (2019) 21 (3) *Reformation & Renaissance Review* 218–38.

——and Sytsma D S, 'A Bibliography of Early Modern Protestant Ethics (ca. 1520–1750)' (2020) Academia <(PDF) A Bibliography of Early Modern Protestant Ethics, ca. 1520–1750 (updated Aug. 27, 2020) | Manfred Svensson and David S. Sytsma - Academia.edu> accessed 1 November 2022.

Swain W, 'Contract as Promise: The Role of Promising in the Law of Contract. An Historical Account' (2013) 17 (1) Edinburgh Law Review 1–21.

Sytsma D S, '"Ethical Theses" in *Theses Logicae, Metaphysicae, Physicae, Mathematicae, et Ethicae* (George Anderson 1646)' (2020) Academia <https://www.academia.edu/44558898/James_Dalrymple_of_Stair_Ethical_Theses_Glasgow_1646_> accessed 15 April 2021.

Tawney R H, *Religion and the Rise of Capitalism: A Historical Study* (first published 1926, Verso 2015).

Thomas J A C, *Textbook on Roman Law* (first published 1976, North-Holland 2012).

Thomas J, 'The Intertwining of Law and Theology in the Writings of Grotius' (1999) 1 (1) Journal of the History of International Law 61–100.

Thomson J, 'Judicial Control of Unfair Contract Terms' in K Reid and R Zimmermann (eds), *A History of Private Law in Scotland*, vol 2 (pp 157–74) (OUP 2000) .

Todd M, *Christian Humanism and Puritan Social Order* (CUP 1987).

Todd, Margo, *The Culture of Protestantism in Early Modern Scotland* (Yale University Press 2002).

Torrance J B, 'The Contribution of McLeod Campbell to Scottish Theology' (1973) 26 (3) Scottish Journal of Theology 295–311.

Trentman J A, 'Scholasticism in the Seventeenth Century' in N Kretzmann, A Kenny, K Pinborg, and E Stump (eds), *The Cambridge History of Later Medieval Philosophy* (pp 818–37) (CUP 1982).

Tuck R, *Natural Rights Theories* (CUP 1979).

——'Grotius and Selden' in J H Burns and M Goldie (eds), *The Cambridge History of Political Thought 1450–1700* (pp 499–529) (CUP 1991).

——'Introduction' in H Grotius, *The Rights of War and Peace* (first published 1645, Liberty Fund 2005).

Tully J, 'Governing Conduct' in E Leites (ed), *Conscience and Casuistry in Early Modern Europe* (pp 12–71) (CUP 1988).

Tutino S, 'Ecclesiology/Church-State Relationship in Early Modern Catholicism' in U L Lehner, R A Muller, and A G Roeber (eds), *The Oxford Handbook of Early Modern Theology, 1600–1800* (pp 150–64) (OUP 2016).

Van Asselt W J, 'Scholasticism Revisited: Methodological Reflections on the Study of Seventeenth-Century Reformed Thought' in A Chapman, J Coffey, and B S Gregory (eds), *Seeing Things Their Way: Intellectual History and the Return of Religion* (pp 154–74) (University of Notre Dame Press 2009).

——*Introduction to Reformed Scholasticism* (Reformation Heritage Books 2011).

Van Dam H-J, 'Second Thoughts: Ordinum Pietas and the Tractatus de Jure Majistratuum' (2013) 34 Grotiana 120–37.

Van den Bergh G C J J, *The Life and Work of Gerard Noodt (1647–1725)* (Clarendon Press 1988).

Van der Merwe D, 'Ramus, Mental Habits and Legal Science' in D Visser (ed), *Essays on the History of Law* (pp 32–59) (Juta & Co 1989).

Van Drunen D and Svensson M (eds), *Aquinas Among the Protestants* (Wiley Blackwell 2017).

Van Gelderen M, 'Arminian Trouble: Calvinists Debates on Freedom' in Q Skinner and M van Gelderen (eds), *Freedom and the Construction of Europe*, vol 1 (pp 21–37) (CUP 2013).

Van Ittersum M, *Profit and Principle: Hugo Grotius, Natural Rights Theories and the Rise of Dutch Power in the East Indies, 1595–1615* (Brill 2006).

Van Ittersum M J, 'The Working Methods of Hugo Grotius: Which Sources did he use and How did he use Them in his Early Writings on Natural Law Theory?' in P J du Plessis and J W Cairns, *Reassessing Legal Humanism and its Claims: Petere Fontes?* (pp 155–93) (EUP 2016).

Viner J, *Religious Thought and Economic Society: Four Chapters of an Unfinished Work* (Duke University Press 1978).

Visser D and Whitty N, 'The Structure of the Law of Delict in Historical Perspective' in K Reid and R Zimmermann (eds), *A History of Private Law in Scotland*, vol 2 (pp 422–76) (OUP 2000) .

Vos A, *The Philosophy of John Duns Scotus* (pp 432–63) (EUP 2006).

Waelkens L, 'La Cause de D. 44,4,2,3 Par' (2007) 75 Tijdschrift voor Rechtsgeschiedenis 199–212.

——*Amne Adverso: Roman Legal Heritage in European Culture* (Leuven University Press 2015).

Walker D M, 'The Structure and Arrangement of the *Institutions*' in D M Walker (ed), *Stair Tercentenary Studies*, vol 33 (pp 100–6) (Stair Society 1981).

——*A Legal History of Scotland, IV* (Tottel 2001).

Wallace V, 'Presbyterian Moral Economy: The Covenanting Tradition and Popular Protest in Lowland Scotland, 1707–c. 1746' (2010) 89 (277) Scottish Historical Review 54–72.

Walzer M, *The Revolution of the Saints* (Harvard University Press 1965).

Waterman A M C, 'Moral Philosophy or Economic Analysis? The Oxford Handbook of Adam Smith' (2015) 27 (2) Review of Political Economy 218–29.

Watson A, 'The Rise of Modern Scots Law' (1977) La Formazione Storica de Diritto Moderno Europa 1167.

——*The Making of the Civil Law* (Harvard University Press 1981).

——'*The Institutions of the Law of Scotland* (1693) by James Viscount of Stair, David M. Walker' 27 (2) (1983) The American Journal of Legal History 214–17.

——'The Evolution of Law: The Roman System of Contracts' (1984) 2 (1) Law and History Review 1–20.

——'Some Notes of Mackenzie's *Institutions* and the European Legal Tradition' (1989) 16 *Ius Commune* 303–13.

——*Roman Law and Comparative Law* (University of Georgia Press 1991).

——*Law Out of Context* (University of Georgia Press 2000).

——'Transformations of Law: Justinian's Institutes 1.2 pr., 1; Stair; Mackenzie' in H L MacQueen (ed), *Miscellany Four*, vol 49 (pp 243–54) (Stair Society 2002).

——*The Spirit of Roman Law* (University of Georgia Press 2008).

Watt D, '"The Laberinth of Thir Difficulties": The Influence of Debt on the Highland Elite c.1550–1700' (2006) 85 (219) Scottish Historical Review 25–51.

Weber M, '*Wirtschaft und Gesellschaft. Grundriß der verstehenden Soziologie* (1922)' in G Roth and C Wittich (trs), *Max Weber, Economy and Society* (University of California Press 1978).

Weir T, 'Contracts in Rome and England' (1996) 66 Tulane Law Review <Contracts in Rome and England — Tulane Law Review> accessed 2 November 2022.

Whitman J Q, *The Legacy of Roman Law in the German Romantic Era* (Princeton University Press 1990).

Williams B, *Essays and Reviews, 1959–2002* (Princeton University Press 2014).

Williams T, 'John Duns Scotus' in E N Zalta (ed), *The Stanford Encyclopedia of Philosophy*, Winter 2019 Edition (Stanford University Press 2016) <https://plato.stanford.edu/archives/win2019/entries/duns-scotus/> accessed 8 April 2021.

Williamson A H, *Scottish National Consciousness in the Age of James VI* (John Donald 1979).

Wilson, A, 'Practicks in Scotland's Interregnum' (2012) 4 Juridical Review 319–52.

Wilson A L M, 'Stair and the Inleydinge of Grotius' (2010) 14 (2) Edinburgh Law Review 239–68.

——'Stair, Mackenzie and risk in sale in seventeenth century Scotland' (2009) 15 (1) Fundamina 168–80.

——'The sources and method of the *Institutions of the Law of Scotland* by Sir James Dalrymple, 1st Viscount Stair, with specific reference to the law of obligations' (DPhil thesis, University of Edinburgh 2011).

——'The Textual Tradition of Stair's *Institutions*, with Reference to the Title "Of Liberty and Servitude"' in H L MacQueen (ed), *Miscellany Seven*, vol 62 (pp 1–125) (Stair Society 2015).

——'The Elchies Manuscript and the Method of Sir Richard Maitland of Lethington' (2018) 62 (1) Manuscripta: A Journal for Manuscript Research 95–146.

——'The Transmission and Use of the Collected Legal Decisions of Sir Richard Maitland of Lethington in Sixteenth- and Seventeenth-Century Scotland' (2018) 19 (3) The Library 325–59.

Winch D, *Adam Smith's Politics* (first published 1978, CUP 2002).

Wolter A B (ed), *Duns Scotus on the Will and Morality* (Catholic University of America Press 1997).

Worden B, *The Rump Parliament, 1648–53* (CUP 1977).

Wormald J, *Lords and Men in Scotland: Bonds of Manrent* (John Donald 1985).

——'Reformed and Godly?' in T M Devine and J Wormald (eds), *The Oxford Handbook of Modern Scottish History* (pp 204–19) (OUP 2012).

Wykes M, 'Devaluing the Scholastics: Calvin's Ethics of Usury' (2003) 38 Calvin Theological Journal 27–51.

Zimmermann R, *The Law of Obligations: Roman Foundations of the Civilian Tradition* (OUP 1990).

Index